The 1929 Sino-Soviet War

MODERN WAR STUDIES

The 1929 Sino-Soviet War

The War Nobody Knew

Michael M. Walker

University Press of Kansas

Published by the University Press of Kansas (Lawrence, Kansas 66045), which was organized by the Kansas Board of Regents and is operated and funded by Emporia State University, Fort Hays State University, Kansas State University, Pittsburg State University, the University of Kansas, and Wichita State University

Library of Congress Cataloging-in-Publication Data

Names: Walker, Michael M. (Colonel), author.

Title: The 1929 Sino-Soviet war : the war nobody knew / Michael M. Walker.
Description: Lawrence, Kansas : University Press of Kansas, [2016] | Series: Modern war studies | Includes bibliographical references and index.
Identifiers: LCCN 2016051187
ISBN 9780700623754 (cloth : alkaline paper)
ISBN 9780700632602 (paperback)
ISBN 9780700623761 (ebook)
Subjects: LCSH: China—Foreign relations—Soviet Union. | Soviet Union—Foreign relations—China. | Chinese Eastern Railway—History. | Joint ventures—History—20th century. | Limited war—History—20th century. | Borderlands—China—History—20th century. | Borderlands—Soviet Union—History—20th century. | Manchuria (China) —History, Military—20th century. | Zhang, Xueliang, 1901–2001. | Soviet Union. Raboche-Krest'ianskaia Krasnaia Armiia—History. | Soviet Union Raboche-Krest'ianskaia Krasnaia Armiia. Osobaian krasnoznamennaia dal'nevostochnaia armiia—History.
Classification: LCC DS775.8 .W3853 2016 | DDC 951.04/2—dc23
LC record available at https://lccn.loc.gov/2016051187.
British Library Cataloguing-in-Publication Data is available.

Printed in the United States of America

10 9 8 7 6 5 4 3 2 1

The paper used in this publication is recycled and contains 30 percent postconsumer waste. It is acid free and meets the minimum requirements of the American National Standard for Permanence of Paper for Printed Library Materials Z39.48-1992.

To the soldiers of both sides and especially those who fought, suffered, and died in a long forgotten war.

Contents

Acknowledgments

No history book is the product of one individual. That is especially true in this case, and this book only adds one more stepping-stone to a path begun by others, notably Felix Patrikeeff, Bruce Elleman, and the late Peter Tang. Research is the heart of history, and a number of people played key roles in that process, earning my lasting gratitude and appreciation. Three in particular are Asada Masafumi of Tohoku University, who generously compiled a master list of Japanese sources on the 1929 Sino-Soviet conflict; Maochun Miles Yu of the US Naval Academy, who forwarded Chiang Kai-shek's August 1929 national address on the CER crisis and brought to my attention the compilation of papers by Chinese scholars presented in Guo Shenjun's *The Chinese Eastern Railway and the Chinese Eastern Railway Crisis*; and Michael Carlson of the National Archives and Records Administration, who helped greatly in gaining access to restricted military intelligence and Office of Naval Intelligence documents.

More than any other individual, David Glantz made this book a reality. Not only did he help in locating the lion's share of the Russian-language sources that got the ball rolling, but he also provided unstinting help and guidance from the inception of this project to its completion. Deep thanks are also due to the military history master's program faculty (especially John M. Jennings of the US Air Force Academy) and the library staff at Norwich University, whose support made possible the thesis that formed the nucleus of this book. The staff at the University Press of Kansas also provided wonderful assistance. The sustained professional assistance from my dear friends, Tim Benbow of King's College London Defence Studies Department, Wayne Downing, and my brother, Joseph D. Walker Jr., proved invaluable, and needless to say, there would be no book without my wife, Megumi, who stood by my side throughout this endeavor.

A Note on Transliteration

For transliteration of Russian proper nouns, a simplified Library of Congress system has been used except for commonly known names. In the case of Chinese proper nouns, Wade-Giles has been selected for two reasons. First, it better reflects the historic period, and second, primary sources often proved impervious to Pinyin conversions. Many English-language sources lacked needed diacritics, while both Russian- and Japanese-language transliterations ended in Wade-Giles, making it the viable option. As an aid, Appendix B matches known pinyin place-names with their Wade-Giles versions.

Abbreviations

CCP	Chinese Communist Party
CEC	Central Executive Committee
CER	Chinese Eastern Railroad
CLC	Chinese Labor Corps
CMNA	Commissariat for Military and Naval Affairs
Comintern	Communist International
FD	Frontier Defense
FER	Far East Republic
GPU	State Political Directorate
IARC	Inter-Allied Railway Committee
IJA	Imperial Japanese Army
KMT	Kuomintang (Nationalist Party)
NEFDF	Northeast Frontier Defense Force
NRA	National Revolutionary Army
NWFDA	Northwest Frontier Defense Army
ODVA	Special Far East Army
OKDVA	Special Red Banner Far Eastern Army
PRA	People's Revolutionary Army
PUR	[Political Administration of the] Red Army
RKKA	Workers' and Peasants' Red Army
RMC	Revolutionary Military Council
RRSC	Russian Railway Service Corps
SMR	South Manchuria Railway
TSRR	Trans-Siberian Railroad
WPA	War Participation Army

The 1929 Sino-Soviet War

Introduction

The 1929 Sino-Soviet conflict was a short and bloody war fought over the jointly operated Chinese Eastern Railroad in China's Northeast between two powers mostly relegated to the dustbin of history, the Republic of China and the Union of Soviet Socialists Republics.[1] A modern limited war, it proved to be the largest military clash between China and a Western power ever fought on Chinese soil. Over 300,000 soldiers, sailors, and aviators served in the war, although only a part participated in the heavy fighting. As a comparison, at the outset of the better-known 1924 Second Fengtien–Chihli War, Chang Tso-lin, the supreme Manchurian warlord, advanced with three armies formed around eleven mixed brigades. In 1929, his son, the Young Marshal Chang Hsueh-liang, arrayed sixteen mixed brigades against the Red Army, the bulk of his army.

The conflict was the first major combat test of the reformed Soviet Red Army—one organized along the latest professional lines—and ended with the mobilization and deployment of 156,000 troops to the Manchurian border. Combining the active-duty strength of the Red Army and border guards with the call-up of the Far East reserves, approximately one in five Soviet soldiers was sent to the frontier—the largest Red Army combat force fielded between the Russian civil war (1917–1922) and the Soviet Union's entry into World War II on 17 September 1939. The 1929 conflict also offered an important look into warfare during the interwar in areas ranging from strategy and tactics to technology. The war is historic.[2]

Because the conflict is absent from many histories dealing with East Asia, scholars have not framed the war by degrees of significance but by extremes ending in insignificance. Jonathan D. Spence did not mention the war in his highly praised *In Search for Modern China,* nor did Nicholas Riasanovsky in his widely used *History of Russia.* James Sheridan gave it but one sentence in two separate works.[3] Unfortunately, this list is both long and impressive. Even scholars who focus on Chinese military history disagree over the war's significance. Bruce A. Elleman, writing in 2001, devoted a chapter to the conflict in *Modern Chinese Warfare, 1795–1989,* while Peter Worthing did not give the war a word of mention in his 2007 *Military History of Modern China: From the Manchu Conquest to Tian'anmen Square.*

This leads to a telling point: military history is important in in own right, and how the 1929 war has been dealt with to date serves as a cautionary tale for historians. While the presentation may be unattractive, as compilation of forces, orders of battle, and tactical analyses are often seen as stale relics of old school military history, the confused, even misguided place of the 1929 war in today's historical debate shows what can happen when, to use Benjamin Cooling's phrase, "traditional drum and trumpet operational history" is jumped over so quickly as to miss its significance.[4] The aim of this work is to try to correct that error by presenting the first extensive treatment of the war and to help resolve the significance controversy by addressing three questions: Why did the political crisis over the CER break out into open warfare? Why was the Soviet Red Army able to decisively defeat the Chinese after a few weeks of fighting? Finally, what were the consequences?

Using Russian, Chinese, and Japanese sources as well as declassified US military intelligence reports, the conclusion is that the war destabilized the region's balance of power and altered East Asian history. A path to war was created when Chiang Kai-shek and Chang Hsueh-liang miscalculated, both diplomatically and militarily, as they viewed the Soviets as politically isolated and militarily weak and were convinced that the time was right to reassert full authority over the CER. For the Soviets, Stalin dominated the action, and he saw war, not negotiations, as the preferred option. Once Stalin approved the large-scale offensive, the Soviet Red Army unexpectedly scored a decisive victory, disproving the assumption that it was incapable of fighting a modern war. With first-rate military doctrine, it possessed the ability to execute fast-paced successive operations and rapidly defeated the determined but divided and unevenly led Chinese forces. This led to significant political repercussions: the Kellogg–Briand Pact or Paris Pact for the outlawry of war failed, the Soviet Union emerged a recognized military power in East Asia, causing Japan to reorient its military policy away from the United States and toward Northeastern China and Soviet Russia, and China was forced to accept the reality that it could not militarily confront either of its two regional rivals, curtailing Nanking's militantly aggressive path in regaining full sovereignty.

Telling this story creates a unique set of problems. As noted, the history of the 1929 Sino-Soviet war is often overlooked, and much of it fits within another obscure subject, the early twentieth-century military history of Northeast Asia. Beyond the 1904–1905 Russo-Japanese War, only the history of the Soviet Red Army in this region has attracted interest, but again, the role of the 1929 war has received scant attention. To help address what Felix Patrikeeff referred to as a "lacunae in our understanding" of this conflict, the book is divided into two parts.[5]

Part I is background. Chapter 1 begins with the 1929 situation in the Northeast, and the chapter's second half, along with chapters 2 to 4, addresses the causes of the war and provides a military-political history of the CER in Northeast Asia within the context of larger historical events that shaped the region's history. For subject matter experts, these chapters are optional. The latter half of Chapter 1 addresses the period from the Boxer Uprising to the eve of the 1911 Revolution. The Northeast's military history from 1911 until 1918, from the dawn of the Republic of China, the 1917 Russian Revolution, and through the World War I is the focus of Chapter 2. The next chapter deals with the period 1919–1924, which saw the rebirth of China's revolutionary movement, international attempts to sustain peace and stability in East Asia, China's further decay into warlordism, and the arrival of the Soviet Union on the Northwest's frontier. The final chapter in Part I explores the changes in the Northeast in the wake of the Second Fengtien–Chihli War and ends in the reunification of China after the Northern Expedition. The role of the CER, the 1929 war's object, is interwoven throughout the chapters. Given the subject's obscurity, by integrating both the Chinese and Russian military history of the region during the 1900–1928 period, these chapters should prove usefully informative to a wide audience and provide needed understanding of the causes of the 1929 Sino-Soviet conflict.

The war is the focus of Part II. Part II covers the 1929 war and its consequences and consists of seven chapters. Chapter 5 addresses the rise of Chang Hsueh-liang as the hegemon of the Northeast in 1928, his submission to the Kuomintang regime in Nanking, and the events leading directly to the 1929 crisis and war. An overview of the Chinese and Soviet armies is provided in Chapter 6, while the 1929 Sino-Soviet conflict is covered in detail in the next three chapters, demonstrating that the war was of significant historical importance. Chapter 10 offers a military analysis of a war fought at the midway point between the two world wars, and the final chapter concludes with a discussion of the conflict's consequences—consequences that often have not been given their due place in the historical discourse.

Part One

Creating Conflict:
The Chinese Eastern Railroad

1 | The Troubled Frontier

Background

Few places in the 1920s captured the public imagination like Manchuria. For outsiders, it appeared to be the ideal land for dreamers, adventurers, and romantics. As Junichi Saga, a Japanese soldier who served on the Korean–Manchurian border in the 1920s, recounted, "There was a feeling in Japan in those days that anything was possible if you went to Manchuria."[1] Businessmen from America and British bankers eagerly sought out their chance to make their mark in the booming economy. The land, especially the northern regions, also held the allure of the American Wild West of the nineteenth century, where trappers could make a small fortune selling furs, outlaws and bandit gangs hid in remote hideouts, prospectors panned for alluvial gold along remote streams and rivers, and bears and Siberian tigers still ruled parts of the forested wilderness. For the large majority of people, however, a more routine yet rewarding life was spent in the cities, villages, and farms. The region remained, as South Manchuria Railway (SMR) officials described it, a "land of opportunities."[2]

Some 940,000 square kilometers in size, larger than France and Germany combined, it was the home to nearly one tenth of China's population, over 30 million people, including 1 million seasonal workers, known as sparrows, who annually migrated from China's northern provinces, especially Shantung. While it boasted of one of Asia's largest multiethnic communities—there were some 2,900,000 Manchus, 350,000 Mongols, half a million ethnic Koreans, 200,000 Japanese, and 141,000 Russians—it was also a magnet for refugees and misfits, as nearly one fourth of the Russian population had arrived in the Northeast during the 1917–1922 Russian civil war, while the number of bandits was put at an astounding 58,000 in 1929.[3]

The Northeast in 1929 could be seen to begin at the southernmost tip of the Liaotung Peninsula on the small Kwantung Peninsula containing the port city of Dairen and then extending up the Liao River north toward Mukden, the first capital of the Manchu Empire (See Map 1 for an overview of the Northeast.) This was the region's economic heart; only the Shanghai metropolis surpassed its concentration of industries and manufacturing plants. Moving northward, the land stretched out into the Central or Tsitsihar Plain, the richest and fastest-growing agricultural region in China. The Greater Khingan Mountains bounded the western edge of the plain; continuing west through mountains, the Northeast then opened onto the plateau of flat marshes and grasslands of northernmost Inner Mongolia until it reached the Argun River and the Soviet border. To the east of the Tsitsihar Plain lay the Yalu River, the Tunghua Mountains, and Tumen River, which together (from south to north) formed the boundary with Japanese-controlled Korea. Continuing north, the plain abutted Lake Khanka with the Ussuri River and the eastern border with Soviet Russia. From the Tsitsihar plain to the north lay the great Amur River basin, the most coveted piece of terrain in Asia—a region that China, Russia, and Japan all wished to dominate.

Troubles along the Amur River began as soon as Cossack expeditions loyal to Tsar Alexis I first reached its banks in the mid-1600s and the river became a flash point between the native Manchus and Russians until the 1689 Nerchinsk treaty delineated a border between the two empires. The treaty served to keep the peace for the next 170 years and helped to define what came to known as Manchuria in the 1920s. The notable exception was Manchu control over the Amur River watershed, which ended with the 1858 Aigun treaty, when the Russians were able to force a prostate Ch'ing China—having been defeated by the British and French in the Second Opium or Arrow War—to cede to Russia all lands east of the Ussuri and north of the Amur River. The Amur was also known as the Heilungkiang, or Black Dragon River. The river basin remained politically charged. Not only was the area contested over by the Chinese and Russian empires, but the Black Dragon Society became the name adopted by Japan's first ultraimperialist association in 1901—a group that urged expansion onto the Northeastern Asian mainland. The arrival of Japan completed the triad of powers that would fight politically, militarily, and economically to control Manchuria during the opening decades of the twentieth century.[4]

These competing interests, combined with Warlord Era (1916–1928) chaos, shaped the governance in the Northeast, and by 1929, it was a complex tapestry of overlapping authorities. The entire Northeast was under the rule of Chang Hsueh-liang, also known as the Young Mar-

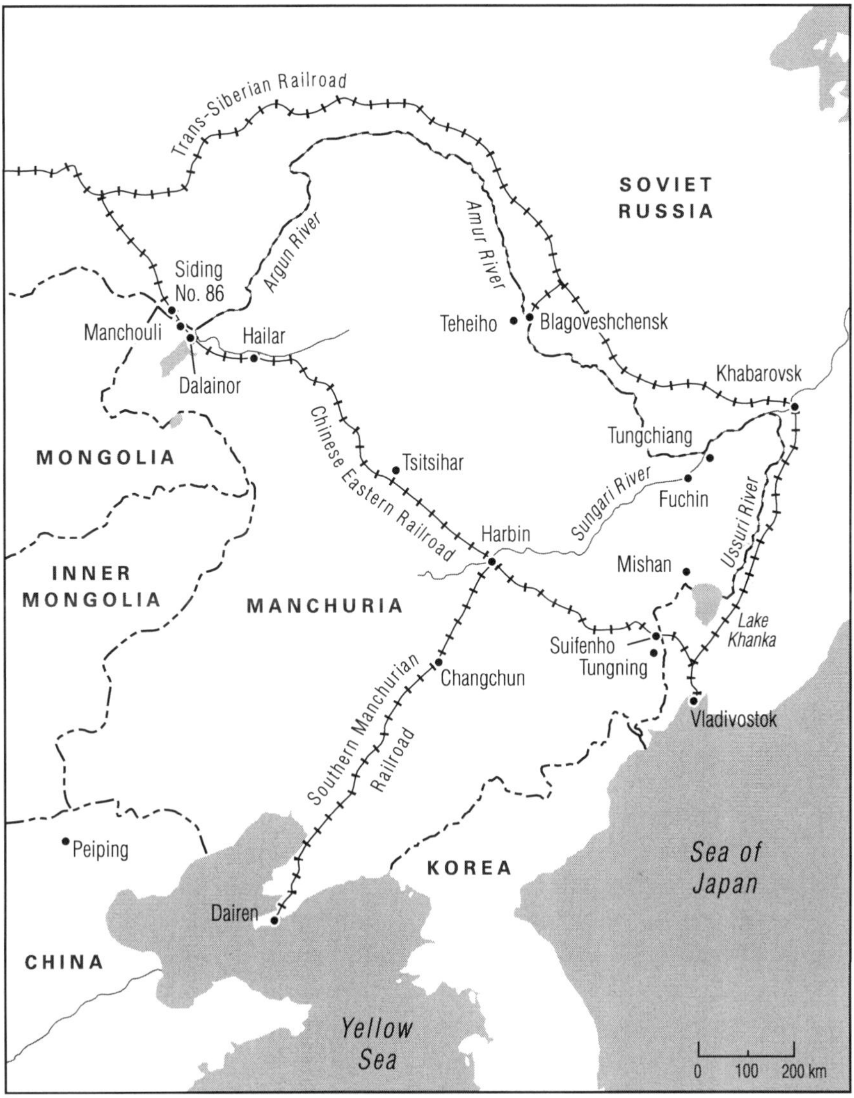

Map 1. Manchuria

shal. Below him were governors-general who ruled the three provinces of Fengtien, Kirin, and Heilungkiang along with the Harbin special administrative area, which included the Chinese Eastern Railroad (CER) Zone under joint Chinese and Soviet Russian management and administered by a general appointed by the Kirin governor (although the Heilungkiang governor had responsibility for the zone in that province). Finally, the Kwantung Leasehold and SMR Zone fell under Japanese jurisdiction.

Of the three Northeastern provinces, Fengtien was the richest and most populous. Much of it had long been part of the Chinese Empire, and the first to have a foreign concession carved out of it: the Russian naval base at Port Arthur and the commercial port of Dairen. The surrounding lands, encompassing some 3,500 square kilometers, was a possession that passed into Japanese hands after the 1904–1905 Russo-Japanese War. Kirin, located northeast of Fengtien, was larger in size but had a smaller population and was less developed. It was the home of Harbin, the multiethnic city and site of the CER headquarters. Heilungkiang, stretching from the Sungari River in the east to the Argun River, 1,200 kilometers to the west, was the largest, most diverse, and least populated of the provinces. It also shared the longest border with Soviet Russia. The population was predominantly Chinese except in the far western border region that followed the Argun, which was home to Bargut–Mongol herdsmen and ethnic Russian farmers of the Starovery (Old Orthodox Believers) who had arrived in the 1880s. During the Russian civil war (1917–1922), other Old Orthodox Believer families fled the fighting in the Russian far east and joined the original settlers.[5]

Economically, Manchuria was China's richest and fastest-growing region, an agriculture dynamo with 30 million acres under cultivation and another 30 million awaiting development. John B. Powell, an American newspaper reporter who covered the 1929 war, reflected on the lands around Tsitsihar, the capital of Heilungkiang province located in the northern end of the plain: "I was constantly reminded of the fertile farm lands and the deep black soil of northern Missouri, Illinois, and Iowa."[6] The range of agricultural goods produced was breathtaking: fruit trees and sugar beets, the traditional staple of *kaoliang* (sorghum), and grains such as barley, corn, millet, rice, and wheat abounded. The greatest source of agricultural wealth, which had only been cultivated on a large scale for a few decades, was the protein-rich soybean, a crop that Manchuria exported across the globe in the form of dried beans, oil, and cakes (hardened bean paste formed into densely packed cylinders measuring roughly two feet in diameter and five inches in thickness). Hemp, tussah, tobacco, and cotton were also produced. Most farmers also possessed a few head of livestock and fowls; the estimated number of domestic animals, flocks, and herds was put at over 20 million, with over 4 million pounds of wool exported annually.[7]

The abundance of land allowed farmers to follow a different path from the rest of China, as it mitigated the ill effects of rural landlordism and helped account for the fact that Manchurian farmers were generally better-off than their counterparts elsewhere. The most richly cultivated region began in the south where the Liao River entered the Bay of Pohai, an area that had been integrated into China for centuries with an agricultural system based on the long-established market town model. To the north, a region populated by newer immigrant farmers, the model changed to larger stand-alone family farms; ethnicity also played a role, as farmers of Korean descent dominated rice production. Geography and climate were the final determinants of Manchuria's unique agricultural profile. The alluvial lands of the Tsitsihar Plain held vast fields of soybeans and *kaoliang*, while corn grew better farther south toward the Liaotung Peninsula and wheat grew best in the northern reaches of the plain. Finally, the valley formed by the upper Sungari River offered soils ideal for cultivating wheat, millet, and soybeans. A variety of *mofang* or local mills, usually employing fewer than ten people, distilled the *kaoliang* or milled the soybeans into oil or cakes and the grains into flour, although large-scale mills, known as *huomo* or fire mills, using steam or electrically powered machinery, often government owned, were becoming commonplace by 1929. One advantage for the farmers was that none of the main agricultural regions was located along the border with Soviet Russia, sparing the large majority of the population from any direct involvement in the war.[8]

Timber was another source of natural wealth, with over five hundred billion cubic feet of timber available that could be easily shipped by rivers and streams, but the numbers were deceiving, as the sustainable supplies were in the north in Heilungkiang while parts of Fengtien province in the south were undergoing a process of afforestation resulting from earlier overharvesting. Mining centered on the two essentials of a modern 1920s economy, coal and iron ore, and Manchuria possessed ample reserves of both, with control over the resources dominated by the CER and SMR. The most productive mine at Anshan, located forty kilometers southwest of Mukden, held a projected 200 million tons of iron ore, while the Fushun open-pit coal mines, stretching fifteen kilometers in length and located forty kilometers to the southeast of Mukden, contained over one billion tons of bituminous coal that supplied not only large quantities of coal and coke but also oil (all under consignment to the Imperial Japanese Navy), natural gas, gasoline, tar, and sulfuric acid. By 1929, the output from the Fushun mines accounted for one third of all the coal produced in China. Together, they made the Mukden region the largest steel-producing center in China, and both had been developed by and were under the control the SMR. The CER controlled the Muleng coal mines near Mishan in northern Heilungkiang, at Dalainor in the far west, and at Koshan, northeast of Tsitsihar in central Manchuria.[9]

Japanese steel mills, both in Japan and the Northeast, fed by ore from Anshan and coal from Fushun, combined with the specialized Ta-Hua Electro-Metallurgical Company, helped explain in part why Japan was both the largest steel producer in East Asia and so insistent on its special position in Manchuria. While the manufacturing facilities in the Kwantung Leasehold and the SMR Zone did make Japan the industrial power in Manchuria, there were extensive Chinese holdings as well. Situated near Mukden was the Penchihu Coal and Iron Mining Company, a joint Sino-Japanese enterprise that employed over 5,000 Chinese miners, and another joint venture, the Chenhsing Iron Ore mining Company, provided jobs for another 3,000 Chinese workers at six facilities in Fengtien province. All told, 95 percent of the pig iron and steel produced in China came out of the furnaces at Anshan and Penchihu by 1929.[10]

The Northeast was a textile center, second only to the Shanghai region, with over 700 looms in operation, and the Chinese-operated Textile Mill of the Three Provinces, employing 1,800 workers, was one of the most profitable in China. In pure dollar terms, the machinery and ceramics manufacturers generated more revenue than the iron and steel industries, with the chemical industry not far behind. The Northeast's rulers influenced the economy through two agencies. The first was the Bureau of Industry, which included agroindustry; it had responsibility for licensing private-sector businesses for the purpose of taxation. The second was composed of a combination of government-sponsored enterprises such as utilities, telephone companies, and the previously mentioned large-scale soybean processing mills, plus a few odds and ends such as the government Sugar Mill in Heilungkiang and saltpeter mines, essential for the manufacture of gunpowder. Finally, there was the Mukden Arsenal, which was actually composed of several arsenals and munitions works; it employed 20,000 people and produced everything needed for a modern army, including heavy artillery and rifle cartridges.[11]

Along with the legal economy, there was an underground economy that ranged from human pipelines for moving people and families fleeing the Soviet Union to illicit dealings in smuggling, opium, prostitution, and gambling. Lawlessness in the sparsely populated wildernesses gave rise to bandit gangs with names like Yellow Spears, the long-established Red Beards or *hunghutzu*, and the Heavenly Gate Society. They roamed the countryside, remote mountain areas, and isolated border areas. Harbin, whose cabarets never closed, had long been known for drunkenness and prostitution since its inception as a wide-open railroad town, and the more isolated stretches of the Sungari appealed to river bandits. They could not only pirate cargo but also pull thousands of freshwater pearls from its waters, while the adjacent lands favored opium cultivation. The rapid growth of the Sungari River town of Fuchin was attributed to its location in the heart of the poppy-growing region, and some argued that the settlement of the lower Sungari was largely due to the attraction of the poppy as a cash crop. Despite this unsavory underside, the Northeast remained a magnet for immigration and investment.[12]

The combination of population, natural resources, agricultural strength, and growing industrial base made the Northeast one of the most coveted economic regions in the world. The value of foreign trade reached nearly $500 million in the year leading up to the 1929 war, and the CER, connected to the Soviet Trans-Siberian Railroad (TSRR) and the Japanese SMR, was a critical tie that held the region together. This was the golden era of railroads. They were the engines of economic growth, and the CER was one of Asia's most important. Stretching some 1,500 kilometers from the Manchouli station in the west to the Suifenho station in the east and linked to the SMR at the Kuancheng station, just north of Changchun, as well as the shipping trade along the Sungari River at Harbin, the CER headquarters, it was the backbone of the economy. The railroad, containing dozens of tunnels and over 1,400 bridges of all sizes and shapes, was divided into three divisions, with Harbin as the hub: the eastern line (550 kilometers in length), the western line

(950 kilometers), and the truncated southern line (240 kilometers). It possessed some 500 locomotives, over 700 passenger coaches, and 11,000 freight cars in 1929. It carried Manchuria's agricultural bounty north to the Soviet border, then along the Ussuri line to the port of Vladivostok or south to Changchun for transfer to the port of Dairen in the Japanese Kwantung Leasehold along the Japanese-owned SMR.[13]

The CER was more than trains and tracks. The railway zone encompassed a quarter million acres. In the far west, at Manchouli, the rail ran in an eastern direction past Dalainor and toward Hailar. Built by the Russians in the 1890s around a thriving fur and pelt trading center, Manchouli sat in a basin ringed with low rolling hills that began five kilometers inland from the Russian border. By 1929, the city was a small but prosperous community housing rail yards, a roundhouse, train repair shops, and a station, along with consular offices, hotels, banks, stores, schools, two hospitals (one run by the CER and the other by the municipality), and hundreds of houses for the town's workers and other inhabitants. Named after Lake Dalai, the much smaller town of Dalainor was located twenty kilometers southwest of Manchouli and just west of its train station. The nearby Dalainor mines employed about 700 Russian and 400 Chinese miners who produced over a quarter million tons of coal per year, almost all for use by the CER but some to run the western region's only electric plant, which powered both western towns.[14]

Fifteen hundred kilometers away, the CER's eastern terminus was near the picturesque town of Suifenho, also built by the Russians in the 1890s and often referred to by its Russian name, Pogranichnaya. In 1929, it was a cosmopolitan city that retained its Russian architectural flavor, and like Manchouli, Suifenho contained a hospital and extensive rail facilities. Some 140 kilometers northwest of Suifenho were the Sino-Soviet Mishan–Muleng coal mines, which opened in 1924 and added another 200,000 tons annually, making the railway self-sufficient. In addition to the hospitals at Manchouli and Suifenho, the CER boasted another five hospitals, augmented by a number of clinics. Together, nearly fifty doctors and 550 other medical personnel staffed the CER system. They represented only a fraction of the over 20,000 mostly ethnic Russian employees who ensured its smooth operation—engineers, mechanics, conductors, stationmasters, accountants, and telegraph operators. By 1929, nearly every major city in the Northeast depended on a CER rail station as its link to the outside. Tsitsihar, Harbin, and Changchun had all blossomed after the arrival of the CER.[15]

Roots of Conflict

The purpose of the CER had always been politically volatile; the Ch'ing dynasty, just defeated in the 1894–1895 Sino-Japanese War, granted Russia building rights as a reward for entering into the secret Li-Lobanov military alliance, which was designed to halt further Japanese expansion. To make the railroad a reality, two Sino-Russian government-sponsored entities were created.

To handle the finances, the Russo-Chinese Bank was established in December 1895. China agreed to deposit 5 million gold taels, to be returned upon completion of the railway. In return, it would obtain a share of the bank's profits. Damning to China's interests, however, CER holdings were kept in the bank's St. Petersburg headquarters, directed by a board composed of eight Russian shareholders with a lone Chinese chairman and under the oversight of the tsar's Ministry of Finance. Because neither country possessed the funds needed to build the railway, Finance Minister Sergei Witte—with the approval of young Tsar Nicholas II—decided that the bank would sell CER bonds on the Paris market to raise the capital.[16]

With the financing in place and the Li-Lobanov treaty signed on 3 June 1896, on 8 September, the bank entered into an agreement with China to form the Chinese Eastern Railway Company to oversee construction and operation of the line. To keep control of the railroad, only 1,000 shares would be issued, with 700 going to the tsar's government and the other 300 going up for sale. As added precautions, only Chinese or Russian citizens could own CER company stock, and the Russian government reserved the right to buy up any unsold stock. The process was a sham. It was not until the day of the offering that the sale was announced, and shares could only be purchased that morning. After a few minutes of inactivity, the sale was pronounced closed, and the Russian government possessed all 1,000 shares by day's end.[17]

The CER would also own the lands needed for the operation of the railway, along with possessing the materials needed for the railway's construction and upkeep. Once construction began, thousands of square kilometers became part of the CER Zone. As for control, the agreement stipulated, "The Company will have the absolute and exclusive right of administration of its land."[18] In addition to the September agreement between China and the Russo-Chinese Bank, the status of the railway also rested on an 1896 second agreement, the Cassini Convention, that strengthened Russian control over the company lands by allowing Russia to station troops and operate mines in the zone.[19]

For the Russians, the CER was not only directed against Japan or a means to simply obtain a shorter route for the Trans-Siberian Railroad from Moscow to Vladivostok (it shortened the trip by over 500 kilometers); the railway could also be used against China. Witte wrote in 1897 that the railroad would "provide Russia with the possibility of transporting her armed forces at all times . . . and of concentrating them in Manchuria . . . at a short distance from the capital of China."[20] Japan's Yamagata Aritomo—general, prime minister, and one of the leading statesmen of his generation—saw the emerging rivalries. He put it bluntly: a Russian railway would turn the Northeast into "a pile of meat among tigers."[21] If anyone was mistaken as to Nicholas's objective, they were disabused by 1898, when he extracted further concessions from the Chinese, permitting the building of the Port Arthur naval base on a leased stretch of land at the southern extreme of the Liaotung Peninsula known as the Kwantung Peninsula, as well as providing a concession to connect the leasehold with Harbin by expanding the CER through the South Manchuria branch line. Japan, who had been forced in 1895 to give up the land during the Russian-led Triple Intervention, was outraged. Even Witte saw this as overreach, calling the acquisition "child's play which would end disastrously."[22]

Cumulatively, the tsar became the de facto ruler of the CER and its associated zone, encompassing vast tracks of land along the railway and the city of Harbin, which came to possess its own administrative, military, and police forces with implied judicial authority, all under Russian supervision. The landscape of the Northeast was transformed: the last great untamed region in East Asia had been opened to the modern world and placed under Russian dominance. The CER became a great success, but the situation in the Northeast would remain unstable, from the 1900 Boxer Uprising and the 1904–1905 Russo-Japanese War, through the fighting during the 1911 Chinese Revolution, the Great War, the 1917–1922 Russian civil war, and beyond. Even the impetus for its creation in the secret Russian-Chinese Alliance was born out of war: had it not been for China's defeat by Japan, there never would have been a CER. With the building of the railway, Manchuria had become, to use Owen Lattimore's phrase, the "cradle of conflict." These conflicts set the stage for the 1929 war, and it is necessary to review the role they played in shaping the rivalries and creating the animosities that led to a tragic war between the Republic of China and the Soviet Union.[23]

The 1900 Boxer Uprising

The West may have equated the 1900 Boxer Uprising with the siege of the Peking Legations, but in the Northeast, it was a full-scale war between China and Russia over control of the CER. The Boxer Uprising, a confused affair from the start, ended in disaster for China and was grounded in the fanatical beliefs espoused by the Yi Ho Chuan (Righteous and Harmonious Fists), or Boxers, so called for their public displays of martial arts drills. It arose at the height of imperialist encroachment in China at the close of the nineteenth century. The catalyst was an intertwining of nationalist frustration and the desperate poverty gripping parts of North China, especially in Shantung. The movement legitimized violent xenophobia, and to the Boxers, their drills were more than a means to conventional military power, as the training claimed to impart to its followers supernatural strength, which included psychic imperviousness to bullets, known as the "armor of the golden bell," a protection acquired after following a months-long ritual. While seen as outlandish to outside observers, they were in keeping with ancient traditional martial beliefs. The *Art of War* and other martial texts dating back to the Warring States Period (476–221 BCE) had remained and still are part of China's military science, but the Boxer's practices were a link to lessons that had been abandoned in the modern era, such as sections of Tai-kung's *Six Secret Teachings*, which emphasized the ability of military leaders to use their mental and spiritual prowess to make battlefield prognostications while identifying and manipulating the chi (roughly meaning the life force) of the enemy, their army, and even nature itself. The Boxer's pseudomystical beliefs were unusual but not unprecedented.[24]

Grounded in this form of mysticism and secret military learning, the goals of the Boxers were to restore traditional Chinese beliefs by overthrowing the Ch'ing dynasty and expelling the "foreign devils" to remove their corrupting influences—ends that were as unwelcome in the capitals of Europe as in the Forbidden City. As the Boxers grew in power, their strong antiforeign beliefs—a conflicted mishmash of justified anger at foreign abuses and distasteful ethnocentrism—came to be embraced by Peking as a means to put the foreign powers in their place. By 1898, after the collapse of the progressive Hundred Days of Reform, an uneasy quasi-official relationship advocated by Shantung governor Yu-hsien had been formed, symbolized by recasting many Boxers groups as militias. A missionary in Shantung noted the change in a slogan, now directed at "supporting the Ch'ing dynasty and eliminating the foreigners." Even though the initial targets were both Chinese Christians and foreigners, the overarching antialien sentiment was always present. Predictably, the first murder of a foreigner occurred in Shantung with the brutal death an English clergyman, Sidney Brooks, on 31 December 1899.[25]

The Powers, save Russia who saw no direct threat, protested the violence.[26] More incidents soon followed. The situation for foreigners and Chinese Christians had become so dangerous in North China by mid-1900 that they began to evacuate the countryside, with many seeking refuge in Peking, congregating in the legation quarter and the nearby North Cathedral abutting the fortified walls inside the Imperial City. The Empress Dowager Tzu-hsi attempted to assuage the fears of the Powers by replacing Shantung governor Yu-hsien with the more capable and aggressive Yuan Shih-kai. Yuan, who was also the commander of the Newly Created Army (one of the only military formations in China that was trained and equipped along modern Western lines), succeeded in suppressing the Boxers, only to see them flee into Chihli and toward Peking, making the situation there all the more precarious for the foreign population.[27]

Faced with a dangerously deteriorating situation that the Ch'ing seemed incapable of correcting, the Powers assembled a fleet of ships off the coast on the Bay of Pohai and landed a military force of several thousand troops, under the framework of an eight-nation alliance, to relieve the 4,000 souls now surrounded and besieged in Peking. When the allied troops advanced from the coast near Tientsin in mid-June without imperial permission, the Empress Dowager ordered the Chinese army to halt the relief column. This was no sign of overt support for the Boxers, but on the grounds that suppressing the Boxers was the responsibility of the Ch'ing, a foreign military strike was unacceptable. The intervention of the superior Chinese army gave the allied force no choice but to fall back, arriving just outside Tientsin on 26 June to await reinforcement. The situation was still perilous for the allies, as nearly two weeks earlier, on 15 June, the Boxers had risen in Tientsin, besieging the foreign quarter there as they had in Peking. In response to the uprising, and to protect the allied rear, the multinational naval force attacked and seized the nearby Chinese Taku forts on 17 July, opening the Pei River from the Bay of Pohai and paving the way for the relief of Tientsin's foreign quarter while securing a base of operations for a future allied relief expedition to Peking. The assaults were met with a declaration of war against the allies by Peking on 21 June, and the city of Tientsin remained in the hands of the Boxers.[28]

By this time, the Boxer movement had also spread to southern Manchuria—an expected outcome given the presence of over 100,000 sparrow laborers from Shantung, many of them CER workers. While the growth of the Boxers was less dramatic than in North China—their calls to violence proved less appealing, in part reflecting the better lot of the typical Northeastern peasant, who was disinterested in revolutionary change—it was enough to alarm the Russians, who had felt that they had a special relationship with the Chinese, thus shielding them from the more extreme forms of antiforeignism. One Russian CER rail guard officer who came upon a secret rally being held by Boxer recruiters in April noted their distinctive yellow sashes, headbands, and martial exercises, but was allowed to observe and walk away unmolested. The Russians also noted that bandits, particularly the Red Beards, were posing a serious danger to the CER. Apprehensions rose again after Boxer attacks against Christians soon branched out into attacks against railways, the hated "iron centipedes."[29]

Chief Engineer A. I. Yugovich feared that the CER would bear the brunt of Chinese anger in the Northeast, where Major General Aleksandr A. Gerngross's 4,500-man CER Independent Border Guard Unit protected the railway. Formed in 1897, it was an unusual organization, as it operated within China but was under the supervision of the Finance Ministry, not the Russian army. Although Gerngross was a career army officer and guards were paid better than soldiers, the army looked down on the unit, whose members were referred to as Matilda's Guards—a disparaging reference to Minister Witte's wife. Major General Vladimir V. Sakharov, commander of the border guard corps at Khabarovsk and Gerngross's superior, was concerned enough to cable Vice Finance Minister P. M. Romanov at St. Petersburg on 6 June, requesting that a force of 11,000 infantry and cavalry be sent to defend the CER. Protecting the CER from the Boxers had become a priority.[30]

June witnessed a dramatic increase in "expel the barbarian" activities in the Northeast—so much so that by 25 June, the War Ministry issued a mobilization order to Governor-General Lieutenant General Nikolai I. Grodekov at Khabarovsk for all Russian army units in the Priamur, containing the Trans-Baikal, Amur, Maritime, and Kamchatka districts. Two days later, the first attack on the CER took place. Witte was in St. Petersburg, along with much of the CER management. They resisted military action, as they feared the arrival of Russian troops would prove counterproductive by inflaming Chinese sensibilities. Eventually the violence demanded action, and even Witte asked the tsar to authorize a military campaign by mid-July. Like outbreaks elsewhere in China, the attacks were widespread and seemingly uncoordinated, but unlike those in China proper, the attacks in the Northeast centered on the physical destruction of the CER.[31]

Until the declaration of war, the imperial policy emanating out of the Forbidden City of overtly vowing to rein in the Boxers while covertly supporting them confused both the Russian and the local Ch'ing commanders. In part a reflection of divisions within the Manchu court, when the declaration of war was announced, it was so vague that General Tseng-chi in Fengtien was not even sure what country or countries were at war with China. Peking had attempted to limit the role of the army, advising the Kirin Governor-General Chang-chun, "If we have to fight against the Russians, let the Boxers be the vanguard, and we ourselves must be most discreet." Committing the Ch'ing army, however, was unavoidable, as there simply was not a credible Boxer force in the Northeast—a reality that accounted for the heavy fighting that followed. Unfortunately, the provincial forces in Manchuria had benefited little from the military reforms that began after China's defeat by Japan four years earlier; there were no modern units akin to those in the Self-Strengthening or Newly Created armies, and although Manchurian forces had been equipped with improved artillery and a few units were armed with first-rate Mauser rifles, they were no match for the tsar's troops.[32]

The conduct of the war was complex, unlike the more straightforward allied drive to relieve the Peking Legations. The fighting in the Northeast was widespread and went through several phases that began with the June CER attacks. The Chinese were quick to take advantage of the departure of over 7,000 tsarist soldiers sent to join the Peking relief expedition. When the Boxer crisis erupted in North China in mid-June, there were three Russian brigades in the Far East. Within a few weeks, the 2nd East Siberian Rifle Brigade had left Vladivostok, and the bulk of the 3rd Brigade departed Port Arthur to join the allied force assembling near Tientsin. The remaining 1st Brigade was sent to Port Arthur, leaving one of its regiments at Vladivostok. The Chinese proved so successful at severing the CER that the isolated Russian guard detachments were cut off and overwhelmed along almost the entire line. In one case, the guards, the railway employees, and their families at Mukden were forced to trek overland to Korea and safety. The Russians abandoned one section of the railway after another, having no choice but to retreat toward their enclaves at Harbin or under the protection of Vice Admiral Yevgeni I. Alekseyev's forces on the Liaotung Peninsula and the nearby treaty port of Yingkow or the border cities of Manchouli and Poganinchnaya at the extremes of the CER.[33]

The attacks were not limited to the CER. The Amur River in the far north of Manchuria became a war front, with the Russian port city of Blagoveshchensk the focal point of the fighting. Troubles on the river between Chinese and Russian ships began in June, and Russian authorities reacted by impressing and arming several paddle-wheel steamers into service to end the often violent disputes. The fighting between Blagoveshchensk and the Teheiho–Aigun region on opposite banks of the Amur River was in many ways a uniquely isolated conflict, and one uncharacteristic of the battles fought along the CER. The two towns held important positions. Blagoveshchensk, with a population of just under 20,000, was the capital of the Russian Amur District, while Teheiho–Aigun was the site of the original Manchu capital of Heilungkiang province, established in the late seventeenth century to monitor Russian activities in the Far East, and had become an important agricultural and lumber shipping hub. War came to Blagoveshchensk on the Sunday afternoon of 15 July with a shelling by Chinese batteries located across the river at Teheiho, an attack that killed and wounded several women and children and threw the civilian population into terrified confusion as they sought shelter.[34]

Two days later, the worst atrocity of the war occurred at Blagoveshchensk when soldiers under Lieutenant General Konstantin N. Gribsky, the local commander, gathered up some 4,000 Chinese civilians living on the Russian side of the Amur, either from Blagoveshchensk or the nearby Chinese community of Hailanpao (also known as the Sixty-Four Villages). The soldiers marched them to the river's edge, where they were given the choice of trying to swim the two kilometers across the river to the Chinese bank or facing execution. Complete terror ensued as the massacre got underway. Only a few dozen survived. Many Russians were appalled. One commentator wrote, "What shall we tell civilized people? We are mean and terrible people; we have killed those who hid at our place, who sought our protection."[35] Over the next several weeks, the two sides bombarded each other, regardless of civilian casualties, and river raids became the norm as the action shifted to Harbin, the CER headquarters and center of Russian power in the Northeast. The damage to Sino-Russian relations in the region was lasting but yielded an important result: it eradicated Chinese settlements north of the Amur River once and for all. Those lands were now the sole domain of Russia.[36]

Harbin had begun to receive refugees as early as 6 July. Four days later, CER officials, led by Chief Engineer Yugovich, lined the docks to bid farewell their wives and children, who were being evacuated to Khabarovsk by steamer while a militia was hastily formed to reinforce the combined police and guard detachment under General Gerngross. Harbin at the time was populated by perhaps 20,000 clustered in three districts: Pristan (the wharves on the Sungari River); New Town, which was under construction; and the Old City, which was populated by Chinese railway workers, who made up more than half the population. Over the next week, Russian civilians and guard detachments from places such as Tsitsihar and Tiehling continued to arrive, often having fought their way through Chinese army units to the west or through soldiers and armed bands of Boxers to the south. Things took a turn for the worse as the news of the Blagoveshchensk massacre spread. Heilungkiang governor-general Shou-shan at Tsitsihar, after hearing of the deaths, informed the Russians that as of 22 July, a state of war existed.[37]

The next night, as merchants attempted to embark their goods, women, crying children, the infirm, and anyone not subject to CER orders—approximately 3,000 people in all—left for Khabarovsk. Surprisingly, only three casualties were suffered when Chinese gunners shelled the steamships as they left the Pristan docks. Yugovich drafted every male CER employee under the age of fifty into the guard with the promise of a 50 percent salary bonus. In order to form a defensive perimeter, Gerngross directed that both Old Harbin and New Town be abandoned in favor of Pristan and to clear fields of fire. Outlying buildings were rigged with demolitions, including the recently built Cathedral of St. Nikolai. The city, now cut off, had been able to muster almost 2,000 men under arms when the weeklong siege began on 26 July with the shelling of docks. The population had plummeted to 4,000 souls.[38]

The Harbin siege signaled the high watermark of the Chinese offensive as the balance of military power shifted to the Russians. The Chinese attacks had swept like a prairie fire that raged along the CER but burned itself out after the initial fighting. Having survived the onslaught, General Grodekov prepared for a counterattack. Russian forces in Manchuria had been organized into two corps, with the overall command of the northern army corps given to Grodekov while Admiral Alekseyev led the southern army corps from Port Arthur. By the end of July, the two had gained control of the Amur, Ussuri, and most of the Sungari rivers, stabilized the situation in the Kwantung Peninsula, and secured the South Manchuria branch of the CER from Port Arthur to Tiehling, sixty kilometers south of Mukden. When reinforcements arrived from European Russia, the two commanders were ready to go on the offensive, opening the final phase of the Boxer Uprising in the Northeast. Military operations were divided between the commanders. The aim of their two-phase offensive was to first have Grodekov's northern forces regain control over the east and west CER lines from Manchouli to Pogranichnaya, which was to be followed by two converging attacks along the South Manchuria line conducted by Grodekov from the north and Alekseyev from the south.[39]

The northern offensive began with a thrust into the western extreme of Manchuria on 25 July, one day before Chinese forces surrounded Harbin, and was the first of a four-pronged penetration of the Northeast from the Priamur. Under the command of Major General Nikolai Orlov, 5,000 Cossacks from the Trans-Baikal District crossed the frontier on a drive for Hailar, some 120 kilometers to the east; Hailar was captured by 6 August. Three days later, Orlov began to march on Tsitsihar, farther to the east with additional reinforcements heading his way. Grodekov had also been building up the garrison at Blagoveshchensk, so that by the end of July, there were nearly 10,000 Russian troops there ready to cross the Amur and carry out the next attack. General Gribsky, the man who ordered the 19 July massacre, went on the offensive on 2 August; within a matter of days, he had successfully crossed the Amur, captured the Teheiho–Aigun district, and sent a force to advance on Tsitsihar to the south under Major General Paul (or Pavel) von Rennenkampf. At the same time, the third and fourth prongs of Grodekov's offensive, aimed at the relief of Harbin, got underway.[40]

On 21 July, a convoy of armed steamships carrying 5,000 troops under General Sakharov prepared to depart Khabarovsk, steam up the Amur to the mouth of Sungari, and from there head upriver to Harbin. Simultaneously, near Pogranichnaya at the eastern terminus of the CER, Major General Nikolai M. Chichagov, with 4,000 troops, advanced west along the CER toward Harbin. By 3 August, Chichagov's cavalry had reached the outskirts of Harbin, and that evening, the first of Sakharov's steamships docked at Pristan. The siege of Harbin had been lifted, and soon the forces under Gerngross were striking in two directions: east along the CER toward Chichagov's main body, and at Tsitsihar, nearly 300 kilometers west of Harbin. Tsitsihar, the provincial capital and the last remaining Chinese stronghold in Heilungkiang, was now facing three converging Russian columns from the east, north, and west. Faced with a hopeless situation, the Chinese surrendered to Rennenkampf's cavalry on 28 August. Governor-General Shou-shan committed suicide shortly thereafter, and Rennenkampf was joined by Orlov's force six days later.[41]

The Harbin column was recalled upon hearing the news of Tsitsihar's surrender, while the ever-aggressive Orlov and Rennenkampf opted to march into Kirin province on 7 September. Organized resistance by Chinese in the north ended within a fortnight, when Prince Ch'ing (Yi Kuang) urged the Kirin governor-general to cease hostilities on 23 September. The province was surrendered to Rennenkampf on the same day. The situation in North China had also turned against the Chinese: on 14 July, one of the darkest days for the Russians in the Northeast, the allied expeditionary force had taken Tientsin, opening the road to Peking, and one month later, on 14 August, the legations were relieved and the defenseless Forbidden City surrounded by the allies.[42] The only remaining center of resistance was the Chinese army in Fengtien province under Governor-General Ching Chang, but Admiral Alekseyev was doing his best to change that. With Grodekov's northern offensive advancing on all four axes, Admiral Alekseyev was still awaiting sufficient reinforcement. Nonetheless, he did order a limited offensive toward Harbin on 10 August that advanced the front along the CER's South Manchuria line, culminating in the capture of Haicheng on 12 August, a city almost 300 kilometers from Port Arthur but still over 600 kilometers from Harbin to the north.[43]

On 6 September, Lieutenant General Dean I. Subbotich and his deputy, Major General Nikolai Fleischer, arrived in Port Arthur with a force of 7,000 soldiers, having sailed halfway around the world after leaving the Black Sea port of Odessa. With sufficient forces now on hand, the pace of operations increased. On 21 September, a little over two weeks later, Alekseyev, with 9,000 troops, launched the final offensive. The last major clash of the war took place three days later at Anshan, the future iron-mining center, which ended in a decisive victory for the Russians. The provincial capital of Mukden surrendered on 1 October without a fight. A few days later, Admiral Alekseyev and General Grodekov's troops joined forces at the Teihling rail station, effectively ending the war. After the initial Chinese raids that destroyed much of the CER, the conduct of the 1900 war in the Northeast proved to be a military anachronism as both armies, with the exception of the widespread use of modern rifles and artillery, fought a Napoleonic war: troops and horses were fed largely through foraging and were supplied by wagon trains; opposing sides formed lines facing each other; cannon fired directly at an enemy arrayed in plain sight; cavalry charged with sabers; and massed infantry dominated set-piece battles. While mopping-up operations continued over the next few weeks, the Russian conquest of the Northeast was complete. The next question to be decided in St. Petersburg was, what was to be done with this vast land?[44]

To end the conflict, the Boxer Protocol was signed in Peking on 7 September 1901. It added greater protections for foreigners in China and was backed up with the right to station foreign troops in Northern China and prohibit the presence of Chinese troops near the legations in Peking and Tientsin. Additionally, an indemnity was included—a financial punishment intended to both recover the cost of damages and to fiscally constrain the Ch'ing government. The thirty-nine-year indemnity was so onerous that the United States thought it could possibly bankrupt China. Because the Boxer Uprising had expanded into a war over the CER in the Northeast, the settlement between Russia and China moved beyond the Boxer Protocol. This is not to say that the Russians did not benefit greatly from the Peking settlement; they were to receive the largest share of indemnity, nearly 30 percent of the total. However, the Russians had more demands to make over the Northeast. For some of the tsar's senior military leaders, the solution was outright annexation into the Russian Empire.

As early as August 1900, after the conquest of Teheiho and Aigun, General Gribsky unilaterally declared the Amur region part of the Russian Empire. Grodekov, his commander, echoed the same sentiment when he declared, "After hard fighting, we have taken possession of the right bank, thus consolidating the great enterprise of annexing the whole of the Amur to Russia's dominions." War Minister Alexei N. Kuropatkin enthusiastically supported the idea of a Russian "Trans-Amur District," the region between the CER and Amur River. Several months later, in March 1901, Vice Admiral Alekseyev argued for Russia to authorize an open-ended occupation of not just the northern Amur region but all of Manchuria, using the defense of the CER as his rationale. Not everyone agreed with the annexation plans: Witte was strongly opposed, and even Alekseyev acknowledged that a deal with Japan over Korea had to be in place if the annexation was to succeed. In the absence of a consensus, high-level discussions of outright annexation of all or part of the Northeast continued into the summer. Peking attempted to thwart the designs, fully realizing that the 1900 Russian victory represented a further weakening of Ch'ing authority within their Manchu homeland. Further, the tsar's commanders on the scene were pushing their military advantage at the local level as well.[45]

First, Admiral Alekseyev unilaterally created a set of "Provisional Rules of Transfer for Fengtien Province" and coerced Governor-General Tseng-chi to sign them, even though they made the province a virtual colony of Russia. Next, St. Petersburg, using Chief Engineer Yugovich as a proxy, drafted the July 1901 "Kirin and Heilungkiang Convention," which was forced on the two provincial governor-generals. The agreements not only expanded Russian authority but also allowed the CER to develop and operate coal mines within fifteen kilometers of the rail lines in those two provinces, most notably the Dalainor mines in the far western reaches of Heilungkiang. The Kirin governor-general was also charged with creating a Department of Foreign and Railway Affairs at Harbin. He compliantly appointed Sung Hsiao-lion to the post. Militarily, the Russians excluded Chinese forces from the CER Zone, to include the Russian section of Harbin while permitting the CER guard corps, which had fought well during the war, to be significantly enlarged. The corps were renamed the Trans-Amur District Border Guards Special Corps in 1903. General Chichagov, who had led one of Grodekov's columns during the Boxer Uprising, took command. By 1904, on the eve of the Russo-Japanese War, the rail guard had expanded nearly sixfold, from under 4,500 troops in 1900 to just over 24,000, including infantry, cavalry, and artillery formations, all wearing new and unmistakably Russian military uniforms. Additionally, a Russian Amur River flotilla had been created, while the Chinese were barred from having men-of-wars on the Amur, Ussuri, and Sungari rivers. The Russian flotilla became one of the most powerful riverine forces in the world with the arrival of eight Typhoon class armored monitors in late 1910.[46]

Alarmed at the Russian attempt to sidestep Peking by negotiating directly with the Chinese governors, Peking effectively fought back: they refused to recognize the Fengtien transfer rules (a document that met with disapproval even in St. Petersburg), delayed the approval of the Kirin-Heilungkiang Convention, and pushed off a scheme championed by Witte that would have made the Russo-Chinese Bank the dominant financial institution in the Northeast. When Tsar Nicholas finally ruled out annexation in the face of Peking's resistance, the way to the 8 April 1902 Chinese-Russian Agreement was opened. Peking fared less well in regaining full control over the three Northeastern provinces. Despite Russia's pledge to return the region to Chinese administration, the tsar's troops remained, taking advantage of the conditions for their withdrawal written into the 1902 agreement: any "actions of other Powers" or "disturbance" could be used to justify a halt. At the close of 1903, all of Manchuria, save the small region abutting the Yingkow treaty port, remained under occupation by the Russian army. The Russians later gained the power to veto future Manchurian concessions offered to other powers or their citizens for mines or other interests and the construction of new railways. Peking's efforts to rein in the growing economic power of the CER also met with limited success: they restricted Russian control of mines developed beyond the fifteen-kilometer boundary and limited CER administration to the Dalainor coal mine, but the CER began a process of unrestrained exploitation of economic resources within the zone.[47]

The Chinese defeat had been felt hard within the ranks of its military in the Northeast. Virtually every regular army unit had been destroyed in battle, creating a power vacuum that was often filled by former soldiers and bandits; indeed, the two were often indistinguishable. One method the Ch'ing authorities used to rein in the bandits was to subvert them by granting amnesty with semiofficial status. One of the bandit leaders to take advantage was Chang Tso-lin, a young man in his midtwenties, a natural leader and the father of a three-year-old son, Hsueh-liang. He caught the eye of a local Manchu official, who won over Chang's loyalty by giving him command of a local garrison in Fengtien. For a man of Chang's abilities and ambitions, the timing was ideal. By 1904, the province became a focus of the Army Reorganization Commission, directed by Yuan Shih-kai, and within a few years, Chang Tso-lin was an up-and-coming figure within the Fengtien provincial forces. The term "Peiyang" (North Ocean) originated with the Ch'ing military reorganization in the 1880s when a foreign invasion along the lines of the Opium Wars was seen as the main threat. The plan had been to create two fleets, a Peiyang Fleet based at Weihaiwei and Lüshun (Port Arthur) with a Nanyang (South Ocean) Fleet at Foochow, each to be teamed with an army and a smaller riverine flotilla. By 1900, the Peiyang Fleet was still replacing the losses incurred during the Sino-Japanese War, the Nanyang Fleet badly needed modernization, and a southern army had never been formed. When the Boxer Uprising began, Yuan Shih-kai and his Newly Created Army were in the Shantung suppressing Boxers, and he refused imperial orders to attack the Allied forces, sparing his force. During the reorganization, the Newly Created Army evolved into the Peiyang Army, the only credible military force in the years immediately after 1900.[48]

The 1900 Russo-Chinese War revealed some painful truths to China and Russia. It offered an abject lesson on the mixed benefits gained through the CER, as they had come with a heavy price in both blood and treasure, and no amount of either on either's part seemed enough to pay the bill. One irony was that the CER had been built to cement a Sino-Russian military alliance aimed at rebuffing Japanese advances on the Northeast Asia mainland, but once the Boxer Uprising began, it instead became the focus of a war that left the local Chinese army in tatters, the railway in ruins, the Russian army in a position of regional supremacy, and a Japan that was undeterred in confronting the new and dangerous threat posed by Russia. The seeds of the next war had been sown, and Russia was about to learn the lesson of imperial overreach with Japan. Undeterred by the war, St. Petersburg continued to make the Northeast the center of its activities in the Far East. In the years after the Boxer Uprising, economic investment there outpaced the Priamur District, it was also home to more Russian soldiers, and to remove any ambiguity, when Nicholas established the Far Eastern Viceroyalty in 1903, he made Port Arthur the capital, not Khabarovsk, and placed Alekseyev, an admiral, in charge.[49]

This aggressive East Asia policy drove Japan to promptly resolve its rivalry with Russia over Korea. When the tsar adopted an unyielding negotiations stance, Japan came to see war as the only solution. Foreign minister Komura Jutaro, like Witte before him, noted in June 1903 that Russian military power stemming from a Manchuria traversed by the CER was of great importance. However, unlike Witte, he saw it as a mortal threat to Japan's interests in Korea. Railroads like the CER came to dominate military planning in Europe, America, and East Asia during the close of the nineteenth century because they allowed for the transfer of troops, equipment, and materials in quantities, all delivered at speeds unthinkable in an earlier age. The Japanese were as alarmed as the Chinese at the failure of the Russian army to leave the Northeast. They concluded that because the Chinese military was impotent in the years after the Boxer Uprising, the substantial Russian army and naval forces in the Northeast had to be directed at Japan. Where St. Petersburg sought to delay negotiations over the Korea question as an effective tactic while expanding Russian military might in response to perceived unreadiness, the Japanese increasingly saw them as examples of Russian duplicity and even deceit.[50]

The 1904–1905 Russo-Japanese War

To the Meiji leaders in Tokyo, that Russia appeared bent on dominating East Asia through force proved the wisdom of a war policy. The Triple Intervention had made clear to Japan the need for a European ally to preclude having to face alone a coalition of powers and the building of an army and navy able to fight and win a war against a Western power in East Asia. With the signing of the 1902 Anglo-Japanese alliance, the first goal had been met. By 1904, the Imperial Japanese Army (IJA) had been increased by six divisions to a total of thirteen, while the navy had grown from a combined fleet built around four dated capital ships to one possessing ten, with six modern, first-rate battleships, all of which had entered service in the last seven years. When the tsar failed to make meaningful concessions over Korea during close of 1903, Japan prepared for war. The ability to transport men and matériel along the CER quickly drew the attention of military planners on both sides. Earlier in June, the Russians successfully transported two brigades to the Far East, an impressive demonstration of the railway's military value. The Japanese officers concluded the CER could carry eight Russian military trains a day, matching their ability to supply their forces by ship, whereas War Minister Kuropatkin, during a 28 December conference with the tsar in St. Petersburg, saw danger in relying on a single line of supply—the CER—to deploy and sustain large forces in southern Manchuria. The Russians opted to delay negotiations with Japan once again, convinced that time was on their side, while the Japanese mobilized. When Tokyo's final offer, issued on 13 January, met with an unfavorable response, war broke out in February 1904.[51]

On the ground, the 1904–1905 Russo-Japanese War was fought almost entirely in the Northeast, commencing in May, when General Kuroki Tamemoto's 1st Army crossed the Yalu River from Korea near Antung and defeated General Sassulitch's along with the bulk of his 2nd Siberian Corps. From that time until the war's end after the Japanese victory at Mukden in March 1905, the Japanese never lost the initiative on the battlefield. After Kuroki's victory on the Yalu, the 2nd Army under General Oku Yasukata landed on the Liaotung Peninsula, splitting the Russian forces. A corps under General Anatoly M. Stoessel was cut off by June and besieged in Port Arthur by August, while the remainder of the army was arrayed between the Korean frontier and Mukden. The CER and SMR proved indispensable, but as Kuropatkin—now the senior commander in the Northeast—predicted, the railways were unable to sustain large mobile Russian forces in southern Manchuria, and a lack of local coal supplies further hampered his operations.[52]

Japan continued to build up its forces. Kuroki was joined by the 3rd Army under General Nogi Maresuke, forcing Kuropatkin to gradually fall back along the SMR, his essential line of communication. By midfall, Stoessel stubbornly held out at Port Arthur, while Kuropatkin had been defeated in two major battles (at Liaoyang in September and along the Shao River in October). Both sides' exhaustion forced a temporary end to the major campaigning, but the war was moving unalterably in Japan's favor. On 1 January 1905, Port Arthur fell to Nogi's badly bloodied 3rd Army, while the decisive land battle of the war at Mukden ended in defeat for Russia in March. Kuropatkin was relived of command shortly afterward, and when the Russian Baltic fleet was destroyed in the battle of the Tsushima Straits in late May, any hope of Russian victory disappeared. By mid-June, St. Petersburg requested an armistice, but Tokyo declined to accept until peace negotiations began on 1 August under the good offices of the United States at the Portsmouth naval yard. The war was over, but at a terrible cost for both sides:

the Japanese saw approximately 60,000 killed in action with another 20,000 dying from disease and close to a quarter million wounded, while the Russian casualties easily exceeded those totals.[53]

Leading Chinese generals like Yuan Shih-kai could only observe at a distance—not that there was a rush to invoke the 1896 military alliance and come to Russia's aid. In some quarters in Peking, there were arguments to walk away from Russia entirely and seek an alliance with Japan, although the idea never gained traction. When war came in 1904, the loose language of the alliance requiring China to commit "forces of which they can dispose at that moment" allowed the Chinese military, still recovering from the losses suffered during the Boxer Uprising, to refrain from direct involvement. Yuan made it clear to his superiors that he commanded a mere twenty thousand soldiers—one-tenth the number available at the start of the Sino-Japanese War nearly a decade earlier. Being a secret alliance in an era of secret diplomacy further played into the hands of a reticent court in Peking; there was little that the Russians could have done to compel the Chinese to enter the war on their behalf even if the tsar desired it, which was not the case.[54]

The war offered insights into the military advances and geopolitics that reshaped not only the future of East Asia but also warfare of that era. Militarily, the clash in the Northeast signified how easy it was slide into a devastating conflict, given the manner the Powers approached war making through bilateral diplomatic ultimatum. The war also represented a quantum leap over that of the Boxer Uprising, as the fighting bore little resemblance to the small-scale combat of that war. It is worth noting, however, that most of the senior Russian officers of 1900 proved capable in fighting the Japanese four years later, and usually at the head of much larger forces, even though Kuropatkin and Alekseyev emerged with tarnished records. In the earlier conflict, no Russian column exceeded 20,000 troops. Every major clash of 1904–1905 exceeded that number; several involved hundreds of thousands of men, and the Russians suffered thousands of casualties, routinely exceeding the total losses of the 1900 war in a single day. Tactically, advances in individual weapons redefined the lethality of war as both rate of fire and range increased, while smokeless rifle cartridges not only improved the ability of soldiers to conceal their firing positions but also removed blinding clouds of smoke, allowing for the better acquisition of targets. The introduction of trench lines protected by barbed wire, rapid-firing cannon, machine guns, and massed infantry formations made the ground a killing field. A young Japanese officer, Sakurai Tadayoshi, described the carnage after a Port Arthur battle: "Dead bodies . . . dyed with dark purple blood, their faces blue, their eyelids swollen, their hair clotted with blood and dust . . . no one dared to go near."[55] The cumulative effect of these innovations contributed to a horror that would be further expanded beginning nine years later, with the outbreak of World War I.[56]

Geopolitically, the Russo-Japanese War ended with the creation of the tripartite alignment of powers that would contend for control of Northeast Asia for the next several decades: China, Japan, and Russia. The Northeast remained a potential flash point for conflict, but the years that followed were surprisingly stable, as Russia and Japan had reached a détente in July 1907 that proved remarkably durable. Many Japanese leaders, such as General Yamagata, were constantly on guard for an anticipated war of revenge, but Russian foreign minister Alexandr P. Izvolsky was confident that war in the short term was highly unlikely. Durability stemmed from a significant degree of agreement in postwar aims between Russia and Japan. Even before the war, Kuropatkin defined Russian vital interests in the Northeast as the Trans-Amur, while Japan's war aims were to ensure its primacy in Korea and regain what had been lost in the Triple Intervention after the Sino-Japanese War: a presence on Liaotung Peninsula to include the South Manchuria Railroad, albeit a railway that lay in ruins in 1905. The treaty of Portsmouth, combined with the July 1907 convention, made meeting the imperialist ambitions of both nations possible and went far in defusing the residual bad feelings between the empires; the signing of the Anglo-Russian entente in August further calmed the waters.[57]

Even China emerged in a better position than it had been in 1904, as the Portsmouth treaty led to the speedy withdrawal of both Russian and Japanese troops into their respective administrative zones at a specified level: fifteen guards per mile of railway. However, there were residual problems for Peking—including a lack of regular Chinese army units and compromised loyalty by high-ranking officials, as demonstrated by Fengtien governor-general Tseng-chi during the Russian occupation—that revealed glaring weaknesses that had to be addressed. As late as 1909, there were only a few thousand regular army troops in the Northeast. To correct this deficiency, Yuan Shih-kai shifted some of his Peiyang units north to augment the provincial forces beginning in 1907. By 1911, they had grown to three divisions and one mixed brigade. One of first units sent was the 3rd Division under General Hsu Shih-chang. In the ranks was a promising young company commander, Feng Yu-hsiang, who later became one of the most powerful military leaders in China. Fixing the administrative problem took longer. By 1905, Tseng-chi had been replaced by General Chao Erh-hsun, and two years later, General Hsu become the first viceroy of the Three Eastern Provinces in an attempt to strengthen Ch'ing control over their homeland. Both were trusted lieutenants of Yuan Shih-kai. Yuan's political career became another casualty of the tripartite rivalry when he was forced to resign in January 1909 for having failed to gain the backing of the United States in a plan aimed at breaking Russo-Japanese dominance over the region.[58]

In the period after the Russo-Japanese War, the Ch'ing finally opted to create a national military, the New Army, using Yuan Shih-kai's Peiyang Army as the nucleus. Designed to reach a final strength of thirty-six divisions composed of two brigades of two infantry regiments each along with cavalry, artillery, engineer, and support troops, the New Army was to be one of the largest in the world. Progress was slow. By 1911, only fourteen division and twenty brigades (that were to expand into divisions) had been formed. In reality, the New Army consisted of two forces. The Peiyang Army, composed of six divisions based in North China, was a true national army designed to meet any challenge. The remaining divisions and brigades took on a more provincial role and intended to deal with local or regional threats. To fill the ranks, provincial governors were directed to create military schools, including an academy for officer training. The use of modern curricula at the preparatory schools and academies attracted qualified candidates who previously would have pursued degrees through the just-abolished civil service examination process. This led to the creation of a provincially centered army as well as an increase in the quality and political awareness of young officers, who began to play a role at the highest levels of local and national governance.[59]

One of those who benefited from the military modernization and expansion reforms in the Northeast was Chang Tso-lin, who soon gained control over five battalions of Fengtien provincial troops, often referred to as patrol battalions and a replacement for the old-style Green Standard formations abandoned years earlier. His ability to recruit and train such a large unit earned him favorable attention from governors Chao and Hsu as well as the provincial military commander, General Chang Hsi-luan. Although still denied admission into the regular army, Chang

Tso-lin used his position to secure promotions for his closest subordinates, like Wu Chun-sheng, who had been with him since the 1900 Boxer Uprising, creating a highly loyal force. Chang's fortunes continued to improve when Chao replaced Hsu as viceroy just before the 1911 Revolution erupted on 10 October in Wuchang. Wuchang, the provincial capital of Hupeh, was one of a three-city metropolis known as Wuhan that also included Hanyang and Hankow; located at the confluence of the Yangtze and Han rivers, it was one of the economic centers of China. It also became the flash point that changed China.[60]

The CER's early years of operation had proven to be a mixed blessing. While being a remarkable economic stimulus, it also created an international rivalry that quickly descended into armed conflicts that failed to settle the competing desires of Japan and Russia to dominate and China to retain sovereignty over the Northeast. The CER played a central role throughout. During the Boxer Uprising in the Northeast, the railway became the focus of Chinese antiforeign anger—an outcome that almost led to its complete destruction. The resulting Russian occupation and CER reconstruction helped lead the way to a military clash between Japan and Russia. The conclusion of the Russo-Japanese War led to a division of the railway while creating a new balance of power, and with it a relative calm for several years. But as China entered a new era during the second decade of the twentieth century, the outstanding issues over control of the CER would be carried forward unresolved.

2 | The Northeast Evolving: The 1911 Revolution and the Great War

The 1911 Revolution

Few realized the gravity of the situation at Wuchang in early October 1911—neither the political powder keg that would soon erupt into revolution nor the role played by the New Army. Since its formation under Yuan, the New Army had become one of China's most important and respected institutions. This caught the attention of Sun Yat-sen and his Tung-meng Hui, or Revolutionary Alliance, which had labored tirelessly, if futilely, to overthrow the Ch'ing—there had been at least ten failed uprisings before 1911. After a failed 1910 attempt to assassinate the prince regent, a co-organizer of the alliance, Wang Ching-wei, was imprisoned. Learning from defeat, the alliance moved to enroll receptive New Army officers capable of leading a force to challenge Peking.[1]

Despite the benefits gained through New Army recruits, the 1911 revolution came close to being one more abortive revolt. Planned to take place in Hankow on 6 October and then delayed, a mishap by bomb makers on 9 October led to the discovery of the rebel headquarters and documents containing activists' names, including New Army sympathizers. Throughout the day, police arrested and often summarily executed the revolutionaries; one bomb maker, shackled hand and foot, was publicly displayed before execution. Zeal undid the police. Suspect troop formations were confined to barracks, a move that ignited the revolution when detained prorepublican soldiers mutinied in the dead of night. Others joined. Soon they controlled the army headquarters and advanced on the government center. By the morning of 10 October, nearly every New Army unit in Wuhan had joined the mutiny, which fell under the leadership of brigade commander Colonel Li Yuan-hung. Li was a sincere republican but a reluctant revolutionary; he had to be persuaded by armed soldiers. The few hundred remaining Ch'ing troops under General Chang Piao awaited help at the Peking-Hankow rail station at Neikow.[2]

Despite the early rebel success, the timing of the rebellion favored the Ch'ing militarily. Imperial troops were in the midst of their annual exercise, formed into three armies and in a high state of readiness. This allowed for the speedy dispatch of troops to aid Chang at Wuhan and to enter western Hupeh. Optimistic that the imperial armies would go over to the republicans, Li—now the rebel general—was not overly alarmed. He was overconfident; the uprising tested but did not sever all loyalties, and both republican and Ch'ing leaders sought the support of Yuan, still the de facto head of the Peiyang divisions and considered best able to win the emerging war. After gaining assurances from his supporters, on 20 October, Yuan sent Peking a list of demands that included full powers as commander and the establishment of a constitutional monarchy.[3]

His demands were hastily, if less than enthusiastically, agreed to by child emperor Pu-yi's advisors, and Yuan joined with the Ch'ing. On 27 October, he came out of retirement and took command of the armies. With the military house in order, the Ch'ing moved on the political front. On 31 October, Peking issued an imperial edict accepting blame for the disturbances while vowing to uphold the constitution and enact reforms. Two days later, it was decreed that Yuan would become prime minister, a move aimed to both appease republicans and assuage Yuan's ambitions. Now fully in charge, Yuan placed his loyalists in command. As the 1st Army neared Neikow, he ordered his loyal subordinate, Feng Kuo-chang, then commanding the 2nd Army, to take over the 1st Army, replacing Yin-chang, the senior Manchu commander, and sent Tuan Chi-jui to lead the 2nd Army. Wuhan became the main and (Yuan hoped) the decisive battleground.[4]

With new leaders in place, the battle for Wuhan began. Feng and Tuan had reached Hankow, and by 27 October, they were threatening Wuchang and the important Hanyang arsenal. In three days of fighting, they gained control of the rail lines and began to encircle Wuchang. The greatest loss of life occurred at Hankow—not in combat but in a massive fire. Thousands perished and more were left homeless. After a brief calm after the conflagration, the fighting began anew. On 5 November, the final push to take Hankow began; the city fell after four days. Feng and Tuan attacked Hanyang on 24 November, opening with a terrific night bombardment followed by the construction of pontoon bridges across the Han River under withering fire. As in the Russo-Japanese War, entrenchments, Maxim machine guns, and rapid-fire howitzers made the battlefields places of almost unimaginable carnage.

After four days of costly fighting in cold, wet weather, imperial forces captured Hanyang. Facing defeat, General Li requested a cease-fire on Yuan's terms on 30 November. Yuan accepted and agreed to send representatives to a republican assembly at Shanghai. By treating directly with Li, Yuan weakened republican authority and created an opportunity to co-opt Li. The effort failed, but Li came to trust Yuan. The cease-fire also recognized a broader reality, while the imperial offensive met with success at Wuhan that was not the case elsewhere.[5]

Beyond Wuhan, and advancing with remarkable speed, the revolution spread. The alliance had succeeded in penetrating the New Army across the nation, and there were uprisings in six other provinces. As many as one fifth of the officers at the Kwangsi Military Academy were republicans. Changsha, the Hunan capital, fell to New Army troops on 22 October, and soldiers in Fukien rose up in early November. Even in the Ch'ing's northern stronghold, General Chang Shao-feng sent the Court a prorepublican manifesto on 30 October demanding its acceptance before advancing on the rebels, and in Mukden, brigade commander Lan Tien-wei openly supported the revolution.[6]

New leaders entered the scene. Several would play a role in the events that ended in the 1929 Sino-Soviet conflict. Feng Yu-hsiang, who had risen to command a battalion in Chang Shao-feng's division, joined an abortive prorepublican mutiny in December and was forced to resign. When Wuhan erupted, twenty-four-year-old Chiang Kai-shek was finishing his military academy training in Japan. With two companions, he departed and found the way to his home province of Chekiang, where he led a rebel attack that seized the governor's residence at Hangchow on 4 November. Chiang then left for Shanghai and gained the attention of revolutionary leaders at the head of a regiment under Chen Chi-mei, the alliance governor in Kiangsu, during the capture of Nanking; he later took command of a newly formed brigade. Colonel Yen Hsi-shan, a Tung-meng Hui member, marched on Taiyuan and became the Shansi military governor.[7]

The Ch'ing continued to resist, but the tide was turning. Steeled by success, Sun Yat-sen departed London on 21 November for Shanghai, and a republic took form as more provinces opted for independence. In December, Wu Ting-fang, the foreign minister for the nascent revolutionary government in Shanghai, made an appeal for foreign recognition, a move that was significant in two regards: the republicans declared control over fourteen of China's eighteen provinces, and they felt confident enough to directly challenge Ch'ing authority at an international level.[8]

The provinces in the Northeast were not included in that total, as the revolution there had met with little success. As the Manchu homeland, the region followed a different path, best seen in the struggle for Mukden. As Yuan withdrew his Peiyang divisions from the Northeast to the south in late October, provincial patrol battalions, like those commanded by Chang Tso-lin, were called on to repress local revolutionaries. The situation was particularly threatening in Fengtien, as the only remaining New Army unit was Lan's prorepublican brigade, and Chang was ordered by Governor-General Chao Erh-hsun to move his forces to Mukden in November and suppress the provincial assembly under the sway of the republicans. Led by Chang Yung, they threatened to declare independence if Chao accepted a Russian loan that the assembly had vetoed on 12 November. At that time, a pro-Ch'ing officer in the brigade initiated a countercoup, forcing General Lan to flee first to Mukden's Japanese quarter and then to Shanghai, while Chang Tso-lin's troops surrounded the assembly building to ensure a secession vote would not take place.[9]

Even though Chang and his troops were ethnic Chinese, their fealty to the Ch'ing was unsurprising. While loyalty to Chang counted most, since the earliest days of the Manchus, the banners had included ethnic Chinese and Mongols; they remained loyal after their dissolution. Fengtien in particular was home to Chinese who had been integrated into the Manchu nation for centuries, such as Governor-General Chao's family, who had been members of the Hanjun Plain-Blue Banner. Chang Tso-lin, whose family had only resided in Fengtien for a century, remained a Ch'ing adherent throughout.

When republican leaders in Mukden persisted in supporting the revolution, Chang carried out a purge in January 1912 that descended into a bloody cycle of nightly raids, arrests, and executions by his men, followed by retaliatory bomb attacks against his forces. The struggle ended in the deaths of several hundred revolutionaries, including their leader, Chang Yung. It was also during this time that Chang received his first Japanese military advisor, Captain Machino Takema, who had been sent by the interior ministry in Peking to assist him in containing the rebellion. After crushing the revolutionaries, Chang Tso-lin was finally allowed to enter the regular army. He emerged as the most powerful military leader in the province when his patrol battalions were combined and expanded into the 27th Division. Yuan conferred upon him the rank of lieutenant general.[10]

Holding firm in the north held little value. The Ch'ing were doomed, and the cost of war hastened the end. Suffering under the Boxer indemnity, in the years leading up to 1911, Peking had been borrowing at seven times the rate of two decades earlier, and the added strain of maintaining a large field army proved unbearable. As in the case of Chang Tso-lin's troops, the army exploded in size during the revolution. On 10 October there were 48 brigades, and by February 1912 the opposing armies mustered 146 with over 700,000 men under arms. Within weeks of the start of the revolution, imperial soldiers were refusing to fight unless they were paid, and the Ch'ing scrambled for resources. An ammunition shortage in December was temporarily solved by a shipment of 40 million rounds; a few weeks later, the press reported that Peking would have to accept any lender's terms to gain more funds. On 21 December, unpaid imperial troops quit Tibet. By month's end, and despite victories at Hankow and Hanyang, Yuan realized that fighting was impossible without paying his soldiers. Failure to obtain an advance from a 150 million franc Anglo–French–Belgian loan drove the Ch'ing to desperation. The Powers opposed new loans to either side. This played into the republicans' hands, as they now largely controlled provincial revenues and had access to Shanghai's sympathetic financial markets along with funds from the overseas Chinese community. With the Forbidden City's coffers nearly empty, the Empress Dowager Tzu-an pledged 3 million taels from her dowry to keep the armies in the field for a few weeks. However, news that Peking was selling imperial jewelry and art treasures in Europe signaled the end was near. The ability of the Ch'ing to continue the war they were losing was rapidly drawing to a close.[11]

Negotiations to end the war began on 18 December in Shanghai as Wu Ting-fang, assisted by Wang Cheng-ting (C. T. Wang), a brilliant twenty-nine-year-old Yale University law school graduate, sat down with Tang Shao-yi. Tang was an experienced negotiator, a close confidant of Yuan and a republican sympathizer. The negotiations started off badly: the unyielding position of the revolutionaries to replace the dynasty with a republic ruled from Nanking led to a suspension of the talks after two days as Tang urgently requested to confer with Peking. The republican drive to end the monarchy was expected. Sun Yat-sen stated on 25 November that the Republic of China should adhere to the United

States' model, with guarantees of provincial autonomy. General Li, sitting at the revolution's center in Wuhan, averred that his vision of a new China was one based on the American republic, a "United States of China." On 28 December, the Manchu court agreed to confer "on a wider basis," an unmistakable signal that the emperor's abdication was acceptable. Moving quickly, republican delegates met and elected Sun as president. General Li was named vice president on 29 December, and Peking made a conciliatory announcement outlining a transfer-of-power process that included a national conference for the formation of a republic. Unwilling to wait, the Republic of China was declared by the revolutionaries on 1 January 1912, and the "Double Tenth" came to be recognized as the national day of independence.[12]

The New Republic and Frontier Imperialism

The revolution began with an army mutiny, provincial secession, and a disjointed military campaign where generals, not politicians, assumed primacy, and ended in a republic. Fittingly, a three-step ritual was orchestrated to transfer the reins of power. When Pu-yi abdicated on 12 February 1912, no central authority assumed power in Peking. Instead, Sun Yat-sen became a caretaker head of state who oversaw the too-hurried drafting of the provisional constitution, followed by his resignation in favor of Yuan Shih-kai, who assumed the presidency on 13 March 1912.

Since coming out of retirement, Yuan had made clear that he sought full executive authority. Having never demonstrated a belief in strong legislative assemblies, his first order of business was to rein in their powers. He watched with unease as the provisional senate enacted laws to hold parliamentary elections by year's end. Worse, Sun's followers formed the Kuomintang (KMT), or Nationalist Party, in August to supersede the Tong-meng hui. When the KMT emerged victorious at the close of the January 1913 voting, Yuan acted with ruthless speed. In March, he had Sung Chiao-jen, the leader who orchestrated the KMT victory and a likely premier, assassinated; he then reestablished Peking as the capital. When the assembly took its seats on 8 April, it was already hobbled. The republicans fought back by launching the second revolution in July, again through a process of provincial secession. Anhwei, Kiangsi, and Kiangsu declared independence. In all, seven provinces rebelled, but they were rapidly crushed by the Peiyang Army. By November, Sun was again living in exile, and the KMT had been outlawed.[13]

Appointed by a rump parliament to serve a five-year term, Yuan took the reins of power on the Double Tenth of 1913 and then rejected the draft permanent constitution on 31 October. He ordered a parliamentary recess on 4 November, followed by its dismissal in January 1914. Operating under a 1 May constitutional compact, he turned the legislature into a political echo chamber by creating the Council of State, consisting of eight ministers under a premier, all appointed by the president. That was followed by the closing of the provincial assemblies and a petition in November from sixteen governors urging they be directly appointed by the president, a power Yuan embraced. By the close of 1914, the republic appeared gone in all but name, save Sun and his followers.[14]

Yuan was left sitting at the top, but without the authority he craved, as the central government was constantly short of funds. The financial problems that had plagued the Ch'ing continued in Peking unabated. Empowered with the ability to tax, the governors sustained themselves indefinitely while starving the national treasury. Without adequate funds, and when the incumbent compromises, deals, and ever-shifting coalitions of provincial governors-general failed to create a stable hierarchy, Yuan Shih-kai ruled not as the undisputed head of state but often as little more than a first among equals.[15]

Beyond the problems in Peking, China's border regions remained in turmoil. The 1912 constitution explicitly preserved the Ch'ing borders, but the indigenous peoples on the frontier and the other Powers saw things differently. The Mongols were the earliest to assert themselves. Reacting unfavorably to talk of a Republic of China, the Mongol princes ousted their Ch'ing overlord, the Amban. In early December 1911, they announced that they would declare independence if the republic became a reality. They made good their threat when they enthroned Javzandamba Hutagt as the "reincarnated Buddhist ruler," or Bogd Khan. Tensions escalated on 8 January 1912 when St. Petersburg demanded that Peking recognize Mongolian independence or Russia would send troops there as a guarantee. The court in Peking, fearful of what would happen not only over Mongolia but also over British designs on Tibet, never provided a meaningful response. The tsar, who had yet to recognize the republic, remained true to his word and dispatched soldiers to Mongolia in March. The Tibetans also rose up. The exiled

Dalai Lama returned in 1913 to an independent Tibet temporarily free of foreign soldiers. On 5 November 1913, Peking settled with the tsar, granting Russia special economic rights in Outer Mongolia. The republic's hold on the old Ch'ing imperial frontier had been shattered.[16]

The Northeast was not exempted. Exploiting regional autonomy also caught the attention of Russian and Japanese expansionists, and the chaos of the revolution opened an opportunity for joint annexation of the Northeast. In November 1911, CER chief manager General Dmitiri L. Horvat in Harbin marshaled about 3,000 railcars for troop deployments on the border at Manchouli, and the generals in St. Petersburg waited for a pretext. The Japanese War Ministry looked hard at annexation, but when a mobilization plan was leaked to the Tokyo press, domestic opinion turned against the expansionists. Left to their own devices, the tsar's agents in Trans-Baikal, in collusion with Horvat, fomented a January 1912 uprising among the Buryat Mongols in western Heilungkiang, who succeeded in capturing Hailar and Manchouli. It took until June for Chinese forces to bring the rebellion to heel.[17]

Tokyo and St. Petersburg strengthened their position in the Northeast vis-à-vis Peking through relationships with provincial commanders. The idea of dealing with autonomous governors in the Northeast had been Russia's desire since the end of the Boxer Uprising, so it welcomed the new arrangement. Japan also saw advantages in local relationships unencumbered by an agenda originating in Peking, and both Japanese counsel Ochiai Kentaro in Mukden and local Kwantung army officers such as Machino found a man they could work with: Chang Tso-lin.[18]

China and the Northeast during the Opening of World War I

While the outbreak of the Great War in August 1914 was greeted enthusiastically by the European powers, the reaction in the Northeast was indifferent. Politically and militarily, the war initially had no real effect. China remained neutral, while Russia and Japan joined the Allied Powers against Germany, leaving the trinational relationship in the Northeast largely unchanged. What little fighting took place in China was brief and not in Manchuria; rather, it was confined to an Anglo-Japanese expedition aimed at the German leasehold at Tsingtao on the Shantung Peninsula. Begun in October and over by November, it cost the lives of some 400 Japanese soldiers with another thousand wounded, and left Japan in control of the German holdings.[19]

The war did kick off the most significant period of economic expansion in the history of the Northeast. The first to feel the demand were the farmers, as the need to feed millions of soldiers strained the world's agricultural supplies, pushing up production of soybeans by over a third compared to the prewar market; soybean flour and oil milling grew at even faster rates. By war's end, soybeans became the dominant cash crop in Manchuria. In 1914, only 24 percent of Manchurian soybean oil was exported, but by 1918, the figure had risen 93 percent.[20]

Not all ventures were successful. A Japanese experiment in rice production failed in 1915. Sugar beets proved profitable while the war lasted, but when postwar prices plunged, the industry floundered; the last mill was shuttered in 1926. The growth also proved uneven: southern Manchuria boomed, while the northern region, dominated by trade with Russia, fell into decline. In 1914, the total value of trade in the north was valued at 41 million Haikuan taels and 150 million taels in the south, but by 1918, northern trade had dropped to 27 million, while in the south, it had grown to 290 million taels. The world war was destroying the Russian economy. The tsar's government was so desperately strapped for cash that it entered into discussions with Japan to sell part of the CER in 1916, although no agreement was reached.[21]

The most far-reaching advances were made in the industrial sector. Steel production in the Northeast, which had been under development before the war, finally entered the market and flourished rapidly, with the blowing of the first blast furnace at the Pehshihu foundry in 1915 and Anshan in 1919. Joint ventures came to the fore. In Kirin province, a Sino-Russian coal mine opened in 1915, and a Sino-Japanese silver and copper venture began operations in 1916. Wartime demand for wool blankets and tussah kicked off the textile industry. It was also during the war that what Asada Masafumi termed the "holy trinity" of railways, ports, and shipping fully integrated the Northeastern economy into the global marketplace. Of the three, railroads—the CER, SMR, and the Peking–Mukden Railway—played the dominant role.[22] The growth in industrialization also increased the need for a literate workforce, driving an expansion in public education; primary school enrollment in China jumped from under 3 million students in 1912 to over 5 million by war's end, and in the middle schools, from under 100,000 to nearly 400,000. The Northeast was booming.[23]

In August 1915, Chang Hsi-luan, one of Chang Tso-lin's earliest mentors, retired as Fengtien governor and saw to it that his protégé replaced him. As part of the 1916 reforms, he was given the new title of tuchun, or military governor. Chang's rise had taken a major leap. Credit for the Northeast's sustained economic success must go in large part to his May 1917 appointment of Wang Yung-chiang as director of finance. Wang created an environment that offered economic opportunity, a strong currency (the Fengtien silver yuan), and fiscally sound administration. The Northeast was now one of China's richest regions and able to finance the ambitions of a man like Chang.[24]

The Leadership Crisis in Peking

In Peking, things were not going as well as in the Northeast. As Europe became fully occupied by its terrible war, Yuan Shih-kai faced his greatest diplomatic challenge when Tokyo issued its Twenty-One Demands in January 1915. In a crude power grab, the Okuma Shigenobu cabinet strove to reshape East Asia's economic, military, and political status quo in Japan's favor and at China's expense. Unable to confront Tokyo militarily, and his counterproposals rejected, Yuan submitted after receiving an ultimatum on 7 May. It was a Pyrrhic victory, as Japan's demands never became a reality beyond rights already attained in the Northeast. Instead, Tokyo alienated the other Powers and irreparably damaged Japan's standing in China. A month later, Yuan's reputation was further tarnished when he accepted the tsar's 7 June 1915 Tripartite Agreement in Regard to Outer Mongolia that confirmed China's superficial suzerainty but granted Mongol autonomy and secured Russia's economic dominance over the region.[25]

A humiliated Peking muddled on until Yuan put everything on its head in an attempt to make himself the great emperor of China on 1 January 1916. Reestablishing the empire was not far-fetched; indeed, all but two of the world powers were monarchies (France and the United States being exceptions), and an imperial system had ruled over China for two millennia. It seemed a logical path in restoring national unity. However, when the idea was put into motion, it failed. Loyalty within the army was Yuan's strength, and he sought the throne by trying to intimidate, bribe, and co-opt a sufficient number of generals to ensure his ascendancy. It was a flawed strategy. His support never transcended the small cadre of leaders personally bound to him, and the effort collapsed. That resistance sprang up at once showed how far republican China had gone along the often contradictory path of centralized power, local autonomy, revolutionary republicanism, and military rule.[26]

Yuan's sudden death on 6 June 1916 left a leaderless and enfeebled administration and gave birth to a strain of warlordism that rewrote the rules of governance. In Peking, Premier Tuan Chi-jui emerged as the de facto ruler. One of Yuan's most capable lieutenants, in addition to having commanded the 2nd Imperial Army during the 1911 revolution, Tuan had earlier served with Yuan during the 1900 suppression of the Shantung Boxers, helped direct the expansion of the New Army, and later served as minister of war during the Yuan presidency before becoming premier in June 1916.[27]

Tuan's goal of entering the war with the Allies brought him into immediate conflict with the isolationist policy of the acting president, Li, and a parliament absorbed in completing a constitution. While able to secure the assembly votes needed to break diplomatic relations with Germany in March 1917, Tuan failed to gain a declaration of war, and Li moved to dismiss Tuan on 23 May. Tuan ignored Li and consolidated his power by unifying a number of like-minded tuchuns, primarily from Anhwei, Chekiang, Fukien, and Shanghai, into the so-called Anfu Clique.[28]

Realizing that votes were not enough to face down Tuan, Li shored up his military power by reaching out to General Chang Hsun. Chang Hsun agreed to move his troops to Peking if Li would dissolve the national assembly, triggering a new election cycle. This was a risky move by Li, as his influence over the assembly made him the front-runner to be the next president after the current term expired on 10 October 1918. He had little choice, however, as Tuan could not be put off until the next year. He dissolved the assembly on 13 June, and Chang arrived with his army the next day. It proved to be a poor decision. On 1 July, Chang Hsun shocked the nation when he moved to restore Emperor Pu-yi to the throne and forced Li to flee the capital. The coup collapsed within a fortnight after Tuan sent in his army. Arriving in Peking as the rescuing hero, Tuan returned to the premiership on 14 July and assumed total power.[29]

Chang Tso-lin Rises as the National Government Fragments

Reaction to the failed restoration reshaped the leadership not only in Peking but also in the Northeast. A number of northern commanders initially supported the effort, and when it failed, they became politically vulnerable. Kirin governor Meng En-yuan and Heilungkiang governor Hsu Lan-chou, among others, had thrown in their lot with Chang Hsun. An exception was Chang Tso-lin. Seeing an opening, he appealed to Tuan to consolidate his control over the Northeast by replacing Meng and Hsu with his own subordinates. Tuan agreed to the replacement of Hsu with Pao Kuei-ching, a relative of Chang and a man trusted by Tuan. However, the matter of replacing Meng, a senior Peiyang Army leader, would have to wait. Why Chang, an ardent Ch'ing supporter in 1911, balked at the restoration remains unclear, but one factor may have been the loyalty earned by Peking's decision to expand the Fengtien force to three divisions, making Chang the Northeast's dominant military commander with an army numbering close to 70,000. In early August, Li's old 1911 Wuhan adversary became acting president: General Feng Kuo-Chang, the second replacement to fill the remainder of Yuan's five-year term.[30]

The change in presidents was more significant that it appeared. Li's removal and the dissolution of parliament ended opposition to entering the war, and on 14 August, China declared war on the Central Powers, although little could be offered in the way of support. In addition, the collapse of the Li presidency left two of Yuan's trusted commanders, Tuan and Feng, vying for control of Peking and splitting the Peiyang Army into factions. It also deepened the political wounds in the south, where Sun Yat-sen declared his opposition to the new Peking regime and left Shanghai for Canton. On 31August 1917, under the protection of General Lu Jung-ting, Sun established a rival government. China became a divided nation just as World War I entered a climactic phase.[31]

The Russian Revolution and the Chinese Eastern Railroad

While the Byzantine ramifications of Yuan Shih-kai's death played out, an event far from China threw the Northeast's stability into confusion. The combined political, economic, and military stresses the war placed on a stumbling tsarist empire reached the breaking point in 1917. On 8 March, a Petrograd rally celebrating International Women's Day erupted into a riot over bread shortages. In the following days, disturbances grew into mass protests that paralyzed the capital. When panicked officials ordered the army to restore order, they refused, and the monarchy's authority vanished. Eight days later, the tsar abdicated. In his place, a provisional government was declared, first under Prime Minister Gregori Lvov, then Aleksandr Kerensky, who took office in July. The March revolution unsettled most Allied leaders save American president Woodrow Wilson, who welcomed the overthrow of what he saw as an unjust autocracy. In the Northeast, the Russian collapse rattled but did not immediately unravel the peace. Things appeared to restabilize when China entered the war on the Allied side on 14 August.[32]

Despite the entrance of China and the United States, the Allies were struggling in 1917 and faced possible defeat, a reality that brought Northeast Asia into the Allied plans. An exhausted France and Britain were determined to keep active a Russian-led Eastern Front that tied down over 2 million German and Austro-Hungarian troops. The French army was nearing collapse, as demonstrated by the May and June mutinies that affected nearly half of the frontline infantry regiments. However, the Russian military faced a direr situation. Russian support for the war was so weak that the newly appointed foreign minister, Pavel Milyukov, could only send a secret reassurance that the provisional government would still abide by the 1914 treaty of London, an agreement that pledged each to fight together and not seek a separate peace with the Central Powers. When the note was made public in May, Milyukov was forced to resign. That, coupled with the failure of the so-called Kerensky offensive and the rise of the Ukrainian autonomy movement in June, sealed the provisional government's fate. The Bolsheviks gained mass support through their policy of "Peace, Land, Bread," and on 7 November (23 October in the old-style calendar), they rose up in Petrograd and stormed the government chambers in the Winter Palace. By the next day, the Kerensky government was out and a Bolshevik regime under Vladimir Lenin stood in its place.[33]

The October Revolution set the stage for the Allied intervention into Northeastern Asia. Grounded in desperation to keep Russia in the war, getting war matériel to the Eastern Front, especially along the TSRR that included the CER, became the focus. The United States was particularly concerned about getting military supplies into the hands of Russian soldiers. To appreciate the railroad's importance, a short study of one of the most obscure United States military organizations of World War I is in order: the Russian Railway Service Corps (RRSC), a group of American railway experts sent to help the provisional government. In the months after the creation of the provisional government, Wilson had sent two missions of railway experts to Russia during May and July (a Railway Advisory Commission and the nascent RRSC) in hopes of finding a better way to transport American war matériel arriving in Vladivostok to the Eastern Front. Central to their mission was the CER.[34]

Things along the CER were faring badly. As events unfolded in Petrograd during the close of 1917, loyalties within the Russian community in the Russian Far East and the Northeast shattered as the supporters and opponents to the Bolshevik movement split into hostile camps. These internal conflicts degraded the efficiency of the rail network and provided impetus not just for the Chinese to intervene in CER operations but for the Allies to intervene in the entire TSRR system. The most telling effect was the shift of rail traffic away from Vladivostok and toward Dairen. Before the revolution, over 70 percent of CER traffic went east to the Ussuri line. Afterward, the roles reversed, with over 70 percent being shipped south on the SMR. While the TSRR did not shut down and many skilled Russians remained, including CER managing director General Horvat, its performance alarmed the Allies as the transportation bottleneck resulted in a massive pileup of war stocks at the port of Vladivostok.[35]

Huge amounts of equipment and matériel, supplied mainly by the United States, had accumulated; dumped anywhere and everywhere in a helter-skelter fashion, it covered several square miles. Items not stored in overflowing warehouses sat in crates or under tarpaulins, or were simply left in the open. Rubber, steel, copper, brass, and lead were available in quantity, as were barbed wire, rails, and machine tools. In addition to weapons and ammunition, there were unassembled cars, trucks, aircraft, and even a submarine sitting in one storage yard. One of the more unassuming goods left exposed to the elements was a large amount of cotton, to be used for clothing as well as for guncotton, an essential ingredient for highly explosive artillery shells. All told, over 700,000 tons of matériel valued at 1 billion 1919 dollars sat idly in Vladivostok.[36]

On the basis of the recommendations of two railway missions, a decision was made in Washington during the summer of 1917 to expand the RRSC to slightly more than 200 officers by recruiting and commissioning professionals capable of managing all aspects of railway operations. Placed under the direction of John F. Stevens, who had been given a colonel's commission, the corps was ready by midfall. Stevens, one of the most distinguished engineers of his day, had not only built the Great Northern Railway in the United States, but he had also been the chief engineer in constructing the Panama Canal. His job was to get war matériel to Russians battling the Central Powers by clearing out the congestion at Vladivostok and opening the rails. The primary transshipment route ran along the CER, and Harbin became the RRSC headquarters.[37]

The task facing the Americans was daunting upon their arrival at Vladivostok in December. As one member, 2nd Lieutenant William Jones, described it, there was an overwhelming backlog of 25,000 railcars in various stages of loading; with crippling Bolshevik labor strikes, only a single forty-car train left per day. The situation was so volatile that the RRSC withdrew to Nagasaki, but with Chinese approval, half the corps went to work along the CER. By March 1918, the RRSC headquarters was established, along with three administrative divisions managing the railway from Suifenho to Hsienilho (a rail station approximately 300 kilometers east of Harbin), Hsienilho to Tsitsihar, and Tsitsihar to Manchouli. RRSC oversight included the telegraph and telephone systems. These moves weakened Russian authority over the CER and thwarted a similar effort by the Japanese to operate the railway—outcomes that indirectly enhanced Chinese control.[38]

The situation in Northeastern Asia remained tense. For the Allies trying to grasp the nature of the Bolshevik revolution, Lenin's actions were discouraging: a "Decree on Peace" was issued in November, and on 2 December, the Bolsheviks signed an armistice that pleased no one. France took it hard, having been instrumental in gaining Romania's entry into the war. When Russia quit, Romania's position became hopeless, forcing them to sign an armistice with the Central Powers on 9 December in the Moldavian town of Focsani. The RRSC mission was transformed as hope of Bolshevik support disappeared. What had been seen as temporary disorder was replaced by a civil war that threatened the Allied war effort. A new player also emerged: the Czechoslovaks, who had been pleading for Allied recognition of their independence from Austro-Hungary since 1916. To prove their worth, by 1917, Czechoslovak POWs had formed a 60,000-man army and joined Russia on the Eastern Front. They came to be known as the Czech Legion, and coming to their aid became a cause célèbre for the Allies.

The Northeast Confronts Multiple Wars

Detailed discussions regarding an Allied intervention into Northeast Asia began shortly before the Romanian armistice, during the Inter-Allied Conference in Paris, which ran from 30 November through 3 December. France's general Ferdinand Foch, leader of the Allied Supreme War Council, drafted a plan designed to prevent further German advances in the east and to aid Romania, and he outlined a military intervention by the United States and Japan to gain control over the TSRR along with Vladivostok and Harbin. The situation was painted in the bleakest of terms. Foch argued that with the collapse of Russia, Germany could wage war on the Western Front and conquer Russia as far as the Pacific and even threaten Korea—points that gained the attention of Japan, who had begun planning an intervention into the Russian Far East a few weeks earlier. Unmentioned in Foch's memorandum was the fate of the Czech Legion, which had been put in limbo by the Soviet armistice. The Czechs reinserted themselves when their leader, Tomas G. Masaryk, declared that the Czech Legion would fight on under the French. In the end, the Allies rejected the Foch plan, but its ideas shaped Allied policy in Northeastern Asia.[39]

China's representatives in Paris were aware that the Foch plan proposed no direct role for their military, but the mention of Harbin and the CER was of direct concern, and China was ready to act. To keep the Russian civil war from spreading into the Northeast, officials banned Chinese enlistment in White or Red forces and closed the custom offices at Suifenho and Manchouli. By late October, Kirin governor-general Meng En-yuan had approved the creation of a special police guard for the Pristan docks at Harbin after a spike in Bolshevik activities. On 28 November, the Allied ministers in Peking urged China to intervene militarily in Harbin. One week later, President Feng authorized local forces to prepare to secure the CER. The Americans urged the Chinese on, arguing that by taking control of the CER, China was defending its own territority. By 17 December, everything was in readiness, and soldiers of Meng's 3rd Kirin Mixed Brigade under General Tao Hsiang-kieu confronted the pro-Bolshevik CER guards. General Tao was aware that overpowering the guard was not the challenge it had once been. At the outset of the war, the Special Border Guards Corps had been a professional formation composed of infantry, cavalry, artillery, and engineer units numbering 33,000 in strength—the single most powerful military force in Manchuria. By December 1917, after most of the troops had left for the Eastern Front, it was a hollow force of 8,000, largely filled by poorly trained reservists, many belonging to units derisively referred to as "invalid battalions." Most were assigned to isolated detachments along the railway, with no hope of reinforcement.[40]

While Horvat, along with a number of CER employees, acceded to Chinese demands, negotiations with the guard commanders failed. The day after, a shooting incident left the Soviet commander dead; Tao's troops surrounded the guards in their Harbin barracks on the morning of 26 December and gave them one day to surrender. Although this was the largest concentration of Soviet troops in Manchuria, their strength did not exceed 1,200 soldiers. Next morning, Tao announced that an attack would commence at once if they did not disarm. A few minutes later, the Bolshevik troops put up the white flag, surrendered arms, and were deported without incident on 30 December.[41]

As a reward, Tao Hsiang-kieu became the commander of the CER Defense Corps. Two of his first acts were to deploy the forces along the length and breadth of the CER to quell intra-Russian violence and to augment his troops with two multiethnic guard battalions composed of Siberian Russians and ethnic Koreans, recruited with the assistance of Horvat. Praise from across China was heaped on Meng; assuming guardianship over the CER likely saved him from removal for having supported Chang Hsun's coup. The accolades were deserved. Both Bolshevik and White forces claimed the CER Zone. It had appeared that the Russian civil war would soon enter the Northeast, but Meng's military presence along the railway forestalled that eventuality.[42]

At the end of December, White Cossacks, along with Buryat Mongols under Ataman Grigory Semenov, were battling unsuccessfully with local Bolshevik forces under Commander Sergei G. Lazo in Trans-Baikal near the CER terminus at Manchouli. Semenov, a decorated and eccentric tsarist officer, had been appointed as a military commissar for the Trans-Baikal by the provisional government that July and was an experienced East Asia hand. Born in Dauria, he had been posted as a junior officer to the Russian forces in Outer Mongolia in 1912 before serving in World War I. He had his hands full fighting Lazo. A young man (he was only twenty-four years old) and a skilled infantry officer who had served at the front in 1916, Lazo was the ideal commander for the fledgling Red Army forces in the Trans-Baikal.[43]

Faced with an ongoing clash at the border, General Lin Fu-man was dispatched to command a brigade-size force at Manchouli and brokered a cease-fire in January 1918. In return for disarming White forces that crossed into China, Lazo agreed not send Red Army troops to the border. Semenov, having been bested by Lazo and not a party to the discussions, had no choice but to accept. For the first time in as long as anyone could remember, Chinese soldiers had confronted Western troops as equals.[44]

Momentous events beyond its borders continued to roil the Northeast as civil war erupted in southern China. The spark was Tuan's attempt to extend his authority by appointing loyalists to senior positions in Hunan and Szechuan on 6 August 1917. In a now familiar step, Hunan governor Tan Yen-kai rejected Tuan's order, declared independence on 18 September, and mobilized for war. Sun Yat-sen threw his support behind Tan, and Tuan countered by invading Hunan and Szechuan. President Feng would not sanction the attack, and generals loyal to him refused to assist Tuan. If Tuan expected a repeat of the rout of the republican forces during the second revolution, he was mistaken. His troops under General Chang Ching-yao were first halted, then driven back as Hunan and Szechuan became battlefields that fragmented provincial governance. The schism widened when Hupeh declared independence, and General Chen Kuang-yuan rebelled in Kiangsi while unrest spread among the troops in Kiangsu. Some pro-Feng Kuo-chang commanders refused to fight; when Feng Yu-hsiang was ordered to march his 16th Brigade into Fukien in November, he simply halted his troops at Pukow. Failure in Hunan coupled with the rebellions forced Tuan to resign on 22 November.[45]

Unwilling to give up, Tuan convened a conference of northern tuchuns at Tientsin on 3 December that included such rising leaders as Chang Tso-lin and Tsao Kun, a Yuan protégé and governor-general of Chihli. Fearing that the southern forces might march into a disunited Yangtze Valley, a number of pro-Feng generals came to support Tuan and formed a "national unification" army. Aware of the shifting loyalties, on 18 December, Feng appointed Tuan to head the War Participation Bureau, the agency directing China's military efforts during the world war, and which controlled the new War Participation Army (WPA). Feng also acceded to a fresh attack on the south.[46]

Chang Tso-lin's reward for allying with Tuan came in February 1918, when, at Tuan's urging, he seized 17 million yen worth of Japanese military supplies intended for the WPA. He justified the theft by proclaiming that the arms were needed to ready his divisions before joining the national unification army. On 25 February, he also urged Feng to create a war cabinet under Tuan and remove the antiwar governors in the Yangtze Valley. Chang arrived at Peking on 16 March and was placed under the command of General Hsu Shu-cheng, Tuan's most trusted lieutenant. A little over a week later, with Chang's troops menacing the capital, Hsu forced Feng to reappointed Tuan as premier. Tuan outraged Feng's followers, who had coalesced into the Chihli clique (Feng's province of birth). As the generals chose sides, the term "Peiyang Army" ceased to have meaning. The rupture widened throughout 1918 as Feng held out for a negotiated settlement with the south while Tuan continued to insist on reunification carried out at bayonet point.[47]

War in the south was not Chang Tso-lin's only problem. The situation within the CER Zone had grown worse. Soon after the Russian civil war began, Chang saw to it that CER operations were reorganized by cutting out the Petrograd governing board and replacing it with an administrative board, the Pravlenie, made up of local Russians and Chinese. Horvat remained as director general, while authority to name the CER president shifted from Peking to the provincial capital of Kirin, where Meng appointed Kuo Tsung-hsi, the figurehead civil governor, to the job. Chang also had to keep an eye on Japan. Already interested in gaining influence over the CER, the Japanese used their influence with Meng to have Admiral Alexandr V. Kolchak appointed commander of a new Russian railway guard with units at Harbin, Manchouli, and Suifenho. Having finished a naval inspection mission in America, he was in Japan en route to Russia when the October Revolution erupted. While in Tokyo, his pro-Allied leanings caught the attention of Japanese army officers, who shuttled to Harbin in time for the CER reorganization. However, Kolchak's force was not intended to rival the Chinese guard; it was to serve as the nucleus of a pro-Japanese White Russian army. The effort fizzled when Semenov refused to accept his leadership and only a handful of recruits responded to the call to arms. An unimpressed Horvat dismissed the admiral on 30 June. Undeterred, Kolchak returned to Tokyo to seek assistance for the White cause at the Allied embassies.[48]

Chang Tso-lin had marched south to join the national unification army under Tsao Kun, and by April, the army—with Wu Pei-fu's 3rd Division in the vanguard—had scored a series of victories in Hunan. To deal with the crisis, on 20 May, General Chen Chiung-ming in Canton pushed aside Sun Yat-sen and formed a military government directed by a seven-man administrative council dominated by General Lu Jung-ting. The war stalemated, and little or no fighting took place throughout the summer. On 26 September, the frontline commanders from both sides issued a circular telegram calling for a cease-fire. Tuan's offensive had failed, again creating a political showdown over continuing the war just as parliamentary elections and expiration of the presidential term loomed in 1918.[49]

Crisis in the West and the Allies in Northeastern Asia

While the war in the south dominated the attention of China's leaders, the consequences of the world war on the Northeast could not be ignored. In the Russian Far East, chaos reigned. The American ambassador in Paris, William G. Sharp, was so unnerved by French reporting in late January 1918 that he proposed to Secretary of State Robert Lansing the creation of a joint American and Chinese corps to address the "extreme gravity of the danger" posed by Germany in the Far East and Allied warships, led by the British cruiser *Suffolk* and the Japanese cruisers *Asahi* and *Iwami*, anchored off Vladivostok that same month. The year 1918 began as the old ended: with deteriorating relations between the Allies and Soviets. While Lenin hoped to transform the war into a global revolution, a goal that undermined relations with the Allies, the Central Powers smelled victory in Russia and pushed hard during the peace talks at the Brest-Litovsk citadel.[50]

On 10 February, the Soviet delegation, headed by Leon Trotsky, declared that they "were removing our armies and our people from the war" while rejecting the peace treaty—a policy of "no peace, no war."[51] Berlin ignored the gambit and announced that hostilities would recommence on 17 February. Soon German troops were marching at will across Russia. Six days later, Berlin responded to a Bolshevik plea for renewed negotiations with a surrender ultimatum. The inexperienced Workers' and Peasants' Red Army (RKKA) that had been hastily formed in January proved incapable of dealing with German force of arms, turning "no peace, no war" into a debacle. On 2 March, Kiev fell, and another advancing German army was no more than 150 kilometers from Petrograd. Lenin ordered the evacuation of the Bolshevik government to Moscow, which became the new capital on 5 March.[52]

The Allies recognized the German advance as a threat to Northeast Asia, a possible realization of Foch's predictions. Lenin saw it as a grave risk to the revolution. What the revolution needed then and there was "breathing room," even if gaining it meant signing the humiliating Brest-Litovsk treaty.[53] Lenin, backed by Josef Stalin, convinced a reluctant Central Committee to recognize the futility of resistance and making immediate peace with the Central Powers a necessity. The treaty was ratified on 17 March. Vladimir Lenin had saved the revolution, but in doing so, he created the political will on the part of the Allied Powers for entering Siberia.[54]

The need to act gained momentum on 21 March, when the Allies' worst fear was realized: the German army launched a massive offensive on the Western Front using troops just arrived from Russia. The situation became dire. With the arrival of the divisions from the East (144 Western Front division were augmented by an additional 52), the Germans had pierced the front and the British and French were falling back to the banks of the Marne. Paris was open to German attack for the first time since the opening weeks of the war in 1914. That month, French prime minister Georges Clemenceau stated that while "Russia has betrayed us," there was no choice but to fight on: "I wage war," he declared.[55] The cost to the Allies was tremendous. Combined, the French and British armies suffered over 800,000 casualties. When the Central Powers forced a harsh peace on Romania on 7 May, France backed intervention and Britain adopted a policy of supporting any and all "anti-German" Russian groups. They were willing to grasp at any straw proffered by a variety of White Russian generals who pledged to reopen the fight on the Eastern Front.[56]

To the dangers on the Western Front and White promises to fight were added Vladivostok war stocks and how to deal with the tens of thousands of German and Austro-Hungarian prisoners of war in Siberia. Rumors, some unfounded or exaggerated, of POWs being armed by the communists and sent along the TSRR toward Vladivostok stoked Allied apprehensions. The imperative at Vladivostok shifted from supplying the Eastern Front to preventing the war stocks from falling into the hands of a hostile Bolshevik regime—or worse, the Central Powers. Even levelheaded leaders, such as American admiral Austin M. Knight, at anchor off Vladivostok on the *Brooklyn*, feared the munitions ashore would be seized. But the pretext for intervention became the rescue of the plucky Czech Legion under General Rudolph Gaida, which had just managed to evacuate Kiev before the Germans arrived. The Czechoslovaks were the good news in that bleak spring: the Czech Legion had bettered the Red Army in a number of engagements, and on 29 June, Gaida's troops occupied Vladivostok. The Czechs sat astride most of the trans-Siberian railway, and Chinese authorities granted them right of passage along the CER. Ongoing discussions between the United States and Japan over an intervention took on new urgency.[57]

The White House decided to act on 6 July, and two days later, Japanese ambassador Ishii Kikujiro received a request for a joint intervention that was followed by President Wilson's 17 July aide-mémoire, which delineated a threefold mission: gain control over the Vladivostok war matériel, assist the Czechoslovakians, and help the Russian people as requested. Japan agreed on 2 August, while the British and French, displeased with Wilson's lack of consultation, ordered in respective forces from Hong Kong and Saigon that had been on alert since the Czech seizure of Vladivostok.[58]

Not surprisingly, the intervention's war aims developed in the Allied capitals differed—so much so that American diplomat George F. Kennan later characterized them as a "fantastic brew."[59] Even Wilsons's goals were confusing. On 3 August, Secretary of War Newton D. Baker met with Major General William S. Graves, the man selected to lead the Americans, instructing him to maintain a strict policy of noninterference in Russian internal matters. Incongruently, the State Department through Counsel General Ernest L. Harris at Irkutsk had discreetly taken steps to support the Whites. This created an overt–covert policy that a conflicted Wilson nonetheless pursued. Britain aligned with France in seeing the reopening of a White-led Eastern Front as the prime objective, a position in harmony with the American State Department.[60]

Japan saw the Bolsheviks as an extremist enemy and Lenin as nothing better than "a cat's paw of the Germans."[61] In November 1917, the *Tokyo Asahi* argued that Lenin was a German dupe, and the next month, the Soviets unilaterally abrogated its treaties with Japan while embarrassing Tokyo by publishing previously secret compacts, including the 4 July 1910 treaty dividing Manchuria into Russian and Japanese spheres of influence. In the minds of expansionists, such as General Tanaka Giichi, who helped plan the intervention and later became war minister in September 1918, the Russian Far East was fair game, spoils up for grabs, and they set about creating a puppet state. This was a departure from previous policy where Japan had often worked with Russia against China's interests in the Northeast. After the onset of the Russian civil war, however, Japan became an eager proponent for intervention and turned to China, securing the Sino-Japanese Joint Defense Agreement on 16 May 1918 with a willing Tuan Chi-jui.[62]

Joining the Allies posed a number challenges and opportunities for China, but the goal of entering the ranks of the world's powers remained paramount. Up to then, China's major contribution had been laborers in Europe, especially the Chinese Labor Corps (CLC), formed before China entered the war and at the request of the manpower-strapped British and French governments. In addition to those working in French and British munitions facilities, the CLC provided over 100,000 laborers who served on the Western Front in a number of roles behind the front lines, but often close enough to be decorated for meritorious service and to suffer casualties. When plans of an Allied intervention neared completion, China opted to participate along the lines of the American force. Italy and Canada, who did not see eye to eye with Japan or Britain and France, adopted missions similar to that of China and the United States: help the Czechs, secure the rails, and do not interfere in domestic Russian affairs. There was just enough overlap in the Allied goals to allow the intervention to proceed, yet too many differences to make the mission a success.[63]

China had other problems. The WPA, headed by Tuan loyalist Ching Yun-ping, had proven a mixed blessing. The only way to fund, equip, and train the army's three divisions and four mixed brigades was by accepting military aid tied to the Sino-Japanese Joint Defense Agreement. This was a solution advocated by Japanese prime minister Terauchi Masatake, who was pleased to see his friend Tuan return to the premiership on 23 March, but bad feelings over the twenty-one demands had not abated. As an added incentive, the Japanese agreed that Hsu Shucheng would personally handle the funding within the framework of the privately sponsored Nishihara loans.[64]

There was also the question of how to use the army. The WPA would not be ready until late 1918, making it ill suited for a leading role in the intervention. Additionally, China's frontier concerns centered on

Outer Mongolia and securing the Russian border, tasks that Chang Tso-lin had reserved for himself. This raised a politically damning question: if the WPA was not intended for participation in the world war, then what was it for? To many, the answer was obvious: Tuan wanted it for the war in the south. In the end, Tuan committed one WPA mixed brigade—a force consistent with the contributions made by the other allies and one that would not threaten Chang's authority.[65]

After the powers accepted Wilson's offer, Tokyo was asked to provide the commander and appointed Lieutenant General Otani Kikuzo, who prepared the plan that would form the basis for initial Allied operations: first, securing Vladivostok and TSRR to the Trans-Baikal region; and second, advancing from Manchouli along the TSRR to Lake Baikal. Japan made the greatest commitment, assigning two divisions and one mixed brigade to the Allied force, with reinforcements at the ready; they also provided military aid to the Czech Legion in the weeks before the Allied landings. Pursuing its own aim of carving out a Japanese-dominated state in the Russian Far East, three White Cossack bands were supported, Semenov in southwestern Trans-Baikal, Ivan Pavlovich Kalmykov and his Ussuri Cossacks, and the Amur Cossacks under Ataman Vasili Gamov.[66]

The Allies Act

On 3 August, the first Allied soldiers came ashore at Vladivostok, Britishers of Lieutenant Colonel John Ward's 25th Battalion, Middlesex Regiment, who were soon followed by the French Colonial Siberian Battalion under Lieutenant Colonel R. Mallet. They landed under the guns of the Allied fleet, including the Chinese-protected cruiser *Hai Yung*, and Czech troops who held the city. The soldiers reported to Generals Alfred W. Knox and Maurice Janin, commanders of the British and Franco-Czechoslovakian Military Missions, respectively. Joining them were detachments of Belgians, Serbs, Poles, and Romanians, the latter three keen on rescuing stranded countrymen, veterans of the Serbian, Russian, or Austro-Hungarian armies. Later, the WPA mixed brigade, led by Brigadier General Yu Yu-ssu, departed Peking by rail for Vladivostok, and Chang Tso-lin's CER rail guards crossed the Russian border at Suifenho to protect the Ussuri line and Manchouli to guard Siding No. 86 on the Trans-Baikal line. Yu's brigade teamed up with Colonel Henry D. Styer's 27th US Infantry Regiment.[67]

After the landings, the Allies prepared to execute General Otani's plan to occupy the Maritime District while Bolshevik forces under Aleksandr A. Taube, about 4,000 Red Guards and 10,000 armed "Internationalist" German and Austro-Hungarian POWs, fought back as best they could. The offensive began shortly after the 18 August arrival of General Oi Shigemoto, the 12th Division commander. Defeating the Bolsheviks north of Vladivostok on 24 August and advancing relentlessly, they captured Khabarovsk on 4 September. There the Allies found the once proud Amur River Flotilla an empty shell, with the ships' engines and guns removed. The Japanese took over the hulks. The Maritime District was secured by 6 September. Taube was captured and sentenced to death; he died in prison. By mid-September, Red power in the Far East had all but ceased to exist, and General Graves wired as much to Washington on 8 September.[68]

The victory ended the unified Allied effort. On 8 September, Graves also informed the War Department that the French, British, and Czechs were advancing beyond the Urals to restore the Eastern Front under the White Russian Omsk regime. In honor of the legion's achievements, on 14 October, the Allies recognized the Czechoslovakian provisional government. The Japanese were busy establishing a puppet regime under Semenov, the Trans-Baikal temporary government. The Chinese and Americans remained east of Lake Baikal as more troops arrived. In mid-October, the Italian Far East Expeditionary Corps under Colonel Gustavo Fossini-Camossi landed at Vladivostok and then joined the Italian "Redeemed" POW legion at Krasnoyarsk (about 800 kilometers west of Lake Baikal). Further west were 12,000 Polish troops under Colonel K. I. Rumsha along with 2,000 Latvian and 1,000 Serbian troops, adding to the Allied formations that clung to the railways. The last major contingent, the Canadian Siberian Expeditionary Corps led by Major General J. H. Elmsley, arrived that fall, taking up positions around Vladivostok. Allied forces now stretched some 7,700 kilometers across Russia.[69]

China maintained an active role. Yu's troops were concentrated at Vladivostok, but shared guard duty at the Suchan coal mines and on the Ussuri line with the Americans and occupied a sector in Khabarovsk along with the Americans and Japanese. Fresh reinforcements arrived in the form of a naval flotilla. One benefit of joining the Allies was the transfer of the German gunboats *Otter* and *Vaterland*, captured at Tsingtao in 1914. Rechristened *Li-chieh* and *Li-shui* and placed under the command of Shen Hung-lieh, they where sent to the mouth of the

Amur River and then on to Khabarovsk, where they assumed river patrol duties on the Amur, Ussuri, and Sungari. There were also advances in the Northeast as the Allies, and particularly the Japanese army, advanced westward. Governor-General Pao Kieu-ching's Heilungkiang troops marched north to reinforce Teheiho, a sign that Chang Tso-lin was expanding his domain into the Russian Trans-Amur sphere of influence. In addition to securing the Chinese bank of the Amur River, Pao reaffirmed the understanding with Lazo that no Red Army or Internationalist troops would advance beyond Dauria, and Semenov continued to be banned from using Chinese territory as a safe haven.[70]

The arrival of the gunboats and Chang's troops on the frontier underscored the need to rein in Semenov's lawless White bands. Earlier they had robbed Chinese merchants in the Trans-Baikal of several million rubles. In retaliation, Peking threatened to halt Boxer indemnity payments to the Omsk government, and they sent in the gunboats to confront the Russians on the Amur. Despite White Russian protests that the warships were banned from the waters by treaty, threats from Peking, the presence of Chang's soldiers, and the arrival of Shen's squadron caused the Omsk regime to make good the stolen monies, and China reestablished its rights over naval navigation in the Northeast.[71]

Armored Trains

The fight along the TSRR raised one the most unusual forms of combat in World War I to an unprecedented level: armored train warfare. Unlike tanks and aircraft, which were firmly footed in the future, armored trains were grounded in the past. Tanks were nonexistent in Siberia, and even aircraft were a rare sight. Railways, conversely, were essential to military campaigns and were too economically vital to destroy. A cousin, the rail gun, saw broad action on the Western Front from the start of the war, but the armored train, a mobile combat platform that had been around since the time of the 1861–1865 American Civil War, was ill suited to static Western or mountainous Italian fronts, although it reached its zenith during the fighting in Russia.[72]

At first, expedients were used to protect the troops running the Siberian rails; early versions used infantry crouched behind sandbags, wooden crates, steel plating, even concrete. The first Russian armored train had been built in 1915, and the Allies battled with a number of Soviet armored trains in the Far East—a threat not eliminated until the Japanese captured the last at Blagoveshchensk in October 1918. More took their place elsewhere. Over time, armored railcars were purpose built, possessing steel turrets housing heavy machine guns and 7.62-centimeter cannon with armored compartments. The Soviets began producing the trains at rail yards located at Bryansk, Moscow, and elsewhere while the Whites and Allies opened shops at yards on the TSRR and CER. Trotsky led the Red Army from a rolling fortress headquarters protected by the "Red One Hundred" guard detachment, Semenov commanded a division of eight heavily armed trains, and the British built a behemoth that carried nine naval guns removed from the *Suffolk*. Eventually there were over 100 armored trains plying Siberian and Manchurian rails, ranging from the purpose-built gun cars and armored locomotives to protected troop and supply transports. They soon migrated into the Northern Chinese warlord armies, often being manned by White Russian mercenaries. Both sides would use armored trains in the 1929 conflict.[73]

Tuan Consolidates His Power and the End of the Great War

As the Allied intervention played out, events in Peking and Europe again realigned the trajectory of events in the Northeast. The inability of Tuan to resolve the civil war had reached the crisis point by mid-1918. Frustrated militarily, he moved to recoup his losses on the political front. In March, Tuan, with the backing of the clique, established the Anfu Club, whose purpose was to elect pro-Tuan candidates during the upcoming May–June parliamentary elections. The effort paid off handsomely: Tuan's supporters won 342 of 470 seats. The new assembly elected Tuan's choice for president, Hsu Shih-chang, who was sworn in for a five-year term on the Double Tenth of 1918. The new president met the usual Northern warlord criteria: a former general, an able and loyal Manchu administrator without a significant political or military base. To distinguish him from General Hsu, Tuan's henchman, the president, as a result of his large stature, was referred to as "Big Hsu" and the general as "Little Hsu." Tuan was now at the height of his power, but the issue of the war with the south would not go away. Tuan's choice for vice president, General Tsao Kun, was foiled when antiwar parliamentarians prevented a quorum from forming, and no candidate was ever elected. Additionally, the Anfu Club's methods created as many problems as they solved: victory was gained through bribery and improper interventions in the voting process. The Anfu Club was a political organization without a political ideology or unifying message, save to support the ambitions of Tuan Chi-jui.[74]

A month later, on 11 November, German armies reached the breaking point on the Western Front, and Berlin agreed to an armistice. For the Allies in Northeast Asia, the problems were that an armistice was not a peace treaty and that no clear winner had emerged in the Russian civil war—outcomes that led to a pause in military operations, not a withdrawal. What would come next largely would have to wait on events in Paris, where the Germans would face the victorious Allies to reach a final agreement to end the war.

Conclusions

It is hard to overstate the importance the seven-year period from 1911 to 1918 had on shaping the future 1929 Sino-Soviet conflict. The 10 October 1911 revolution in China, the onset of World War I, the rise of warlordism, the 1917 Russian October Revolution, the Allied intervention into Northeast Asia, and the 11 November 1918 armistice all played a role as these cascading events redefined the balance of power in the Northeast.

On the Chinese side, the leadership that shaped China and the Northeast in the years leading up to the 1929 conflict entered the scene. Chiang Kai-shek was firmly ensconced within Sun's KMT, Yan Hsi-shan ruled Shansi, and Feng Yu-hsiang had gone from leading a battalion to commanding a brigade. Finally there was Chang Tso-lin. In 1911, Chang was an undistinguished commander of provincial auxiliaries. In January 1919, President Hsu, with Tuan's concurrence, appointed him inspector-general of the Northeast and promoted him to full general in honor of his service to the Allies in the Great War. Chang Tso-lin was now one of China's most important leaders. His Northeastern domain would become the battleground and the army he created during this period the nucleus of the force that would face the Soviets in 1929. For Russia, the success of the 1917 October Revolution thrust both Lenin and Stalin into new heights of power, and both would shape the dynamics that led to the Sino-Soviet clash.[75]

Politically, the effects were equally telling. The 1911 revolution ended in a Republic of China hobbled by a weak central government that was loosely federated and dominated by New Army generals whose power only grew in the ensuing years. China's entrance in the Great War on the Allied side raised its international stature to a new level—and with the armistice, its first victor's seat for the upcoming Paris peace negotiations. For Russia, it led to destruction of the centuries-old Romanov dynasty, the rise of the Bolsheviks, and descent into bloody civil war. These events, coupled with China's participation in the Allied intervention, allowed Peking to erase much of the Russian sphere of influence in the Northeast—the pre-1911 dream of a Russian Trans-Amur District in northern Manchuria was dead by 1918. While Tokyo's position remained stable in the Northeast, the rise of Chinese power forced an often reluctant yet potent Japan to recognize China's expanded authority.

The Great War ushered in an unprecedented period of growth in the Northeast that proved enduring. The rise of Chang, with his ability to pick gifted administrators like Wang Yung-chiang, accelerated the expansion. The economic value of the CER was reconfirmed; Stevens noted in December 1918 that whoever controlled the railway controlled the trade in Manchuria and Siberia. The Northeast's expanded wealth and economic strength would help drive the regional ambitions of China and Russia that would end in the 1929 conflict.[76]

Militarily, in 1911, China's Northeastern forces were inferior to both the Russian Special Guard Corps and the Japanese Kwantung Army and SMR rail guards. That changed. By 1918, Chang had expanded a hand full of battalions into a multidivision army while subordinating the Kirin and Heilungkiang forces. Down the Sungari and on the Amur, the Sungari River Flotilla protected Chinese lives and property, and Chinese troops moved freely throughout northern Manchuria without needing Russian consent, leaving only Japan as a military threat. China also had become an equal to Russia within the CER Zone. The Russian guards were gone, replaced by the Chinese CER Defense Corps, and the operation of the railway was no longer the exclusive right of Russia. The CER remained the great prize, and rivalry for control over the railway would be the driving cause of the 1929 conflict.

3 | Talks, Wars, and Railroads (1919–1924)

The Versailles Peace Treaty and the May Fourth Movement

Peace. The word was on the minds of millions as the world's leaders descended on Paris and the magnificent palace of Versailles in early 1919. Peking was equally optimistic that a new era was dawning. In November 1918, Westel W. Willoughby, the father of American political science and finishing a year as a constitutional law advisor to the Chinese government, wrote a memorandum for the American delegation on the positions Peking would likely take in Paris. He presented two sections, "The Treaty or Treaties of Peace" and "Determinations Tending to Establish International Justice and Perpetual Peace."[1] Despite the hope proffered by the subtitles, reality undermined exuberance, as even sending a Chinese delegation to Paris proved difficult.[2]

To show a unified face, Peking reached out to Canton. Foreign Minister Lou Tseng-Tsiang asked C. T. Wang, a senior Sun advisor, and C. C. (Chao-shu) Wu, the son of Sun's Foreign Minister Wu Ting-fang, to attend as plenipotentiaries. Canton rebuffed the outreach. Wang accepted, but not as Sun's representative, while Wu refused and led a rival delegation to Paris that was never recognized. Alfred Sao-ke Sze, another delegate, reflected the diplomats' conflicted loyalties. A Sun follower, he willingly accepted the post of minister to Great Britain during Yuan's presidency. Also harboring republican leanings while serving Peking was Wellington Koo, the minister to the United States and another plenipotentiary. Wang, Sze, and Koo represented an attempt by career foreign service officers to create a transcendental international policy designed to move China into the ranks of the world's powers no matter who governed in Peking.

Matters got off to a disappointing start after the Chinese established themselves at the posh Left Bank Hotel Lutetia in the heart of Paris, as most initial meetings were held by the Big Five (France, Britain, America, Japan, and Italy) behind closed doors. China was also left in the cold when the preliminary conference for drafting the peace treaty began on 18 January. Designated a "special interest" party, China could only attend plenary meetings or sessions addressing the Far East. Even then, their wishes often fell on deaf ears. Despite the obstacles, the delegation succeeded in laying down three objectives that became the cornerstone of Chinese foreign policy for the next decades: restoration of territorial integrity, restoration of internal sovereignty, and economic freedom.[3]

Recovering the German Shantung concessions became the immediate objective, and C. T. Wang fought to have China heard. As one of the Big Five, Japan was able to make its case first. Baron Makino Nobuaki held that in light of its soldiers lost in battle and treasure spent, the concessions were hard-earned war reparations. Japan was arguing from a position of strength as well; before the Paris deliberations, it had secretly secured written support from Britain, France, and Italy, and even Peking had signed an agreement accepting Japan's claim on 24 September 1918. Unaware of these dealings, on 28 January Koo presented China's case, asking the powers to recognize its sovereignty over a region that ranked as "the heart of Chinese civilization" and noting that China had the right to demand "direct restitution" of the lands taken from it.[4] Based on their participation in the Great War and Wilson's Fourteen Principles, the return of the German territories was a cut-and-dried issue for the Chinese delegation; however, their Versailles dream died when the fifth plenary session declared on 28 April that Japan would be awarded the concessions.[5]

China's reaction was not long in coming. On the day the peace treaty went to the printers in Paris—4 May—student-led marches began in Peking. In the following days, they exploded in size as thousands took to the streets across China, ushering in the May Fourth Movement. As one early Chinese Communist Party historian wrote in 1926, "Its impact was singularly profound," and the "humiliation of Versailles" was a "special phenomena of China in 1919."[6] During the next session on 6 May, a shocked Lou took the unusual step of publicly condemning the decision. In Peking, American diplomats cryptically noted on 25 May, "Chinese persons stirred as never before," and the legations were inundated with petitions and telegrams from across China.[7]

Two weeks later, Shanghai was wracked by a general strike, followed by an embargo of Japanese goods. On the next day, 10 June, the Shanghai International Settlement municipal police fired on a crowd in an incident that killed several people and created the cause's first martyrs. When the 26 June Paris peace treaty signing ceremony was held, the Chinese delegation stayed in their hotel while Chinese students studying in France rallied outside. A stung Tokyo announced on 18 July that it would send a delegation to Peking to negotiate the retrocession of Japan's Shantung rights after China's signing of the treaty. To clarify its intent, the Japanese foreign ministry stated on 29 July that the aim of the negotiations was to restore China's sovereignty over Shantung. While less than successful, the initiative calmed the waters to a degree and the boycott began to recede in September. However, the movement had changed China. It signaled the rebirth of revolutionary nationalism.[8]

The Shanghai Peace Conference

Simultaneous with the Paris conference, peace negotiations to end China's civil war began on 20 February in Shanghai, where the Big Five tried to mediate a reunification based on the 2 December 1918 joint aide-mémoire. They saw the first two steps as a halt to the fighting, followed by demobilization. They hoped to influence the two sides through a stick in the form of an arms embargo combined with the carrot of a Four Power (Britain, France, Japan, and the United States) loan for economic development. The embargo came first. The Great War ended in a glut of war matériel, and arms manufacturers looking for new markets found war-torn China an appealing destination. Peking's diplomatic corps looked to shut them out and embargo discussions by the Big Five got underway in Peking during October 1918. The embargo on the sale of arms to China went into effect on 1 March 1919.[9]

To enter the peace talks, Sun's Nationalist Party set three preconditions on 13 February: a halt to the renewed fighting in Shensi, the disbandment of the WPA, and a halt to arms shipments to Peking. The Anfu Clique (Chang Tso-lin and Tsao Kun each had a representative) dominated the Peking delegation and was equally intransigent. Tuan neutralized the WPA issue by redesignating it the Northwest Frontier Defense Army (NWFDA) on 24 February while quietly approving the creation of four additional brigades, a move that outraged his critics. More deftly, he skirted the armaments issue by arguing that the Paris treaty had not been signed and that a possibility of resuming hostilities remained, which necessitated equipping the NWFDA. The Powers supported disbandment and proposed to use loan monies to pay for discharged troop stipends.[10]

After several desultory meetings, the Peking delegation resigned en bloc on 28 February, and Canton then insisted on the removal of Shensi tuchun Chen Shu-fan within forty-eight hours as a condition for further dialogue. The conference was thrown into confusion. To pressure the parties to return, the Powers announced that no new loans would be forthcoming until the country reunited; the effort was thwarted when Japanese private banks made loans to Peking in March. Tuan did sack Chen, but the Shensi fighting continued. By the end of the month, formal talks were over, and after a series of unproductive private meetings in April, meaningful discussions ceased altogether. With no path to progress open, the conference collapsed under its own weight. In mid-May, the Peking delegation departed Shanghai, and the tuchuns supporting Tsao concluded that if Tuan would not make peace with Canton, then perhaps it was time for him to go.[11]

Unresolved Conflict in Northeast Asia

The 11 November armistice threw the Allied intervention into disarray. Japan opted to stay the course and continued to build its puppet state. The British and French were in a spot; trying to reopen the Eastern Front had meant siding with the Whites, plunging them into the Russian civil war. They too stayed the course. With British support, Kolchak overthrew the Omsk regime, declaring himself Russia's supreme leader in mid-November. The Czechs were caught off guard. On 20 December, their National Council came out against Kolchak; the troops refused to advance on the Red Army, declaring that they would not be involved in Russia's war. They left the front by 20 January 1919. Unwilling to be drawn in deeper, and aware of the progress at Paris and Czech withdrawal, the remaining Allies formulated their exit strategies.[12]

It would take over a year for most of the troops to leave. The first to head home were the Canadians, who were gone by 5 June 1919. Yu's brigade left for Chihli at midyear as well, although Chang's rail guards remained. General Graves gave them high praise: "The Chinese troops in Siberia were very faithful to the obligations they assumed, attended strictly to their own business and did not meddle in the affairs of other people."[13] The British left in September, though Knox's advisory mission, like that of the French, did not leave until 1921. The Italians were gone in February 1920 and the French battalion in March. The first ships for the Czechoslovaks arrived in February, and they were gone by June. The last of the American Expeditionary Force set sail on 1 April.[14]

As the Allies departed, the CER assumed greater importance, as it was the quickest and safest route to Vladivostok and home. To maintain order along the rails, the RRSC mission had to be revisited. The Allies meeting in Vladivostok in January and February 1919 formed an Inter-Allied Railway Committee (IARC) to coordinate the withdrawal.[15]

Almost immediately, Japan and China tried to sidestep the agreement by acceding to IARC control over the TSRR in Russia while claiming special privileges over the CER. A Japanese IARC official, Nagao Hanpei, sought two goals: to control the CER line from Changchun to Harbin and to place Semenov as CER director general. He largely succeeded in the former but was blocked in the latter. China's actions were more complex. Peking argued for sole control, absent a recognized Russian government. The Allies countered, stating that the CER was under joint control as long as the intervention lasted. In Peking, communications minister Tsao Ju-lin then moved to assign a railway expert as copresident with Stevens, only to be rebuffed, but the Chinese did convince the Allies "that wherever possible Chinese technical assistance should be utilized" along the CER.[16] The IARC also agreed in April that only the CER Defense Corps should protect the railway. The CER guard was reorganized, with control divided at the Kirin–Heilungkiang boundary and the guards falling under the command of the military governors. This erased the last vestiges of the Russian guard force. The era of purely Russian administration over the railway zone was over, and the Chinese were there to stay.[17]

Kolchak's Defeat

When the armistice was announced, who would win the Russian civil war remained uncertain. Kolchak proved the naysayers wrong by scoring a victory over the Red Army at Perm in December 1918 in which the Bolsheviks lost thousands of troops and quantities of precious artillery pieces and machine guns. The defeat forced Lenin to send in Stalin to steady the front, while Trotsky sent the armies of Mikhail V. Frunze and

Mikhail Tukhachevsky, two of the Red Army's best, to take on Kolchak. The Eastern Front became the most important battleground of the war. In 1919, Kolchak was advancing against the Red armies arrayed before him. In two months, he recaptured an area half the size of France; during one stretch in early April, his army advanced over 100 kilometers in six days. It was a high-water mark, as his forces suffered a decisive defeat in a summer offensive led by Frunze, who now commanded four Red armies. That began a death spiral of defense, defeat, and retreat for Kolchak that brought the Red Army into the Urals by September and into utter defeat by December. He was captured in Irkutsk on 20 January 1920, tried, and sentenced to death. On 7 February, Admiral Aleksandr Kolchak was executed by a firing squad, but the Russian Far East remained in White hands.[18]

Allied Incidents on the CER

As the Allied withdrawal picked up steam, a wide variety of Allied military trains along with the Whites were crisscrossing the rails, leading to friction among the various forces. Adding to the tensions, in June 1919, the Japanese assigned soldiers to guard their military telegraph line, which had paralleled the CER since the intervention's start. In July, during the height of the May Fourth disturbances, an otherwise minor incident between Chinese and Japanese troops where the SMR and CER met at the Kuancheng station, some ten kilometers north of Changchun, shattered the peace among the Allies. When Japan was awarded the SMR after its victory in the Russo-Japanese War, the rail gauge was shifted from the wider Russian track to the narrower international standard, creating a transfer problem where the SMR and CER met. The solution was the construction of two overlapping rail lines to ensure "direct communication for passengers and merchandise." After the CER Defense Corps replaced the Russian guards in 1917, Chinese soldiers came into constant contact with Japanese SMR guard troops. On 19 July, while emotions related to the May Fourth Movement were running high, several CER Guard Corps soldiers beat a Japanese laborer.[19]

After being notified by the SMR police, Japanese soldiers accompanied them to the CER Guard Corps barracks, where the dispute escalated into a gunfight that ended in the death of more than a dozen soldiers on each side and an equal number of wounded. Ordinarily the dispute, bloody as it was, would have been quietly settled. Japanese army officers initially demanded apologies, a withdrawal of Chinese troops from the train station, and the punishment of local Chinese commanders; American diplomats in Peking noted that the incident appeared to be of no political importance. Kirin governor Meng En-yuan attempted to weather the troubles by acceding to Peking's demand that he sack his nephew, Brigadier General Kao Shih-pin, who served as his chief of staff and handled Kirin's affairs with the Japanese army. Kao was removed from his posts and sent to command of the 1st Kirin Mixed Brigade.[20]

During follow-on meetings in Changchun, the Japanese further demanded Meng's resignation, and when Peking directed that the incident be handled locally, Chang Tso-lin saw an opportunity to take the province. The die was cast. Chang pushed the resignation issue, and Peking acquiesced by shifting Pao Kuei-ching from Heilungkiang to replace Meng, while a Chang stalwart, Sun Lieh-chen, became Heilungkiang tuchun. Pao, no stranger to warlord politics, quickly ousted Tao Hsiang-kieu, naming himself CER Defense Corps commander, and replaced Kuo Tsung-hsi by appointing himself as CER president. Chang Tso-lin was the big winner, however, having finally placed a loyalist in charge in Kirin, thus advancing his control over the Northeast.[21]

In April 1920, it became Chang's turn to weather a CER incident with the Japanese when a confused shoot-out erupted at the Hailar station. The gunfight began when an angry crowd of pro-Soviet Russian rail workers attempted to stop Japanese troops escorting several Bolshevik prisoners who faced almost certain execution. The Hailar station was crowded with the Czech Legion's rear guard, comprising seven military trains (including the armored train *Orlik*), which had just arrived from Chita, marking their complete exit from the Trans-Baikal. Also on hand was a Chinese rail guard detachment, a disarmed battalion of Semenov's troops, and an American, Major D. S. Colby, of the IARC. In the aftermath, the prisoners escaped and several Japanese soldiers were wounded.[22]

To save face, local Japanese commanders blamed the incident on the Czechs—conveniently the one party interested in leaving Hailar as quickly as possible. General Oi sent a force to seize the *Orlik* in retaliation. Well aware of the fates meted out to their fellow officers caught up in the 1919 Kuancheng station incident, the Chinese commanders quietly urged the Czechs to accept the Japanese claim, disappointing the Czechs and Colby. In siding with the Japanese army, however, Chang

Tso-lin defused a serious incident and got the Allied departure back on schedule. He inherited the *Orlik*.

Chang Hsueh-liang

Having observed Chang Tso-lin's troops during the southern campaign, the War Ministry ordered the reopening of the Mukden military academy to improve officer quality. The episode revealed one reason why Chang rose to power; although unschooled, he saw the directive's value and set the tone by enrolling Chang Hsueh-liang in the first artillery officer's course, marking his eldest son's entry into the army. Only nineteen years old, Hsueh-liang was well educated and grounded in both Chinese and Western traditions. During English tutorials at the Harbin YMCA in 1916, he attended a lecture by Chang Po-ling, perhaps the most renowned educator of his generation, who expressed a powerful optimism for China's future; alluding to René Descartes and citing himself as an example, he argued that as long as the Chinese people could think for themselves, there would always be a China. The young Chang took the lesson to heart. Over seventy years later, he stated that Chang Po-ling teachings had had the greatest influence on him.[23]

While at the academy, Hsueh-liang excelled under the tutelage of Colonel Kuo Sung-ling, a respected Peking war college graduate, who came to be his most trusted confidant. After graduation, Chang Tso-lin promoted his son to colonel and procured a sinecure in May 1920 as aide-de-camp to his old mentor, President Hsu. The appointment, which gave his father an ear within the presidential offices, afforded the new officer an opportunity to learn firsthand about Peking's political machinations during the peak of the warlord era. Hsueh-liang was a welcome arrival for Hsu, but the posting was brief as war threatened. He returned home to command the 3rd Guards Brigade on 2 June.[24]

The 1920 Anfu–Chihli War

If 1919 was a failed year of peace, then 1920 became a year of crisis that ended in war. The causes were several. After Feng Kuo-chang's death on 28 December 1919, Tuan hoped the Chihli clique would fade away, creating an opportunity to defeat Canton at the hands of a reunified Peiyang military. Instead Tsao revitalized the clique. His success stemmed in part from the failed Shanghai talks. Tuan's unwillingness to end the war and abolish the NWFDA alienated Tsao and his key subordinate, Wu Pei-fu. Tsao also held Tuan responsible for Tsao's failed bid for the vice presidency, and Wu was embittered over the Hunan fighting. He won the province, but Tuan named Chang Ching-yao, the commander of the failed 1917 Hunan offensive, as tuchun. To add to the injury, Wu's troops had not been paid for ten months. The two worked to undermine Tuan.[25]

The Tsao–Tuan split climaxed in the 19 April Paoting conference, where dissident Yangtze Valley tuchuns along with Chang Tso-lin united under Tsao. With the lines drawn, the Chihli clique issued a demand for the abolition of the NWFDA bureau, the placement of the NWFDA under the War Ministry and the dismissal of Little Hsu. True to form, Tuan ignored the demands. Seeing no hope for resolution, on 25 May, Wu advanced his troops along the Peking–Hankow railway as far north as Paoting.[26]

As clouds of war loomed, Chang tried to mediate, meeting variously with Tuan, Tsao, President Hsu, and Little Hsu. It failed to heal the split. He left for Mukden, deciding to side with Tsao in the coming war. Big Hsu dismissed Little Hsu on 4 July. On 9 July, Tuan responded by having Tsao censored and Wu dismissed from the army. Three days later, Tuan closed the government by suspending parliament and placing guards around the president's residence. Declaring themselves the nation's defenders, Tsao and Wu marched north. The first skirmish was reported on 11 July south of Peking at Chochow, a Peking–Hankow railway town near the Yungting River. The next day, the Chihli clique issued a declaration against Tuan, vowing to "exterminate the traitors and strengthen the country," opening a war that both sides fought in the conviction that victory was theirs.[27]

Where they would fight was a strictly modern affair. In this era, military movements centered on the railways, and the North China network provided the logistical lifeblood for the warring armies. It consisted of five main lines. The Peking–Hankow (Pinghan or Kin-Han) railway ran from Peking south to Chengchow, the capital of Honan province, to Hankow; the Peking–Tientsin branch line connected those metropolises, running north of the Yungting River; the Tientsin–Mukden branch line similarly served to link North China and the Northeast; the Tientsin–Pukow (Tsinpu) railway ran south from Tientsin to Tsinan,

Hsuchow, and Pukow (across the Yangtze from Nanking), where a ferry connected it to the Nanking–Shanghai line; and the Lunghai railway, which ran from the port of Lienyungkiang in Kiangsu to Hsuchow, where it crossed the Tsinpu line, to Chengchow, crossing the Pinghan line, and to Sian, the Shensi capital.

The overall strategies were simple. Tuan planned to remain on the defensive, with his army centered near Peking but ready to counterattack if the opportunity arose. He placed two divisions at Chochow, two more divisions and several brigades nearer Peking, and Lung Chi-kuang's two divisions at Tientsin. The Chihli faction sought to crush the Anfu forces by advancing on the capital along two converging axes. Chang, with two divisions and his son's brigade, would drive on Tientsin, then pivot west and advance along the Peking–Tientsin line to the capital while bypassing Tuan's isolated division in Chahar. From the south, Tsao troops combined with Wu's battle-hardened 3rd Division would advance north along the Pinghan to Peking.[28]

The conflict was a limited one because of the war in the south. Feng Yu-hsiang's brigade sat out the war in Changte, and Wang Cheng-pin, Wu's replacement in Hunan, convinced the frontline troops not to enter the conflict. The pro-Chihli Kiangsu tuchun Li Shun played a key role by preventing the Tsinpu railway from being used by pro-Anfu troops in Anhwei, Chekiang, and Shantung, a move that—while not requiring battle—cut Tuan off from reinforcement and protected Tsao's rear.[29]

The fighting held closely to the plans. By 14 July, Chang was at the Great Wall, and to protect his flank during the advance on Tientsin, Chang Ching-hui's division shifted from Mukden to Shanhaikuan. Wu executed a more complex maneuver that tripped up Tuan. Tuan's two divisions, located near Chochow, held a strong position, and when they defeated Wu's advance forces, they went onto the offensive on 12 July. Wu retreated twenty kilometers to Kaopeitien. A confident Tuan then offered Wu the governorship of Hunan on 13 July in a bid to end the fighting. Wu's retreat was a ruse to draw Tuan's divisions into the open, allowing Wu to hit their flank. After heavy fighting, he routed them on 16 July. The Anfu army unraveled. Two brigades of Feng Kuo-chang's former troops went over the Chihli side, and after renewed combat on the next day, two more regiments switched sides while a Frontier Defense (FD) brigade sent from Peking surrendered without a fight. On 18 July, the Anfu troops beat a hasty retreat to Peking, only to find the gates sealed and the city's garrison in open rebellion against Tuan.[30]

Chang sealed Tuan's fate. Driving from the Great Wall, he met little opposition as Lung fell back in disorder below Tientsin. Closing in for the kill, Chang Hsueh-liang experienced his baptism of fire in capturing two brigades. His father was free to advance on Peking. In desperation, Little Hsu ordered the last two uncommitted brigades to halt Chang, and the forces clashed at Yangtsun on 18 July. The combat was inconclusive—both sides claimed victory—and irrelevant; further resistance was impossible. Tuan resigned, and on 22 July, a cease-fire was declared. The war ended in just eleven days.[31]

The 1920 war ended Tuan's 1917–1920 war on the south. It also ended an era. Tuan was the last of the "big four" generals who emerged from the 1911 revolution with the potential to rule China. Li Yuan-hung passed up his chance by becoming Yuan's vice president, and Yuan died in 1916 and Feng Kuo-chang in 1919, leaving Tuan, who was swept away and relegated to the role of a useful figurehead. The war's tragedy, however, was that it taught the victorious warlords the wrong lessons.

In the 1920 Anfu–Chihli War, the casualties were few, the cost not excessive, and the spoils many. None gained more than Chang Tso-lin. He was given Chahar. The troops stationed there were placed under his trusted lieutenant, Chang Ching-hui; meanwhile, Fengtien soldiers under his chief of staff, Chin Hua, manned Peking's garrison. New Japanese and Italian equipment from the disbanded FD divisions was snapped up, and formations were incorporated whole into his army. His army had swelled to twenty-eight brigades, although the additions were of dubious loyalty and quality. To top off his gains, on the Double Tenth of 1920, Chang was elevated in rank to marshal.[32]

The war did nothing to unify China or secure its borders. Tsao and Chang came to see themselves as rivals, and just before the war, Canton's last KMT member, Foreign Minister Wu, departed for Shanghai to join Sun. Internationally, the Western powers found little comfort in Peking's new leaders. Tuan's demise ended some bad feelings with Tokyo, and the abrogation of the Sino-Japanese military alliance on 7 September 1920 was a positive step. Yet the frontier still posed a threat. Renaming the WPA the NWFDA had not been entirely a game of semantics. The Russian civil war continued, forcing Peking and Mukden to continuously work to secure the old Ch'ing borders. One consequence of Kolchak's defeat was renewed struggle in Northeast Asia.[33]

Controlling the CER

The arrival of the Red Army in the Trans-Baikal in early 1920 was strongly felt by Peking and Mukden, but what to do about the CER remained a central problem. Difficulties began earlier, in the summer of 1919, when the assistant commissar for foreign affairs, Lev M. Karakhan, issued a 25 July manifesto that declared, "The Soviet government restores to the Chinese people without exacting any kind of compensation, the Chinese Eastern Railroad, as well as all concessions of minerals, forests, gold and others that were seized from them by the government of the Tsars."[34] A month later, on 26 August, Moscow retreated by issuing an edited version that reinstated Russia's CER rights. The Chinese, believing they were betrayed at Versailles, clung to the July manifesto and looked warily at Soviets who insisted the second August declaration was the true document. The issue sowed new seeds of resentment and distrust that would culminate in the 1929 war.[35]

The continued presence of the Allies and the death throes of the Whites in the Far East increased the tensions. Chang Tso-lin had his hands full with the Russians. In January 1920, before the departure of the Allies, the uncontrollable Semenov laid claim to Kolchak's mantle as the supreme leader in Siberia, then began moving his troops into and out of Manchuria without permission. Adding to Chang's woes, fleeing officials from the collapsing White regime arrived in Harbin, leading Horvat to assert governmental authority over the CER. The railway suddenly appeared to be for sale. At the end of the month, Peking inquired about a purchase loan from the United States, and the Japanese approached Horvat with the offer of 20 million yen to buy the CER outright in early February. The issue was put to bed when Washington turned down the loan request, Peking made it clear that Horvat had no power to negotiate, and the Allies decided to keep the IARC active until the last Allied soldier left. The struggle to control the CER dragged on.[36]

In many ways, the situation along the CER was less stable in 1920 than it had been during the Great War. Peking's 1 March claim assuming "full responsibility for the protection of the CER" proved a challenge.[37] That month, the Marshal had to order his soldiers to suppress a pro-Bolshevik railway strike, disarm White Russian troops in the CER Zone, and direct General Pao, the Kirin tuchun and CER president, to replace Horvat. Troubles continued. Only a few months after the 1920 Anfu–Chihli War, Chang had to send his son's 3rd Guards Brigade to

Kirin province on a bandit-suppression campaign to clean out the lawless gangs, many composed of ex-soldiers who had fought in Siberia. The fighting was often hard, and Chang Hsueh-liang gained valuable experience.[38]

The withdrawal of most Allied troops created new opportunities for Chang. The transition to normalcy led Stevens to report in June 1920 that commercial traffic dominated the rails and that the CER had returned to profitability. By August, revenues reached prewar levels. With his coffers beginning to fill, Chang took a major step in consolidating Chinese authority on 31 October, when he had the railway president redesignate the CER Zone as a special region under Chinese administration, while the Russian judicial system was abolished and replaced by Chinese-supervised courts of procuration. This fell on the heels of the October reorganization by the CER's owners, where the board of directors abolished the Russo-Chinese Bank and replaced it with the Paris-based Russo-Asiatic Bank, and the regional branch office opened in Peking.[39]

The Far East Republic

While things began to look up in the Northeast, the frontier continued to pose problems and peace remained elusive. When the Red Army halted in 1920, it faced an Imperial Japanese Army prepared for combat and in support of Semenov. For the Soviets, fighting the Whites was one matter, but entering a conflict with Japan was unthinkable for a people who had been at war for seven years. To break the impasse, Lenin struck upon the idea to create an artificial political construct, the Far East Republic (FER), to deal with Japan and the other Powers. The Allies' first hint of what he had in mind arose when the Czechs, who had signed a cease-fire with the Red Army in February, informed them that the Soviets were looking for a "temporary buffer state" to avoid "immediate direct contact" with Chinese or Japanese forces.[40] A diplomatic feeler from Moscow also went out to Tokyo on 24 February, proposing talks to create a favorable modus vivendi in the Far East. Four days later, a congress at Verhneudinsk established the FER.[41]

To end the fighting, the FER leaders proposed amnesty to White soldiers and promised that the Red Army would not enter the republic. They also demanded that Japan cease support to Semenov and withdraw its troops. Raising concern in China, they also claimed control over the CER. The republic was a tortured creature, and its military, the People's Revolutionary Army (PRA), reflected the difficulties. To avoid the appearance of a Red presence, the 5th Army enlisted in the PRA. Bolsheviks, along with guerrilla groups of all political persuasions, joined with Whites to form a disunited organization with loyalties largely set by the areas under Soviet or Japanese control. In the sector controlled by former Red Army troops, the PRA was loyally Bolshevik. Within the Japanese sector, Soviet supporters, maintaining covert organizations and partisan bands, faced off against White troops and struggled to take over local non-Bolshevik governments. Despite internal dissentions and structural flaws, the FER became the catalyst to realize Lenin's goal of national reunification. The creation of the buffer state ended any hope for a White victory, opening a new path to regaining Russia's Northeastern Asia domain. To further that goal, Moscow recognized the FER as an independent state on 14 May. Regaining what was lost also resonated in Peking, with Outer Mongolia the object.[42]

War in Outer Mongolia

Outer Mongolia was ruled in name by the Bogd Khan, and despite—or perhaps because of—his political and military weakness, the Bolsheviks saw Outer Mongolia in a revolutionary light. In May 1919, they expressed the hope that its lands would "fall into the sphere of Soviet influence."[43] When the Red Army entered Siberia that summer, Moscow renounced the Sino-tsarist treaties that had made autonomy synonymous with Russian domination and declared Mongolia a free country. Peking grew alarmed.[44]

Chinese control in Mongolia was feeble in 1919, but Moscow's actions demanded a response. That summer, Hsu Shu-cheng marched the 1st FD Brigade to the capital city of Urga and sent garrisons to Uliasutai in west-central Mongolia, the walled city of Kobdo in the far west, and 250 kilometers north of Urga to the Maimaicheng trading village, which lay across the border from the Russian towns of Kyakhta and Troitsosavsk and near the Selenga River, which flowed to Verkhneudinsk and the TSRR. As he neared Urga, Mongol soldiers burned their barracks. Most fled; those who remained were disarmed. Hsu then established the 23rd FD Brigade at Ude, the Gobi Desert oasis midway along the 1,000-kilometer-long Urga–Kalgan caravan route, and coerced the Mongol princes to repledge their loyalty to Peking on 15 November. The Bogd Khan was confined under guard in his palace, and Hsu confiscated his seal of office on 1 January 1920.[45]

It was a substantial achievement for the Tuan regime, and the Russians reacted. The White ambassador in Peking, Prince Kudachev, insisted that Russia's special rights in Mongolia remained unchanged, but Kolchak's defeat rendered his threats meaningless. Meanwhile, the Bolsheviks courted Mongols opposed to Chinese rule. Recognizing the vulnerability, Hsu sent reinforcements in early 1920 and proposed merging his brigades to form the 4th FD Division under General Chu Chi-hsiang. As part of the well-equipped WPA, Chinese aircraft, motor vehicles, machine guns, and a battery of modern field guns were on display at Urga. That support came to an abrupt halt after Tuan's defeat in the Anfu–Chihli War. Much of the NWFDA was disbanded, and efforts to form the 4th Division were abandoned in late July. The Chinese garrison in Urga had lost its protector.[46]

The city became a prize fought over by Chinese, White and Red Russians, and an assortment of Mongol bands. There were rumors that Semenov might head to Urga, but it was nothing new. Semenov had tried to excite the region in early 1919 with talk of a pan-Mongol movement, but no action followed the words. The first real sign of trouble surfaced in September 1920, with reports that renegade Whites numbering perhaps 1,000—the Asiatic Cavalry Division—were on the move after breaking from Semenov in the Trans-Baikal. Its leader, Roman F. von Ungern-Sternberg, was a decorated former tsarist officer who practiced Lamaist Buddhism and was known as the Mad Baron for his capricious bloodlust. Ungern felt at home; a veteran of the Russo-Japanese War, he had served in Dauria as a Cossack cavalry officer and as an advisor to the Mongol army at Kodbo.[47]

Aware of the danger, Peking's new government moved. On 30 September, Chen Yi was named the pacification commissioner for Mongolia. Chang Tso-lin's subordinate, Chang Ching-hui, the new Chahar tuchun, directed a brigade from his division at Kalgan to support Chen, and the general assumed overall responsibility for Urga's defense. Chang Ching-hui's pledged support was of dubious value. Crossing the Gobi to reach the capital might take only two days by automobile, but it would take his cavalry weeks under the best of conditions. With winter approaching and hostile horsemen on the loose, the offer was largely symbolic. The two Chinese brigades in Outer Mongolia were on their own.[48]

In early October, Ungern clashed with Chinese cavalry to the east of Urga. On 14 October, Chen banned foreign travel and declared martial law as his troops hurriedly dug their entrenchments. The makeup of Ungern's army was dismal. Observers noted that Semenov attracted the dregs of the Russian officer corps, and Ungern drew on the worst of that lot in forming his polyglot force of White Russians, Cossacks, Tibetans, and Chinese mercenaries as well as Chahar, Bargut, and Buryat Mongols. He attacked Urga on 26 October and was beaten back by Chu. Also beaten back were a second attack on 30 October and two more assaults on 2 November. Defeated, Ungern quit the field three days later, leaving behind much of his equipment, and retreated to the Russian village of Aksha. He regrouped, made good his losses, and prepared for a winter offensive. In the wake of the attacks, Chu's soldiers became even more repressive. They pillaged the countryside, further alienating the population and driving able-bodied men into Ungern's arms. By early 1921, Ungern's ranks had swelled to several thousand men, dominated by Mongol cavalrymen and including the khan's bodyguard, eager to attack Chu. They did not have long to wait.[49]

Under cover of darkness on the evening of 31 January 1921, Ungern launched a bold raid that freed the Bogd Khan. The main attack began the next day. When the strength of Ungern's army was revealed, Chu abandoned his soldiers and fled the city in a column of motorcars. Leaderless and isolated, the Chinese put up an uneven defense. After captured field guns and machine guns were turned against them, they were quickly defeated. The city fell on the afternoon of 3 February. At Maimaicheng, the Chinese garrison fled across the border to Troitsovask and pleaded for the Red Army's help. Atrocity followed in victory's wake as the garrison was massacred, along with Jews and any deemed undesirable by the Mad Baron. Ungern then advanced on Ude, taking it by midmonth, having defeated an Urga relief column in the process. His troops were now halfway to Kalgan, a fiasco that brought allegations of negligence against Chang Ching-hui.[50]

Moscow had been keenly watching the events in Mongolia. One week after the Mad Baron's failed offensive, on 11 November, the commissar for foreign affairs, Georgi V. Chicherin, proposed to Peking a joint campaign to eliminate Ungern. The Chinese declined and restated their right of suzerainty over Mongolia. Their defeat at Urga changed everything; the Soviets moved, notifying Wellington Koo in London on 4 May that they were prepared to cross into Mongolia. The PRA had just been placed under the command of Vasily Blyukher, a proven leader and the first Red Army soldier to be awarded the Order of the Red Banner. Acting swiftly, he readied the army and placed a number of detachments near the Mongolian border under Albert I. Lapin. Peking protested, and later that month, during the Tientsin conference, Chang Tso-lin was directed to replace Chen Yi and form a three-division army to recapture Urga. The Marshal set September as the start date for his offensive and designated Manchouli to be the staging area. This caused immediate friction among the Allies, as his officers ignored IARC directives and commandeered CER trains without coordination or permission.[51]

Unaware of the forces being assembled against him, on 8 May, Ungern vowed to restore the Russian monarchy. He marched his cavalry north in two columns toward Russia. He took a direct overland route while the second column, under General Boris P. Rezhukin, followed the Selenga River. Both converged on Kyakhta and Troitsosavsk. Without waiting for Rezhukin, Ungern attacked the PRA's 106th Rifle Regiment at Kyakhta on the morning of 5 June. Only one battalion was with the regimental headquarters, along with the peasant militia, but they held the town. The next day, the two remaining battalions rejoined the 106th Regiment, and Red Army cavalry under Konstantin K. Rokossovsky arrived at Troitsosavask. The tide turned. Ungern was defeated after suffering heavy losses in three days of fighting and beat a hasty retreat. Rokossovsky was wounded and later awarded the Order of the Red Banner. Several weeks later, the Mad Baron linked up with Rezhukin on the Selenga, but the reunion was not a happy one. A PRA force from Kyakhta had crossed the frontier and captured Urga by 6 July. Accompanying the PRA was the Mongolian People's Revolutionary Army (MPRA), led by Damdin Sukhbaatar, a former Mongol who quickly established a pro-Soviet regime.[52]

With the Red Army in his rear and his troops deserting, the Mad Baron entered the Trans-Baikal. On 30 July, he engaged the PRA's 104th Rifle Regiment near the north shore of Lake Gusinoe, site of a revered Buddhist monastery (known as the Lake of the Priests to the Mongols). Perhaps Ungern hoped for divine intervention or Buryat support, but no succor was to be had. After fierce fighting, the PRA gained the upper hand, and Ungern began a long retreat to Mongolia. In the aftermath of the defeat, morale plummeted, and when he proposed to march 2,000 kilometers to Tibet, mutiny ensued. Rezhukin and other loyalists were murdered on 19 August. The next day, Ungern, along with a handful of officers, was seized and turned over to the Soviets. After being taken back to Russia, Ungern was executed on 15 September 1921 at Novonikolaevsk.[53]

The Mad Baron's death proved to be a setback for Peking. The defeat of Kolchak had allowed China to regain control over Outer Mongolia, lost since the 1911 revolution. White fragmentation, however, led to Ungern and ended in China's defeat. He proved less a problem than the aggressive action of Blyukher's PRA, which rendered moot Chang Tso-lin's offensive. Going through the motions, Chang sent a senior officer to Manchouli to inspect the preparations, but nothing came of it. Mongolia fell to the Soviets, culminating three years later with the creation of a pro-Soviet puppet regime, the Mongolian People's Republic, on 26 November 1924.[54]

Soviet Progress and a Massacre

With the Mongolian campaign concluded, winning the civil war in the Far East was Moscow's imperative. Blyukher reorganized the PRA, cashiering over 10,000 men and leaving a more fit fighting force of nearly 80,000 men, and prepared for battle while the FER worked to establish relations with the Allies. Surprisingly, a terrible incident at Nikolaevsk in 1921 helped to lead to a diplomatic breakthrough with Japan.

Nikolaevsk was a trading center eighty kilometers upstream from the mouth of the Amur River. As guerrilla warfare spread during the 1920–1921 winter, the town was besieged and captured by Yakov Triapitsyn's Red partisans. After the siege, the White garrison was slaughtered while a contingent of Japanese troops who had taken part in the fighting was left alone until 10 March 1921, when it was ordered to surrender its arms. Opting to fight instead, the soldiers were overwhelmed and killed to a man. After the news reached Japanese headquarters in Vladivostok, an anti-Red purge began on 4 April, leading to the death of as many as 3,000 Bolshevik partisans and sympathizers, including Commander Sergei Lazo, who was burned alive after being thrown into a locomotive's firebox by Cossacks allied with the Japanese. Chinese gunboats reached the town in May to take away Chinese nationals, including the counsel. Their departure triggered an even greater orgy of killings. When the

Japanese relief column reached Nikolaevsk, they found the city burned to the ground with every man, woman, and child dead. Among the rotting bodies were several hundred Japanese civilians.[55]

For the Japanese, the scale of death was unprecedented: nearly 300 soldiers and sailors had perished, compared with just under 200 for 1918 and 400 in 1919. But what made it such an outrage was the civilian deaths, some after terrible mistreatment; in the blackened shell of the prison, a pair of woman's underwear was found nailed to a wall in the guard's area. Japan seized northern Sakhalin Island in retaliation, and the Soviets found justification to execute Triapitsyn, who had acted without orders.[56]

The bloodletting opened a door to cooperation between General Oi and FER war minister Vladimir S. Shatov. By 29 April 1921, an agreement had been reached where the Japanese army would quit the Trans-Baikal, Amur, and parts of the Maritime districts while forming a Russo-Japanese boundary commission to head off incidents between the forces. Oi also returned the Amur River flotilla warships. Influencing the decision was the reality that Japan paid a heavy price for becoming involved in Russia's internal affairs; H. C. Smith, the US IARC representative, noted in November 1919 that there were ten times as many attacks on Japanese railway guards as on Americans or Czechs. By the fall of 1921, the Japanese withdrawal was complete.[57]

The Soviets made further diplomatic advances. The FER was invited to send E. K. Ozarnin as an extraordinary representative to the IARC technical board in Harbin, and in August, FER diplomat Ignatius L. Yurin announced that he would meet with Japanese representatives in Dairen to try to normalize relations. Yurin then headed to Peking to attempt to gain recognition from China. He had some success. On 10 September, Peking withdrew the diplomatic status of the White Russian legation. A week later, all Russian diplomats departed China. On 23 September, President Hsu announced that, given the "contending factions," it no longer recognized a Russian government.[58]

Soviet Victory in the Far East

Soviet military victory was near. Ordered to attend the Dairen talks in November, Blyukher did not return to the front until 17 December, where he had to restore a faltering PRA. Blyukher arrived too late to prevent the recapture of Khabarovsk on 22 December by Viktorin M. Molchanov, the new and talented White commander who had taken over from Semenov in May, but he was able to halt Molchanov's advance near the small village of Volochaevka, thirty kilometers west of Khabarovsk. The two enemies, dug in, with a combined strength of over 20,000 troops, faced each other across a series of trench lines stretching sixteen kilometers and anchored to the Amur River to the south and the Tunguska River to the north. Blyukher's offensive began on the evening of 11 January and continued for two long, bloody days. Molchanov was battered but held, forcing Blyukher to regroup before launching a second offensive on 4 February. After eleven days of fighting, the PRA broke Molchanov's main defensive belt. The Whites retreated. The PRA marched into Khabarovsk on 18 February. Over the next two months, Blyukher pressed the retreating Whites—and urged Molchanov to join the Bolsheviks—until they reached Spassk, the northernmost town within the Japanese zone.[59]

Troops from two Japanese divisions triggered a halt, whereupon everyone except die-hard Whites realized that the PRA had won the war. The only remaining task was to arrange the exit of the Japanese Expeditionary Force to complete the Red victory. Japan accepted the inevitable and announced on 15 July that it would withdraw. Later that month, Blyukher departed, having been appointed as the Petrograd Military District commissar and commander. On 26 September, the last Japanese detachment departed Vladivostok and the Japanese troops along the CER returned to their Kwantung Leasehold barracks. This was also the cue to close down the IARC, which officially ceased operation on 1 November. On 15 November 1922, the FER was peacefully absorbed by Soviet Russia. The role it played had proved crucial for Moscow.[60]

The 1921–1922 Washington Conference

To build on the spirit of international cooperation begun at the 1919 Paris peace talks, the United States hosted its first international conference. It opened on 12 November 1921 in Washington, DC, and was composed of concurrent sessions addressing naval disarmament and the Far East. When the latter talks opened, the China situation dominated the proceedings. The Chinese were again led by Koo, China's minster in London, who was joined by Alfred Sze, the minister in Washington,

Wang Chung-hui, and Hawkling L. Yen, with W. W. Willoughby serving as a technical expert. The delegation was able to push its 1919 policies forward slightly by obtaining resolutions to form an extraterritoriality committee, conditionally abolish foreign post offices by 1 January 1923, enter into discussions over foreign armed forces in China, tie future rail development to a unified rail system under the Chinese government, and, in an effort to kill secret agreements, publish all treaties between the Powers and China.[61]

Concurrent with the conference, the other Powers pushed Japan and China to resolve the divisive Shantung dispute. An agreement was hammered out and signed in Washington on 4 February. It was a success for China, as Article I flatly declared, "Japan shall restore to China the former German Lease Territory of Kiaochow."[62] Japan would be compensated for the Tsingtao–Tsinan railway, and a second agreement stipulated that the Japanese troop withdrawal was to be completed by 30 April 1922. The failure to gain immediate Japanese capitulation was used by Wu Pei-fu to criticize the pro–Chang Tso-lin government, opening a bitter feud between the generals that again threatened war.[63]

The conference marked the last direct attempt to resolve the CER issue by the Powers as a group, and deliberations did not begin until 18 January 1922. The United States argued that the railway was too important not to allow free access for all; it also recognized that it was Russian property and that China ultimately held reversion rights. Counter to the American position, ownership was contested by China and France. Yen initially claimed ownership on the basis of Russian default, to which the French quickly countered that the owner of the CER also owned the bond debt owed to French investors. Facing insurmountable difficulties in repaying the French, Koo fell back on the 1896 agreements, stating that Chinese control was temporary, pending recognition of a Russian government, and stated that the CER was a joint concern between China and Russia. This created a dilemma when Elihu Root, a senior American delegate, made clear the impossibility of sending "notice to Russia or to collaborate with Russia," a statement reinforced by Chicherin, who had denounced the entire Washington conference in December, confirming that the CER issue could only be resolved between Moscow and Peking.[64]

Only two issues remained, and China's position prevailed in both. The first concerned policing the CER. The idea of a multinational guard was raised. China, with American support, rejected the idea, arguing that the issue had been settled during the 1919 IARC talks. Yen added that the former Russian railway guard had been a violation of the original CER agreements and could not be reestablished. China would exclusively provide for railway security. The second and less important issue aimed to establish China's sovereignty over emerging radio technology, especially the use of public commercial and informational broadcasts. A resolution passed giving China authority over nondiplomatic transmissions and, in a sign of China's growing equality, the right to take over unauthorized radio stations. Aside from the reaffirmation of China's right to guard the CER and the recognition of its authority over radio broadcasts, the major issue of railroad control remained unresolved. In the end, the Powers adopted a diplomatic if toothless resolution on 4 February 1922 regarding "a more careful selection of personnel to secure efficiency of service, and a more economical use of funds to prevent waste of the property" in the conduct of CER operations.[65] Going forward, the struggle over the railroad would be waged between China and Soviet Russia.[66]

The First Fengtien–Chihli War

Tsao Kun remained the head of the Chihli clique, but Wu Pei-fu would lead the effort for war with Chang Tso-lin in 1922. Chang and Wu had never been close; the Marshal had publicly snubbed Wu after the 1920 Anfu–Chihli War, stating, "I deal with Tsao Kun only. Wu is only the chief of a division."[67] By 1921, Wu was his equal, having been appointed inspector general of Hunan and Hupeh. An uneasy truce emerged after the April–May 1921 Tientsin conference, where both refused to recognize the 20 April election of Sun Yat-sen as president after the reconvening of the 1913 national assembly in Canton. The rapprochement was short, as Wu used the 1922 Shantung treaty as a political cudgel to beat Peking's pro-Mukden officials and label them traitors. That broke the few remaining bonds, and Wu's continuing condemnation of Sun also opened the door to a Sun–Chang alliance, which advanced after Dr. C. C. Wu visited Mukden to consult with Chang. Later, in the March 1922 "National Unification" Tientsin conference, Chang solidified the opposition against Wu, and war planning began.[68]

The strategy to defeat Wu called for attacks from the north and south. The Marshal would hold the Peking–Tientsin area by defending a 150-kilometer front along the northern bank of the Yungting River. He would also pressure Wu by driving south from Tientsin into Anhwei. Sun planned to advance north into Wu's rear with two columns, one from Kwangsi under Sun and the second under General Chen Chiung-ming in Kwangtung. As an added measure, Chang obtained the support of a Honan tuchun, Chao Ti, who promised to rise up and attack Wu. Trapped between enemies and facing an internal uprising, Wu would be forced into capitulation. Wu's strategy was to first defeat Chang, the more dangerous foe, by a three-pronged attack while holding off Sun. To breach Chang's Yungting River defenses, Wu's prongs would progress as follows. In the west, he would drive on Peking along the Pinghan railway; in the center, his forces would attack Kuan, with its river bridge; and to the east, his forces would march up the Tsinpu line to Tientsin. Like Chang, he also looked to weaken his adversaries internally. In Marshal Chang's ranks, Wu found an ally in Kao Shih-pin, the general ruined during the 1919 Kuancheng station incident, who would rebel in Harbin and take over the CER. To stymie Sun Yat-sen, he approached Chen, who had no ambitions beyond Kwangtung, and it was reported that Wu and Chen had reached an understanding in April not to fight each other regardless of what Sun ordered. As Wu envisioned it, with Chang Tso-lin beaten on the Yungting and Chen refusing to enter the battle, Sun would have to make peace on his terms. Wu would emerge as the ruler of China.[69]

The Marshal's plan did not start well. The army's movement—fifty-two train cars of troops departed Harbin on 1 April—alerted Wu, and he mobilized his army. The Fengtien deployment nonetheless proceeded smoothly, and Chang established his headquarters at Chunliangcheng, twenty-five kilometers east of Tientsin. The 1st Army, under Chang Tso-hsiang, occupied the front's eastern half, and the 2nd Army, under Chang Ching-hui, the general who botched the 1921 defense of Mongolia, took charge in the west. Chang Hsueh-liang, with three brigades, would serve under him.[70]

The war unfolded slowly at first. Chang Ching-hui did not repeat Tuan's mistake of crossing the Yungting. Instead, he strengthened his defense at Changhsintien. While Wu prepared, hostilities began at the front's eastern end on 18 April, when Chang's 1st Army moved on Anhwei and Tsao's troops fell back. At 3:00 AM on 20 April, Wu assaulted Changhsintien without success. In the east, by 27 April, Chang Tso-hsiang had reached Macheng, 65 kilometers south of Tientsin, where the Chihli forces had formed a line; fighting raged all the next day. The war had begun in earnest. At Macheng, Tsao's troops retreated under a Fengtien assault backed by an artillery bombardment. The Chihli casualties were estimated at 1,000. After a failed second Fengtien assault on 1 May, the casualties also mounted for Chang. The same day, the Chihli attack on Kuan succeeded, and Chang's defenders were driven to the Yungting bridge. One observer noted, "The war that is now in progress seems to be the most business-like in China's modern history and modern implements of warfare, such as machineguns and heavy artillery, are being employed with telling effect."[71]

As Wu attacked, he ordered Feng Yu-hsiang in Shensi to protect his Loyang capital. After he arrived on 26 April, he further directed Feng to send one brigade to aid the Changhsintien attack. Its arrival proved decisive. The brigade conducted a difficult night march that allowed it to fall on Changhsitien's weakly defended western flank on 3 May. The attack shattered the defense. Hearing of the crisis, the Marshal left his headquarters and arrived at Fengtai in time to see his troops beaten off their line of defense.

With his army in trouble, Chang militarized the Peking–Tientsin railway, in violation of the Boxer Protocol. Despite international protests, he kept control, as it offered the only hope of saving even part of the 2nd Army. After ordering his son to safety, Chang pulled back his troops at Macheng—they were now on the wrong side of the Yungting. A general retreat was ordered on 4 May. Three days of rearguard fighting allowed Chang to save much of his army—the trains ran through Tientsin around the clock for two days—but a number of troops were lost, and only the 1st Army withdrew in good order.[72]

Two other hopeless battles were waged. In Honan, Chao Ti rose up on 4 May but was soon crushed by Feng. The successes in Honan and of his brigade at Changhsintien catapulted Feng into the highest tier of Wu's lieutenants, ending in a promotion to Honan tuchun. In the Northeast, Kao rebelled but was suppressed by loyal troops led by Chang Tsung-chang. Chang "Dog Meat" Tsung-chang was rewarded with a brigade command and became a favorite of the Marshal.[73]

The war in the south never got off the ground when Chen balked at advancing north. Sun pleaded, but Chen refused, declared Wu Pei-fu a patriot, and sat out the war. This ended the southern offensive before it began, just as Wu had hoped. After Chang's retreat, Sun was briefly expelled from Canton. Sun and Chen, allies since the 1911 revolution, never reconciled. Needing a new military advisor, Sun called on one of his capable acolytes, thirty-five-year-old Chiang Kai-shek.[74]

Wu publicly pledged to crush Chang. On 10 May, and at the urging of Wu, President Hsu stripped Chang of his official positions, honors, and rank while his adherents in the cabinet were sacked. A Shanghai press report stated that the Marshal had "definitely passed from the political stage of China." The outlook in Mukden was grim.[75]

Just as things looked hopeless, Chang Tso-lin pulled off a miracle. Two days after being sacked, he declared his independence, reestablished his headquarters midway between Tientsin and the Great Wall, and rallied his troops. In days, Chang was able to establish a defense, with two lines of trenches and artillery in the hills to his rear. Wu advanced north and launched a series of assaults in early June, but none succeeded. Stalemated, Wu agreed to an armistice on 17 June. On 19 June, the Marshal took his battered but unbroken army back into "Fortress Manchuria."[76]

Wu Pei-fu and Tsao Kun could be forgiven in thinking that they were a hairbreadth away from reunifying China. The two had proven their ability to defeat southern, Anfu, and Fengtien armies almost at will and now controlled Peking. President Hsu was out, replaced by Li Yuan-hung on 11 June. Who could stop them? Unfortunately, obstacles remained. Tsao was not unchallenged, as Wu used his Loyang group to expand his influence within the Chihli clique; Sun Yat-sen possessed a nationwide political base; and an autonomous Chang stood at the head of an army in the Northeast. It was at this inopportune time that Soviet Russia turned its gaze toward China.[77]

The CER and Sino-Soviet Relations

The struggle for control over the CER soon came to the fore; the Allies failed to resolve the question during the Washington conference, so now it fell to China and Soviet Russia to find the answer. The FER's Yurin had opened the issue, but it would be the lack of success by two Soviet diplomats, Aleksandr K. Paikes and Adolf A. Joffe, that would help nudge China and Russia toward the 1929 war over the railway.

With warlord strife peaking, Peking in late 1921 was not an ideal setting for a new diplomat from an unrecognized nation to gain success, and Paikes seemed an odd choice. A long-serving Bolshevik, as head of the Food Commissariat during the civil war, his duties entailed supplying the Red Army with rations and munitions, and he supported Frunze's 1919–1920 offensive that crushed Kolchak. In that capacity, he often was in direct communication with Lenin, further enhancing his reputation. When he arrived on 14 December, just as the Washington conference was getting underway, the split between Chang and Tsao had become irreversible, and their struggle crippled rule in the capital. Paikes's logistical experience with railways during the civil war, however, made him a strong candidate for his carefully defined mission: resolve the Sino-Soviet disagreement over the CER so that diplomatic relations could be restored.[78]

Peking welcomed two-party negotiations. Paikes's task was quickly undone, however, when the Chinese ignored his agenda and pushed for the removal of the Red Army from Mongolia as a precondition. Paikes countered, repeating Chicherin's position that the Red Army would leave as soon as Peking and the pro-Soviet government in Urga reached an understanding. When the 5 November 1921 Soviet–Mongolian agreement (which ignored China's rights) was made known after Paikes had denied its existence, his standing was irreparably diminished. It was of little consequence; he had become a messenger, not a negotiator, and his message was that the 25 July 1919 Karakhan manifesto was dead and that only the amended 26 August version that favored the Soviet position was acceptable. Just as the 1922 Fengtien–Chihli War was getting underway, Paikes took matters further by informing the foreign ministry on 26 April that while the tsarist treaties had been "abolished," their underlying "basis" was not; nor were they "unconditionally canceled." This applied to the secret agreements as well.[79] While publicly proclaiming solidarity with China, behind closed doors, the Kremlin held that the tsar's treaties remained in full effect until new agreements could be concluded or the old treaties revised. The Soviets took a hard line. The question was, could a Peking government embroiled in a civil war be as tough?[80]

The Chinese diplomats proved to be hard negotiators by talking about many things but agreeing to little. With the CER in Chinese hands, the delaying tactics were especially effective. When Adolf Joffe replaced Paikes in October, no agreement on any issue of substance had been reached. An experienced diplomat and medical doctor, as well as an ally of Trotsky's, Joffe was in frail health. Split between responsibilities in both Japan and China, he made little headway in the face of unwavering opposition. He departed Peking in January 1923. An unwillingness to make significant concessions to the Russians was perhaps the only policy on which the Chinese were united.

Chang Tso-lin also competed with the Soviets. After the end of the 1922 Fengtien–Chihli War, Chang moved to rebuild his army and create an autonomous regime. The departure of the Japanese army and the closing of the IARC by November allowed him to increase his authority in the CER Zone. Wellington Koo in Peking noted that the railroad continued to expand (the number of trains, total freight shipped, and distances traveled all increased) while expenditures shrank and profits grew. Before departing for home, Stevens noted that Peking claimed to control the CER but Chang ruled in the Northeast. As if to prove the point, the Marshal used an obscure section of the Washington conference to seize the Harbin CER radio station on 2 October. It was not the railway's owners, the Russo-Asiatic Bank (which obeyed the conference precepts) that objected, however; it was the Soviets who demanded its return. Chang kept it.[81]

Not everything was to Chang's liking. He had lost influence in Peking, and he protested vigorously when the Russo-Asiatic Bank held its board meetings there instead of Harbin, as he held that CER matters were under his purview. Surprisingly, Chang found himself on the same side as the Soviets, as Joffe also protested the bank's actions. Opposing the bank was nothing new for Chang; he had objected to its attempt in July to gain financial independence by issuing new bonds. Fortunately the railroad's future was too uncertain to attract investors, and the sale failed. In a less successful effort, he tried in 1923 to seize the CER land office, which managed the railway's vast holdings, but he backed down in the face of opposition from the other Powers and Soviet Russia.[82]

American diplomats noted the change in Moscow's dealings with Peking, from the idealistic July 1919 Karakhan manifesto to the tense negotiations over recognition and the protest over the radio station seizure. Joffe declared that "the Russian Government alone has the right practically to interfere" in CER issues.[83] That the Red Army might be used to regain the CER became a possibility, and the American consul in Harbin reported that such an eventuality was being contemplated in late 1922. Cooler heads prevailed. It was rumored that Ozarnin, formerly of the IARC and now the ranking Soviet official in Harbin, led the opposition to intervention. In any event, no military action was taken as Moscow's attention focused on a new revolutionary force in China.[84]

The Emergence of the Chinese Communist Party

Communism had a late start in China. The first Marxist study group, led by Li Ta-chao, began only after the 1917 October Revolution. The May Fourth Movement stirred the group into greater action, yet it was only after the arrival of Communist International, or Comintern, organizers in late 1919 that things got off the ground, beginning with the formation of the Socialist Youth League in August 1920. Key among the early revolutionaries was Ch'en Tu-hsui, the first secretary general of the Chinese Communist Party (CCP), which was formed under Comintern auspices in Shanghai during the summer of 1921. Ch'en and Li nurtured the CCP from a membership of less than 100 to nearly 1,000 by 1923, but its influence—despite inroads into trade unions in 1921 and adopting an ambitious proposal to create a Red Army in 1922—was mainly limited to a small circle of intellectual ideologues.[85]

Efforts to form a Northeast CCP branch proved equally difficult. The first cadre, Chen Wei-jen, arrived in Dairen in February 1923. Chen was exceptionally qualified, having helped set up the Socialist Youth League and CCP and led the Pinghan railway workers until Wu Pei-fu crushed them just weeks before his arrival in Manchuria. After forming a worker's study group, he was joined by Li Chen-ying and established the Harbin cell in October. Li held that the railroads were key to CCP success, writing in late 1923, "The future revolution cannot depart from the Chinese Eastern and South Manchuria Railways."[86] Although the region possessed a strong union base, it was also one of China's most hostile environments for communists. Chang Tso-lin saw Bolshevism as a mortal threat and had forcefully ended CER labor strikes in May 1920; his police brutally suppressed communist agitators as soon as they appeared. The Japanese in the Kwantung Leasehold and in the SMR Zone were equally efficient. Even in the countryside, the CCP faced difficulties. The farmers were better off and likely as not owned their land, making calls for revolution unappealing. They were also difficult to reach; beyond the long-settled Liao River region, the wheat and soybean farm families lived in greater isolation. To adjust, the CCP Central Committee set low recruitment goals. Yet even those proved impossible when the police moved. The CCP survived but never thrived in Manchuria.[87]

The United Front

Facing a stone wall in Peking, the Soviets chose not send a replacement for Joffe but turned to Sun in Canton. It was a renewal of an old line of communication. First writing to Lenin in 1918, Sun expressed openness toward the Bolshevik regime, but no real progress was made until Chen Chiung-ming's betrayal and defeat in the 1922 war. The setback sent Sun on a quest for a KMT army, and Soviet Russia presented a solution. In 1921, he contacted Moscow through the agency of Maring, a talented Comintern operative. After a meeting between the two in August 1922, Sun became convinced that an alliance with the Soviets was needed to complete the Chinese revolution, and the Soviets held that an alliance with CCP was equally critical. This led to a final conference with Joffe in Shanghai on 24 January 1923 that cemented a KMT–CCP alliance. The public announcement, made two days later, praised the partnership, but it was every bit as much an alliance between the KMT and the USSR—in effect a tripartite agreement.[88]

Soviet aid, in the form of military equipment and supplies along with political and military advisors, gave Sun Yat-sen the tool he had always lacked: an army whose first loyalty lay with the Chinese republic. Mikhail M. Borodin headed the mission, arriving in September. It was during this period that the first four Soviet military advisors arrived in Canton, and things progressed rapidly. In January 1924, the 1st KMT Congress established the National Revolutionary Army (NRA) under Chiang Kai-shek. Another major step forward was taken in May, when the first officer's class was enrolled at the new Whampoa military academy. P. A. Pavlov, a distinguished civil war cavalry commander, was selected as the senior Soviet military representative and reached Canton in mid-June 1924, bringing along a second detachment of officers to serve as academy instructors. Earlier, on 2 June, Sun proclaimed a KMT Republic of China, and Pavlov helped the NRA get off to a good start before he tragically died in a boating mishap in July. Vasily Blyukher was chosen as his replacement; he adopted the Comintern cover name of "Galen" and took his place at Whampoa early that fall. On 7 October, a shipment containing quantities of ammunition and small arms, along with ten military advisors, arrived. The creation of the NRA and Whampoa's opening, combined with the arrival of Soviet weapons and Blyukher's advisors, freed Sun from his total dependence on the southern tuchuns. The NRA was still so woefully small—numbering no more than 1,500 men by year's end—that Sun continued to seek the aid of willing warlords.[89]

Breakthrough in Peking–Moscow CER Talks

Moscow returned to the issue of recognition, and the decision to send Karakhan to Peking presented a new opportunity. The Kremlin had also tentatively agreed on a CER policy by 1923. Initially, Trotsky and Stalin argued bitterly; Trotsky wanted little to do with a railway that he saw as a "tool of imperialism," while Stalin countered with a proposal for joint CER operation. Stalin ultimately won when fellow Central Committee leaders Grigory E. Zinoviev and Lev B. Kamenev closed ranks against Trotsky.[90] After Lenin died on 21 January 1924, Stalin's authority increased at the expense of Trotsky, and the push for joint operation was on.

With Sun Yat-sen supporting Soviet recognition, Peking was ready to revisit the issue. Tsao Kun had maneuvered himself into the presidency, but his inauguration on the Double Tenth, when Li Yuan-hung handed over the keys of government, was shunned by the Peking diplomatic corps. It served more as a eulogy, marking the beginning of the end of Tsao. The Soviets could not have hoped for a better outcome. Karakhan had arrived a month before to a warm welcome. Speaking to the press, he averred that only Soviet Russia "would like to see China, known as the 'sick man,' become strong and united," but under whom was unsaid.[91] In the following negotiations, an objective observer might have concluded that it was not a China led by Tsao.[92]

Dr. C. T. Wang headed up a commission on Sino-Russian affairs to handle the talks. Although it operated outside normal foreign ministry channels, the change did nothing to resolve the underlying dispute over the CER. Wang was still attempting to get the Soviets to honor the 25 July 1919 manifesto as late as January 1924, while the Soviets were equally adamant in holding to the 26 August 1919 manifesto. CER joint management was the only solution. In late 1923, Karakhan even had hinted at military action if progress was not made. The Chinese position was not as unreasonable as Karakhan portrayed it; on 26 February 1921, the Soviets had signed a treaty of friendship with Persia that turned tsarist railways, telegraph lines, canals, and even steamships over to the Shah without cost. No such magnanimity was in the offing for China, and the talks deadlocked.[93]

In February 1924, Karakhan moved to break the impasse by adding concessions: joint administration would be temporary, as China could buy the railway or gain full ownership without cost in 1976. No real favors were offered; the railway was grossly overpriced at 700 million rubles. It was twice the estimate reached by independent observers. It included the cost of the SMR and ignored the fact that the CER had been built using French funds that Moscow would not repay. The price was moot—there were no funds—and Wang pushed back one last time before he folded, acceding to Karakhan's terms on 14 March. Opposition within Tsao's cabinet arose at once. Wang was forced to resign, and his commission was abolished. Foreign Minister Koo assumed responsibility while Karakhan, upset that the agreement had not been acted on, issued an ultimatum with a 19 March deadline. Responding coolly, Koo informed him that he had no power to set deadlines for the Chinese government. The delay changed nothing. The pact was signed on 31 May.[94]

The treaty was actually two documents. The fifteen-article Agreement on General Principles restored diplomatic relations, renounced both the Russian share of the Boxer indemnity and special rights for Soviet citizens, called for a conference to replace the tsarist treaties with new agreements based on "equality, reciprocity and justice," and set a date for Red Army withdrawal from Mongolia. The agreement also devoted a lengthy article to the CER and another to the seemingly unusual topic of propaganda, which pledged the two states to "not permit, within their respective territories the existence and/or activities of any organizations or groups whose aim is to struggle by acts of violence against the Government of either Contracting Party" and "not to engage in propaganda directed against the political or social systems of either Contracting Party."[95]

Its inclusion was no mistake. Propaganda in the 1920s was not much different from propaganda today. Words and images were used to gain and bolster support or demoralize the opponent, and a new facet—influencing foreign parties—had come into its own during World War I. It need not be false, only biased to push forward the objective. The 1920s meaning differed from its modern version in important ways. Today's pejorative undertone was not as pronounced, as propaganda was a legitimate undertaking, the outcome of which was not to simply influence a targeted audience but rather to spur them to action. Its activities—speeches, wall posters, handbills, telegraphs, and radio and newsprint messages—were intended to produce results. When called for, boycotts, rallies, strikes, protests, and sacrifice by the soldiery were to translate into victories for the cause. In 1920s China, no leader could afford to take propaganda lightly.[96]

Added to the treaty was an eleven-article Agreement for the Provisional Management of the Chinese Eastern Railway. It addressed the board of directors, senior management, and auditors; it also provided a directive to revise the 1896 CER statutes to put them in compliance with the new agreements. The language implied truly joint management based on a "principle of equal representation between the nationals" of the two states.[97] At noon on 8 September 1924, Karakhan reopened the Russian legation in Peking and became the first Soviet ambassador to China.[98]

Having made Manchurian autonomy a reality, the Soviets also moved to negotiate with Chang Tso-lin, who zealously guarded his CER prerogatives; the Marshal rejected the Peking accords out of hand, putting the entire agreement in jeopardy. Aware of another looming war with Tsao and Wu, and mindful of the rumored Soviet military action over the CER in late 1922 as well as Karakhan's threat of a military strike in 1923, the Marshal wished to come to terms with the Soviets. Unbeknownst to Chang, the Kremlin had created a special commission to study seizing the CER under Vladimir Antonov-Ovseyenko that had concluded that "under no circumstances" should military action be taken.[99] With both parties eager to reach a deal, Karakhan and the Marshal's representatives signed the treaty on 20 September 1924.[100]

The resulting Agreement between the Autonomous Three Eastern Provinces of the Republic of China and the Union of Soviet Socialist Republics was an abridged combination of the two Peking treaties. Outwardly, the only meaningful difference provided for the free transfer of the CER to Mukden in 1956, twenty years earlier than the date agreed to in Peking. Unknown to the public, Chang and Karakhan's advisors had penned a secret clause that granted Chang the authority of the Chinese government for the proposed two-party conference.[101]

The Soviets broke precedence; while the other Powers had worked out a modus vivendi with Mukden, only Moscow engaged in treaty writing, and concluding a secret agreement ran counter to the policy of condemning such actions. It now appeared that some tsarist practices were being reintroduced. In addition to the secret pact, recognition of dual authority was in keeping with Russian policy of weakening Peking's control over the Northeast dating back to the Boxer Uprising and put almost all of China's authority in the hands of Chang, leaving Peking holding nearly valueless pieces of paper. The Marshal had no time to enjoy the diplomatic success as civil war again wracked China.

The Kiangsu–Chekiang and Second Fengtien–Chihli Wars

With the war in Kiangsu that began on 3 September 1924, China had reached its "turning point," as Arthur Waldron put it.[102] As with Tuan's 1917–1920 war, it began when Peking attempted to expand its authority, this time into Shanghai ruled by the last Anfu tuchun and ally of Chang Tso-lin, Lu Yung-hsiang of Chekiang. Chi Hsieh-yuan, inspector general of Kiangsu, Anhwei, and Kiangsi, led the Chihli advance on the city. When battle began, Lu had little trouble fending off Chi. Wu then ordered in Fukien tuchun Sun Chuan-fang, and he broke the deadlock by overrunning Chekiang. As Lu's defense faltered, Tuan sent Little Hsu to help in September, but he was no match for Sun, who reached Shanghai at the same time. After a bloody four-day assault, Sun broke though Lu's lines on 7 October, and by 13 October, Chi and Sun emerged victorious. Chi occupied the massive Lunghua Arsenal two days later. Little Hsu attempted to regroup the defenders but was captured and deported. The last of Lu's troops surrendered on 19 October, and Lu ignominiously retired, seemingly ending another dubious tuchun war. This was different, however, as it served as prelude to a far greater conflict, the Second Fengtien–Chihli War, for on 7 September Chang Tso-lin declared war on the "traitors" Wu and Tsao, citing their "wickedness" that had "destroyed" the republican system.[103]

Wu feared a larger war, and mobilization in North China had begun on 1 September. His strategy was ambitious. Having won decisive victories in 1920 and 1922 through flanking attacks, he now planned a massive double envelopment. Part of his 1st Route Army at Shanhaikuan and the nearby port of Chinwangtao and the 2nd Route Army under Wang Huai-ching at Chengte (160 kilometers to the northwest) would drive at Chang's army. Feng Yu-hsiang's 3rd Route Army, based at the Great Wall, passing north of Chengte, would advance to hit Chang from the northwest. In a daring move, troops would be embarked at Chinwangtao and would land to Chang's northeast, completing the encirclement.[104]

The plan was foiled when Chang Tso-lin struck first. Also initially using three armies, he sent his 1st and 3rd Eastern armies toward Shanhaikuan and the 2nd Eastern Army on a long march to Chengte. To the north, near Chifeng, he deployed cavalry to screen his armies from Feng. The war began on 17 September when the 2nd Eastern Army defeated a Chihli brigade at Chaoyang, 260 kilometers northeast of Chengte. The next day, an eight-day barrage of artillery and aerial bombings began at Shanhaikuan. A Chihli relief column bound for Chaoyang met and was defeated by the 2nd Eastern Army on 22 September. On 3 October, the army marked its halfway point to Chengte when Dog Meat Chang captured Chien Ping.[105]

Heavy fighting erupted at Shanhiakuan on 29 September as the 1st Eastern Army repeatedly threw itself against the Chihli defenses without success; the rebuff was a reminder of the how the Great Wall, built on advantageous terrain, could still confound a modern army. Both sides rushed in reinforcements; the total number of soldiers reached 400,000. Chang sent the 5th Eastern Army to Shanhaikuan, and the 6th Army joined the cavalry opposite the idle Feng Yu-hsiang. To break the stalemate, on 7 October, Chang Hsueh-liang's 3rd Army launched an enveloping attack through the Yan Mountains, about fifteen kilometers to the city's north, and broke through the Chihli defenses at Chiumenkuo Gate. After breaching the line, the 3rd Eastern Army had an opportunity to march through the pass and turn the flank on the Chihli 1st Route Army, tied up at Shanhaikuan. Wu, at his Fengtai headquarters outside Peking, saw the peril and rushed to the Shanhaikuan front on 11 October just as the battle peaked.[106]

During the fighting, Chang Hsueh-liang's chief of staff, Kuo Sungling, ordered the artillery brigade at Shanhaikuan north to exploit their breakthrough. Han Lin-chun, in command at Shanhaikuan, countermanded the order. Angered, Kuo halted his infantry, creating a dangerous gap in the Mukden lines. Only the intervention of the Marshal and Chang Hsueh-liang persuaded Kuo to reenter the battle. Once back, Kuo led his forces to a series of victories ending in Chinwangtao's capture, signaling Wu's defeat, but the rash act tarnished Kuo's reputation. While the fighting of the Eastern Army, exemplified by Kuo, did much to help their cause, the decisive act of the war occurred away from battle when Feng marched his army to Peking on 21 October.[107]

The Feng Yu-hsiang Coup d'État and Peace

By midnight on 22 October, Feng's troops, along with Sun Yo's garrison, were in control of the capital, and troops were deployed to block any move on the capital by Wu. The next day, Tsao was made a prisoner in the presidential residence and telegraphic and telephonic communications were severed; only radio reports got through. Feng met with the diplomatic corps, declaring that a negotiated settlement to the war must be reached while demanding that Tsao issue two mandates, one ending the war and another dismissing Wu. Wu answered on 26 October with a counterattack on Chang's armies at Shanhaikuan.[108]

The coup was not entirely unexpected. On 9 October, the press published rumors of a Wu–Feng split. Feng had never been a member of either Tsao or Wu's inner circle, and after his mentor General Lu's death in 1918, he had to rise by his own abilities. Having been hedging his bets since the 1911 revolution, he decided to look out for himself before fighting began. The protracted war soured Feng, as quick victory and spoils were what motivated his participation. He was ripe for rebellion. Just days before the war erupted, Feng had won over Sun Yo, deputy commander of the Peking garrison, and Hu Ching-i, a 3rd Route Army commander whom Wu had sent to keep Feng in line; he also gained the support of Shansi tuchun Yen Hsi-shan. Feng was positioned to take advantage of a victory by either side. Chang Tso-lin, aware of Feng's unease with Wu, approached him with an offer of power and riches. For a general of few resources and little loyalty, the offer was too good to pass up. The Marshal, through his Japanese backers, cemented the alliance by transferring several million dollars to Feng in the days leading up to the coup. The betrayal was complete, but Wu Pei-fu refused to yield.[109]

Wu's intransigence was unexpected, but his battlefield success perplexed his foes. Chang had his hands full, and Feng had to eat his words about peaceful negotiations while marching on Tientsin and Wu. Chang and Feng's combined weight proved too much, even for a skilled tactician like Wu. By 30 October, Wu's troops were forced to abandon North China. However, the twenty ships he had amassed for a canceled landing in Chang's rear saved his army. Remarkably, he was able to transport a sizable number troops to the mouth of the Yangtze River and reestablished a base of power in Hupeh and Honan.[110] Tsao Kun resigned as president on 2 November, barely a year into his five-year term. The war had ended. Where China would go in its aftermath was anyone's guess.[111]

Conclusions

The five-year period from 1919 to 1924 reshaped the Northeast into much of the form that existed when the 1929 Sino-Soviet conflict erupted.

The international accords fared badly. The Versailles treaty failed China, but the pent-up frustration over what had not been accomplished in Paris found an outlet in the May Fourth Movement, as the movement reinvigorated the Chinese revolution with a new vision that turned away from Wilsonian democracy and toward the rising Soviet Union; it ended with the creation of the CCP and the United Front. The KMT and CCP became potent political forces, and both remained as such in 1929. The Shanghai peace conference and the arms embargo did not end the violence, and the Washington conference did nothing to end the CER dispute between China and Russia, thus keeping the option of armed resolution alive.

The Allied intervention altered the region. It made the CER an internationally known commodity; soldiers from a dozen countries had ridden its rails, and its strategic military value was obvious. The intervention rewrote the Russian–Chinese rivalry, as it allowed Chang Tso-lin to expand Chinese authority over the CER and dismantle the Russian sphere of interest. It also sharpened the rivalry with Japan, as witnessed by the armed clashes during the Kuancheng station and Hailar incidents. The Nikolaevsk and Urga massacres offered windows into the brutality of the era's warfare; much has been written of warlord-era atrocities, but these incidents demonstrated that terrible depredations were not a characteristic unique to Chinese soldiery in the 1920s.

Ongoing wars in China and Russia during these five years had direct consequences for the 1929 Sino-Soviet conflict. The tuchun wars honed the growing sophistication and lethality of the Chinese armies, particularly those of the Northeast. The Chinese army that fought the Soviets in 1929 was largely formed in the crucible of war during the 1919–1924 period. Chang Tso-lin's 1922 defeat also led to the autonomous state that basically remained in place when the 1929 conflict erupted. The Russian civil war that ended in a Soviet victory opened the difficult road to reconciliation with China as the clash over Outer Mongolia wrested that region forever out of Peking's grips. Conversely, the establishment of the FER created an entry point to better relations that ended in the 1924 CER agreements and diplomatic recognition. These events strongly influenced the 1929 conflict; the agreements framed the railway dispute that led to war, while the fighting in Russia and Mongolia gave rise to three of the conflict's leading Red Army commanders: Vasily Blyukher, A. I. Lapin, and Konstantin Rokossovsky.

4 | Warlordism in Decay, CER Troubles, and the Northern Expedition

Warlordism in Decay

Expectations that the Second Fengtien–Chihli War would augur a better era were quickly dashed. Given the breadth of the front and the size of the forces engaged, the war was unlike its predecessors. Had it not been for Feng Yu-hsiang's betrayal, the outcome might have been different. As it was, competing warlords still dominated the political arena, and the old imperial vision of one China ruled from Peking, with its international legations and the sole base both for obtaining foreign loans and national taxes (however limited), remained the great prize. Wu Pei-fu had survived. Chang Tso-lin was once again advancing south of the Great Wall at the head of a victorious army, and Feng Yu-hsiang had taken a step forward as a national leader. In an attempt at reunification, a little over a week after Wu fled to the Yangtze Valley, on 11 November, Chang sponsored a national reconciliation conference in Tientsin.[1]

In the conference's wake, the warlords decided to reinvent themselves. The creation of the NRA and Feng's October decision to build his own military, the Kuominchun (National People's Army), were followed by the disbandment of eleven New Army divisions, and with it the facade of a unified army. Misrule had debased the rank of tuchun from that of a military official to one of contempt. Similarly, the rank of inspector general came to represent unrestrained warlord ambition. So in January 1925, "tuchun" was replaced by *tupan*, or supervisor, and the rank of inspector general abolished. *Tupan* became as discredited as its predecessor—becoming a distinction without a difference—and critics adopted the term *junfa*, a more literal translation of the Western pejorative. Governmental reform fared no better. To make a clean break, the generals reengineered Peking with the Six Articles that did away with the president and premier, adding more nails to the coffin of constitutional rule. The head of state became the chief executive, and Tuan Chi-jui was given the job. The appointment of the powerless Tuan, followed by Feng's resignation from his cabinet, confirmed the obvious: the chief executive was to be an administrator and figurehead. An unimpressed diplomatic corps granted the regime only de facto recognition.[2]

Sun Yat-sen Heads North

In an attempt to heal the north–south split, Sun Yat-sen was invited to the conference. Although he agreed to visit, Sun showed no interest in the conference, departing Canton on 13 November and taking a circuitous route that included stops at Hong Kong, Shanghai, and Kobe, Japan, before arriving at Tientsin on 4 December. Sun conferred with Chang Tso-lin but declined to recognize Tuan's government, dashing reunification hopes. That Chang and Sun were unable to find common ground was unsurprising. A few days before Sun's arrival, during a meeting with American chargé d'affaires Paul W. Mayer in Peking, the Marshal let it be known that he was "openly, extensively and hostilely" opposed to Bolshevism and avowed he would never support Sun as long as the KMT remained partnered with the CCP.[3] Chang welcomed reconciliation, but on his own terms.

On 31 December, a frail and openly defiant Sun arrived in Peking. Met by a mass of supporters including many students and invoking the 1911 revolution, he addressed the crowd as the "masters of the Republic," declaring that China's freedom had been "sold" to foreign powers and therefore "we must save the nation."[4] It was his last public appearance. Outside observers noted Sun's foresight; a few months later, US minister Jacob G. Schurman wrote to newly appointed Secretary of State Frank B. Kellogg that the students were "a most powerful factor in the existing political situation."[5]

Chang's Spoils of War

Oblivious, the *tupans* clung to their methods. Chang had won the 1924 war, and on 11 December he began distributing the spoils. Li Ching-lin was given Chihli, and Kan Chao-hsi, an ally since Chang's bandit days, was ensconced in Jehol. Both faced Feng's armies. Kuo Sung-ling, Chang Hsueh-liang's stormy chief of staff, had to settle for a division.

On 13 December, the Marshal undid the Chihli Kiangsu–Chekiang War victory by ousting Chi Hsieh-yuan. Wu's ally, General Sun Chuan-fang, attempted to hold firm against Chang's advances on Kiangsu and Shanghai but retreated when Dog Meat Chang marched on the city in January 1925. As a reward, Dog Meat Chang was given his home province of Shantung and Chang Tso-lin continued to reshape the political landscape in northern China. Mourning after Sun Yat-sen's 12 March death lasted only five days before the Marshal declared he would take Peking and was prepared for war with Feng or other "hosts of Bolshevism." The threat worked. In May, Feng vacated the capital.[6]

The Soviets in the Northwest

Feng's earlier resignation from the Tuan government and withdrawal from Peking masked a drive by the general to enter into the highest tier of the Northern warlords. By December, he had reorganized the Kuominchun into five armies spread across his northwestern realm. The reorganization was important, but what really enhanced Feng's power was his outreach to the KMT and Soviet Russia, as he had come to the opposite conclusion of Chang: he saw both as potential partners, not enemies. Feng was open to a goal Sun Yat-sen had expressed in a 1923 letter to Karakhan about the need for a military force northwest of Peking to defeat the Northern warlords. In December 1924, with Feng still in Peking, Karakhan wrote Chicherin urging an alliance with Feng. What had proved impracticable in 1923 became reality when the Kremlin approved the proposal. Feng left Peking for Chahar in January 1925 and established his headquarters at Kalgan. The city that had served as the Chinese base of operation during the 1921 fighting against the Mad Baron had little to offer. It was a rough-hewn, semilawless caravan center filled with hides, furs, and carpets, but it put the Kuominchun in contact with the Soviet Red Army in Urga, an attribute that Feng was eager to exploit.[7]

During the conference with Borodin held in the city the next month, Feng agreed to accept RKKA assistance. After further talks that included the KMT, the Soviets agreed to dispatch advisors under Vitovt K. Putna. Ivan Korneev, an advisor in Canton, also was dispatched at once and joined by A. I. Lapin, the military attaché in Peking. The two laid a foundation of trust with Feng before the first members of the group arrived during April. Initially numbering thirty-three and composed of military advisors accompanied by four translators with a small political cell, it grew significantly over time.[8]

Feng's role as a counterweight to Chang was clear to Moscow, adding urgency to the Soviet mission. In May 1925, Karakhan wrote of the looming war between the two, stating, "His [Feng's] defeat will be qualified as our defeat, his victory—as ours."[9] Fending off political work, Feng benefitted from the Kalgan Group. Nil T. Rogov trained his logisticians, Konstantin D. Kalinovsky, an expert on armored vehicles, helped field armored cars and first-rate armored trains, while Aleksandr A. Argentov schooled the combat engineers. They also restructured the 1st Kuominchun to better handle Chang's Eastern Army. To offset Mukden's advantage in cavalry, they organized five brigades by October 1925, transforming them from simple mounted infantry into true cavalry. And military aid arrived. Feng received quantities of rifles, machine guns, and ammunition worth millions of rubles to include 15,000 rifles, 9,000 pistols, and 9,000 grenades.[10]

Earlier in June, the Kaifeng Advisory Group under Lapin and A. Y. Klimov had been formed to help the 2nd and 3rd Kuominchun armies in Honan. The reception by General Hu Ching-i was warm, and he was open to political training for his troops—Klimov rated him the most pro-Soviet of the Kuominchun leaders—but his unexpected death in May 1925 prematurely ended the relationship. His replacement, Yueh Wei-chun, proved as distrustful as Feng but not as good a leader; his obsession with quantity over quality led to two swollen armies—300,000 troops of poor fighting ability. The arrival of the Soviets, if not an unmitigated success, was of great benefit to Feng, but its significance had been eclipsed by an event in distant Shanghai that riveted the nation.[11]

The May Thirtieth Movement

Chang Tso-lin's occupation of Shanghai was a sorry affair. It left governmental agencies weakened and public safety suffering as funds were diverted to his military and troops came and went; Dog Meat Chang's brigade left in April. The city became an ideal recruiting ground for KMT–CCP activists as antiforeign protests and strikes roiled Shanghai. Japanese businesses were especially hard hit; in February a Japanese manager was killed, and on 15 May a Japanese manager killed a Chinese worker. When protests over the worker's death entered the International Settlement on 22 May, over 100 were arrested and a trial set for eight days later. With the Fengtien garrison away, CCP labor leader Li Li-san called for immediate action. On 30 May, a major rally was held where police locked up student leaders at the imposing Louza station. By afternoon, a crowd advanced on the station; chaos reigned when they stormed the entrance. Police opened fire, slaying four students outright and wounding over a dozen. Eight later died.[12]

The violence ushered in national protests and boycotts that came to be known as the May Thirtieth Movement. On 2 June, Foreign Minister Shen Jui-lin protested to the Powers that the victims were "young men of good family, very patriotic and unarmed."[13] The next day, mass demonstrations began in the capital. Led by Li and Chou En-lai, the Shanghai protest strikes peaked on 4 June with 74,000 workers taking to the streets. Chang Tso-lin denounced the Shanghai shootings and declared the students innocent. He also dispatched two guard battalions under Chang Hsueh-liang to restore order. By late June, with the arrival of Hsing Shih-lien's brigade, there were 6,000 Fengtien troops in Shanghai. The boycott spread to Canton on 22 June. During a Canton rally held the next afternoon, gunfire again erupted, and dozens of Chinese lay dead.[14]

Always the filial son, Chang Hsueh-liang moved to crush his father's foes, going so far as to offer a joint campaign with the International Settlement to crush the communists. It was declined. Chang soon left, leaving Lu Yung-hsiang to reassume control over Kiangsu, but the old Shanghai was gone. Lu departed after two months and was replaced in August by Yang Yu-ting, Chang Tso-lin's chief of staff. Gradually order was restored. The last strike against the Japanese ended on 25 August and at the British factories five days later. By September, the Shanghai General Labor Union had been closed and Li Li-san arrested. The movement was far from over, however.[15]

The Emergence of the National Revolutionary Army

Even before the May Thirtieth Movement, the NRA had made good progress. The end of the 1924 wars rekindled southern warlord ambitions, and the KMT became a target. The NRA had shown its mettle earlier in October when it crushed the Canton Merchants Corps. In December when Chen Chiung-ming threatened, the army marched. Infused with Whampoa officers, it stunned and routed Chen at the battle of Mienhu outside Canton. Chen beat a hasty retreat. The victory proved the NRA could defeat a local warlord, and it was tested again with an eastern expedition that began in February 1925. Lasting nearly six weeks, during which most of eastern Kwangtung fell under KMT control, a thoroughly defeated Chen fled to Hong Kong. By mid-May, the KMT, backed by its NRA, broke relations with southern tuchuns who would not submit to KMT control and who openly opposed the Peking and Mukden governments.[16]

The May Thirtieth Movement thrust the NRA onto an even higher trajectory. Aroused patriotic sentiments helped turn the army into a potent force. In April, before the incident in Shanghai, the NRA numbered 3,000 soldiers. In July, 9,000 troops stood in its ranks, and by November, it had exploded to 30,000 soldiers. However, the rapid growth produced mixed results. Of its five undersized corps, the 2nd Corps was nothing but a collection of regiments, and the 5th Corps was little more than a warlord force that submitted to the KMT. Only the 1st and 4th Corps were first-rate fighting organizations. Prepared or not, the NRA reentered the fray in June when the Yunnan and Kwangsi warlord troops rose up in Canton, only to be crushed in one week by the 1st NRA Corps under Chiang Kai-shek. His much smaller force took 17,000 prisoners along with a large quantity of arms. Four months later, the Second Eastern Expedition was launched. It ended in complete defeat for the Kwangtung warlords despite Wu Pei-fu's support.[17]

The victories ushered in a new era, signaling the return of the first national army since before the 1911 revolution, and one that won offensive battles against numerically superior foes. The Powers noted the change. In the United States, during July discussions over China, British chargé d'affaires Henry Chilton informed Secretary Kellogg that the Whampoa officers were "a nucleus of a military force" of such potential that they could "seriously affect the whole Chinese situation."[18] If the 1925 NRA battles represented the future, then the renewed fighting in the north represented the failed past.[19]

The 1925–1926 Fengtien–Kuominchun War and the Kuo Sung-ling Rebellion

Throughout 1925, the northern warlords jockeyed for position. Chang took Anhwei, appointing Chiang Teng-hsuan as *tupan*, completing his dominance over the coastal region from Korea to the Yangtze. Wu had regrouped in the Central Plain, and with Soviet assistance, Feng was growing stronger by the day. Meanwhile, Sun Chuan-fang sat in the unenviable position of facing Wu to his northwest and Chang to his north. By summer's end, two rival blocs had formed. Wu, seeking revenge against Feng, made peace with Chang, who, already distrustful of the Soviets, feared the Kuominchun. Sun had little choice but to ally himself with Feng, and the generals grew eager for the fight. Earlier, on 8 April, a *Times* correspondent in Peking had argued that chaos and anarchy ruled China, with the country on a "downward path."[20] Never had the futility of the northern warlord adventures been more prominently displayed, yet conflict continued unabashedly.[21]

As in 1924, the war began over Shanghai, and again, Sun prevailed. Hostilities began on 14 October when Hsing's outnumbered Fengtien brigade faced Sun's advancing columns and beat a retreat. Feng then declared war on Chang and marched the 1st Kuominchun Army to Peking. Three days later, Sun declared himself commander of the Army of the Five Provinces. A not fully prepared Chang had 50,000 soldiers in Jehol and 70,000 at Tientsin in addition to Yang and the Shantung army. Little happened over the next few weeks as Yang's Fengtien forces from Anhwei and Kiangsu massed at Hsuchow and were later joined by Chang Tsung-chang's Shantung forces. Sun, bolstered by provincial forces, pushed Yang out of Hsuchow on 7 November. Having secured his Five Provinces hegemony, Sun halted. Yang and Dog Meat Chang fell back to Tientsin. A tentative peace sponsored by Tuan—whom Feng held under house arrest—was reached after Hsuchow's fall. The Tientsin pact, ceremoniously signed on 12 November, Sun Yat-sen's birthday, required the Marshal to recognize Sun's gains and cede control of western Chihli to Feng. With that, a precarious calm returned.[22]

Chang Hsueh-liang departed Tientsin on 20 November to attend a conference with his father in Mukden. Command of his 3rd Eastern Army, stationed near Shanhaikuan and Chinwangtao, temporarily passed to his trusted subordinate, Kuo Sung-ling. Three days later, Kuo issued a circular telegram demanding Chang Tso-lin and Yang Yu-ting's resignations, and a well-orchestrated coup to overthrow the Marshal got underway. To control Mukden, Kuo had quietly dispatched 2,000 troops north by rail, and the Marshal's rear was threatened when Chang Huan-hsiang and his CER rail guards joined Kuo. Sitting astride the Mukden–Tientsin railroad, Kuo had cut the Eastern Army into pieces, with Dog Meat Chang holed up in Shantung and Yang trapped in Tientsin while the rest of Chang's troops were dispersed closer to the frontier. On 25 November, Feng again declared war on the Marshal, and Kuo now could count on the Kuominchun. The press opined that the coup was "immensely strengthening" Feng and put Chang in a nearly fatal position.[23]

Kuo had to be pleased, but despite a near-perfect beginning, things began to unravel as Kuo failed to enlist Chang Hsueh-liang. Entreaties urging him to replace his father fell on deaf ears. There was never a doubt as to Chang's loyalty; he wrote to his father, "If I cannot stand against Kuo then I am not your son."[24] More blows landed; Kuo's troops sent to Mukden were disarmed, and control over the 3rd Army unwound. On 26 November, Chang Hsueh-liang returned to Chinwangtao and convinced some of the troops to desert the rebels. The next day, he wrote a letter that pleaded with Kuo to stop and had it delivered by a trusted aide. With head bowed, listening quietly as the letter was read, Kou replied with tears in his eyes that there was no turning back. To regain control, Kuo executed General Chiang Teng-hsuan and arrested over thirty senior officers, including three of seven 3rd Army brigade commanders. Determined to destroy a man who had been his closest ally, Chang sailed to Dairen and proceeded to Mukden. General Yang had also arrived, and the two worked to rally the Eastern Army. Kuo's troops, now the 4th Kuominchun Army, advanced victoriously north of the Great Wall.[25]

Then the unexpected occurred again. Japan weighed in on the Marshal's side. Alarmed by Kuo's anti-Japanese proclamations and fearful of a victory that would advance the pro-Soviet Feng, the Kwantung Army commander, Lieutenant General Shirakawa Yoshinori, refused to allow Kuo near the Kwantung Leasehold and the SMR. Kuo's situation continued to deteriorate. On 2 December, Li Ching-lin in Tientsin switched back to Chang, freed the captive pro-Chang officers, and formed an army to oppose the rebels. Now it was Kuo's turn to face enemies to his front and rear. The Marshal's position was still precarious; the US counsel in Mukden, William F. Nason, predicted his imminent fall on 4 December. Nason was not alone. Kirin governor-general Chang Tso-hsiang, fearing the worst and aware of the CER guard rebellion, sought a modus vivendi with the Soviets while a buildup of Russian troops along the border was reported on 10 December. Back in Mukden, the situation had improved. Yang and Chang Hsueh-liang decided on 7 December to make a final stand on the Liao. Kuo's advance guard reached the river two days later. The Eastern Army stood ready.[26]

To aid Kuo, Feng ordered the Kuominchun to advance on Tientsin. Li repelled the Kuominchun at Macheng and was engaged in heavy fighting at Yangtsun on 13 December. Two days later, the Liao River battle began. On 20 December, a severe winter storm ended the combat for two days while Chang Tsung-chang in Shantung advanced toward Tientsin to relieve Li. On December 23, the weather cleared and Chang Tso-lin's army went on the offensive, scoring a decisive victory after hitting the rebels with a terrific artillery barrage followed by an enveloping attack on Kuo's flank by cavalry who had maneuvered undetected during the blizzard. The rebel army collapsed almost at once, surrendering wholesale to their former comrades. Too late to matter, the Kuominchun crushed Li at Tientsin, but the Marshal had won the war.[27]

The repercussions were felt at once. Kuo was quickly captured. Chang Hsueh-liang interceded with his father, but the reply was cold and final: "The Kuo Sung-ling execution order has been carried out."[28] His corpse was put on display in Mukden for three days, beginning on Christmas. Chang Tso-lin did not purge the mutinous leaders—a wise decision, as their loyalty became unwavering. It was small comfort that Hsueh-liang's role in the victory added to his reputation, but he never got over the loss of an officer he saw as a brother. He later commented in trying circumstances, "If Kuo Sung-ling was here, I could have done this without difficulty!"[29] For a young leader, the rebellion was a harsh lesson on how tenuous warlord rule could be and the ruthlessness required to survive.[30]

The showdown with Feng took time. Winter played a role, and to put off the inevitable, on 1 January 1926, Feng resigned from his governmental posts. Chang also delayed, needing time to rebuild his forces. His best, the 3rd Army, had been rent apart and bloodied in combat, and Li's army had been crushed fighting Feng. The burden fell on Wu Pei-fu, who attacked the 2nd and 3rd Kuominchun armies in Honan in late February. He quickly smashed both within a few weeks and controlled the province by early March. The remnants of Feng's armies retreated into Shensi; they were trapped and besieged at Sian by mid-April. It was not until 3 March that the Marshal was able to counterattack the 1st Kuominchun at Tientsin. By 21 March, Feng's army was in retreat toward Peking.[31]

Peking was no obstacle for the two advancing armies. The fighting around the city's outskirts began five days later as Wu advanced along the Pinghan railway. Beginning on 2 April, Chang Hsueh-liang's air forces bombed Kuominchun positions as the Eastern Army joined with Wu. On 15 April, General Lu Chung-lin, the 1st Kuominchun Army commander, withdrew toward Kalgan and the Nankow Pass. Tuan was removed by a pro-Wu coup d'état. Feng first departed to Urga before entering the Soviet Union, where he would spend the next four months. The Six Articles were discarded, and Peking came to be ruled by the regency cabinet, composed of four northern tuchuns dominated by Chang. On 21 April, Hsueh-liangs's 3rd Army entered the capital and a siege of the Kuominchun began at Nankow Pass. Chang Tso-lin had little time to savor his victories as the struggle to control Manchuria's railroads was renewed. Earlier, on 20 January, Japan and the Soviet Union had established diplomatic relations that reconfirmed their respective authority over the SMR and CER zones, an outcome that Chang had dreaded, and more importantly, joint management of the CER had become one endless problem. The reason was plain: the Soviets had bested the Chinese negotiators in 1924.[32]

The CER: Renewed Rivalry

According to the Provisional Management pact, joint administration consisted of a Chinese director general, former Kirin governor Pao Kuei-ching, a board of directors (composed of five Russian and five Chinese, including Pao as president), and a Soviet general manager, Aleksandr N. Ivanov, to oversee operations. Pao and Ivanov took office on 3 October 1924 and the condominium era began. On paper, power was shared. In practice, Ivanov ran the CER as the board—not Pao—had authority over him, leaving the decision making to Ivanov. If the Chinese agreed, the manager's decisions were approved, but if they disagreed, the board froze in a split vote that passed the issue to the respective governments for lengthy resolution. Meanwhile, Ivanov's decision stood. Either way, the Soviets won, leaving the Chinese no effective recourse. By enacting the Provisional Management agreement, which provided sufficient guidance to run the railway, Moscow could maintain its advantage indefinitely. China's goal was to reach a final settlement, but the language of General Agreement Article II only required the parties to "confer," foiling the effort. Eventually Peking was able to convene the conference on 26 August 1925, ten months after the agreed start date, but only on a pro forma basis as Karakhan left the next day for Moscow, ending any chance of meaningful progress.[33]

This created the worst of all worlds for Peking: it covertly gave the Kremlin control over the CER that approximated that of the tsar while overtly fostering a pretense that China was a coequal partner. Chang Tso-lin had admitted as much when asked why he entered into an agreement, stating he was forced to support "an obligation which the Chinese Government had assumed, but which it was unable to carry out."[34] Stalin aided and abetted in the duplicity, and not just in regards to the CER, ordering Karakhan "to conceal all the activities in China as much as possible," a task the ambassador found unrealistic, noting that the secret arms shipments to Feng in remote Inner Mongolia had quickly become common knowledge.[35] The tsar's dominance over CER affairs had been resented by the Chinese but was an unambiguous fact; however, the 1924 agreements implied that a more just beginning was in the offing—a falsehood intentionally obfuscated by Stalin that rankled at a time when Chinese nationalism was coalescing into a force to be reckoned with. C. C. Wang, former CER president, referred to the 1924 agreements ruefully in 1925 when he noted, "It must have required much skill [on the part of the Soviets] to frame the terms in such a pleasant and elastic way."[36]

Soviet thirst for the CER was also a sore point for the CCP. Signing the 1924 agreements garnered strong resentment within some Chinese revolutionary circles. At the Whampoa military academy, no less a personage than Chou En-lai struggled to defend the Russians against criticism from young officers who could not understand why Karakhan had not supported the transfer of the CER to China and were dismayed when the Kremlin entered into the separate pact with a hated warlord like Chang Tso-lin. Unsaid was the conclusion drawn by many in Moscow, who saw success in any agreement that led to a CER condominium. Grigori N. Voitinsky, the senior Comintern operative in the Far East, held that the CER "will become the main road for a great victory march," destroying the pretense presented in the 1924 agreements that the CER was a purely commercial enterprise.[37] For the Soviets, the agreements were not binding contracts but a means to advance their revolutionary objectives in China.[38]

At first, the Soviet moves were limited and raised few concerns. Senior anti-Bolshevik Russian CER managers were expelled in early October; the Orthodox Church department was closed in November and teaching religion was banned the next month. But as Chang Tso-lin realized that shared governance had no meaning, he used every opportunity to limit Soviet reach. Over Kremlin protests, Chang acceded to the construction of the SMR spur line into Heilungkiang that began in March 1925 and was completed in thirteen months; in 1927, the spur was further extended to Tsitsihar. Chang could now avoid the CER when shifting his forces from Mukden into Heilungkiang.[39]

One month after the start of the new SMR line, Ivanov attempted to purge the railway of all non-Soviet Russian employees and set a 30 May 1925 deadline. Because these were the Russian employees most loyal to the Chinese, the Manchurian authorities opposed the decision and CER president Pao, backed up by bayonets but not legal authority, refused to let the order be enforced. A rough compromise appeared to have been reached when the Soviets dropped the policy and Pao resigned as railway president. General Lu Yung-huan replaced Pao as CER *tupan*, but tensions continued to build. Mukden signed a tariff agreement with Japan in May that gave highly favorable rates for goods sent along the SMR for transshipment from Dairen, putting the CER–Ussuri route to Vladivostok at a marked disadvantage. The Soviets proved equally underhanded; no sooner had Pao resigned than Ivanov dismissed the targeted Russian workers again in June. Mistrust and bad faith came to define the relationship.[40]

Things did not get better when Ivanov refused to transport Eastern Army troops on credit, effective 1 December 1925. When he blocked transit of Chinese soldiers on 16 January, troops of the 26th Kirin Mixed Brigade seized a CER mail express in Harbin while Chinese officers ignored Ivanov's order and commandeered trains as they saw fit, going so far as to sell tickets at the Kuancheng CER–SMR transfer station. In retaliation, Ivanov ordered the station closed on 21 January, and Chang Tso-lin had him arrested the next day. Had Ivanov closed the railway during Kuo's rebellion in December, he might have logistically crippled Chang's army before the decisive Liao River battle. Instead, the shutdown became a temporary inconvenience. Strongly worded protests from Moscow and Karakhan in Peking followed, combined with a strike by Soviet Russian rail workers, and the Marshal finally relented and released Ivanov. Chang did win a concession; he was allowed to continue to transport his troops on credit; not giving up the struggle, he shifted to less direct efforts to undermine Russian authority.[41]

Vishniakova-Akimova in Kalgan sensed the continued hostility by noting that while the crisis ended, anti-Soviet activities in the Northeast extended into mid-1926. In March, Soviet Russian municipal councils in the CER Zone were disbanded and replaced by Chinese assemblies; that month, the British War Office noted that Chang "genuinely hates the Russians," and the feeling was mutual.[42] Several months later, the Comintern executive committee branded the Marshal "the worst enemy of the Soviet national revolutionary movement."[43] Karakhan was especially vehement in his renunciations, referring to Chang Tso-lin as a "primitive vulture," among other things.[44] Mutual bitterness poisoned the relationship between the Soviet and Chinese authorities in Manchuria.[45]

Even though Trotsky had suppressed his misgivings and ceased open opposition to Stalin's joint management position, the ongoing CER problems redivided the Kremlin over how to proceed. In March 1926, a CER special commission headed by Trotsky, which included Red Army leader Kliment Y. Voroshilov, State Political Directorate (GPU) and Supreme Council of National Economy head Felix E. Dzerzhinsky, and Chicherin, concluded that to avoid imperialist control, they had to focus on "strictly keeping the actual apparatus of the CER in the hands of the Soviet government" even if that meant "creating an impression of Soviet imperialism."[46] Four months later, during the plenum of the Central Committee, the railway was alternately presented as "a 'blister' on our foot" to be rid of and the essential "revolutionary forefinger pointed into China."[47] The CER would remain under Soviet dominance, but one blister the Kremlin had grown tired of was Karakhan and Ivanov's constant tit-for-tat warring with Peking and Mukden.

The decision was made to remove Ivanov first. His replacement, Aleksandr I. Emshanov, unlike Ivanov, was both an engineer and a rail expert, as well as a party to the 1923 Berlin mission that procured hundreds of modern locomotives for the Soviet Union. Residual resentment plagued Emshanov after his arrival. That the Soviets were using the CER to advance a revolutionary agenda was clear to the Chinese, and for the first time, Chang raised Article V of the Mukden agreement prohibiting propaganda to justify placing the CER commercial schools under his control in early August. Later that month, CER-owned vessels, the largest shipping fleet to ply the rivers of the Northeast, were seized by Mukden on the grounds that they were not part of the railway.[48]

In late August 1926, a frustrated foreign ministry in Peking threatened to declare Karakhan as persona non grata due to interference in China's internal affairs and engagement in "subversive propaganda."[49] Moscow avoided a confrontation by agreeing to order him home and named the low-key and able Semen I. Aralov as a replacement on 30 December. The timing was fortunate; tensions eased along the CER as war—not railways—came to dominate the action in China. Once more, Marshal Chang had to look south, this time to face his greatest threat yet: the Northern Expedition.[50]

The Birth of the Northern Expedition

With the growing might of the KMT–CCP alliance, the road to national reunification was open. The NRA, which was vital to KMT–CCP ambitions, had matured to the point where it could take on the warlords—an unthinkable concept only a few years earlier. The rising power of the Canton regime and its message of reunification, rights recovery, and self-strengthening proved attractive to militarists who, having witnessed the failure of warlordism, desired a new path, one that put the needs of the nation first. Tang Sheng-chih in Hunan was one of those generals. In early 1926, he went over to the KMT; his army was incorporated into the NRA in April. This was not a repetition of earlier KMT–warlord alliances. Tang remained in control but under KMT–CCP direction, and political officers were assigned to his forces to instill discipline and revolutionary vigor. Tang's decision created a new conflict, as Wu was unwilling to cede control of Hunan, the place where he had made his reputation during Tuan's on-again, off-again 1917–1920 war against South China. The KMT–CCP response to Wu was the Northern Expedition.[51]

Planning the expedition began that spring and finalized in May. Chiang initially proposed a two-pronged attack against both Wu and Sun. Because they considered themselves unready to enter into combat on two fronts, the KMT Central Executive Committee (CEC) opted to concentrate the NRA on Wu. It was a prudent decision. Wu was ill-positioned, as the bulk of his army was with Chang Tso-lin battling the Kuominchun at the Nankow Pass (1,800 kilometers to the north), but Wu was confident in the ability of his Hunan soldiers to win one more victory over the KMT. In May, he ordered Governor-General Chao Heng-ti to destroy Tang. A capable former KMT officer, Chao pushed

Tang back toward the Kwangtung border, but the gains were reversed when two NRA divisions arrived in June.[52]

With Wu still tied up to the north, there was no better time to strike, and the CEC approved the offensive on 23 June. The campaign plan was complex. Tang's Center Army would drive over 500 kilometers north to Wuhan. To protect his eastern flank from Sun, Chu Pei-tei's Right Army would advance with Tang. Yuan Tsu-ming's Left Army would advance on Tang's west and seize Chingchiang in Shensi and Hsiangyang in Hupeh (150 kilometers north of Wuhan on the Pinghan line). Blyukher wrote that the armies would "move together, like a fist." The reserve in Kwangtung would support the advancing armies. Finally, the elite 1st Corps would invade Fukien if Sun entered the war. Separately, Feng was to march east from Kansu into Shensi along the Lunghai railway toward Chenchow, a key Honan transportation hub 500 kilometers north of Wuhan. It was hoped that the NRA and Kuominchun would link up in Honan or Hupeh. In its totality, it was the most ambitious military plan since the days of the High Ch'ing.[53]

The Initial 1926 NRA Offensive

The NRA was mobilized on 1 July, and when Tang captured Changsha nine days later, the KMT CEC opted to launch the expedition. The NRA attacked north in force on 19 August. Wu's troops were soon retreating in disorder toward the Hupeh border with the Center Army in pursuit. Fortunately for Wu, Feng had given up the fight at Nankow Pass three days after the NRA offensive began, allowing Wu to shift his best divisions south to meet the NRA head on. Their arrival changed nothing; Wu suffered twin defeats at Yochow on 22 August and Tingssuchiao (40 kilometers south of Wuhan) on 27 August. The road to Wuhan was opened; Hanyang fell on 6 September, and that evening, Wu, with 294 carloads of troops, headed north by rail. Hankow was captured the next day; only the walled city of Wuchang, defended by General Liu Yu-chun, offered stiff resistance, holding out against the Center Army until the Double Tenth.[54]

While the siege of Wuchang got underway, Sun Chuan-fang began shifting his forces toward the border between Kiangsi and Hupeh and attacked the 1st NRA Corps at Swatow. Chiang Kai-shek ordered a sweeping counterstrike that began on 6 September. In Honan, the

NRA Right Army advanced into Kiangsu and the 7th "Flying" Corps was pulled from the Wuchang siege to march on Kiukiang in northern Kiangsi. The 1st NRA Corps invaded Fukien on 19 October. Foochow fell on 12 December, and the province was secured by the end of December. The NRA reserve also entered Kiangsi, capturing the provincial capital of Nanchang on 9 November after heavy seesaw fighting. The reserve then entered Chekiang in early December, advancing the front lines to Hangchow by midmonth. Sun's Five Provinces domain was on the brink of total collapse when winter intervened, halting further operations.[55]

Feng Yu-hsiang's 1926 Shensi–Honan Offensive

The August retreat from Nankow Pass sorely tested the Kuominchun, but Feng was determined to fight on. Some soldiers defected to Yen in Shansi; others turned bandit. But even those who remained found themselves strewn across a 1,600-kilometer-long arc stretching from the Chahar–Suiyuan border to Kansu. Additionally, the remnants of the Kuominchun armies defeated by Wu in February remained trapped in Sian. Feng left Moscow just as the Nankow retreat began, reaching his Kansu headquarters at Lanchow in time to save the army. On 22 August, he sent a delegation to Canton to coordinate the attacks on Wu, and in a sign of subservience, Feng joined the KMT the next day. He could not join the Northern Expedition until Kansu was sufficiently pacified, and his attack against Wu's general in Shensi, Liu Chen-hua, did not begin until 2 November.[56]

Liu, once a protégé of Yuan, relied on one division reinforced with provincial troops to halt Feng. Feng pushed him back repeatedly. Within a few days, Liu was retreating toward Sian and attempted to organize a defense at Tungkuan Pass on the Shensi–Honan border where the Yellow and Wei rivers met. Feng kept up the pressure; Soviet military aid arrived from Urga, and the Sian siege was lifted on 27 November. The city suffered grievously during the siege as countless houses and businesses were looted and gutted. During the final weeks, the population devoured every animal from horse to stray cat, yet thousands starved to death. Despite cutting down the city's trees for firewood, thousands more died of exposure when the cold weather arrived.[57]

War in Shensi continued unabated for the next several weeks. Feng now fielded the outlines of three armies, marched the bulk to

Tungkuan Pass, and defeated Liu during four days of intense combat (7–10 December). The drive into western Honan began at once, and by the end of the month, Feng was within 200 kilometers of Chengchow, the primary objective. The full effects of winter and the arrival of reinforcements for Lui forced Feng to halt, ending the hope of either capturing Chengchow or joining with the NRA.[58]

Chang Tso-lin Enters the War

With Wu battered and Sun barely holding on, Chang Tso-lin assumed ever-greater importance, but warlord mistrust undermined their ability to work cooperatively. Unlike the hard-pressed Liu, who welcomed intervention, Wu asked for funds and munitions but refused the offer of troops. Chang in turn offered excuses instead of aid. In Shansi, Yen made himself appealing to all while avoiding involvement. To forge a degree of unity, Chang hosted a conference in Tientsin on 13 November, and it was agreed to form a unified military, the Ankuochun (Pacify the Country Army), under Chang Tso-lin with Wu, Sun, Dog Meat Chang, and Yen named deputy commanders, although Yen was not in attendance. It also was decided that Chang should position his armies to aid Sun and Wu if asked. On 20 November, Sun asked for support and offered Kiangsu in payment.[59]

The offer was accepted. Three of Chang Tsung-chang's armies entered northern Anhwei, followed by the dispatch of two more armies to Kiangsu. Chang Tso-lin ordered his troops south, shifting the 4th Eastern Army to Tientsin while his son, in command of the 3rd Eastern Army, arrived in Peking. By early December, both armies began to advance toward the Yangtze battleground but remained north of the Yellow River. The relentless political maneuverings within the Ankuochun's senior ranks continued to hamper the efforts needed to defeat the combined NRA–Kuominchun armies.[60]

The 1927 Offensive Plan

The gains made by the NRA during the 1926 campaign were unprecedented in the republican era. What looked to be a deadly replay of the contest over Hunan—which had been going on since 1917—turned into a series of NRA victories ending in the fall of Wuhan. The 1927 NRA goal was more ambitious: complete victory. Swollen by new soldiers and by Wu and Sun's defecting units, the old corps became full armies, and new leaders took charge. The Center Army, with its Left and Right Route armies, came under Chiang Kai-shek's direct command. Tang's Right Army became the Western Route Army, while Ho Ying-chin, the 1st Corps commander, took over the Left Army, now called the Eastern Route Army. General Pai Chung-hsi commanded Ho's assault troops.[61]

The campaign was to be conducted in two phases. First, the Center and Eastern Route armies would sweep east across the lower Yangtze Valley. The Center Army would take Nanking and the Eastern Route, Chengchow. Both armies would then converge on Shanghai. Simultaneously, Tang in Hupeh would drive north, join forces with Feng at Chengchow, and then position their forces along the Peking–Hankow railroad. To bolster the Kuominchun's revolutionary spirit, on 12 January, Feng accepted twenty CCP cadres as political officers. During phase two, the Western Route Army would drive up the Penghan to Peking while the rest of the NRA struck north along the Tsinpu line, taking Hsuchow, Tsinan, and Tientsin before pivoting west for the decisive march on Peking.[62]

Growing Problems between the KMT and CCP

The KMT–CCP political campaign had not developed as smoothly as that of the military, and the two movements drifted apart, hindering reunification both externally and internally. After the draining 1926 battles, the KMT-Left (the noncommunist KMT faction led by Wang Ching-wei, who continued to work with the CCP) and CCP chose Wuhan as their headquarters, while Chiang led from Nanchang and refused to subordinate himself to Wuhan. Internationally, these divisions, coupled with antiforeign agitation by the KMT-Left and CCP, crippled efforts to gain recognition from the Powers. Internally, the advance of the revolution required an ever deeper penetration of society that created state enemies. By late 1926, there were three expanding classes: warlords, Chinese working with foreigners, and rural landlords.[63]

The KMT–CCP factions sought different methods for handling them. Chiang's NRA followed Sun Yat-sen's course of molding warlords into soldiers of the state, and warlord troops that threw in with the KMT were accepted en masse. The KMT-Left and the CCP balked at this. As NRA propaganda chief Kou Mo-jo noted, "Old-style warlords, with crimes to their account for which they should have died ten thousand times over . . . had with one bound become revolutionary heroes."[64] A CCP demand for economic self-reliance turned Chinese working with foreigners into enemies while alienating many city dwellers as well as overseas Chinese. Peasant associations and land redistribution policies proved equally divisive as the rural gentry fought against both. Mao Tse-tung, the CCP leader who helped mobilize the agrarian masses, encouraged violence against the rural gentry, further splitting the NRA, as many officers came from that class. Joining two revolutionary movements together had worked when both needed each other to survive, but as they grew in power, a drive to dominate the revolution became inevitable.[65]

The Opening of the 1927 Campaign and CCP Purge

As political success proved elusive, the battlefield again dominated the action. The NRA campaign to capture Shanghai got off to a slow start. During the first week of January, Ho's army drove on Hangchow but was met with unexpectedly stiff resistance, and Liu kept both Tang and the Kuominchun at bay well beyond Chengchow. In Peking, Chang Tso-lin remained confident. During a dinner with the legation ministers, he railed against Chiang and referred to Sun Yat-sen as a sincere visionary whose policies could only "be realized, if ever, in the distant future."[66] He also attempted to woo the Powers through his anti-Red rhetoric, referring to the KMT–CCP as "this disturbing political party" that was "inflaming" the Chinese people "with Russian madness."[67] To show his ardor, on 17 February, he announced an offensive to recapture Wuhan. Chang spoke, but the NRA acted. They captured Hangchow the next day. Sun Chuan-fang failed to reorganize his defenses near Lake Tai, and Shanghai fell on 22 March.[68]

The NRA plan for victory in 1927 was succeeding, but the next day, Cheng Chien's 6th NRA Army captured Nanking from Dog Meat Chang, and everything changed. Antiforeign demonstrations that had resulted in earlier evacuations again erupted. When Nanking fell, radicalized NRA soldiers went on an antiforeign rampage, looting and destroying foreign property, ransacking consulates, and killing foreigners.

Hundreds of terror-stricken foreigners awaited rescue ships. Cheng restored order, but the Powers, envisioning what American minister John Van Antwerp MacMurray termed a "new Boxer movement," reacted strongly.[69] Thousands of American and British troops sailed for China. The Japanese formally declined to participate as Foreign Minister Shidehara Kijuro assured the United States that the KMT would stop the violence for fear that the Powers would shift their support to Chang Tso-lin. Chiang hurried to Nanking, where he vouchsafed the security of the foreign community. Chiang was not alone in opposing the CCP's antiforeign violence; Borodin feared a confrontation with the Powers, noting that their intervention "could bring about the destruction of the Revolutionary Army."[70]

What no one outside Chiang's innermost circle knew was that the Nanking rampage was the final straw in his struggle with the CCP. During an earlier 19 February speech, he had tipped his hand: "Being known as a faithful believer in the doctrine of Dr. Sun Yat-sen, I have the right to say that every true member of the party must be just that and nothing else. Whoever goes against the aims and methods indicated by Dr. Sun Yat-sen will not be a comrade but an enemy who must not remain among us."[71] Chiang ordered KMT officials to suppress CCP-controlled labor unions, who went so far as to execute CCP union leader Chen Tsan-hsien. Outraged, the CCP–KMT-Left moved to rein in the general, and on 30 March, they enacted a law subordinating him to its military council.[72]

Unfazed, Chiang created a governing council at Nanchang, and during a closely guarded meeting on 7 April, he issued orders to purge the CCP; it would start in Shanghai. On the evening of 11 April, the murder of the communists began. Hundreds were hunted down and executed, with the survivors driven underground.[73] The purge quickly extended to Canton and beyond. The communists were safe only in areas controlled by the KMT-Left. To show a centrist intent, on 12 April, the rightist Western Hills Group was suppressed, and those who refused to support Chiang were expelled from the KMT. However, unlike the CCP, Western Hills Group members were not killed, and the group was reinstated in June. Moving past the party upheavals, Chiang continued the Northern Expedition, but the second phase of attack, north along the Tsinpu railway, quickly stalled.[74]

Chang Tso-lin added political pressure on Chiang by keeping the peace in the north, as American consul Samuel Sokobin in Mukden was quick to note, and hit KMT–CCP activists. On 6 April, the Peking metropolitan police raided the Soviet-controlled Dalbank and CER offices as well as the Soviet embassy, where police arrested thirty-six local KMT and CCP leaders, including Li Ta-chao, the CCP's cofounder. All the CCP prisoners and several KMT prisoners were executed. Chiang's crackdown on the CCP muted Chang's actions. MacMurray in Peking noted that after Nanking was proclaimed the KMT-Right capital on 4 May, "popular sentiment appears to strongly favor Chiang Kai-shek."[75]

The 1927 Campaign Continues

On 10 May, Feng from the west and Tang from the south opened the drive on Wu's last stronghold, Chengchow. During the fighting, the casualties for both sides were terrible. Feng finally entered the city on 30 May, but both his and Tang's armies were so exhausted that the attack on Peking had to be postponed. Instead, Feng sent Kuominchun elements east against slight resistance until they halted at Kaifeng on 1 June. The loss of Chengchow marked the end of Wu Pei-fu, the first of the great warlords to give up the fight. Bereft of troops or territory, he announced his retirement.[76]

To the south, the KMT's struggle against the communists received a boost from an unexpected quarter that nearly doomed the CCP. On 1 June, Stalin ordered Borodin and CCP leader Ch'en to form a 70,000-man Chinese Red Army and purge the KMT-Left. Both requests were impossible, and after learning of the betrayal, Wang's KMT-Left broke relations with the Soviets. Tension remained high as the CCP-led worker's militia was disbanded and trade unions suppressed. On 20 July, Wang approved a CCP purge. The Chinese communists went into hiding to organize uprisings in Hunan, Honan, Kiangsi, and Kwangtung. The KMT-Left spotted unusual troop movements. The 4th NRA "Ironsides" Army left the front for Nanchang and on 29 July uncovered the uprisings plot. It was too late. On 1 August, much of the 4th Army revolted, giving birth to the Chinese Red Army. It took several months for NRA troops to regain control, but the ensuing chaos allowed Mao to form a guerrilla base in the remote Chingkang Mountains.[77]

The CCP survived, but the Soviet-KMT alliance was destroyed. A dejected Borodin concluded, "All any of them want is rifles."[78] He retained some goodwill, and as he left Hankow on 27 July, Wang and other KMT-

Left dignitaries warmly saw him off. Other Russians were not so lucky. Lapin's Kalgan Group was marooned. Feng intervened and guaranteed the group and Borodin safe passage home by way of Outer Mongolia. Soviet Red Army NRA advisors were exempted from retribution and were allowed to leave, often with expressions of gratitude, as was the case with Blyukher, who had an amicable parting with Chiang. No niceties, however, could hide the fact that Stalin's China policy lay in ruins. Soviet Russia had fallen from being the most influential foreign power in China to near insignificance, its presence reduced to its Northeastern consulates and the CER.[79]

As events played out that summer, Chang Tso-lin saw an opportunity to strike a divided NRA. While Chiang still commanded the bulk of the NRA, Tang had proven troublingly independent. Feng had pledged his loyalty to Wuhan, and the KMT-Left NRA was locked in combat with the Chinese Red Army. On 8 August, Chang struck. Sun advanced down the Tsinpu railway toward Nanking, and Chang Hsueh-liang attacked down the Lunghai railway in hopes of retaking Chengchow. Further helping Chang, the CCP expulsion set in motion a KMT reunification, but Wang would agree only if Chiang stepped down. In the face of the Ankuochun assaults, Wang won out. On 11 August, Chiang resigned. The KMT became whole again, but the NRA lost its commander.[80]

Chiang's absence on the battlefield was felt. In Honan, Tang and Feng had some initial luck in holding back Sun but soon fell back to Pukow and then across the Yangtze on 17 August. Sun crossed the river on the night of 25 August, ushering in the battle of Longtan just to the east of Nanking. Fighting raged for six days; the two armies suffered an estimated 10,000 casualties before the NRA gained the upper hand. Although Sun escaped, 30,000 of his troops were forced to surrender. After two months of rebuilding, Tang and Feng struck north again, capturing Hsuchow, at the juncture of the Tsinpu and Lunghai railroads, before winter ended the fighting in December. To the west, when Chang Hsueh-liang advanced on Chengchow, his father demanded that Yen join the attack. Yen refused, and when some Ankuochun troops entered Shansi in late September, Yen fought back. Chang Tso-lin declared war on 3 October, and his son led a counterattack that pushed Yen back to Shansi's Ladies' Pass before both sides halted operations. The 1927 campaign was over. The NRA had fallen far short of its goal.[81]

The Final 1928 Offensive

The year 1928 looked unpromising for the nationalists. Not only were the 1926 warlords, with the exception of Wu, still standing, but also the CCP had become an enemy and the KMT schism had healed unevenly. American military attaché John Magruder noted that the fighting spirit among the Fengtien troops now equaled that of the NRA, as high casualty rates among the Whampoa graduates and the loss of CCP officers took their toll. To no one's surprise, no major military operations occurred in the year's opening months. The two sides needed a respite; the nation looked as divided as ever.[82]

Frustrated by the lack of progress, the KMT CEC invited Chiang to return as supreme commander with virtually unlimited powers on 6 January. He quickly shored up morale and reorganized the army for a final offensive. The core of the NRA became the 1st Army Group, Feng's Kuominchun became the 2nd Army Group, and Yen's army was renamed the 3rd Army Group. To battle the communists and serve as reserve, the 4th Group was placed under Li Tsung-jen. The realignment took time, but things had come together by the spring. The changes to the 1927 plan were minimal: Yen would attack north toward Peking while Chiang and Feng would advance along the Tsinpu toward Tsinan and Tientsin before moving on Peking. The Ankuochun held a strong front from below the Yellow River in Shantung westward to Shansi's Taihang Mountains. Chang's armies held the center and west while Sun's troops anchored the east. With Sun was Dog Meat Chang, whose divisions were little more than an armed mob. Chang Tso-lin was undefeated and confident.[83]

That did not remain true for long. Chiang Kai-shek launched the push north on 18 April, and the offensive rapidly gained momentum. Yen slowly advanced and captured Shihkiachuang in central Chihli, which opened the way to Paoting and on to Peking, but the main action was in the east, with the drive by Chiang and Feng on Tsinan. The decisive battle took place on 19 April, when Sun attempted to attack Feng's left (western) flank. The maneuver weakened his lines. Feng struck and broke into Sun's rear. Fearful of encirclement, Sun's army panicked in retreat, losing 50,000 troops, and Dog Meat Chang's rabble melted away. It was Sun's worst military defeat, and he never recovered; by the next day, NRA artillery was in range to shell Tsinan while Feng and Chiang converged on the city. Sun's defeat was a catastrophe for Chang Tso-lin.

With his army shattered, the entire eastern front was in peril, rendering the defense of the center and Peking tenuous at best. The Fengtien forces rushed east could not stem the NRA advance on Tsinan.[84]

The uncertain situation in Shantung and fresh memories of the Nanking incident compelled Japan to send a brigade to protect Tsinan's predominantly Japanese International Settlement. The decision seemed justified; in April, Ankuochun soldiers had killed two American missionaries as the fighting entered the peninsula. Tsinan remained calm after Ankuochun forces withdrew on 30 April, and when NRA troops arrived two days later, Japanese soldiers began to remove their barricades. Unexpectedly, over 3 and 4 May, clashes erupted after NRA soldiers began pulling down Japanese flags. Soldiers on both sides were killed and wounded; worse, the fighting left many Chinese and Japanese civilians dead. An alarmed Tokyo sent the rest of a division to Shantung.[85]

Chiang was unwilling to risk final victory by entering into a conflict with Japan. He wrote in his diary, "If one does not bend, how can one extend?"[86] He hurried to the city and brokered a peace deal on 5 May; calm returned. Four days later, Chang Tso-lin tried to use the incident to gain political favor from the Powers by reiterating his anti-KMT policy and rejection of attacks on foreigners (belied by the murder of the American missionaries). It had no effect. The nationalists were advancing north along three axes: Yen advancing up the Pinghan railway, the 1st Army Group advancing along the Tsinpu railway toward Tientsin, and Feng marching toward the old 1922 Yungting River battle line. By 7 May, Chang's divisions were north of the Yellow River. A little over two weeks later, Yen completed a deep envelopment of Peking and captured Nankow Pass.[87]

The nationalists had won the war. With Sun's army in tatters, the 1st NRA Group joined with Feng, and Peking was now threatened by attacks from the south, southeast, and northwest. Although Chang Hsueh-liang was able to stabilize the southern front at Paoting, it only ensured an orderly Fengtien withdrawal. On 30 May, his father issued the order to retreat to the Northeast, and four days later, in the early hours of 3 June, and with great fanfare, Marshal Chang Tso-lin departed Peking for Mukden as his armies continued their withdrawal north of the Great Wall.[88]

To keep order in Peking, Pao Yu-lin's Fengtien brigade remained behind and was granted safe passage to Mukden on 8 June when Yen's subordinate, Sun Chu, entered the city. Designated by the KMT CEC as the Tientsin–Peking garrison commander, Yen arrived on 11 June and set up headquarters at the War Ministry, a move that prevented Feng from occupying the city. Yen was soon backed up by the arrival of several NRA divisions, although he was more distrustful of Chiang than Feng. The alliance composed of Chiang, Feng, and Yen was already fraying. KMT officials closed the foreign office and took control of the archives two days later. On 30 June 1928, Peking was renamed Peiping, and China had only one capital, Nanking, for the first time since 1917. The 1928 offensive had led to the complete defeat of the Ankuochun in just under eight weeks.[89]

Conclusions

The four-year 1925–1928 period after the Second Fengtien–Chihli War through the Northern Expedition rocked the Northwest. The sequence of events—the implementation of the 1924 CER agreements, the death of Sun Yat-sen, the May Thirtieth Movement, and the rapid rise of the NRA under Soviet Red Army tutelage—had caught Chang Tso-lin and his son flat-footed. Focused on northern warlord struggles with Feng Yu-hsiang backed by the RKKA as the main enemy, the idea that the NRA's 1926 Northern Expedition in the far south would become an existential threat to their Manchurian fortress was beyond their ken. Although the NRA defeated the warlord alliance led by Chang, the expedition was not an unqualified success. Both Yen Hsi-shan and Feng Yu-hsiang had joined with the KMT but remained their own masters, while Chang's army—and Northeastern autonomy—survived.

In a more direct outcome, the success of the 1926–1928 Northern Expedition put China on a collision course with the Soviet Union. The 1927 KMT–CCP split made the Soviet Union an enemy of both Nanking and Mukden. For the Marshal, defeat at the hands of the KMT, coupled with a hostile RKKA on his border and an aggressive Soviet presence within the CER Zone, left his Northeastern realm more vulnerable than at any point since 1922. Nanking's victory set the stage for the 1929 conflict as the wrestling match over the CER now included the nationalists. One certainty remained on the minds of the victorious nationalists and the defeated Changs: the Soviets would not dominate the CER. Bitterness over Soviet exploitation of the 1924 agreements fanned the fires of war.

Part Two

Crisis and War

5 | The Rise of Chang Hsueh-liang and the Coming CER Crisis

The Assassination of Chang Tso-lin

Japan understood that China's reunification was at hand after the Ankuochun defeat at Tsinan and on 18 May, Tokyo sent identic notes to Peking and Nanking making it known that it would not allow the fighting to spread into Manchuria. Japanese Kwantung Army staff officers under General Muraoka Chotaro not only prepared for a defensive war against Chinese excursions into either the Kwantung Leasehold or SMR Zone but were also ready to seize the whole of the Northeast if allowed. They were not. On 26 May, the army ministry in Tokyo directed them to "suspend completely" any such invasion plans while the foreign ministry contemplated recognition of the Nanking regime.[1]

Enraged by the 26 May order to stand down, radical Kwantung Army officers rejected a peaceful accommodation with Nanking, and under the leadership of staff planner Colonel Komoto Daisaku, they plotted the Marshal's assassination. The officers believed the chaos and political upheaval stemming from his demise would create a pretext for the Kwantung Army to gain control over Manchuria. The invasion would be ordered in the name of preserving peace and order while protecting Japanese lives and property. Once the Marshal's retreat into Manchuria began at the close of May, the conspirators knew that Chang Tso-lin would return to Mukden. By 1 June, they had completed their preparations to strike him down soon after he left Peking.[2]

At approximately 5:20 A.M. on 4 June, just a few kilometers from Mukden, a rail-side bomb detonated next to the posh Blue Express private car carrying the Marshal, severely injuring him in the legs and chest. Chang, realizing he was fatally wounded, sent an order calling for Chang Hsueh-liang to return immediately to Mukden; he died a short while later. The loss was a profound blow. With a laissez-faire approach to administration and the economy, good judgment in selecting military commanders and civil officials, and a willingness to accept Japanese military support and advice, Chang Tso-lin had created the largest and best-equipped warlord army in China. His insatiable appetite for power—to rule all of China—led to his ultimate downfall, as the Marshal was devoid of a compelling political or ideological vision, depriving him of popular support. After the onset of the Northern Expedition, his attempt to rule solely through force of arms finally led to financial bankruptcy, military defeat, and death.[3]

The plot succeeded, but nothing else went according to plan for the Kwantung Army conspirators. Prime Minister Tanaka Giichi was appalled, calling Komoto and the others "fools." Realizing the damage it would wreak on Sino-Japanese relations, he put a press blackout on the incident and initiated a full-scale cover-up of Japanese army involvement.[4] Tokyo's attempt to hide army involvement failed badly. As part of the plot, three unknowing Chinese dupes, ironically procured by a former Kuo Sung-ling loyalist, were to be bayonetted to death by Japanese soldiers and blamed for the attack. When Japanese soldiers went to kill them after the blast, one escaped and later told Chang Hsueh-liang everything. The plan to seize Manchuria was foiled, but Komoto did accomplish one other limited goal besides killing the Marshal; in Mukden, chaos reigned when Chang Hsueh-liang arrived on 4 June, and he was immediately confronted with a number of challenges where failure could mean the end of his rule and perhaps his life. That chaos left a glimmer of hope in the hearts of the Kwantung Army radicals. What Komoto and his followers did not expect was that Chang Hsueh-liang was up to the challenge.[5]

The Rise of Chang Hsueh-liang

During a tightly guarded meeting on 17 June, the Mukden generals chose twenty-nine-year-old Chang Hsueh-liang as the new commander in chief and acting military director of Fengtien province, releasing the news two days later and only after the delayed announcement of Chang Tso-lin's death. Chang retained sole control over military affairs while a Peace Preservation Committee oversaw governmental administration during the emergency. He assumed his father's mantle and promised to form a constitutional government along the lines of the KMT. He was immediately referred to as the Young Marshal as a result of his age.[6]

A veteran of five campaigns by 1928, well educated, and groomed for leadership since birth by his father, Chang had been given ever-increasing responsibilities since he accepted a commission in 1919. He led a brigade in the 1920 Anfu–Chihli War and later conducted an antibandit campaign. In 1922, he commanded three brigades and the 3rd Eastern Army in 1924. He witnessed the 1925 May Thirtieth Movement in Shanghai and during December 1926 formed the Ankuochun air corps while still leading the 3rd Army. In 1927, his troops participated in the battle of Chengchow and later fought against Yen's Shansi army. By the end of the Northern Expedition, the Young Marshal had been elevated to lead the Ankuochun army group defending the Pinghan railway. A proven leader, when battling the NRA, he did not hesitate to shunt his father's officers off to the side and assigned the key commands to younger officers like Hu Yu-kun, whom he appointed to command the17th Eastern Army. His youth was seen as weakness, yet few officers could boast of a more impressive record.[7]

In the immediate aftermath of his father's death, the Young Marshal had to deal with a number of rivals vying for control over the Northeast. The most dangerous were army chief of staff and head of the Mukden arsenal Yang Yu-ting and railway telegraph communications director and Fengtien governor Chang Yin-huai. Both were trusted confidants of the late Marshal, and they held the next two most powerful positions in Manchuria after the Young Marshal. Another potential threat came from Chang Tso-hsiang, the self-serving Kirin governor, who had cravenly approached the Soviets during the height the Kuo rebellion and hungered to become an independent tuchun. External forces were not to be ignored; both Nanking and competing Japanese political and military factions were actively seeking out supporters in the ranks of the Fengtien leadership, and it went without saying that the opportunistic Feng Yu-hsiang would exploit any infighting to his advantage. With the future of the Mukden regime at stake, unity was the priority that summer. The Marshal's commanders had pledged their loyalty, and that, coupled with the tediously slow-to-act Peace Preservation Committee, neutralized his internal rivals and bought time at a critical juncture when his seat remained tenuous.[8]

Beyond keeping control in the Northeast, the Young Marshal had to decide whether to pursue an autonomous Manchurian regime or join the Nanking government. Autonomy was contingent on strong Japanese backing, but the assassination of his father poisoned the relationship, and Chang never avidly pursued the goal. Highlighting the dysfunctional nature of the radical Japanese officers, after the hoped-for incident that would trigger an invasion of Manchuria failed to materialize—the result of both the pluck of the Young Marshal and stiff opposition from saner parties in Tokyo—the radicals' influence quickly receded. Military intervention was out, but opposition to unification remained the center of Prime Minster Tanaka's Manchuria policy.[9]

Two days after the Young Marshal took the helm, Tanaka had a private communiqué delivered to Chang by Mukden consul Hayashi Hisajiro strongly urging the Young Marshal not to join with Nanking. To assume that he had a special relationship with the Young Marshal and to have so misunderstood the resentment and distrust toward his father's killers was stunning, yet the politician militarist Tanaka was the embodiment of Japan's interwar schizophrenia; the reasoned diplomat in him saw the almost certain futility of following an aggressive Manchuria strategy, but the proud general saw Japan as the region's rightful overlord—a dream not to be denied. Tanaka's ill-conceived diktat fell on deaf ears and quickly failed. Chang Hsueh-liang coldly informed Hayashi that the matter was out of his hands; the will of the people would not be ignored.[10]

A unified China became Chang's objective. Unquestionably ambitious and jealously guarding his position in the Northeast, the Young Marshal was also a nationalist. He had been open to Sun Yat-sen's goals early on; in 1922, he had funded a pro-KMT periodical, *The Three Eastern Provinces People's Paper*, had maintained contact with Chinese nationalists like Chang Po-ling throughout his career, and had been an advocate of the China's rights recovery movement since 1924. During July, American minister MacMurray in Peiping wrote Secretary of State Henry L. Stimson that the recognition of Chang Hsueh-liang as leader of the Northeast boded well for Chiang Kai-shek, as the Young Marshal was "more amenable" to the KMT than his father.[11] Reaching out to Nanking soon became an imperative.[12]

As the message from Tanaka drove home, the real challenge was to affect a union with Nanking while avoiding a military strike by the Japanese Kwantung Army. Equally important, the Young Marshal intended to remain the ruler of Manchuria in a KMT-ruled China. Assuaging Japan's fears after rejecting autonomy was essential in achieving that goal. Chang seized on the heightened tensions between Nanking and Tokyo after the KMT's 7 July 1928 pronouncement that the thirty-two-year-old Sino-Japanese commercial treaty would end in two weeks, with no replacement expected. Bringing Manchuria into the diplomatic fray two days later, Tanaka publicly declared that he would not oppose Mukden's reunification with Nanking, but Japan would accept neither any infringement of its acquired rights in the Northeast nor any breach of the peace. The Young Marshal avoided becoming embroiled in the dispute by meeting with Consul Hayashi, thus reaffirming friendly relations with Tokyo. With Japan momentarily placated, it was time to open negotiations with Nanking.[13]

Preliminary reunification talks with the KMT began that week, but as neither party had a clear position, the negotiations formally ended on 25 July without resolution. They were not renewed over the following weeks, yet the Young Marshal continued to advance his political agenda by keeping the promise he had made in June: the enactment of a provisional constitution for the Northeastern provinces that aligned with the KMT reforms recently adopted in Nanking. It included a nullification article to take effect once "China becomes unified," and American observers in Peking assumed the article's intent was for Manchuria to come under the control of Nanking in the near future.[14] Despite his public pronouncement and Chang's offer of friendship, Tanaka clung to the hope that he could stop the alliance between Mukden and Nanking; he saw an opportunity when it was announced that Chang Tso-lin's state funeral would be held on 4 August.[15]

To represent Japan, Tanaka sent Minister Hayashi Kensuke from Peking with orders to entreat the Young Marshal. After the ceremony concluded, the two had a private meeting where a last attempt to pressure Chang into rejecting Nanking was made. Again, the Young Marshal politely but firmly cited the inviolacy of "the will of the people."[16] His position would not be altered. The Young Marshal repeated his justifications to Consul Hayashi during a meeting on 9 August: "The reason why I would like to compromise with the national government is to complete the reunification of China."[17] Tokyo had no choice but to accept his decision and agreed the next week to the idea of the nationalist flag being raised over Manchuria in mid-November. Having finally gained the grudging acquiescence of Japan, the Young Marshal now had to reach an agreement with Chiang Kai-shek.[18]

In contrast to the fitful start in July, finding common ground in late August presented no difficulty, as Chiang's terms were generous to the Young Marshal. He would become a KMT member and be given a high governmental posting, while the Eastern Army would be incorporated into the NRA as the Northeast Frontier Defense Force (NEFDF) and remain under Chang's personal control. The KMT would not assign political officers to the NEFDF or send party organizers to Manchuria. He would continue to administrate the Northeast; he was also given control over the Inner Mongolian district of Jehol, with one of his followers, General Tang Yu-lin, appointed governor. Reunification proceeded smoothly. On the Double Tenth of 1928, the new KMT government was officially inaugurated, and the Young Marshal was appointed to the sixteen-person state council, with Chiang Kai-shek as the chair. As a sign of fealty to the KMT—and to the alarm of Japanese officials—in December, Chang proposed to end direct bilateral discussions between Mukden and Tokyo, deferring further negotiations over Japan's Manchuria rights to Nanking, although he took no immediate action.[19]

Chang Hsueh-liang's efforts had not met with unconditional success; relations with the Soviets remained openly hostile. Even during the Northern Expedition in January 1927, RKKA units had made repeated military demonstrations along the Manchurian border that were seen as an attempt to tie down Fengtien forces in the Northeast and keep them from moving south to fight the combined NRA–Kuominchun armies. The Soviets also sought to take advantage of the death of Chang Tso-lin by increasing their influence among the Manchurian Mongols, excusing the interference in China's internal affairs on the principle of self-determination by national minorities. In Moscow's view, when the Soviets declared Mongolia a free country in 1919 and helped establish a "people's government" in Outer Mongolia in 1921, they created the justification for spreading the revolution into Chinese-controlled Mongol lands to include the far west of Manchuria.[20]

In early August 1928, Barga Mongols with Red Army officers from Outer Mongolia crossed into the Arshan–Nomonhan border area in western Manchuria, incited the local Bargut tribes to rise up, and drove east as far as the CER line, temporarily disrupting rail traffic. Even with revolutionary trappings, the military advance was reminiscent of the tsarist conniving orchestrated by Horvat during the 1911 revolution. A sharp response by Heilungkiang troops pushed the Outer Mongolian raiders back across the border by 20 August. Angered by Moscow's meddling, the Young Marshal ordered a crackdown on the Soviet activities, and the CER vice president, Mikhail M. Lashevitch, was arrested later that month. Documents implicating Soviet participation in the uprising were found in his possession, sealing his fate. Lashevitch later died while in Chinese police custody, and relations with Russia continued to sour.[21]

By the close of 1928, the uprising collapsed. Soviet support for the Barguts had ended in fiasco, and the political repercussions continued. M. Gekker, Lashevitch's deputy and acting Harbin consul general, was immediately recalled to the Soviet Union, and within a few weeks, the Soviet director of the CER education department was expelled by Mukden for disseminating communist propaganda in the railroad zone technical schools. On 29 December, the white star, blue-sky flag of nationalist China was raised across the Northeast. In the CER Zone, it replaced the railway's ensign, which had been a combination of the Soviet and five-bar Fengtien flags. Joint CER administration had been put on notice. Driving the point home, Kirin office of education director Chang Kuo-chen gave an interview to Russian-language Harbin newspapers after the flag-raising ceremony where he stated that if the Soviet citizenry in Manchuria did not demonstrate loyalty and obedience to Chinese law, and if "full parity" in CER employment was not introduced, then the local authorities might take actions against the Soviets similar to those exercised by the KMT in 1927.[22] Chinese patience was nearing its end.[23]

Having forcefully dealt with these Soviet-sponsored intrigues, on 1 January 1929, the Young Marshal moved to eradicate Russian influence within the Fengtien leadership by dismissing the long-serving CER rail guard commander, General Chang Huan-hsiang, and his supporters, who were judged to be pro-Soviet. Just under two weeks later, the Young Marshal secured unchallenged control in Mukden by murdering Yang Yu-ting and Chang Yin-huai on the evening of 10 January 1929. It was a violent beginning for a violent year in Manchuria, but the lessons learned from the bloody end of the two men who had shaped his life—the assassination of his father and Kuo Sung-ling's execution as a traitor—gave him the strength and judgment to act. Chang Hsueh-liang had little difficulty in doing away with his two rivals.[24]

The primary official justifications given were plotting against both China and national reunification. In more direct language, the two engaged in a scheme to eliminate the Young Marshal and take over Manchuria. A circular telegram in support of the Young Marshal and signed by Mukden's senior leadership legitimized the killings. The *Japanese Advertiser* speculated that the two had been co-opted by Feng Yu-hsiang after Chang Hsueh-liang threw in his lot with Nanking, although the *Peking Weekly* argued the opposite, naming Yang as a leading unification advocate. The nuances were irrelevant; it was a life-or-death struggle for power. Yang and Chang were also found guilty of the lesser charge of corruption in their duties as heads of the arsenal and government railway, and of the telegraph, telephone, and radio agencies, respectively, resulting in the arrests of eight subordinates. While the international press sensationalized the killings, painting a picture of the Young Marshal akin to that of American gangster Al Capone, the efficiency and thoroughness of the arrests and executions, coupled with the supportive circular telegram and no sign of opposition, spoke powerfully to Yang and Chang Yin-huai's guilt and the need for immediate and harsh measures.[25]

With the Young Marshal now sitting securely as the ruler of the Northeast, the political intrigues disappeared, and the early months of 1929 became a time to rest and recover after years of war. Even though fighting the Northern Expedition had bankrupted the Mukden treasury and the CCP continued to work for his downfall, Chang Hsueh-liang had to feel confident as he took the oath of allegiance to Nanking on 4 February. He had defused the situation with Japan, stood up to the Soviets, effected a peaceful reunification with Nanking, and put his own house in order with a minimal amount of bloodshed. As the political tumult sorted itself out in Manchuria and storm clouds formed over the CER, the Americans, far across the Pacific, were putting in place what they believed was a treaty that would end war forever.

Perpetual World Peace

The Treaty for the Renunciation of War as an Instrument of National Policy, often referred to as the Paris Pact or the Kellogg–Briand Pact (named after US secretary of state Frank B. Kellogg and French foreign minister Aristide Briand), was born out of the revulsion over the horrific losses incurred after the outbreak of World War I. That outcome led a number of American progressives to seek a way to make war unlawful, beginning with the formation of the League to Enforce Peace in Philadelphia in 1915. Frustration over its failure to stop the fighting did not deter the movement, and by February 1918, Salmon "Sol" O. Levinson, a respected lawyer who had specialized in international financial law, published a tract entitled "The Legal Status of War" with the object of ending all war. The American antiwar groups, however, were never unified in their actions, and when the split between the internationalists and isolationists subsequently arose over League of Nations membership, the fragmentation became permanent, leaving the movement weakened.[26] The pleadings of Levinson and others gained no traction.

It was not until 1923 that the effort that ended in the Paris Pact began to show results when Senator William E. Borah of Idaho, at Levinson's constant urging, introduced a resolution for the outlawry of war on 13 February. Borah was a dubious instrument. A staunch isolationist, one of the most powerful senators in the nation, and gifted with a profound intellect, he had never lived outside the United States, deemed himself an expert on foreign affairs, and seemingly conjured up a vision of the outside world to suit his politics, accurate or not. The resolution met a tepid response by his fellow senators and languished for the rest of the congressional session. With 1924 being a presidential election year, Borah's resolution remained tabled. The problem of enlisting support was formidable. In addition to divisions over ideological lines, there were disagreements over the concepts of the right of self-defense, the application of sanctions, what constituted an aggressor, and what form the proposed international court to adjudicate disputes should take.[27]

Levinson himself was part of the problem. Unlike an engineer who would obsess over a solution to a problem, Levinson approached the task of creating perpetual peace as a lawyer who sought to best adversaries and score a win. This led to the formation and breakup of coalitions through endless political maneuvering and infighting as the legalists often ignored or opposed potential allies who made different arguments, such as addressing war's root causes. The movement also suffered from a lack of institutional support. There was no champion in the White House or in the state department, and while both political parties opted to include noncommittal outlawry planks when they drew up their national platforms for the 1924 election, no follow-up action was taken. Even Congress looked away: the Senate voted for membership in the Permanent Court of International Justice at The Hague in January 1926—a step seeming to advance the outlawry cause—but added so many preconditions that the United States was never able to join.[28]

The burden then fell on leading citizens. While Levinson toiled tirelessly and quietly behind the scenes, the public face of the antiwar movement largely rested with well-known academics like James T. Shotwell and Nicholas M. Butler, both associated with the Carnegie Endowment for International Peace, and noted Protestant theologian Charles

Clayton Morrison, who published *The Outlawry of War: A Constructive Policy for World Peace* in 1927. That all were caught up from time to time in internecine antiwar wars only gave American politicians greater cause for inaction.[29]

The situation in Europe was less convoluted. In England, Lord Robert Cecil, one of the architects of the League of Nations, led the way, while in France, Briand, a political giant, dominated the scene from inside the government at the Quai d'Orsay. It would be Briand who unintentionally broke open the logjam in the United States when he disclosed, during an April 1927 interview with the Associated Press, a desire that France and the United States enter into a "mutual engagement tending, as between those two countries, to 'outlaw war,' to use an American expression."[30] He followed up the next month during a lunch in Paris honoring Charles Lindberg after his historical 20–21 May solo flight across the Atlantic by asking American ambassador Myron T. Herrick to begin formal outlawry talks. Support for the cause among the American people grew. That June, Briand sent Washington a draft bilateral proposal seeking the limited objective of an "anti-alliance," where the two states agreed to renounce the use of armed force to resolve any conflict between them.[31] The French and American objectives differed greatly. France looked across its border and knew it could not fight another war with Germany without allies. It was continuously trying to isolate Germany and build a defensive coalition. America remained staunchly isolationist and had no interest in overseas power struggles.[32]

In Washington, Borah turned cool toward the French offer; an aggressor could use a series of such neutralizing treaties to both isolate a victim and protect the aggressor from armed retaliation. Borah concluded by late October that the solution was not a bilateral arrangement but a comprehensive pact to outlaw war among the major powers. President Calvin J. Coolidge grudgingly agreed in the face of strong public support for outlawing war, and the die was cast. Even though the topic had been discussed and written about for over a decade, it did not diminish the reality that the Americans sought a breathtakingly ambitious goal: the global outlawry of war.[33]

After five years of desultory progress, the advancement of a pact to ban war took on a feverish pace after Kellogg handed French ambassador Paul Claudel a note on 28 December 1927 that argued for "a more signal contribution to world peace by joining in an effort to obtain the adherence of all the principal Powers of the world to a declaration renouncing war."[34] By January, Briand had come around to a multilateral treaty, and after a series of questions and answers between Paris and Washington, on 13 April, a draft was sent to the other major powers: Germany, Italy, Japan, and the United Kingdom. The negotiations rapidly gained momentum, additional countries were invited to join in the deliberations beginning in mid-May, and with great ceremony the pact was signed on 27 August 1928 in Paris.[35]

The final agreement consisted of a preamble with three brief articles that combined to rule out war in favor of pacific settlement of disputes and an invitation for other nations to sign on in the future. The preamble offered whatever teeth the pact possessed, stating that any signatory who resorted to war in the future would "be denied the benefits furnished in the treaty"—those evidently being the perpetually peaceful and friendly relations between the peoples of the world. Kellogg held that war could be avoided through an "aroused public conscience" and a shared "peaceful mind."[36] In all, it was a thin gruel. Further undermining the treaty, the Powers staked out a number of claims, conditions, and interpretations during the negotiations, overlaying the treaty with a degree of intricacy that was missed by those who put their faith in the wording alone. Adding another strike against it, of Levinson's three tasks (outlawry, codification, and adjudication), the signing of the Kellogg–Briand Pact only signaled that the first had been completed; the second consisted of a simplistically vague treaty with a disordered pile of communiqués, and nothing had been done to address the last. Briand stated on 27 August 1928, "Peace is proclaimed: that is well, that is much. But it still remains necessary to organize it. For solutions of force, juridical solutions must be substituted. That is the work of tomorrow."[37] A glaring lack of process and enforcement was the trap the Powers had laid for themselves.[38]

The end of war had been declared, and Soviet Russia and China became signatories; the USSR announced the pact would enter into effect on 27 September 1928, and China gave a date of 8 May 1929. Neither had been a party to the preratification discussions between the Powers, and both raised issues after joining. A week after the Paris ceremony, Maxim Litvinov, the Soviet ambassador at large, while complaining that the Soviets had not been invited to help draft the treaty, expressed a desire for a follow-up agreement addressing world disarmament and argued in favor of bilateral nonaggression pacts. With the Siberian intervention fresh in their memory, Moscow further held that, by their interpretation, the Paris Pact prohibited interventions or military occupations and included a ban on governments using force in suppressing domestic "movements for the liberation of peoples," citing China as an example.[39] Soviet Russia made it known that it would adhere to its own interpretation of the pact. Nanking, while ignoring the argument against the use of force in suppressing domestic movements, echoed some of Moscow's concerns in September, urging that the unequal treaties be abolished and also urging an end to foreign military occupation in China. Minister Alfred Sze in Washington repeated the same message, noting that the true path to peace in East Asia, the goal of the Kellogg–Briand Pact, equated to a free and independent China.[40]

China's Rights Recovery and the Looming Crisis over the CER

Events in Manchuria quickly, if temporarily, swept aside musings over the sanctity of perpetual peace for China and Russia. A confrontation over the CER was in the making, and the architects were Chang Hsueh-liang and Chiang Kai-shek. The Young Marshal's relationship with Chiang was unique among the former warlords, and the shared goal of rights recovery helped foster a cooperative attitude between the two men. Additionally, Manchuria's physical isolation from China proper, the border with Soviet Russia, and CER coadministration, coupled with Japanese presence in the Kwantung Leasehold and the SMR Zone, created a complex political, military, and economic dynamic that required Chiang and the Young Marshal to coordinate policies that affected China's relations with Japan and Russia. Those efforts were expected to be eased to a degree as the Young Marshal reaffirmed his December 1928 vow to shut down the Mukden foreign office under Tsai Yun-sheng by October 1929 and hand over all diplomatic activities to Foreign Minister Wang. In the meantime, Tsai would inform and consult with Wang on a regular basis. This completed another step toward national unification that displeased Japan and was less than welcomed by Russia.[41]

Soviet internal polices kept the Young Marshal's attention as well. To make "socialism in one country" a reality, Stalin ordered a radical transformation of the Russian state in the 1920s. Facing a harvest that would produce shortages, Stalin had given the secret police a free hand to boost grain procurement during the first week of 1928. Two weeks later, and without Central Committee approval, he spoke to party officials in Siberia, a region he felt lacked revolutionary zeal, and announced his collectivization and dekulakization policies. The actions misfired as parts of the Soviet Union barely avoided famine, and while Stalin came under organized criticism led by Nikolai Bukharin, he refused to back down even as food shortages continued.[42]

Stalin's new policies profoundly affected the Soviet Far East; the Buryat–Mongol federation, numbering over 200,000 and mostly concentrated between Lake Baikal and the Manchurian frontier, was hit particularly hard. Proponents of the policy, like Walter Duranty, the *New York Times* correspondent in Moscow, wrote that "collectivization spells civilization," but it proved equally true that collectivization spelled cultural eradication.[43] The Buryat, who were primarily nomadic cattle grazers, were unsuited for Soviet-style sedentary agrarian consolidation, and increased state supervision disrupted their traditional hierarchy. As the program was instituted, unrest spread across the Buryat lands, and the Kremlin took severe countermeasures. The Communist Party made an official pronouncement condemning Mongol nationalism (within Russia) and the widespread practice of Buddhism. Monasteries were closed; the one at Lake Gusinoe—the scene of the Mad Baron's crushing 1921 defeat—was razed, and the number of lamas was cut in half. In the end, Soviet collectivization meant confiscation, submission, and the destruction of traditional culture.[44]

The Buryats were badly divided. Some embraced the new Soviet era, others clung to traditional ways, and many revolted. Some rebels fought the GPU and paramilitary forces; thousands died in a losing battle. More simply slaughtered their herds as the collectivization deadline neared in 1929, but a number sought refuge, which disrupted the peace along the western Soviet–Manchurian border. In March 1929, sixty Buryat families, along with 10,000 head of livestock, entered the Barga region of Manchuria and set off a scramble by the Russians and Chinese to seal the frontier. Soon armed bodies of troops from both sides patrolled the border. Further large-scale emigrations ceased, although crossing by small parties continued for years. The border had assumed a new political prominence.[45]

Cooperation in ending the illegal border crossings aside, the Young Marshal's conflict with Moscow only intensified. The heavy-handed approach of the Soviets over joint management of the CER came to dominate every other issue. By 1929, Soviets headed twenty-four of the twenty-six CER departments, despite the agreement's equal representation language. Finding the situation unacceptable, the Young Marshal followed his father's indirect strategy by seizing the CER's Harbin telephone system on 9 January. The Soviets protested, to no avail. On 1 March, CER president Lu Yung-huan delivered to the Soviet consulate a formal complaint over propaganda violations and the failure to assign Chinese managers to positions of authority. Later that month, the new Soviet consul general in Harbin, an experienced China hand, Boris N. Melnikov, met with the Young Marshal to protest the telephone seizure. Chang Hsueh-liang replied that telephones were not covered under the railroad agreements and countered that the Soviets had not responded to Chinese complaints. Melnikov then offered to renegotiate the CER agreement with Mukden. Chang coyly referred him to Nanking, stating that he too had to answer to "the Party," a reference both to the common Soviet diplomatic delaying tactic of claiming matters had to first be approved by the Kremlin and to the fact that Chang was now a member of the KMT. Melnikov dropped the topic, not wishing to give Nanking a voice on CER management issues.[46]

The Soviets in turn frustrated the Young Marshal's efforts to have financial information submitted to the CER board. From 1924, when joint management began, until 1928, CER profits vanished; revenues continued to grow at healthy rates, increasing by 70 percent during the period, yet net profits fell by over 90 percent, from over 7 million gold rubles in 1924 to 563,000 rubles in 1928. Making the losses more confounding, the railroad was well run, as seen in the ratio of operating costs to revenues, which improved during the 1924–1929 period. The problem stemmed directly from the joint agreement: controlling the railway's management allowed the Russians to manipulate the CER's revenue and expenditure accounts at will and to use the additional funds as they saw fit.[47]

In the spring, the focus of China's affairs briefly shifted away from the Sino-Soviet CER troubles and toward what became known as the Kwangsi rebellion. The conflict arose in February 1929 over control of provincial revenues, what James E. Sheridan termed "the lifeblood of a regional warlord," and as Nanking asserted power over provincial purses, the die-hard warlords rose up.[48] The chief instigator was Kwangsi general Li Tsung-jen, the 4th Army Group commander who had held back his troops during the 1928 offensive. Still in Wuhan with 60,000 soldiers, Li attempted to retain control over the finances in Hunan;

this necessitated the dismissal of General Lu Ti-ping, who was taking his orders from Nanking. Another Kwangsi general, Pai Chung-hsi, in Peking also threw his support behind Li. Chiang Kai-shek was having none of it and soon had 150,000 troops from the 1st NRA Army Group poised to strike Wuhan. Li and Pai quickly caved under the pressure, and their so-called Kwangsi Clique broke apart. On 26 March, the two were stripped of their commands and expelled from the KMT. Chiang Kai-shek marched peacefully into Wuhan on 5 April.[49]

This turn of events unraveled the plans of Feng Yu-hsiang, who was attempting to solidify his control over Northeastern China by expanding his authority into the Shantung Peninsula. The insurmountable problem was that the 1st NRA Army Group sat victoriously in Central China. Chiang Kai-shek pushed his advantage through diplomatic maneuvers with Tokyo that delayed the withdrawal of Japan's Shantung forces until after Li's collapse at Wuhan. The nationalists then moved to wrest both Shantung and Honan provinces away from Feng in April. Feng prepared to put up a fight, but when Chiang Kai-shek positioned the NRA for battle, he quietly withdrew into his Northwestern stronghold at month's end and took no stronger action than to transmit anti–Chiang Kai-shek telegrams during May.[50]

The center of rebellion then shifted south, to Kwangsi and its governor-general, Huang Shao-hsiung. Huang had been disgusted with the foolish and destructive ambitions of his fellow clique members, Li and Pai, but was unwilling to bow to Nanking. The final battle with the Kwangsi Clique was not long in coming: the fighting began on 5 May when Huang marched into Kwangtung and began to encircle Canton. Local KMT forces quickly gained the upper hand, and as more NRA troops arrived, the Kwangsi army collapsed and Huang sought refuge in Hong Kong in June. Although Nanking had successfully weathered the storm, this first major outbreak of the plague of residual warlordism did not bode well for the immediate future of China. The British War Office noted that Chang Kai-shek's unification efforts "may only be temporary," as "there are many elements within and outside the Government who are conspiring for his downfall."[51] The display of disunity was unfortunate because the Sino-Soviet dispute in Manchuria was heating up again.[52]

The Raid on the Harbin Soviet Consulate

Chinese attempts to gain equal control over the CER had ended in failure after railway president Lu's 1 March proposal to restrict the powers of the Soviet managers was rejected. Over the next few weeks, the situation simmered until the political war between Chang Hsueh-liang and the Soviets erupted afresh. On 27 April, the CER meteorological office was taken over by Mukden, and a short time later, Chang become aware of a 27 May Comintern meeting, to be held at the Soviets' Harbin consulate, aimed at destabilizing the Young Marshal's regime. Harbin had transformed itself from a rough frontier town in 1900 to a booming metropolis of over 300,000 inhabitants by 1929. With sizable Russian and Chinese communities combined with smaller clusters of foreigners from Japan and the other Powers, it was one of the most diverse, fascinating, and exotic places on earth. The old town was famous (or perhaps infamous) for its raucous nightlife; the bars and clubs never closed. New Town, completed after the Boxer Uprising, had a different reputation. Boasting stately houses, upscale stores along broad, tree-lined boulevards reminiscent of Paris, and pleasant parks for leisurely strolls and picnics on weekends, it was one of the grandest communities in China. New Town was also the home of the expansive CER administration building and the Soviet consulate, the target of Chang Hsueh-liang's wrath. On the day of the meeting, the Young Marshal again stole a page from his father's handbook and raided the consulate.[53]

At the time of the raid, the Comintern was under the personal control of Stalin. An attack on its members inside a Russian diplomatic compound was a major escalation in the political struggle and a turning point in Soviet relations with Mukden. Chang was motivated by a diverse set of reasons beyond the complaint of aggressive anti-Mukden propaganda emanating from the consulate and the Soviet CER staff. Japanese consul Yagi Genhachi in Harbin noted that a contributing cause was the recent split between Feng Yu-hsiang and Chang Kai-shek, which signaled a renewal of the Feng–Soviet alliance, a view echoed in the *North-China Daily News*, which assumed that a secret agreement between Feng and the Soviets had been reached—an outcome certain to unsettle the Young Marshal. Chang wanted to send the Soviets a forceful message to stay out of his affairs.[54]

The remaining justifications centered directly on the CER: the discovery of an illegal diversion of $500,000 in CER funds to the Soviet-controlled railway workers' union, as well as a growing frustration and anger over the Soviet attitude in resolving CER management issues and the hope that the raid would become the catalyst to finally fix the problem. The American minister in Riga who monitored events in Moscow, F. W. B. Coleman, saw it as the prime cause; the raid stemmed directly from the struggle over control of the CER—a theme that soon appeared in the Japanese press. The official rationale made by Chang Hsueh-liang in a report to Nanking after the raid stated that it was carried out to preserve public order after the Soviets violated a nationwide order banning public meetings during the 26 May–1 June burial week for Sun Yat-sen. Chang also argued that the participants were communists and reactionary elements—a violation of the 1924 CER agreement.[55]

The raid began around noon, an hour before the scheduled start of the Comintern meeting, stretched into the night, and had all the elements of a cloak-and-dagger spy novel. The local Chinese police claimed to have been tipped off a few days earlier by an informant, a Chinese employee working at the consulate who barely escaped discovery. Similarly, Soviet lookouts spotted the Harbin police assembling before the raid and were able to warn the consular staff. By the time the police arrived at the scene, and despite the warm May weather, all the windows and doors had been bolted shut, and billowing clouds of black smoke poured out of every chimney. The Soviets had learned from the 1927 sacking of their Peking embassy grounds and had set aside quantities of oil and newspapers by each fireplace and kitchen stove for the emergency destruction of sensitive materials.[56]

While police battered their way in through doors and windows, the Chinese commanders on the scene placed a number of urgent calls to the local fire brigade and police headquarters for assistance. By 1:30 P.M., the chief of police, General Mi Tseng-jeng, along with thirty additional officers, arrived to take charge. In the midst of the confusion, Consul General Melnikov, captured while burning documents in his private upstairs office, vigorously protested the blatant infringement of diplomatic inviolability and calmly refused when ordered to open his office safe. The Harbin police, ignoring Melnikov's complaints and aided by the timely arrival of firemen, moved on with their search, and by 5:00 P.M. they had amassed enough documents to fill two trucks, including classified messages to Melnikov, Japanese consular seals and envelopes, and American consular bronze stamps, apparently used to forge documents for clandestine communications. Another surprise awaiting the police was the discovery of a hidden wireless set in the third-floor attic—proof to the Chinese that the Soviets were transmitting secret radio messages.[57]

Of the more than 100 people detained by the Harbin police, 39 Soviet citizens, most found hiding in the basement, were arrested; the rest were released into the custody of Consul General Melnikov. The Soviet prisoners ranged from CER general manager Emshinov and his deputy, A. A. Eismont, to customs and security officers, union leaders, three merchants suspected of being spies, and diplomatic officials from Manchouli, Tsitsihar, Muleng, and Changchun. Three women were caught in the net; they gave their names as Paula, a union official; Glorias, a representative from Hailar; and Khored, a customs official. The Chinese released the former Soviet consul general in Mukden, M. Kutznetzov, but in return, he was ordered to leave the country. The Harbin authorities went out of their way to ensure that the prisoners were well treated, arranging for the delivery of food from a nearby Russian restaurant along with tea and tobacco. They were also given access to a large office and chairs, supplied with soap, towels, and Western bedding with sheets, and were free to move about except during questioning.[58]

The raid spurred follow-on sweeps by Chinese authorities. At 1:00 A.M. the next day, the pro-Soviet Harbin newspaper *Novostizdizny* was closed by the police, and the investigation was extended to other Soviet offices in Harbin. The Soviet consulate at Suifenho was raided a few days later. To present a feeling of a return to normalcy, Chinese authorities announced that the Soviet consulate at Harbin was operating as usual, but behind the scenes, Mukden authorities worked closely with Nanking to exploit the intelligence coup. Soon Russian linguists in Peiping were on their way to assist in translating the captured documents. Additionally, the Harbin authorities sought to contain the Soviet attempt to air their version of the events of the 27 May raid. They shut down the consulate's telephones on 4 June, the same day that the official police report on the raid was released. Chinese actions were not limited to fighting a propaganda war; on 7 June, the attorney general for the Harbin Special District announced that the thirty-nine Soviet prisoners were to be tried under the 1928 laws dealing with communist plots against the Chinese revolution.[59]

The Soviets protested, without success. What steps to take in retaliation were strongly contested within the walls of the Kremlin; during a Politburo meeting, Red Army commander Voroshilov argued for military demonstrations on the Manchurian border. Bukharin opposed any military action. In the heated exchanges that followed, Voroshilov erupted, shouting at Bukharin, "You liar, bastard, I'll punch you in the face."[60] Bukharin walked out of the meeting, but Voroshilov did not get his way. Moscow settled for expelling the acting Chinese minister to show their displeasure. Soldiers were placed outside the Chinese consulates at Khabarovsk and Blagoveshchensk to intimidate the diplomats, and Chinese travelers inside the Soviet Union were harassed, but the Russians took no stronger action.[61]

The reaction in Nanking and Mukden was much different. By June, anger toward the Russians was palpable. According to Nanking, the seized documents revealed a "campaign of terrorism" and a commitment to help Feng Yu-hsiang. The information confirmed what they already believed: that the CER was being used to both fund and organize anti-KMT activities in North China and the Northeast. As for the charge of a secret alliance with Feng, even in Moscow it was accepted as true, although the Kremlin would not publicly admit it. Chiang and the Young Marshal felt no need for further justification to act against the Soviets, and the British minister in Peiping, Miles W. Lampson, was informed by William H. Donald, an Australian advisor to the Young Marshal, that seizure of the CER was being contemplated.[62]

Nanking felt it was in a strong position. Externally, Japan resigned itself to the inevitable and recognized the nationalist government on 28 June. Internally, Chiang had brokered a rapprochement with his archrival, Feng Yu-hsiang, canceled Feng's arrest warrant on 5 July, and, as a sign of continuing good faith, appointed a number of his allies to important government positions over the following weeks. China also saw vulnerability when it looked toward Russia: the Soviets were not in the League of Nations and Washington did not recognize Moscow, while Britain had severed relations in May 1927 during the Arcos affair—a political debacle for the Soviets that mirrored the same type of Comintern meddling in Britain's internal affairs that had partially motivated the 27 May Harbin raid.[63]

The Road to War

On 24 June in Washington, Chinese minster C. C. Wu, while meeting with Stimson, hinted at was being planning for the CER by asking about the use of force to protect China's rights under the Paris Pact. The United States was unsure of how to handle the question; as state department official W. R. Peck wrote in a memorandum about the meeting, "Is China to be debarred from the use of it own forces in its own territory to protect what it regards as China's rights, on the grounds that to do so would not be 'pacific'?"[64] The direction of the conversation was revealing: it showed that Nanking was transitioning from rhetoric to action. While Wu was talking in Washington, the Young Marshal met with his senior commanders. He concluded that the use of force to recover the CER was warranted and that the Soviets would not fight. On 27 June, Chiang Kai-shek agreed to meet with Chang in eight days at Peiping. As Lucien Pye noted, during the 1926–1929 period, anti-imperialism and the unequal treaties had been the focus of KMT propaganda efforts, and seizing the CER ideally addressed both these goals.[65]

On 6 July, Chiang and Foreign Minister C. T. Wang met with Chang Hsueh-liang in Peiping at the Grand Hôtel de Pékin to finalize the plan to recover the CER. To assist in the effort, the Young Marshal was promised $1,600,000 in cash and Nanking's revenues from the Peiping–Mukden railway to cover any expenses associated with the seizure. Providing military aid proved problematic. General Tang Shen-chih, a man neither Chiang nor Wang fully trusted, was to lead the NRA troops that Chiang Kai-shek had tapped to reinforce the NEFDF. Tang had proven loyal and capable but staunchly independent during the Northern Expedition, and he held a low opinion of Chiang Kai-shek. When the two had first met at Changsha in August 1926, Tang was unimpressed with Chiang, either as a military or political leader. The two worked together but were not close allies. While accepting the military support, the Young Marshal was less than enthused. Tang had played an active role in defeating his father in 1928, an outcome that led to the collapse of Chang Tso-lin's power in North China, the driving force behind his assassination by Japanese officers. The Young Marshal was also sensitive of his prerogatives in the Northeast and would deny the entry of Tang's NRA troops into Manchuria except under the direst of circumstances.[66]

After the decision was finalized, the Young Marshal telegraphed General Chang Ching-hui, commander of the CER rail guards and a trusted confidant of his father's who proved equally faithful to him, and Lu Yung-huan, the CER *tupan*, directing them to prepare to seize the CER. The next day, Chiang Kai-shek traveled briefly to Tientsin and met with the press, where he laid a political foundation for what was to come: "The position on our rights, within the [CER] Agreement, should be tough. We cannot give up."[67] Although the two men were deeply bound—the Young Marshal later stated that he had given "all my heart and soul" to supporting Chiang—the declaration identified both a common goal and marked differences in method.[68] That July, Chiang told the KMT CEC, "This is the first bullfight, we want to cancel the unequal treaties and the first is recovery of the CER."[69] While Chiang was eager for the fight, the Young Marshal sought a different, less confrontational path; he hoped the seizure would spur a resolution within the framework of the 1924 agreement. However, both were of the same mind: the time to reestablish China's CER rights had come.

6 | The Chinese and Soviet Russian Forces

The Chinese and Soviet militaries, while sharing the commonalities of any army, were distinctive fighting organizations in 1929. The Young Marshal's army was in a state of transition. Unlike Wu and Sun's forces, it had survived the 1926–1928 Northern Expedition largely intact, and as it prepared to join the NRA, the stirrings of nationalism grew but had not fully taken root. The army had yet to shed fully its recent warlord past. The 1919 arms embargo only just had been lifted, and the reforms after the defeat in the First Fengtien–Chihli War remained unchanged. While it was moving toward the future, there had not been enough time to transform it into a truly national army.

As the product of World War I and the Russian civil war, the Soviet Red Army had followed a different path. The trauma of World War I kept Red Army planners firmly within the realm of modern total war, while the civil war forced the Soviets to confront the myriad of problems associated with fighting along multiple fronts and over vast distances. Building on those experiences, the idealistic vitality of the early revolutionary years instilled a sense of confidence and created a culture of innovation unlike any seen in the tsarist armies of the past.

The Northeastern Frontier Defense Force

Leadership and the 1922–1924 Reforms

When the Sino-Soviet CER dispute reached the crisis stage, Chang Hsueh-liang led the NEFDF without interference from Chiang Kai-shek, and the army compared well with the NRA. Like the NRA, the NEFDF possessed a competent general staff, and the quality of its officer corps was above the norm. While Whampoa remained the premier military academy (which moved to Nanking after the end of the Northern Expedition), the 1922–1924 reforms had made significant improvements at the Mukden academy, and the more senior NEFDF officers had attended many of the same staff schools as those in the NRA, including a significant number of Peking war college and Japanese military academy graduates.[1]

Like other warlord armies, and unlike the NRA, the officers lacked a culture of subordinated service to the nation since the start of the republican era. Historian Jerome Chen argued that the fall of the Ch'ing had "eviscerated the concept of 'loyalty to the throne,'" and as the actions of Kuo Sung-ling and Yang Yu-ting demonstrated, no unifying sense of loyalty replaced it.[2] Subservience to the tuchun proved inadequate. Missing a transcendental purpose had put the NEFDF at a disadvantage when it faced the NRA in the Northern Expedition. It lacked the fighting spirit the NRA had gained through the presence of patriotically animated Whampoa graduates and political officers who put the Chinese revolution before all else. A 1926 Soviet report attributed to Nikolai V. Kuibyshev, Blyukher's successor at Whampoa, averred that the NRA's greatest weapon was "political consciousness and political enlightening."[3] The nationalist victory stimulated those emotions, but the NEFDF could not match the NRA's élan in combat.

While the execution of Yang and Chang Huan-hsiang had solidified Chang Hsueh-liang's authority within Fengtien province, the senior NEFDF leadership remained splintered. The Heilungkiang and Kirin brigades, a third of his army, answered to military governors Wan Fulin and Chang Tso-hsiang, respectively. Additionally, Chang Chin-wei commanded the Harbin Special District that included the CER rail guards. Because their loyalty was not absolute, the Young Marshal was careful in his support while husbanding resources for his own brigades, a necessary but inefficient stratagem. The overall outlook in 1929 was promising, however. Chang Hsueh-liang's successes after ascending to the leadership had calmed the waters, and the NEFDF possessed one of the most capable contingents of battlefield commanders in China.[4]

The outlines for the professionalization of the 1929 NEFDF officer corps were drawn during the 1923–1924 reforms instituted by the elder Chang after Mukden's 1922 defeat and overseen by the Chang Hsueh-liang. During the conflict, a troubling number of top commanders had proven ineffective and that led to a postwar purge of the old *hunghutzu* bandit leaders, opening up a new rivalry between the officers educated at Paoting and Peking who followed the Young Marshal and Kuo Sung-ling and those who graduated from the Japanese military academy and looked up to Yang. Although divisive to a degree, the change was for the better as it created a competition within the officer corps directed toward military excellence as opposed to one of personal fealty to Chang Tso-lin. For the officer ranks, this strongly reinforced the two pillars of NEFDF stability: the traditional cultural ties of loyalty between officers and soldiers through a father–son relationship and between senior and junior officers through teacher–student bonds. By 1924, the army had been set on a better course, with five years of professional development that benefited the Young Marshal, when the CER crisis erupted in 1929.[5]

Recruitment, Training, and Doctrine

To procure soldiers, China never adopted a modern conscription–mobilization system during the warlord era. It was the right solution; the country was too vast, the population too large, and the central government too weak to develop a national *levée en masse.* Local recruitment by various means ranging from voluntary enlistment to forced impressment stood in its stead, and authority to recruit—the path to power and money—became a cherished warlord prerogative. There were national standards set by the army ministry regarding age, height, weight, and other criteria, but the decentralized system never assured the quality of the inductees or controlled the number of soldiers. The NEFDF fared well in this process; Manchuria possessed an ample population and sufficient resources to make recruiting appealing, although the army also continued into the 1920s the expedient of enjoining bandit gangs into its paramilitary forces, creating a potentially lawless band within the ranks.[6]

The peace stemming from the 1928 recognition of Nanking allowed the NEFDF to rearm and ready itself after the losses incurred during the Northern Expedition. The long series of wars from 1920 through 1928 had earned the NEFDF a reputation of producing soldiers who would fight, although there was concern among observers that some units, like the Heilungkiang troops, had not seen major action since 1925. The army possessed veteran officers who led from the front—only the NRA's Whampoa-trained officers were held in greater esteem—but there were problems. Lacking a standard training system, the Chinese armies adopted their own methods, and those used by the NEFDF differed from either those of the Kuominchun or the NRA; the worst of the tuchun armies possessed many units that were little more than armed gangs. The better armies, like the NEFDF, adhered broadly to some common policies. All continued in one form or another the regional military schools created during the 1904–1905 New Army reforms. Doctrine was based on traditional Chinese military texts, such as the *Seven Military Classics*, and translations of German and Japanese military regulations.[7]

In addition to classical and borrowed military texts, the NEFDF benefited from a growing body of modern Chinese doctrine that was begun by Yuan Shih-kai with his *Training and Drilling Methods* and that was best exemplified by the writings of General Chiang Fang-cheng (also referred to as Chiang Pai-li). Chiang was an exceptional officer who had served under Chao Erh-hsun in Mukden after the Russo-Japanese War and went on to direct the Paoting military academy. He first gained attention with a 1915 republication of Sun Tzu's *Art of War* that incorporated the writings of Carl von Clausewitz and Helmuth von Moltke the Elder before writing *Common Knowledge of Military Science* in 1917, the most widely used Chinese military text of the era. The introduction of Chinese military texts was one of the few authentic advances in military science during the early republican era.[8]

Career officers possessed the midlevel command and staff skills that allowed the NEFDF to conduct the large unit operations vital to the survival of the regime. Until 1922, they also masked the incompetence of Chang's bandit generals, and as discussed previously, Chang Tso-lin did not initially value formal military schools. The Mukden military academy had been reconstituted in 1919 only because of orders originating in Peking, but it proved its value immediately, graduating a steady stream of capable young officers. This created an educated cadre of junior officers that provided battlefield cohesion to the platoons and companies, but beyond infantry training, specialized schools were lacking.

There was no national artillery school. Mukden created its own course—the Young Marshal was a distinguished graduate of its first class—and accurate artillery fire eventually became the norm. During the 1922 war, Fengtien artillery was able to mass its guns on key objectives, although fire was aimed directly at a visible enemy and often at ranges under one mile in size. By the time of the Second Fengtien–Chihli War, day and night indirect fire controlled by forward observers became routine, and Fengtien artillery became a force to be feared. By the mid-1920s, the NEFDF had mastered most forms of modern warfare: machine guns became commonly used, aircraft were in use, and tanks saw limited action as early as 1925. Whole armies could be transported large distances and logistically sustained by rail. Unfortunately, there were few qualified combat engineer or communications officers—deficiencies that kept the NEFDF from reaching equality with the militaries of the other Powers.[9]

The foreign factor provided the final dimension to officer training and military education. Large numbers of promising officers were sent abroad for training, and when the 1922 reforms were initiated, some 100 officers were recalled to help spearhead the efforts. Foreign advisors were also common and assisted in raising professional standards; Francis A. Sutton, a former British army officer, oversaw operations at the Mukden arsenal, Frenchmen helped with the air force, and White Russian officers were used as planners and for specialized skills in engineering and artillery. Advisory duties were dominated by the Japanese army. The numerous Japanese officers wielded a great degree of influence, and in 1928, over fifty were assigned, introducing Chang's officers to the latest tactics and techniques used by the imperial army.[10]

In the ranks, as with the officers, infantry drill dominated training. Discipline was harsh, and floggings with sticks continued into the 1930s. Gendarmes or military police kept the troops in line by any means necessary, and executing deserters or mutineers was common practice. Despite its disadvantages, joining the army offered a route for social advancement that was impossible in most professions and was one of the few examples of an egalitarian meritocracy in the warlord era. The normal path for officer candidates was passing a written entrance examination, but the NEFDF successfully gambled on "raising soldiers from the ranks" by giving superior but illiterate candidates a basic education before reporting to the academy. This did much to motivate individuals with ability and ambition, but outside the selected handful, the cultivation of enlisted leadership was neglected.[11]

There was no professional NCO corps for much of Chang Tso-lin's reign of power. Under his system, NCOs were nothing more than veteran soldiers with little or no leadership responsibilities. When junior officers were killed or otherwise incapacitated, the platoons and companies became leaderless and often ineffective in combat. To address this shortcoming, Kuo Sung-ling established a NCO school at the Mukden academy as part of the 1922–1924 reforms. By 1929, progress had been made, but the creation of a skilled NCO cadre was still years away.[12]

Equipment

NEFDF weapons and equipment came from an almost dizzying variety of sources; German- and Austrian-designed artillery, Russian rifles and machine guns, French fighter-bombers, and Japanese weapons of all types were common, along with those designed and produced in China. The NEFDF also maintained armored trains and a number of French Renault FT-17 tanks whose origin remains unclear. This allowed the Young Marshal to keep his army amply equipped, but the lack of weapons standardization created a nightmare for the armorers to maintain and the logisticians to keep armed. The NEFDF held an advantage over most Chinese armies by being able to produce many of its own weapons and munitions. China's major arsenals were at Canton, Chengte, Hanyang (Wuhan), Kiangnan (Shanghai), Kinghsien (Loyang), Nanking, Tsinan, and Mukden, with two dozen lesser facilities spread across the country, like the one in Yunnan that produced 20,000 cartridges daily for Japanese-model rifles.[13]

The more capable Canton arsenal could produce as many 125,000 cartridges, fifty to eighty rifles, and one machine gun daily. Yen in Shansi had also greatly enlarged the Taiyuan arsenal, putting it just behind the Hanyang complex. All paled in comparison to Mukden's Three Eastern Provinces Arsenal, the nation's largest, where roughly half of the weapons manufactured in China were produced. When Sutton took charge in 1922, it covered over 700 acres and employed some 30,000 workers; it only grew in size and capability in the years that followed.[14]

While on a wartime footing during the height of the Northern Expedition, 150 rifles a day came off the Mukden assembly line, along with 300,000 rounds of ammunition for the variety of rifles and pistols used by the NEFDF. Although the arsenal produced a Chinese version of a Mauser rifle, many of the troops were armed with the readily available Japanese Type 99 7.7mm and Russian Mosin-Nagant 7.62mm rifles (also used by the Soviets in 1929), while their Hotchkiss and Maxim machine guns were locally manufactured at a rate of two to three per day, with additional guns acquired overseas, although a lack of ammunition limited their use. Two types of mortars and four types of artillery pieces were also manufactured; the most common were the 76.2mm Stokes mortar, the 76.2mm field gun, and a modern 152mm howitzer. To keep them in action, 4,000 shells of all types were produced daily, a feat made possible by the importation of high explosives from Norway. The NEFDF was the best-equipped army in China, but it had never faced a foreign army in combat.[15]

Embargo on the Sale of Arms to China (1919–1929)

An important episode in the Chinese military history of the era, and one tied to the equipping of the NEFDF, was the 1919 arms embargo. As discussed in Chapter 3, the Powers hoped that the threat of an embargo would help bring the militarists to terms. The Americans took the firmest stand, demanding a halt to current deliveries of military arms and munitions while banning future orders.[16]

The other Powers were not in full agreement, and a number of exceptions were put in place. "Sporting" arms under $1,000 in value were excluded, a move that sharply limited the size of, but did not stop, the shipments. Warplane sales were banned. Airplane sales were not, and the Americans failed to push through sales restrictions on converted warplane models sold as civil aircraft. Italy did not join in the embargo until the other Powers agreed that its existing arms contracts were to be held harmless, and Japan made a similar claim regarding shipments for the WPA. By early April, Tokyo agreed to cut off its military support of Tuan's Anfu faction because the majority of the promised WPA arms had been delivered—a concession by the other Powers that allowed Japan to remain in the talks and the pact to proceed.[17]

On 5 May 1919, with no prospect of ending the civil war through the Shanghai conference, the five Powers informed Peking that the embargo was to remain in effect until China reunified. The Americans then demanded that Dairen in the Japanese Kwantung Leasehold be included in the list of embargo ports. Surprisingly, Japan agreed, and on 10 May, all parties agreed that the ban on armaments and munitions would include all Chinese ports of entry. Soon after, Belgium, Brazil, Denmark, the Netherlands, Portugal, the White Russian government, and Spain agreed to join the pact. As China had an inherent right of self-defense, Peking demanded in August that arsenals be permitted, and that in turn sanctioned the selling of materials and equipment needed to produce modern weapons and munitions. The Americans opposed the idea, but the other Powers sided with China. Arsenals were exempted, paving the way for the colossus erected at Mukden. More damaging than the loopholes were the armament and munitions manufacturers who did not sign the pact, such as Soviet Russia and Norway, who ignored the embargo at will, and while Germany and Austria were forbidden by postwar treaties to export arms, machinery to produce their weapons, especially artillery pieces, eventually found their way into China's arsenals.[18]

At first the embargo had no effect. The French worked around the small arms ban by shipping quantities of rifles and pistols as police weapons. The English aircraft manufacturer Vickers began equipping the Chinese air force and developing their airfields in the fall of 1919. In all, violations by Belgium, Italy, Japan, the United Kingdom, and the United States were reported during the first quarter of 1920. In July, just days before the start of the Anfu–Chihli War, the Italians shipped 2,124 tons of military supplies to Shanhaikuan and 2,460 tons to Tientsin. As a result of Japan and Italy's exemptions, Tuan's army was well equipped in modern arms and munitions when war broke out in mid-1920. With Chang Tso-lin's victory, the Anfu air force procured by Japan was quickly transferred to Mukden as spoils of war. On 23 November 1920, the American merchantman *Woudrichem* delivered several Curtiss seaplanes and machinery for the manufacture of rifles and cartridges to the Canton arsenal. The embargo appeared to be failing.[19]

Eventually the Powers took firmer steps. In January 1921, they met to discuss the violations, and each justified its actions but agreed to do better. Although no new written restrictions were enacted, the Powers did move to enforce the existing embargo. American authorities began to crack down on the arms running and foiled an attempt to ship 3,000 rifles and 1,500,000 rounds of ammunition from the Philippines to Canton in September. The loopholes remained in place, however. Aircraft were still excluded from the ban, and the British made substantial shipments: Vickers sent sixty Avros and forty Vimy bombers, while Handley-Page delivered fourteen aircraft of various types by early 1921. In a replay of 1920, during the nights of 21 and 22 November 1921, the Italians delivered eighty train carloads of weapons and munitions to the Chihli army at the Shanhaikuan Pass barracks.[20]

Earlier in May, during Japan's first Eastern Regions conference to map out a national policy for China (to include Manchuria) and Mongolia, Prime Minister Hara Kei ruled out supplying arms to China and directed compliance with the 1919 embargo but authorized assistance in developing Chang Tso-lin's Mukden arsenal. Japanese army officers working with Chang urged a change to the embargo policy in early 1922 but were rebuffed. With that door closed, in the weeks and months before Vladivostok came under Soviet control, the eyes of Chang's Japanese army advisors turned to the port's remaining military stockpiles.[21]

At that time, a CER employee reported that a shipment of military supplies of US manufacture had been sent from Vladivostok to Wu Pei-fu. The British raised concerns over the weaponry in early September, believing that Japanese army officers would try to transfer the stocks to Chang Tso-lin. A few weeks later, on 27 September 1922, the British fears were proven true when the Japanese press broke the story that Vladivostok munitions were going to Chang Tso-lin. By 4 October, the Japanese army was being publicly criticized over the "lost arms."[22] Later that month, as the last remnants of the White Russian bands disintegrated before Vladivostok, a court-martial found Major Hara Soichi, a midlevel staff officer, guilty of mishandling the Vladivostok munitions—a clear example of what the Japanese press termed the Japanese army's "double diplomacy" of working at cross-purposes with the government in Tokyo.[23]

There were additional attempts to sustain and even strengthen the restrictions. On 24 January 1922, during the Washington conference, Arthur Balfour, the chief British negotiator, introduced a resolution to rid the 1919 agreement of its exclusions but was met with unexpectedly strong opposition. Dr. Wellington Koo, China's representative to the discussions, saw the embargo as an infringement of sovereign rights and asked for it to be abolished within two years. Italy declined to give up its 1919 reservations protecting preexisting arms contracts, and Japan declared that it would cease its voluntary ban on similar contracts if Italy's request was granted. With the entire framework at risk, the resolution was withdrawn without action. The United States held firm to a complete embargo. A few weeks later, on 4 March 1922, immediately after the repeal of the Espionage Act of 1917, which had provided the legal authority to enforce the embargo, President Warren G. Harding enacted a joint resolution of Congress that banned sales to China of arms or munitions, to include "aeronautical material or equipment" and raw materials and machinery related to war.[24] In July 1923, one of the few years without a major conflict in China, the Powers agreed to embargo aid to Chinese naval facilities such as shipyards, dockyards, and naval arsenals.[25]

The flow of weapons and munitions continued. Italy delivered $4 million in arms to Wu's forces in late February 1924, and on 24 October, the French mail steamer *Chantilly* delivered aircraft and machine guns to Dairen that were passed on to Chang Tso-lin. Over time, French aircraft became the mainstay of the Fengtien air force. Discussions over aircraft sales proved fruitless. All the Powers, save the United States, rejected any limits on commercial aircraft sales, but the Americans saw it as a meaningless distinction; civil aviation in China was nonexistent making all aircraft de facto warplanes. Aeroplane sales continued unabated despite continuous efforts by the United States throughout 1924. On rare occasions, violators were punished; the American captain of the *Talbot* was given a one-year sentence for shipping arms to China in 1925. It had virtually no deterrent effect, and little progress was made in stopping the gunrunners.[26]

The Americans were disheartened. On 3 April 1926, MacMurray wrote from Peking that the embargo, which he played a part in enacting seven years earlier, was "wholly ineffective" given the Russian material support to the KMT and Feng's Kuominchun.[27] Rather than constraining the violence, the embargo simply allowed the Soviets to gain influence by equipping those factions in sympathy with the Kremlin's goals. By 5 August, as the Northern Expedition picked up steam, Kellogg decided to discreetly discuss ending the embargo, but he did so without conviction and nothing came of it. Reflecting on the efficacy of the embargo in 1928, Joseph E. Jacobs, the American consul in Shanghai, held that only the Italians and French failed to uphold the pact while noting that the Japanese had been lax earlier but not during the late 1920s. Neither that reality nor the massive flow of Soviet arms moved Kellogg; his support of the ban remained virtually unchanged as the Northern Expedition entered its closing months. It was only after reunification, that the embargo, in a piecemeal process that began in the summer of 1928 and extended through the first six months of 1929, ended as each participating nation gave full recognition to the nationalist government in Nanking.[28]

What did the embargo accomplish? While historian Stephen Velone argued that the primary purpose of the 1919 embargo was to limit Japan's influence in China, the collapse of the Tuan regime in the wake of the 1920 Anfu–Chihli War largely rendered that aim moot. Afterward, the Japanese government adhered to the policy at least as diligently as other Powers. The Soviets benefited the most by being a nonsignatory to the agreement, but they lost their hard-gained influence during the 1927 KMT–CCP split. From the perspective of international efforts to gain advantage in China, the embargo produced no clear winners.

Working against success, the loopholes were eagerly exploited by both the warlords and Powers. The Italians and Japanese used 1919 exclusions to continue arms shipments, the Kwantung Army violated the agreement outright in 1922, and the French simply redefined military aid as police aid. Norway provided the TNT needed to keep the manufacture of munitions and grenades flowing. Outside the Americans, aviation materials were delivered without hindrance; militarizing aircraft proved challenging but not impossible for the Chinese. Despite continuous American protests to the contrary, the presence of warplanes was irrelevant, as airpower never played a major role in any of the warlord conflicts.

One benefit of the embargo was the accelerated development of arsenals, allowing the Chinese armies to grow in size and strength. Conversely, it thwarted the development of high-quality modern weapons. Most armaments produced in China were based on models from World War I or earlier, while its Japanese and Soviet rivals marched into the future by fielding aircraft, armored vehicles, and artillery superior in range, accuracy, and lethality. The Soviets began manufacturing warplanes and tanks in the 1920s, while China relied entirely on imports. The frontline 75mm howitzer used by the Fengtien forces was based on a pre–World War I Krupp design, while the Japanese army introduced new guns at the rate of one every two years during the period 1914–1929; they were far ahead of the Chinese in aircraft and tank development. The piecemeal embargo efforts did nothing to deter the tuchun wars or to assist in a uniform development of the Chinese military. The net effect only served to slow needed modernization.[29]

When the embargo ended in 1929, China was left with an army that relied too heavily on rifle-armed infantry, preventing the adoption of offensive maneuver tactics that would have been unavoidable if the widespread use of up-to-date machine guns, artillery, and aircraft had been present on the battlefield. The Chinese army was not backward; in most respects, it was sophisticated by any standard of the day. The injury stemmed not from an absence of but a scarcity of modernity. As the major Powers developed mechanized forces supported by aircraft, the Chinese were mired in a form of warfare dominated by foot-mobile riflemen. Had there been a smaller national army—one organized, equipped, and supplied along Western lines—it would have devastated the poorly trained tuchun formations in short order. The rise of warlordism did the major damage, but the embargo further perverted the natural evolution of war fighting, putting China and the NEFDF at a disadvantage when facing a modern army.

NEFDF Size and Organization

In February 1929, during Nanking's disbandment efforts to reduce or even eliminate the tuchun armies, the NEFDF strength was put at 160,000 soldiers. This number was designed to appease Chiang Kai-shek but was not an accurate reflection of the size of the Young Marshal's army. The American military attaché in Peiping put the size of the force at 329,500 soldiers in June and 360,000 by October 1929, but it was smaller then the massive forces enlisted during the Northern Expedition. The disbandment efforts did make the NEFDF stronger in two ways. First, a return to peacetime military expenditures allowed for the rebuilding of the army, and second, officers and soldiers who had not measured up during the hectic wartime expansion during the Northern Expedition were purged from the ranks, immediately improving the overall quality of the troops.[30]

Structurally, the 1929 NEFDF was built around twenty-seven mixed brigades that were grouped together into armies (beyond the early years of the NRA, China never adopted the corps formation). The mixed brigade structure was another key part of the 1922–1924 reforms. The most important change was the abandonment of the division formation. Of the five divisions that fought in 1922, none came out with a distinguished battle record—their size proved too difficult to control—and it was decided to make the mixed brigade the building block of the army. Infantry divisions were temporarily formed after 1924, but the brigade repeatedly proved itself the best combat grouping. By 1929, an army had begun to resemble those of the other major Powers. Headed by a general or lieutenant general and supported by a staff of approximately 200, it possessed a radio communications company and a number of logistical support units. To augment the fighting power of the mixed brigades, an army contained one or two artillery regiments of seven or eight three-gun batteries and a brigade or more of cavalry, normally composed of three regiments of 650 troops each. Pioneer or engineering units were in short supply, and an army would be lucky to possess even a single battalion.[31]

The 5,200-man mixed brigade was the heart of the army. Commanded by a colonel or major general, it possessed three infantry regiments that did most of the fighting. The rifle was the dominant weapon, while most NEFDF mixed brigades held as many as twenty heavy machine guns (light machine guns were virtually nonexistent). The term "mixed" referred to the addition of a headquarters section, cavalry squadron, pioneer company, and support troops that allowed the brigade to operate independently. Artillery was scarce. Many Fengtien brigades had one battalion of two two-gun batteries along with mortars, but most, like the Heilungkiang mixed brigades, had none and were equipped with twenty 76.2mm Stokes mortars for the delivery of indirect fire on the enemy. Finally, there was the 1st Heavy Artillery Regiment, 3rd Guards Mixed Brigade, and an armored force composed of several dozen French FT-17 light tanks that all answered directly to Chang Hsueh-liang.

While the army dominated the NEFDF, there was also a small navy and air force. Equipped with some 100 aircraft organized into squadrons of five to nine aircraft, the force was a source of great pride for the Young Marshal. He had been its commander and champion since the First Fengtien–Chihli War of 1922. During the subsequent 1923 army reorganization, the force increased in size and in quality as well through the procurement of new aircraft (primarily the first-rate French Breguet 19). Battle experience had been gained during three wars, but only in the areas of bombardment and scouting. Its pilots had no skills in aerial combat, and as a result of the withdrawal of the Soviets after the 1927 KMT–CCP split, the Fengtien air forces never encountered RKKA pilots in the air. These limitations, coupled with the great cost associated with acquiring and maintaining an air force, led the Young Marshal to be cautious, if not overprotective, of his planes and pilots. They would not be risked in the air except under the most advantageous conditions.

The core of the navy was the Sungari River Flotilla. China had long maintained a naval presence on Manchuria's rivers; since the 1660s, war junks built at Kirin on the Sungari River defended the Manchu homeland from Russian encroachment. After the 1900 Boxer Uprising, only Russian warships sailed the rivers. As discussed in Chapter 2, as a reward for entering World War I on the Allied side, two German gunboats were transferred to China and eventually made their way to the Amur River, forming the nucleus of the flotilla. Additional patrol boats were stationed at Yingkow on the Bay of Pohai, but the Sungari Flotilla remained the primary naval force. By 1920, the flotilla was under the command of Captain Yin Tsu-yin and summer ported at Tungchiang where the Sungari and Amur rivers met before moving south to Harbin for the winter, when the northern rivers froze over. By 1929, command had passed to Shen Hung-lieh and the flotilla had grown to four gunboats, the *Li-chieh* and the *Li-shui* (the two former German gunboats) along with the *Lu-chi* and the *Kiang-heng*, which served as the flagship. Augmenting the gunboats were seven patrol craft.[32]

Organization, equipment, training, and leadership meant little without soldiers who would fight, and the NEFDF entered 1929 with a motivated army. This was a break with the past. If China's descent into warlordism roiled loyalties within the officer corps, then it devastated the soldier's will to fight long and hard, and at great personal risk. The 1928 reunification reinstilled a sense of devotion to the nation, and the opportunity to face foreign imperialism gave the NEFDF soldiers a new sense of mission and determination. Mercenary wants were being supplanted by emerging patriotic pride, sense of duty, and sacrifice.

The NEFDF was unmistakably a product of the warlord era, and one that only could have come to fruition in Manchuria. Warlordism allowed Chang Tso-lin to create a massive private army ruled by heredity leadership and personal loyalties. Defeat in the 1922 Fengtien–Chihli War led to a military reorganization that, among other things, abandoned the New Army division model for that of the mixed brigade, making a clean break with the past. Such a reformation could never have happened outside the Northeastern sanctuary, which possessed the economic resources to make the vision a reality. The NEFDF in 1929 was a potent military machine that had just begun to transition into a national army. Chang Hsueh-liang could take comfort in the knowledge that, aside from Chiang Kai-shek's elite NRA divisions, he commanded the best military in China.[33]

The Workers' and Peasants' Red Army

Leadership and Mission

The Chinese were not alone in improving their military during the 1920s; the Soviets made even greater strides. Russia, like China, had undergone a profound and tragic political transformation. Unlike the miseries of warlordism, the Russian people faced a new terror as the Soviet Union moved from rule by an authoritarian tsar to control by a totalitarian dictator; Josef Stalin was the unrestrained leader over a society seduced by a violently radical ideology. By the close of 1928, as E. H. Carr put it, Stalin "stood at the summit of his ambition."[34] Interparty democracy was dead, and the authority of Communist Party organs, such as the Central Committee and the Politburo, were reduced to little more than advisory bodies. Stalin did allow for decentralized decision making and readily delegated authority, but once an issue caught his attention, his dictates were to be followed unquestioningly. Stalin's December 1924 speech arguing for "socialism in one country" changed the direction of the nation, and in the months to come, the pursuit of the world socialist revolution advocated by Trotsky was brushed aside. This had immediate consequences for the Red Army.[35]

Even before Stalin's new initiatives, the RKKA had become a military organization not before seen in Russia's long history. To grasp that uniqueness, Lenin's vision of the Red Army must be understood. Until World War I, Lenin had preached that world peace was the logical blessing of the socialist movement, but with the failure of European socialists not just to prevent war in 1914 but in many cases to become vocal national champions of the conflict, Lenin began to rethink his conclusions. By 1915, he had abandoned them altogether. The pacifist became the student of Clausewitz, the eighteenth-century military genius and author of the classic *On War.* By 1916, Lenin saw the victory of socialism as the result of a global conflict against imperialism. The road to peace now followed the path of revolutionary war. It could be argued that his military epiphany was the spark that ignited the "wars of radical socialism" that consumed most of the remainder of the twentieth century.[36]

With his new philosophy in place, it became inevitable that Lenin would create a Red Army to secure victory after the collapse of the tsarist regime and the Bolshevik uprising. The RKKA, established on 15 January 1918 under Trotsky's command, was to be composed of "class-conscious" workers. The enlisting soldier had to be "ready to give his life and strength for the defense of the achievements of the October Revolution, the Soviet Power and socialism."[37] More militia than army, by the close of the civil war it had become an unwieldy mass of 5 million poorly trained soldiers—a force more akin to the tuchun armies than those of the other World War I participants, and an army to be neither feared nor respected.

After the end of the civil war, discharging the bulk of the enlistees while turning the RKKA into an army oriented on defensive operations became Trotsky's objective. As Lenin lay dying in January 1924, the triumvirate led by Stalin acted to break Trotsky's hold over the Red Army by removing his ally, Antonov-Ovseenko, as head of the Political Administration of the Red Army (PUR). Andrei S. Bubnov took the helm, and control of the PUR was shifted from the RKKA to the Central Committee of the Communist Party. The move was a serious blow to Trotsky. Communist dogma demanded that the army serve the party, and political reliability was mercilessly maintained through PUR commissars who acted as co-commanders. With Antonov gone and the PUR no longer under his command, Trotsky lost his hold on the ideological loyalty of the army.[38]

The political attacks on Trotsky continued. Six weeks after the 21 January death of Lenin, Stalin orchestrated the replacement of Trotsky's long-serving deputy, Ephraim M. Sklyansky, with Mikhail V. Frunze. A Lenin loyalist who had brilliantly led several armies during the civil war, Frunze was responsible for the defeat of Kolchak in Siberia and played a key role in defeating Wrangel on the Southwestern Front. After the war, he earned a reputation as one of the ablest military thinkers and strategists in the Red Army. He was also an outspoken critic of Trotsky, a trait Stalin found valuable in 1924, and in that light, Frunze was directed to head a special commission to investigate RKKA administration and readiness. Its purpose was twofold: to develop a plan to reform the army and to discredit Trotsky. Frunze accomplished both, finding that "neither the Red Army or the country is ready for war" and developing a blueprint for RKKA improvement.[39] Trotsky's authority within the army was fatally compromised.[40]

The term "cult of personality" described the influence of Josef Stalin; no other person so dominated the Red Army. By the end of 1924, the RKKA's newly created controlling bodies answered directly to Stalin: the Commissariat for Military and Naval Affairs (CMNA) and the Revolutionary Military Council (RMC); his loyalists, known as the Tsaritsyn group, held important posts. Kliment Y. Voroshilov was given command of the vital Moscow Military District with Grigory I. Kulik as deputy, and Semyon M. Budyonny became inspector of the Red Army cavalry with A. E. Shchadenko as senior commissar. In the face of unrelenting political assaults by the triumvirate and the special commission's scathing indictment, Trotsky resigned from his military posts on 17 January 1925 and began his slow descent into powerlessness. Nine days later, Frunze took his place as both the RMC chairman and CMNA commissar, ushering in a period of military strengthening. The choice reflected Stalin's caution: although Frunze was not a member of the Tsaritsyn group, he was a loyal communist who possessed no political power base. He was an able soldier acceptable to the party and, above all, no threat to Stalin.[41]

Frunze immediately made great strides in developing doctrine and reorganizing the army. In his paper "Front and Rear in Future War," Frunze attacked the idea of separate public and military economic sectors; he saw only a war economy—a total national effort in case of attack. He also challenged the assumption on how such a war should be fought. Although the RKKA mission of strategic defense remained unchanged, Frunze moved to emphasize the importance of the attack in any defensive campaign, and he worked to create a regular army guided by the principles of maneuver and offense. The international revolution was not completely forgotten; in August 1925, Frunze exhorted the war college graduates to be ready to "aid the world's proletariat in defeating their internal class enemies," a challenge soon realized with the dispatch of Soviet military advisory groups to China.[42] Regrettably, his work was left unfinished when he died unexpectedly after heart surgery in late 1925. Voroshilov took his place.[43]

With the passing of Frunze, the development of new strategy, theory, and doctrine went into a decade-long decline. John Erikson noted that no text on strategy was written after 1926, and David Glantz observed that the development of new doctrine ended in 1935. Voroshilov was no visionary. Lenin once stated, "He has the NCO's bravery in his soul; Marx somewhere in his mind; and a revolver in his hand." Whatever his limitations, he was unshakably loyal to Stalin and fully dedicated to the Red Army.[44] His contemporary, General Aleksandr I. Todorsky, noted the obvious: "Everyone knew Voroshilov was Stalin's arms bearer, his spokesman and mouthpiece."[45] The appointment reflected the totality of Stalin's power. His men were in charge, and the army would answer to Stalin and Stalin alone.

Recruitment, Training, and Doctrine

Red Army recruitment and training were not exceptional except in two areas—obtaining soldiers and keeping their loyalty—and revolutionary ideals influenced both objectives. The size of the RKKA necessitated a peacetime conscription and mobilization system to support both active and territorial military formations. The territorials, as their name implies, were reserve forces recruited from specific geographic regions. To possess a large mass of trained soldiers, the Soviets conducted an annual draft of twenty-one-year-olds. Those found physically and mentally fit were sent to either regular or territorial units. Bitterness from the civil war was still strong, and the term "workers and peasants" was taken literally in the 1920s; kulaks ("tight-fisted" farmers with hired hands), churchgoers, and other nondesirables were banned from service.

Fear of the politically unreliable peasant led to a quota system designed to enlist the largest number of proletariat workers possible. Not all military branches were treated equally; no less than half of the troops selected for tank units had to be from the proletariat, compared to a mere 8 percent for the infantry. Political reliability also gave rise to concerns over the roles of military specialists who had served as tsarist officers. Lenin and Trotsky were realists who enrolled the specialists both during and after the civil war. Stalin, who undervalued their expertise and distrusted their class status, had them gradually purged after he took power. The moderated loss of experts did not have a significant impact because the number of specialists needed had decreased during the army demobilizations of the mid-1920s, and RKKA training and education programs filled the vacancies.[46]

The RKKA had to compete for manpower with the GPU. Under the direct command of Vlacheslav I. Menzhinsky, its members were often referred to as the secret police and were responsible for internal and border security. Its needs were not insignificant: it contained over 200,000 soldiers formed into brigades and regiments, and the GPU sought to expand its military power. Not content with controlling railway guard units, in 1928 it created its own armored train unit with the commissioning of the *Felix Dzerzhinsky* and established an armored train headquarters and school at Minsk. To fulfill its growing needs, the GPU officers siphoned off the best candidates from the annual army drafts; those chosen held elite status, all at the expense of the RKKA.[47]

The second factor that made the Red Army stand apart was indoctrination by the Communist Party. The focus on political reliability was nothing new to those who had observed Soviet advisors with the NRA, but its role in RKKA training was hard to overstate. The *1929 Field Service Regulations* adopted that June laid out its importance: success in combat "is secured most by . . . the political training of the troops."[48] For active units, the daily goal was 5.5 hours for training and 4.5 hours for political indoctrination, while in the territorials, only tactics and marksmanship training had more allotted time. The ideal may have fallen short—no standard small unit training regulations were implemented until 1933—but if training missed the mark, there was always the barracks lecture, and the commissars still controlled the libraries, soldiers' clubs, military newspapers, and army party cells. Their influence was so pervasive that it became a point of contention when more and more officers became party members in the 1920s. Communist Party RKKA commanders saw their commissars as superfluous, while the PUR viewed them as essential to the subordination of the military to the party. As a compromise, the 1925 Frunze reforms limited the PUR's powers: commissars remained at the small unit level, but for regiments and larger units, a party-member commander could assume both duties.[49]

The conscription system had its weaknesses. Given the political constraints and the losses to the GPU, there were not enough qualified recruits available to fill the RKKA quotas, leading to a chronic shortage of soldiers and leaving first-line units under strength. The term of active service was short—two years for regulars—before being sent to the reserves, and territorials only received initial training. After the training, territorial reserves were sent home and were required to complete one month of active duty each summer in addition to periodic training during the rest of the year. As a legacy of the revolution, there were no ranks in the RKKA; leaders were identified by their position, such as brigade commander or platoon leader. The lack of ranks meant there was no cadre of professional NCOs, putting an added burden on the small unit commanders.[50]

The Frunze reforms produced an adequately trained force, but its strength lay in numbers in the event of a national mobilization. The Red Army in 1929 was not a highly trained regular army like those in Japan, the United Kingdom, or the United States, but its active-territorial conscript army produced a large number of military-age civilians who possessed basic military skills, allowing the RKKA to rapidly expand in time of war. Once enlisted, the Red Army subjected its soldiers to a physically demanding life, but it valued the individual soldier, sailor, and airman. Corporal punishment was banned, and illiterate peasant recruits were offered classes in reading and writing. In the Far East, the Amur River flotilla established a program to routinely recognize outstanding sailors, and there was an emphasis on rewarding leadership in combat. Respect for the achievement of soldiers served to create a pride in individual performance, and the efforts of Communist Party commanders and commissars ensured that a belief in the soldier's patriotic duty took hold. The Red Army soldiers sent to the Manchurian frontier were motivated and determined to win on the battlefield.[51]

When the possibility of going to war with China became a reality in 1929, the RKKA benefited from a strong doctrinal base. It began in 1920 with Aleksandr A. Svechin's "The Foundations of Military Doctrine," which introduced the notion of deep offensive battles, a concept that would eventually dominate Soviet military thought. It was his argument for the strategic defense as Soviet policy that had the greatest immediate impact on the Red Army. It is no exaggeration to state that the Frunze reforms built on the work of Svechin or that the works of Svechin and Frunze allowed the next generation of RKKA theorists, Sergey S. Kamenev, Vladimir K. Triandafillov, and Mikhail N. Tukhachevsky, to take the next steps forward—efforts that led directly to what came to be called operational art, arguably the most significant strategic-tactical innovation of the interwar years.[52]

Operational art constructed the missing bridge: the alignment of tactical operations with strategic objectives. The theory was groundbreaking. It demanded that strategy drive tactical actions and advocated for rapid-paced successive battles to be carried out not simply by traditional divisions or brigades but by task-organized infantry–cavalry–artillery combat groups combined with air and tank units. Although operational art was unformed at the time, the practice of combat grouping was embodied in the *1929 Regulations*. Like operational art, the 1929 manual was ahead of its time. Written under the supervision of Triandafillov and, surprisingly, by Red Army officers who were largely veterans of the Imperial Russian Army, it was not a continuation of the linear advances made since the publication of the *1925 Regulations*. It represented the cutting edge of military science in two areas: consecutive engagements and tank employment.[53]

Tactically, the ideas were advanced but not unique. Commanders were directed to plan for the sequential capture of enemy positions to neutralize individual elements of the enemy's order of battle, a concept similar to the "methodical battle" technique used by the French. At the operational level, the concepts again appeared to be nothing novel—a focus on envelopment and encirclement. The RKKA had moved beyond the basics, however. The real emphasis was placed on breakthrough and rapid pursuit through successive operations by mounted and motorized troops supported by aircraft. The goal was to penetrate deeply into the rear battle zone and annihilate the enemy before it could reorganize. This was a new approach that ran counter to the attrition-based defensive orthodoxy professed by most of the world's military establishments in the 1920s. Only Germany embraced similar concepts.[54]

Armored warfare was the second area of doctrinal innovation. The development of RKKA tank combat was dissimilar to that of any other army in that, like the use of armored cars, it was an offshoot of the armored train forces. By 1929, tanks had eclipsed both armored trains and cars. The trains were still in use, but there was only one brief paragraph dedicated to their employment, and armored cars received similar short shrift in the new regulations. Their decline was due to one factor: mobility. Trains were tied to rails and cars to roads and "unbroken fields."[55] Because of their mobility in rough terrain, tanks, on the other hand, were dealt with extensively. Given that a secret joint German–Soviet tank school only had opened at Kazan in 1924 and that the first serious RKKA focus on tanks began to emerge in 1927, the extent of their doctrinal inclusion in the *1929 Regulations* was impressive—doubly so given the frequent mechanical problems discovered during training exercises.[56]

Tanks, working with infantry and "strategic cavalry units," were deemed key to maneuver in general, and especially in meeting engagements and the all-important breakthrough attack. According to the precepts of the *1929 Regulations,* "Long Range" armored echelons were seen as able to strike "deep in the enemy's defensive zone."[57] Nonetheless, the RKKA had no real armored forces in 1929, and reality tempered theory. The role of the tank was still seen as tentative and limited. They were "help" for the infantry primarily and cavalry secondarily, at best a surrogate form of mobile artillery and not as a separate force to lead maneuvers on the battlefield.[58] Even if they penetrated the enemy's rear area, after destroying the enemy there, they were to return to the reserve and not occupy the ground or advance further.[59] Even given the constraints, to appreciate how advanced the *1929 Regulations* mechanized warfare concepts were, a decade later, in the 1939 edition of the US Army's *Tactics and Technique of Cavalry,* there was no mention of tank–cavalry cooperation, and a mere fifteen pages in an 875-page manual were devoted to the employment of armored cars. The 1929 RKKA was a world leader in mechanized warfare theory.

There had been advances made in aerial warfare as well. In 1918, a technical institute for aviation was established, along with a school to train military aviators. Cooperation with the Germans formally began on 22 July 1923 when Arkady P. Rozengolts, head of the RKKA Air Force committee, arrived in Berlin. This was followed by visits from retired colonel Hermann von der Lieth-Thomsen, the former head of the German air forces in World War I. By 1924, an aircraft experimentation and training base had been established at Lipesk, and it became a school for German as well as Russian aviators. The shared training was responsible for the similar development of doctrine used by the RKKA Air Force and later the Luftwaffe: a focus on tactical air support. The RKKA had looked at an independent bomber command. Aleksandr N. Lapchinsky published the first writings on strategic bombing in 1926 and the RKKA Air Force had experimented with the concept during the 1928 maneuvers, but Lapchinsky saw the strategic bomber as an element of a larger air force focused on support of the ground forces. There was no independent bomber force in 1929.[60]

The *1929 Regulations* gave the RKKA a significant advantage over its Chinese foes, but they were new and little time was available to implement its tenets. Collaboration with the German army, begun in earnest in 1924, had yet to bear significant fruit. It was not until late 1929 that Heinz Guderian, the leading German tank theorist, developed the concept of a combined-arms panzer division as the key tactical battle formation in future wars, but some operational art ideas were in place before the Red Army confronted the NEFDF. The unanswered questions were, would any of these forward-thinking concepts be put into practice in 1929, and would they succeed?[61]

Equipment

The weapons and equipment used by the Red Army were not that different from that used by the NEFDF. Infantrymen carried the Mosin-Nagant rifle and were supported by gunners using the Maxim machine gun. Similarly, most Soviet artillery designs dated from World War I or earlier. Unlike the NEFDF, the guns were available in quantity, and more importantly, ample ammunition allowed the RKKA to fully exploit the weapons' lethality. That underlined the material advantage of the RKKA. In November 1925, all of Russia's armaments factories were consolidated under the Military–Industrial Directorate, which answered to Dzerzhinsky, chairman of the Supreme Council of the National Economy and head of the GPU. While the NEFDF had to fend for itself, the

RKKA benefited from a unified national effort to equip and supply its troops.

In 1926, there were thirty-five arsenals and military factories to include seven plants devoted to artillery that produced close to 500 guns per year. The Red Army's 76.2mm field gun or 100mm and 107mm cannons held no advantages over their Chinese counterparts, and many of the Chinese 76.2mm guns were Russian. However, the RKKA's 122mm, 155mm, 200mm, and 203mm howitzers were superior to the few heavy guns held by the Chinese, giving the Red Army a decisive advantage. Smalls arms manufacturing also dwarfed that of China, with a quarter million rifles, 800 high-quality Maxim machine guns, and over 5,000 light machine guns manufactured annually, principally at the Izhevsk and Tula arsenals. Expansive munitions factories produced 6 million artillery shells and 100 million rounds of rifle ammunition every quarter, keeping the RKKA's magazines well stocked.[62]

There were technological advances as well. Some plants specialized in optics and medical supplies, and the presence of military research facilities spoke to resources that the NEFDF could only imagine. A month after the arsenal consolidation, during the December 1925 party congress, it became the open aim of the nation to become producer, not an importer, of arms; the start of Red Army mechanization was the most significant development. The RKKA still relied on foreign technical assistance in its modernization efforts, and in 1926, a joint German–Soviet tank warfare base was established at Kazan, where the first experimental tank unit was formed. Four years later, the Soviets adopted the American Christie tank, becoming the BT-1, which evolved into the T-34 and the British Vickers tank renamed the T-26.[63]

During this period, the first experimental armored units were formed, consisting of three tank regiments: the 1st and 3rd assigned to the Moscow Military District, and the 2nd in the Leningrad District. They were composed of heavy and light tank companies, and the mainstay was the MS-1 tank—the first manufactured in Russia—which entered service on 6 June 1927. The MS-1, an improved World War I French FT-17, was later redesignated as the T-18. The tank was armed with a longer-barreled 37mm main gun along with a machine gun and possessed greater speed (22 kilometers per hour) and maneuverability than its French predecessor. Production was just coming online when the CER crisis arose, with forty-eight MS-1s leaving the assembly line during 1928–1929 and another 100 scheduled for delivery in 1929–

1930. The MS-1s were augmented by English-made Carden-Lloyd tankettes (T-27), along with obsolete British Mark V heavy and Mark A Whippet medium tanks that had served in the tsarist army. Despite these advances, the numbers available were small, and the Red Army remained a "foot and hoof" army in 1929.[64]

Even better progress had been made in aeronautics. Advances began with the creation of the technical institute, and in 1929, it came under the direction of renowned engineer Nikolai Tupolev, who had designed the twin-engine TB-1 heavy bomber. The air force had started to rely on Soviet-built equipment. The workhorse was the Polikarpov R-1, a model based on the British de Havilland DH.9 bomber. It was used in the reconnaissance, bomber, and seaplane squadrons. Foreign-produced aircraft were nonetheless still common; in addition to R-1s, the RKKA was armed with late-model British Martinsyde F.4 and Dutch Fokker D.XI fighters.[65]

The Soviets had a clear advantage in arms and munitions manufacturing, including small arms, artillery, tanks, and aircraft; further, they had not been hobbled by an international arms embargo like the NEFDF, and they had ready access to the latest technological developments, especially those from Germany. Despite its reliance on stocks of World War I–era weapons, the RKKA was transitioning into a modern military that was better armed and supplied than its Chinese opponent.

Size and Organization

With an active force of some 560,000 soldiers in 1929, the RKKA was the world's second largest military—only China had more men under arms—and was composed of seventy-seven rifle and eleven cavalry divisions. It was a mixed army in that only twenty-eight of the rifle and nine of the cavalry divisions were active while the rest were territorial. Unit structures were in transition: the two-division corps remained in the 1914 tradition, while the triangular three–rifle regiment division reflected a new, dynamic formation. The rifle division was the key fighting organization in the Red Army. An active-duty division held 2,400 regulars with a wartime strength of approximately 13,000 soldiers, while most territorial divisions (with the same wartime strength) contained a mere 604 to 622 active-duty personnel, and the cadre territorial divisions had only 190 active-duty soldiers assigned.[66]

All the remaining soldiers were territorials, and only a fraction of these forces were located in Northeastern Asia. The border with Manchuria spanned two Red Army military districts, the Pacific and Trans-Baikal, containing approximately 34,000 troops. Military districts had a dual purpose; in peacetime they were administrative and training organizations, and in wartime they served as front commands. The major Pacific formation was the 19th Rifle Corps, and the Trans-Baikal District held the 18th Rifle Corps. Both were first-line active-duty units and had a history of success in the Far East. The 19th Corps contained the 1st "Pacific" and 2nd "Amur" Rifle Divisions, the 9th Cavalry Brigade, and support troops. The 1st Division had been formed as part of the FER's People's Revolutionary Army on 18 April 1920, and the 2nd Division was created not long after. Both were incorporated into the Red Army with the dissolution of the Far Eastern Republic in 1922.[67]

The 18th Corps contained the 35th and 36th Rifle divisions and the 5th Cavalry Brigade. The divisions contained formations that had distinguished themselves earlier; the 35th Division included the 104th Rifle Regiment, which had crushed the Mad Baron's army at the battle of Lake Gusinoe in July 1921, while the 36th Division held the 106th Rifle Regiment, which had blunted Ungern's attempt to capture Kyakhta earlier that same year. In Siberia, the 12th Territorial Rifle Corps at Irkutsk (26th Territorial Rifle Division) and the 21st Territorial Rifle Corps, headquartered at Novsibirsk (12th and 21st Territorial Rifle divisions), stood by in reserve. Finally, armored trains had not been forgotten: the 9th Armored Train Division was formed in the Far East in 1925.[68]

Lagging behind the more conventional military branches, the RKKA Air Force Directorate had only been established in 1926 and was undergoing a period of rapid growth from a low of under 300 aircraft in 1924 to just under 800 by 1927, with a goal of 1,200 by 1929. The Far East was a neglected area. The 18th Corps possessed two twelve-plane squadrons with 300 personnel, and the 19th Corps contained two understrength squadrons of four planes, each with 100 personnel assigned. The most versatile Red Army force was the sea–air–land Amur River Flotilla, built around monitor, gunboat, and fast patrol boat divisions, a minelayer and minesweeper group, the 68th Seaplane Squadron, and the 2nd Battalion, 4th Rifle Regiment, which had been training with the flotilla for three years and whose members were experts in riverine operations. With a combined strength of approximately 130 officers and 800 sailors and soldiers, the Amur River flotilla was arguably the most potent riverine force in the world. While the Russian gunboats were similar to those seen elsewhere on China's major rivers, the four-ship monitor division, whose heritage dated to the *Monitor* of the American Civil War, was unprecedented.[69]

Gutted during the Russian civil war, the four river monitors were rebuilt, modernized, and given revolutionary names. The *Storm* reentered service as the *Lenin*, the *Blizzard* became the *Sverdlov*, and the *Squall* was recommissioned as the *Liebnecht*, in honor of the German communist leader martyred in 1919, before being changed to the *Sun Yat-sen* in 1925. Similarly, the *Hurricane* first became the *Trotsky* until his fall from grace, when it became the *Red East*. Like all monitors, a shallow draft, flat decks, minimal superstructure, and gun turrets characterized the warships. Of the other three monitors returned by the Japanese in 1921, the *Whirlwind* was in such poor condition that it was converted into the seaplane tender *Amur* to support the 68th Squadron, and the *Tornado* and *Typhoon* did not return to service until 1932. The four-ship gunboat and three-vessel fast patrol boat divisions were comparable to their Chinese counterparts in the Sungari River Flotilla, while the minesweeper group and minelayer *Strong* gave the Soviets the ability to open or close Manchurian river ways at will.[70]

All of the RKKA units in the Far East were under strength, and a mobilization order from Moscow would be necessary if they were to assume a wartime posture. Beyond the 68th Squadron, only a handful of aircraft were assigned to the region—and no tanks, another glaring weakness. There was, however, one last group of forces that could augment the Red Army along the Manchuria frontier: the GPU border guard regiments and brigades. These units served as both a police force and military formations capable of conducting combat operations, although they lacked the heavy artillery, aircraft, and tank units found in the RKKA. As a rule, the GPU worked independently of the RKKA, and joint military operations required "military political conferences," a friction point with the Red Army, which preferred to directly control the GPU regiments in the event of war.[71]

Conclusions

The Red Army acknowledged the abilities of the Chinese army. In 1917, they parleyed as equals on the Manchurian frontier to keep the peace. In 1920, one of the reasons for the creation of the FER was to avoid a military conflict with the Chinese, and in 1924, the CMNA concluded that a war with China had to be avoided at all cost. By 1929, the Red Army opinion had changed; the reasons were twofold. First, beginning in 1925, the huge untrained militia of the civil war had been replaced with a more compact and better-equipped professional army. Second, the experience of Red Army officers in China during the Northern Expedition gave the Soviets valuable insights into the strengths and weaknesses of the Chinese forces. The RKKA also had the opportunity to closely study the NEFDF when Colonel Grinevsky and Lieutenant Colonel Garutsos filmed a documentary movie on Chang Tso-lin's Eastern Army during the 1925 fighting for Tientsin. Having evolved into a potent military force that understood the enemy, the Red Army was ready to confront the Young Marshal's army on the battlefield.[72]

7 | The CER Incident and War

On the evening of Tuesday, 9 July 1929, L. H. Lamb, the British consul in Harbin, sent a transmission to Peiping noting that the Harbin Special District authorities were apparently preparing for trouble with the Soviets over the CER. At 7:00 A.M. on the following day, in a manner that was as swift as it was comprehensive, two parties of senior Chinese officers arrived by motorcar at the Pristan and Harbin telegraph stations with orders to take over the operations, although the Soviet managers and employees were allowed to retain their positions. Simultaneously, other Chinese officers occupied the telegraph stations along the railway and General Shen Chia-chen, head of the Harbin telephone system, arrived at the CER central telegraph office to oversee the coup.[1]

With communications in their hands, General Fan Chi-kuang arrived at the imposing CER administration building, assumed control of the railroad, and "temporarily" appointed Chinese managers to a number of key CER departments while placing Emshanov and Eismont under guard. Fan was an ideal choice, having been educated in Russia and fluent in the language. To make the Chinese position clear, a Sungari River flotilla gunboat had taken up a position across from the CER's Pristan workshops to prevent violence there while the Harbin police moved to shut down all Soviet offices and commercial activities.[2]

Railway *tupan* Lu then arrived at the administration building and handed the Soviet railway directors a note predated to 6 July containing four demands: abolition of the Soviet CER unions, an end of propaganda work in the CER Zone, Soviet payment in silver to make good the worthless 1918 Bolshevik paper script given to the CER, and the transfer of diplomatic authority from the CER control department to the board of directors. This last demand was intended to place the CER's international border crossings and customs more fully under Nanking's control. The propaganda issue was not a minor complaint. Mukden later identified four areas of abuse: using CER commercial agencies to disseminate propaganda, using Soviet department heads to advance communism, misdirecting railway funds to Soviet-controlled CER organizations, and subsidizing pro-Soviet newspapers with CER funds. Lu's note required a response by 20 July.[3]

That afternoon, the Young Marshal, under heavy guard, departed Peiping for the seaside resort of Peitaiho as a second wave of arrests was underway in Harbin. Soon the number detained rose to over 100, while the first trainload of expelled Russians left for the Soviet frontier that evening. Lu then issued a second list of demands to Emshanov, announcing that orders from the general manager were unenforceable unless countersigned by the Chinese assistant general manager and the appointment of Chinese as the heads of five departments then led by Soviet managers. When Emshanov refused, Lu suspended him from office on 11 July. The long-simmering dispute over the CER had reached the boiling point.[4]

In the following days, the Chinese continued to roll up Soviet operations in Manchuria; the CER land department and Dalbank were closed, although the bank managed to transfer its funds to New York before the Chinese arrived. The July seizures made clear the extent of Soviet agencies beyond the CER. The properties of the Soviet textile syndicate, mercantile fleet, and naphtha syndicate were seized, while Chinese authorities moved against the Dalastorg (Far Eastern State Trading Organization), Trogpredstvo (Soviet Trade Commission), Soviet-controlled newspapers, cooperatives, and trade unions to include Dorkom (the Soviet Railway Workers Committee). As American consul George C. Hanson noted, the operation had to have been thoroughly planned in advance. Surprisingly, both sides showed restraint and no blood was spilled.[5]

The cause of Soviet restraint was tied in part to the severing of the telegraph lines; Moscow was unable to get accurate information on what was happening and slow to understand the scope of events. Its first response was to treat the incident like the others before it. An offer to send a midlevel railway expert to discuss any problems was put forward on Thursday, the day Emshanov was sacked, but soon the expelled Soviets arrived in Russia and were able to describe the situation in Harbin and along the CER. Once Moscow realized the gravity of the situation, it reacted swiftly: on 13 July, an ultimatum, under the name of Karakhan, now the deputy people's commissar for foreign affairs, was issued, with three demands: a call for an immediate conference to resolve the dispute, a return to the status quo ante on the CER, and the immediate release of Soviet citizens.[6]

The foreign affairs commissariat was under unsteady leadership, as Chicherin was seriously ill. Stalin filled the gap by taking the dominant role in directing the action. He teamed Karakhan with the capable Litvinov to manage the day-to-day diplomatic efforts to resolve the crisis. Vyacheslav Molotov, one of Stalin's most trusted underlings, would assist. Stalin was intent on following an integrated political-military strategy to enforce the ultimatum, and an order to mobilize Red Army Far East forces soon followed. Both military districts responded with the 19th Rifle Corps in the Pacific and the 18th Rifle Corps in Trans-Baikal, calling up reserves and preparing for movement to the frontier. At the same time, the Amur River flotilla prepared for combat operations, while in Siberia the mobilization of the 12th and 21st Territorial Rifle corps also got underway.

That Friday, the Soviet military attaché in Tokyo let it be known that Russia was prepared to use force to take back the CER, and three days later, on 16 July, passengers arriving in Harbin reported Soviet troops mobilizing at Chita and Irkutsk. The Soviets had no fear of fighting a ground war on the Asia mainland. The 18th Corps was ordered to the Western Front facing Manchouli and Dalainor, and soon trains were arriving at the rate of six or seven a day at Siding No. 86, near the Chinese border. Within a week, the 35th Division had arrived, to be followed by the remainder of the 18th Corps, while the 19th Corps deployed to the Eastern Front. The press reported that N. V. Kuibyshev, head of the Siberian Military District, had arrived in Blagoveshchensk to take command of the forces there.[7]

To fill the ranks, reservists in the Far East born in the years 1902–1904 were called to service. They would join the regulars—the 1929 draftees who had reported for initial training in June and the older territorial soldiers who had been awaiting their discharge. The orders meant that every able draftee who had previously entered the Red Army in the Far East (ranging in age from twenty-one to twenty-seven) was soon on active duty. Beyond going after former soldiers from the civil war era, a more complete mobilization of the local RKKA was not possible. To free up Red Army forces for frontline duty, worker militias were formed for the protection of internal order throughout the border zone and rear areas. IJA military observers compared the speed and efficiency of the Russian mobilization with that of August 1914 in Europe. Major Kanda Masatane, one of the observers, noted it took only two days of around-the-clock work to stand up both the 35th Division and 9th Calvary Brigade; the brigade's lead elements had arrived on the Eastern Front by 16 July.[8]

The war zone was overwhelmingly vast at first glance. The Russian–Manchurian border was approximately 3,000 kilometers long, and all but 560 kilometers followed the trace of three rivers: the Ussuri, Amur, and Argun.[9] The potential areas of conflict were divided along three fronts: Northern, Western, and Eastern. The Northern Front was the longest and ran along the Amur for approximately 1,300 kilometers, but geography limited the fighting, as only one fourth of that length was suitable for combat operations. The westernmost 600 kilometers abutted the Greater Khingan Mountain range, covered with birch and pine forests and unfit for warfare. To the east, along the river region extending from Blagoveshchensk to Khabarovsk (also called the Hsinganling region), the mountain ridges of the Lesser Khingan range lined both banks prohibiting military maneuvers for another stretch of 400 kilometers. That left the 300-kilometer stretch of the river centered on the opposing towns of Teheiho and Blagoveshchensk, the scene of the 1900 massacre. The Soviets held a logistical advantage: while Blagoveshchensk was linked to the strategic Trans-Siberian Railroad, Teheiho relied on the Amur River. Without the Amur, Teheiho's link to the rest of Manchuria depended on trails that could accommodate vehicles during the winter, but during the rest of the year, they were only open to pack animals. This was combined with limited navigation along the Nonni River after the spring thaw freed the mountain streams.[10]

The Western Front covered some 25,000 square kilometers (Map 2). It stretched along the border for eighty kilometers, near the towns of Abagaitevskya on the Russian side and Manchouli–Dalainor on the Chinese side, then extended across open grasslands and marshlands into Manchuria as far as Hailar, located at the foothills of the Greater Khingan Mountains, 160 kilometers to the east. Manchouli was located in a basin surrounded by rolling hills, while the area around Dalainor, located about twenty kilometers farther down the railway, was interspersed with marshes that covered the region from Lake Dalai, located fifteen kilometers southwest of the town, to the headwaters of the Argun at the border ten kilometers to the northeast. The dominant piece of terrain was a triangular hill, perhaps a thousand meters in length on each side, identified as Hill 1005. Part of a range of small hills, it was located about seven kilometers south of Manchouli, nine kilometers southwest of the CER, and eighteen kilometers west of Dalainor. To the

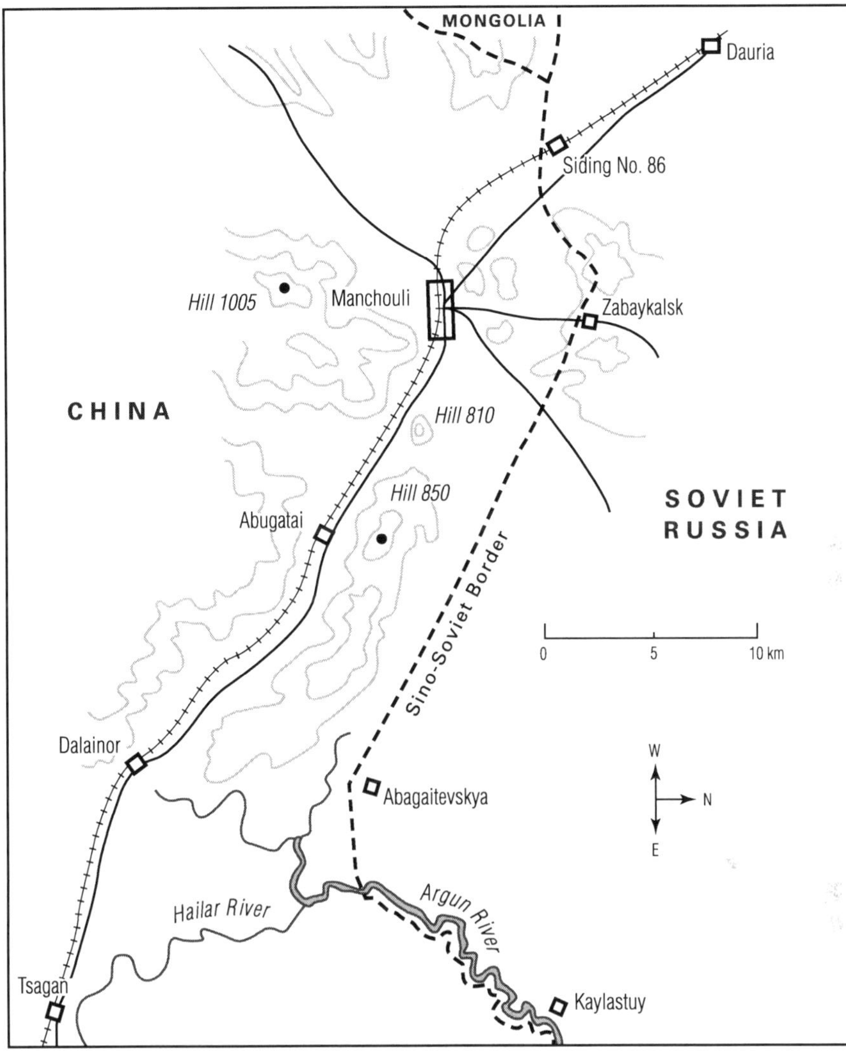

Map 2. Manchouli-Dalainor Battleground

northeast of the towns, both Chinese and Russian soldiers also patrolled a 100-kilometer stretch of border along the shallow and easily forded Argun River, the scene of the 1928 Buryat anticollectivization exodus. On the opposite riverbank, Soviet agricultural communities dotted the border.[11] There the towns of Borzhya and Dauria sat adjacent to the Trans-Baikal branch of the TSRR, which joined the CER at the frontier. Sino-Russian relations among the local people were open and amicable. When the 108th Rifle Regiment of the 35th Division arrived at Borzhya after mobilization, the soldiers found the city densely packed and were shocked to see that almost all the shops and restaurants were operated by Chinese who, although wary of the soldiers, were well treated by the Russians and remained with their businesses after the crisis erupted.[12]

The Eastern Front ran along the Amur's easternmost 230 kilometers until it met the Ussuri River. It then extended south along the Ussuri River to its source at Lake Khanka, and from there, it followed forested hill country until meeting the Korean border. It was in this region that the CER reentered the Soviet Union near Suifenho. On the Soviet side, the wheat fields that dominated the region were intruded upon by the installation of Red Army border watchtowers, searchlights, and trenches. Emplaced to improve observation, the watchtowers and searchlights proved to be of no real military value because the hills and forests on the Chinese side restricted visibility and movement, making the area less than ideal for offensive operations. The Chinese border town of Tungning, forty kilometers to the south, was the only other significant border settlement (Map 3).[13]

To the north were two additional areas of military interest. The first was the town of Mishan located near the Muleng coalfields, about 140 kilometers to the northeast of Suifenho, and the second was the Sungari River, which led from the confluence with the Amur at the port of Tungchiang upriver 500 kilometers to Harbin and the CER headquarters. Off limits on the Eastern Front was the Chiantao (Kando) region, which ran along the Tumen and northern headwaters of the Yalu rivers. Populated by some 400,000 ethnic Koreans, compared to just over 100,000 Chinese inhabitants, it was under the protection of Japan, a foe neither side could afford to antagonize. With the exception of Chiantao, these fronts became the flash points between China and the Soviet Union in the following weeks and months.[14]

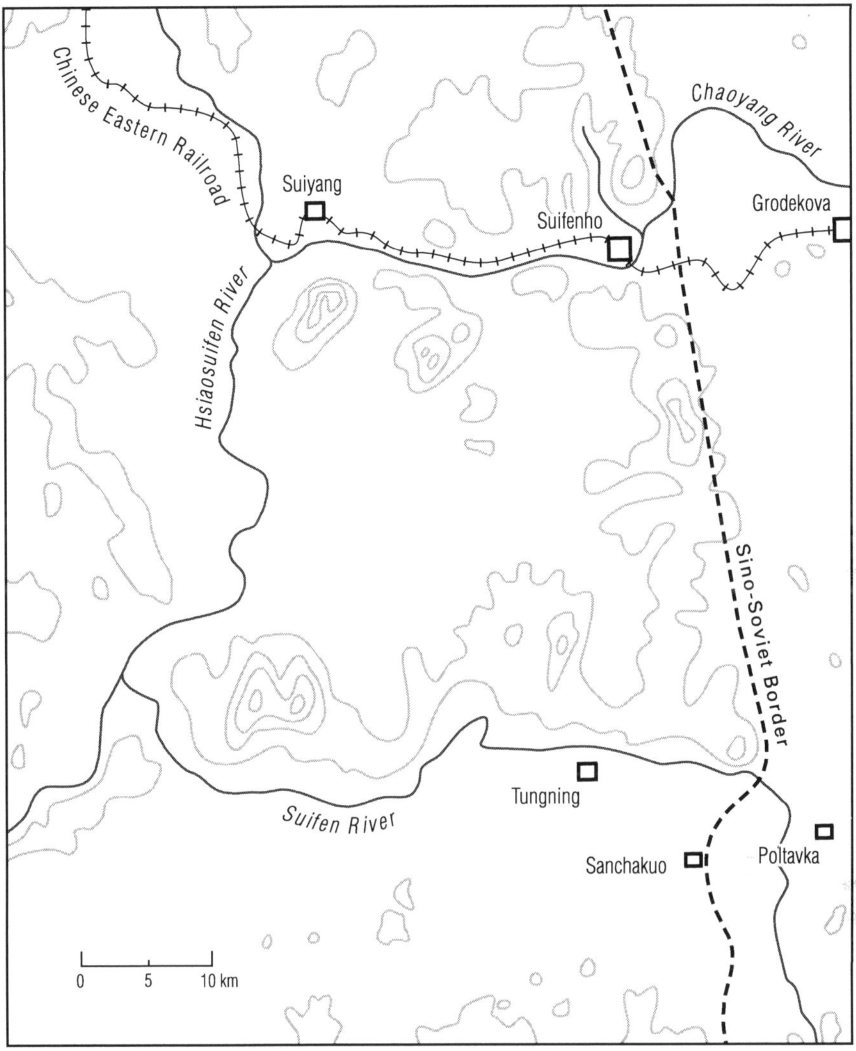

Map 3. Suifenho-Tungning Battleground

Military Posturing and Propaganda

The positions taken by China and the Soviet Union appeared far apart in the immediate aftermath of the CER seizure and the subsequent ultimatum by the Kremlin. The propaganda campaigns were in full swing, and it had not been without reason that Dr. C. Guangson Young, assistant director of KMT intelligence and propaganda, had accompanied Foreign Minister Wang to Peking on 8 July to join Chiang Kai-shek and the Young Marshal for the finalization of the plans for the seizure of the CER. Chiang Kai-shek, addressing the cadets at the Nanking military academy on 15 July, stated provocatively that the seizure was just the "first phase," that China was going to "go farther," and that "the imperialist Powers are greatly alarmed." He closed by arguing, "As long as we Chinese are united ourselves, we need not fear from any oppression."[15] The Russians were in an equally bellicose mood. On the same day as Chiang's speech, the Soviet propaganda effort picked up steam when a Moscow crowd of thousands marched through the streets with banners proclaiming heated if lengthy slogans such as, "We demand that our government take decisive measures against that rusty old Chinese counterrevolution" and "We don't want war but are willing to leave our machines and take up arms in defense of the proletariat fatherland." Newspapers printed cartoons ridiculing Chinese leaders.[16]

The Kremlin decided to follow up its rhetoric with action. On July 17, the border was closed, CER trains and railcars on Soviet lines were seized, and the Red Army made the first show of military force. As a sign of Moscow's concern, General Budyonny arrived to review the military preparations. Russian military aircraft flew over Suifenho; four warships of the Amur River flotilla, with seaplanes circling overhead, took up positions at the mouth of the Sungari River near Tungchiang and evacuated the town's Soviet customs officials. The Amur and Ussuri rivers were closed and a number of islands occupied by GPU border guards. On the Northern Front, Soviet forces at Blagoveshchensk established sentry posts for several miles on either of the town, set up searchlights, prepared firing positions for at least ten artillery pieces, and a few days later conducted a live-fire drill with the guns as a show of strength.[17]

In response, the Chinese forces across the river at Teheiho assembled a brass band to try to drown out the noise of the Russian artillery while provincial reinforcements were dispatched from Tsitsihar. Ignoring the RKKA military demonstrations on the frontier and hardening their diplomatic position, Nanking responded to the Kremlin's ultimatum by demanding the release of Chinese citizens recently arrested by the GPU before it would enter negotiations. The nationalists blamed Moscow for the crisis, stating the Russians both violated the prohibition against propaganda in Article 6 of the 1924 Peking agreement and attempted to undermine the authority of the Chinese government. The Soviets were having none of it and severed diplomatic relations on 18 July.[18]

In Mukden, the Young Marshal established a supreme headquarters, opted to militarize the border, and proved equally adept at the rail movement of troops to the frontier. The decision was made to hold fast on the borders at each end of the CER. Soon a continuous stream of fifty-car troop trains moved across the CER lines, each car carrying either thirty soldiers or ten Mongol horses—a Chinese version of the French World War I *quarante-et-huit* train cars. On 18 July, 2,000 troops from the 21st Kirin Mixed Brigade were transported to the Eastern Front near Suifenho to reinforce the 200 border guards stationed there, and the combined force was soon placed under the command of General Ting Chao. Heilungkiang forces were also on the move; 20,000 troops began arriving at the Western Front under the command of General Liang Chung-chia. Liang directed that the 17th Mixed Brigade commanded by General Han Kuang-ti remain at Hailar while he advanced on Manchouli with the 15th Mixed Brigade.[19]

After assessing the border situation, Liang divided the 15th Brigade. The headquarters was established in railcars at Manchouli, the expected objective of any Soviet attack, with the 43rd and 51st Infantry regiments occupying defensive positions astride the CER and on the commanding high ground between the city and the Russian frontier, while the 38th Infantry Regiment was tasked with defending the smaller town of Dalainor to the southeast. General Liang was one of the new breed of professional Chinese officers; he believed in leading from the front and relied on his chief of staff, Colonel Wei Chang-lin, to oversee the day-to-day operations of the brigade as he directed the defense on the Western Front. Wei was a good example of a career NEFDF officer and was well prepared for his assignment. Aged forty-eight, he was an experienced officer, having served in the earlier Fengtien–Chihli wars as well as graduating from the second class of the Paoting military academy in 1915. The Chinese forces were ably led.

Reacting to the NEFDF military buildup, the Kremlin decided to increase the political pressure inside China and ordered the Comintern to issue an appeal to the CCP on 19 July to support Soviet Russian efforts to recover the CER. The CCP dutifully complied five days later. It was tapping a weak resource. On the plus side for Moscow, the CCP under the leadership of Soviet-trained labor organizer Li Li-san was witnessing a period when the influence of the Soviet Union was at its zenith; on the negative side, however, the party's fortunes were near their nadir. Ever since the crushing and fragmenting of the CCP in 1927, the party had been on the defensive. The KMT–CCP alliance had ended disastrously, while the formation of an authentic Chinese communist movement under the leadership of Mao Tse-tung had yet to be realized. In 1929, only a glimpse of the future had begun to emerge in the Chingkang Mountains as Mao forged the 4th Red Army into an effective political-military force. In the Northeast, the CCP situation was desperate.[20]

Adding to the internal difficulties was the poor relationship between Soviet authorities and CCP cadres in the Northeast, which went back several years. Early on, local Chinese communists saw the CER as fertile recruiting grounds. The key labor issue was the two-tiered pay scale, where Soviet Russians were paid more than their Chinese counterparts for the same work. The Soviets quickly quashed CCP attempts to organize the Chinese CER workers for an equal pay strike in late 1927.[21] In another incident, a low-ranking Russian comrade was able to veto the appointment of the union leader of the Chinese CER workers as the head of the CCP's Harbin committee. The union leader left the party in frustration, and CCP activities among the Chinese railway workers fell dormant.[22]

Despite these obstacles, the CCP's Northeastern committee under Chairman Chen Wei-jen had been able to open up five active cells in Dairen, Mukden, Changchun, Kirin, and Harbin. Most were short lived. In the wake of the national repression that began after the April 1927 purge, the police were able to wipe out the cells in Changchun, Kirin, and Dairen, while the Mukden cell lost two-thirds of its members, falling to about 30 comrades; a similarly small number survived in Harbin from a high of 130 activists. By 1928, virtually any CCP agitation or propaganda effort in the Kwantung Leasehold became almost suicidal. The issuance of a May Day declaration resulted in the annihilation of party organs by Japanese authorities within a few weeks. While the CCP in the rest of China had been able to slowly rebuild its strength, the Manchurian branch had been crushed anew by police raids in 1929, while the local party cells were in poor communication and occasionally at odds with the Central Committee, which demanded a focus on industrial centers like Dairen and Harbin.[23]

Into this cauldron arrived Liu Shao-chi in June 1929 to lead the party forward. However, it proved impossible to make meaningful headway against the entrenched Mukden regime. All that could be done in the short term was a 1 August announcement by the Manchurian executive committee declaring against war and for the overthrow of the KMT. Repeated directives from the CCP Central Committee to engage students, workers, and even the business community could not overcome the predictable patriotism of the Chinese in Manchuria who supported the recovery of the CER. Even though Liu personally took charge of the propaganda operations, the efforts failed.[24]

Outside the Northeast, the CCP fought back with more vigor. In Shanghai, the communists scored the first blow on 14 July with a pro-Soviet protest combined with the distribution of anti-Nanking posters across the city, which carried messages such as, "Let us ally ourselves with the World's Proletariat and Soviet Russia." Two days later, wall writings demanded the overthrow of the KMT and encouraged a 1 August protest, the anniversary of the 1927 Nanchang uprising. The KMT countered on 19 July with a manifesto issued by pro-Nanking students praising the "absolute control by China" of the CER. On 22 and 24 July, the propaganda department of the KMT's First District met to organize an anti-Soviet campaign. These efforts led to almost daily anti-Soviet rallies opposing "the imperialist aggression of Soviet Russia" with slogans declaring, "Down with Soviet Russia! Long Live the Chinese Revolution!" One KMT rally held at the Shanghai public recreation grounds drew a crowd of 10,000, of which 10 percent were said to be female students and workers. Not to sit by idly, the CCP distributed handbills condemning "imperialist aggression against Soviet Russia" and bearing the slogan, "Restore the friendship between China and Soviet Russia." A CCP cartoon posted on Shanghai's Bubbling Spring Well Temple depicted Chinese soldiers led by a KMT officer being ridden by a Japanese women marching on the CER. The caption had the woman saying, "My boy, have courage to proceed with your Chinese railway case. I am back of you."[25]

While the KMT–CCP propaganda war raged, the Young Marshal had returned to Mukden on 21 July to command the CER operation. The first armed clash occurred that day on the Eastern Front when Red Army troops crossed the border near Suifenho. More incidents were reported to the north, near Turi Rog by Lake Khanka. Liang's troops began digging trenches on the Western Front, while Soviet warships seized Chinese vessels on the Amur, Sungari, and Ussuri rivers. This caused a small international row when the family of an American diplomat stationed at Teheiho, Roy Talbot, was detained after GPU officers boarded the Chinese steamer *Ilan*. The Americans were well treated and released, but the fate of the White Russians and Chinese nationals was not as pleasant; detained White Russian ship's officers were summarily executed. Within a few weeks, over 1,100 Chinese sailors and passengers in the Amur region were arrested and interned by the secret police, and the seized ships were converted into military transports. The term "White Russian" had lost its meaning by this time. It no longer just applied to the supporters of the White movement or even the opponents of the Soviet regime but to all ethnic Russians in China who were not Bolshevik adherents. In the wake of the seizures and arrests, Mukden responded by issuing public protests and halting Chinese ships from sailing on the Amur and Ussuri rivers while laying electric contact mines to seal off the Sungari from Russian warships.[26]

Red Army forces continued to make their presence known. By the close of July, there were numerous reports coming from the Eastern Front, including that of a Soviet aircraft overflying Taichungkiang and that of a company of infantry digging in near Tungning while a formation of over twenty aircraft was spotted over its skies. The planes traveled on to Santaotungtze for a further demonstration of RKKA might. In a larger show of force, 1,000 troops prepared ten kilometers of trenches near Tangpichien and the local inhabitants told to move away.[27]

All the while, Nanking and the international community downplayed any possibility of Soviet military action. Diplomats in Moscow were convinced that war was unlikely.[28] The Japanese foreign ministry "did not for a moment" believe that things would end in war.[29] Even the military experts ruled it out; the British War Office Far East intelligence chief stated that the crisis would be resolved by "diplomatic negotiations without resort to war," and Colonel Archen, the French military attaché at Riga, added, "We all know, of course, that Russia is unable to wage war." At the time, Riga served as a listening post for the Americans and other nations that did not have diplomatic relations with Russia.[30] The spokesman for the Japanese army general staff in Tokyo downplayed the possibility of a shooting war, although one Japanese general, Tatekawa Yoshistugu, soberly told Major Magruder in Peiping that if war occurred, then "two good divisions could go anywhere in Manchuria."[31]

That Stalin meant business was seen in the ultimatum, in the mobilization, in the Tokyo attaché's comments, and in the supporting public and diplomatic messages emanating from Moscow. If further proof was needed, Stalin's reaction to antiwar comments by Politburo members on 17 July left no doubt. Aleksandr P. Smirnov, a ranking agricultural commissar, "expressed hope for peace, because the grain-stocking campaign would be upset," and fellow Politburo members Sofia Smidovitch and Nikolai Brukhanov agreed.[32] Stalin did receive some good news: on the same day, *New York Times* correspondent Walter Duranty favorably reported from Moscow that "no single Russian soldier will step foot on Chinese territory," but the Politburo utterances were opposed to policies strongly backed by Stalin.[33] Smirnov's remarks were especially stinging; Stalin had been one of the chief proponents of the agricultural price-control regime that had led to widespread grain shortfalls in 1928, and the 1929 harvest was even worse.[34] This raised the need to buy grain abroad, but the Kremlin lacked the necessary foreign currency reserves. On 19 July, *Pravda* announced that there would be no foreign grain purchases for the rest of the year. There would be shortages, but for Stalin, the issue was closed. The last thing he wanted was the Politburo discussing a grain-stocking problem as he was implementing a more radical and disruptive plan for farm collectivization.[35]

Of more immediate concern, the peace remark flew in the face of his political-military strategy to compel the Chinese to accept the CER ultimatum. For Stalin, the stale pre–World War I communist view of pacifism had been put to rest when Lenin had adopted the objective of an armed world revolution. Stalin saw the use of force to resolve the CER crisis as an application of his concept of a Red Army created to protect socialism in one country—in this case, the protection of Soviet CER rights. Stalin expressed immediate displeasure with the mutterings of Smirnov and the others; there were even rumors that the speakers were to be expelled from the Politburo, and as a result, no dissenting voice was heard again. For Nanking and Mukden, things had also not developed exactly as planned. The Russians had not stood idly by, as they had during the previous seizures of CER assets, when notes of protest were the strongest measures taken. More distressingly, the Chinese were surprised by the international support for the Soviets over the charges that China had wrongly violated the 1924 agreements.[36]

The British War Office in London let it be known that it "favoured the Russian contentions."[37] The foreign office found the Chinese actions predictable, given the Soviet denial of the July 1919 Karakhan manifesto and the breach of propaganda prohibitions, but it concluded that China had violated the 1924 agreements. Tokyo's *Asahi Shimbun* had taken the Soviet Union's side early on by referring to China's actions as a "hijacking," and in Washington, Stimson informed Minister Wu that China's actions "might well be interpreted as an attack on Russia."[38] Washington had shifted completely away from its militant World War I stance when it had encouraged the seizure of the CER. It stated at the time, "China is entirely within her rights in employing troops to protect her sovereign and territorial integrity."[39] Ironically, while Moscow's position was favorably received among the so-called imperialist and anti-Bolshevik Powers, some on the European left had only condemnations. In Germany, the *Banner of Communism* ran an article that blamed the CER crisis on Soviet "encroachment on China's right of self-determination," and a piece in the French Marxist journal *Against the Current* laid the cause on "the adventurist policy of the Soviet bureaucracy."[40] Their support was of no help to Nanking.[41]

An Attempt at a Negotiated Settlement and Invoking the Kellogg–Briand Pact

To rebut the claims that China had violated either the 1924 agreements or the peace pact, the Young Marshal published a statement on Monday, 22 July, respecting the CER agreement that was also hand delivered to Soviet consul General Melnikov by Mukden commissioner for foreign affairs Tsai Yun-sheng in Harbin. Nanking moved on the next day to reassure the Powers that Russia's rights had not been abrogated. Later that Tuesday, Kirin governor-general Chang Tso-hsiang, having met with the just-returned Young Marshal, left Mukden by rail for Changchun to head up an effort to peacefully resolve the crisis, while Tsai and Melnikov departed Harbin together by motorcar for the rendezvous. The three conferred for several hours at the Changchun train station in the early morning of 24 July, and both sides agreed to contact their respective superiors to argue for a negotiated settlement.[42]

Along the fronts, hastily deployed RKKA units continued air and artillery border demonstrations. On the Amur River, an exchange of gunfire between Chinese troops and the Soviet gunboats *Buryat* and *Peasants* was reported. The Soviets also shelled the border near Manchouli, where General Liang's soldiers had impressed local civilians to dig trenches, and by the end of the day, the Manchouli station sold over 8,000 tickets as the citizens prepared to flee. Stimson was concerned enough to circulate a draft aide-mémoire to invoke the Paris Pact and proposed an "international commission of conciliation" to resolve the crisis peacefully on 25 July. What Levinson had described as "inconceivable" only a few months earlier was happening: two signatories of the 1928 Kellogg–Briand Pact were preparing to go to war.[43]

The United States, having been the driving force behind the pact, considered the CER crisis and adherence to the treaty to be inseparable issues and formulated its responses accordingly. To make matters more awkward for the Americans, President Herbert Hoover was scheduled to hold a celebratory ceremony at the White House on 24 July to declare the treaty of perpetual peace in full force. Ironically, the competing interpretations of the Kellogg–Briand Pact were used to justify the 1929 conflict. China was redressing an underlying cause for war—unequal treaties that led to continued imperialist Russian encroachment through the CER—and the Soviets were reacting to an armed Chinese seizure of their sovereign property. Under the right of self-defense, the Soviets were convinced that they were entitled to recover the railway, by force if necessary.[44]

The invocation of the peace pact was problematic from the start, and it was thus no surprise that Stimson's draft generated an intense flurry of diplomatic communiqués between the Americans, British, French, and Japanese over what to do next. While sympathetic to Washington's plan for peace, London did not want to act precipitously, preferring to proceed slowly. The French aims were twofold: support the Kellogg–Briand Pact, and do nothing that would damage the standing of France's CER bond claims against the Soviet Union. While no one was interested in signing onto a joint communiqué tying a CER settlement to honoring financial transactions, it did not harm the process. Paris was quickly in harmony with Stimson's initiative, and it was at this time that the policy of Japan's foreign ministry began to be understood.[45]

When the crisis first erupted, Japan's position was far from clear, as the Tanaka cabinet had resigned on 2 July over the army's involvement in the assassination of Chang Tso-lin and the new cabinet under Hamaguchi Osachi was trying to find its footing. Rumors regarding Japan's intentions immediately began to swirl. Hanson in Harbin speculated that "perhaps there exists some sort of understanding between Soviet and Japanese officials" supporting the Russian side—possibly based on protecting their mutual spheres of influence—while Minister MacMurray in Peiping wrote to the contrary—that the Soviet government seemed convinced that Japan was behind China's seizure of the CER.[46] Belying both assumptions, the new foreign minister, Shidehara Kijuro, one of Japan's most experienced diplomats who had previously held the post from 1924–1927, was actually reaching out to both China and Soviet Russia in an attempt to resolve the crisis.[47]

If Japan's foreign ministry was assuming the role of peacemaker and go-between, the IJA had become a faction-riven entity working at cross-purposes. In Tokyo, representatives from the War Ministry had joined an interagency committee that followed the lead of Shidehara in finding a pacific solution to the CER dispute, while in Manchuria, officers of the Kwantung Army were still planning for a war to safeguard Japan's dominance over Northeastern China. The leader of the war faction, Lieutenant Colonel Ishihara Kenji, had begun a fact-finding tour that took a select group of Japanese army officers across the Northeast. Overtly, the Ishihara group was studying how to fight Soviet Russia if they invaded Manchuria—a goal that was welcomed by the Mukden regime and led to improved relations between the NEFDF and the Kwantung Army staffs. Covertly, the Ishihara group was simultaneously refining a campaign plan for the Kwantung Army to seize large parts of Manchuria. Their plotting would have to wait, as both the army general staff and War Ministry in Tokyo were unreceptive and a negotiated Sino-Soviet settlement dominated policy discussions.[48]

Because the Soviets had already rejected separate offers of mediation from both Japan and France that week, the American draft was tabled, and the international diplomatic consensus formed around the idea that two-party talks offered the best hope for a settlement. It appeared that the diplomats had got it right as the crisis showed signs of abating. Following up on the Changchun discussions held five days earlier, the Young Marshal announced on Monday, 29 July, a willingness to release the Soviet prisoners and to negotiate a solution. The Soviets promptly agreed. Tsai met again with Melnikov that Monday in Harbin, and both agreed to open negotiations at Manchouli the following day. Tsai saw success, going so far as to make a statement to the press on 31

July that the Soviet prisoners would soon be released before the start of formal negotiations over the outstanding issues.[49]

While Mukden had acceded to all the Soviet demands in the 13 July ultimatum, they also exercised their right to declare CER manager Emshanov and his assistant, Eismont, as personae non grata in accordance with Article 1, Section 8, of the 1924 Mukden agreement. The Chinese held the two responsible for corrupting CER operations while aiding and abetting armed revolution. While Manchouli was a pleasant place to negotiate, Siding No. 86 on the Soviet side of the border was a stark piece of dirt composed of "only three railway tracks and several small wooden houses," and perhaps it was appropriate that the talks died there on 2 August. The outcome was unexpected, as the Chinese were confident that a resolution was at hand.[50]

Melnikov quickly dashed Tsai's optimism. Mukden's position regarding the CER mangers was rejected out of hand. More damaging, there were new and more punitive demands from Moscow. The Red Army was to enter Manchuria on a permanent basis in the form of a revitalized Russian rail guard, to be staffed on an equal basis with Chinese rail guards. All White Russian CER employees were to be fired, and White Russians living within 100 kilometers of the border were to be removed (especially those at the Trekreche, or the Three Rivers District, on the Western Front). Further, *tupan* Lu was to be dismissed as CER head and the telegraph department immediately returned to the control of its suspended Soviet director. Unlike the first meeting between Soviet and Chinese officials at Siding No. 86 in March 1918, when the two sides had successfully defused the fighting between White and Red forces along the border while arranging for the reopening of the CER, there was no agreement in the offing this time. The situation had shifted dramatically, and discussions were at an impasse.[51]

As soon as the talks stumbled, the alliance between Nanking and Mukden began to fray as Chiang and the Young Marshal followed paths of convergence toward rights' recovery but began to diverge in how to achieve that goal. While Chiang Kai-shek was making warlike speeches like the one at the military academy, Chang had been working behind the scenes to reach a quick settlement, even if that meant giving in to the Soviet 13 July ultimatum. Chiang remained a revolutionary at heart, as his academy speech showed, and even though he quickly backed off the more radical statements, he was never comfortable with Chang

Hsueh-liang, who was a traditionalist, even a bit of a Confucianist, and a man always willing to compromise in seeking a solution. Neither course had proven successful, as the harsh new Soviet demands caught Mukden off guard while intransience in Nanking gained nothing but mutual failure. The Kremlin took immediate steps to further divide Chiang and the Young Marshal, stating on one occasion that they would adhere to a 25 July communiqué from Nanking but not the 1 August signal from Mukden, while later entreating with Tsai at Siding No. 86 but refusing to parlay with Chu Shao-yang, Nanking's emissary and former chargé d'affaires in Moscow, who arrived on 7 August.[52]

The tactic may have worked too well and was too transparent. The French were already sharing with the international diplomatic community their presumption that the Soviets were manipulating a disagreement between Nanking and Mukden—and, as became apparent, for no gain. Shocked by the severity of the new Soviet position, the Young Marshal fell in line with Nanking's position. Soon the Soviet and Chinese delegations were not even meeting face to face, relying instead on telephone conversations. On 16 August, Tsai and Chu, who had waited in vain for over a week to resume the dialogue at Manchouli, returned to Harbin. The crisis moved toward war as the military option replaced negotiations.[53]

Initially, the RKKA's leaders had not devoted their full attention to the crisis. When it erupted, they were in the midst of correcting a shortfall in the original 1928 five-year plan. In 1928, the supreme objective had been the modernization of the Russian economy, and national defense was not addressed. To correct that omission, the RMC and CMNA worked throughout the first half of 1929 to develop a corresponding five-year plan to address the needs of the RKKA and military industries. By early summer, their work was finished, and just five days after the CER seizure, on 15 July, the Politburo passed the "State of Defense" and "On Military Industry" programs that began the militarization of Russia. The Red Army leadership began to concentrate on events in the Far East. A number of meetings addressing the Manchurian situation took place between the leaders of the army general staff and military commissariat at Moscow in late July. After one meeting at the commissariat headquarters, Triandafillov, deputy RKKA commander, invited Aleksandr I. Cherepanov, an experienced China hand and former senior Russian advisor at the Whampoa academy, to present his opinion. In addition to Triandafillov, V. N. Litunovskim, Triandafillov's chief of staff, and Yan K. Berzin, RKKA director for intelligence and a staff academy classmate of Cherepanov's, were present.[54]

Although Cherepanov was just thirty-four years old, he was a seasoned veteran. In addition to service in China with the NRA (1924–1927), and having just returned from fighting the *Basmachi Jihadi* along the Afghan border in Tajikistan, he had seen combat during World War I, the Russian civil war, and the Soviet–Polish war. When pushed by senior commanders, Cherepanov stated that the Far East forces were inadequate and needed reinforcement. This assessment aligned with Triandafillov's and the following day, another series of meetings chaired by Voroshilov took place that included a number of China-service veterans. At its conclusion, the decision to establish the Special Far East Army (ODVA) was set. During the meetings, Cherepanov also recommended his former commander in China, Vasily Blyukher, to lead the army to defeat China.[55]

Blyukher's availability proved a lucky break. His time in China had been physically demanding, and he had suffered two bouts of prolonged illness, one a flare-up of earlier war wounds. Upon his return from China, he was sent to recuperate while studying at the German general staff college, an apparent prelude to assignment as the senior military attaché in Berlin. Relations between the two countries were at a low point after the politically motivated arrest of several German engineers in Siberia. The German foreign ministry objected to Blyukher's appointment—his German name and revolutionary fame were deemed too controversial—and the nomination was quietly withdrawn. Instead of walking the halls of the palatial Soviet embassy on Unter der Linden Boulevard, a fit and rested Blyukher sat as the deputy commander of the Ukraine Military District, ready for immediate service in the Far East.[56]

His appointment as ODVA commander still faced a final hurdle: the nomination was challenged. PUR head Bubnov had also served in China and had not gotten on with Blyukher. The falling-out centered on the 1926 Northern Expedition. Blyukher had reservations, but he accepted the KMT CEC decision and worked hard on the planning. Bubnov opposed the expedition and wanted to push Soviet support toward Feng Yu-hsiang, a position that angered Chiang Kai-shek and led to his recall by Moscow. When Blyukher's name came forward, Bubnov argued for other China veterans to take the command, noting that the well-connected N. V. Kuibyshev (his brother, Valeryan, was a close confidant of Stalin's) was already in the Far East, as was A. I. Lapin. The senior

RKKA leadership disagreed, and Blyukher became the commander. A few months later, Bubnov was replaced as PUR chief.[57]

On 6 August, the order was issued. The creation of the ODVA represented three changes in policy. First, in light of the failed attempt by Melnikov to get the Chinese to unconditionally accept Soviet dictates, the order made clear that the Soviet Union was prepared to go to war to resolve the crisis. Second, ODVA leaders were to be handpicked by Moscow—some of the RKKA's best officers were sent to the Manchurian frontier—and Blyukher was not given a free hand; he would answer directly to Voroshilov, who would personally approve the army's operational orders. To free up Voroshilov, Tukhachevsky would oversee RKKA operations in Moscow for the duration of the crisis. Lapin would serve as Blyukher's deputy, and Vasily I. Chuikov—another veteran both of China and the anti-Kolchak campaign—would serve as ODVA chief of operations, while Kuibyshev remained in Blagoveshchensk. ODVA headquarters was established at Chita. Stepan S. Vostretsov replaced 19th Corps commander Graisnov on the Western Front, and the corps was redesignated the Trans-Baikal Group, while on the Eastern Front, Cherepanov would take command of the 1st Division of the 18th Corps (Pacific Group). Vostretsov had previously served under Blyukher in 1922 during the civil war, being twice awarded with the Order of the Red Banner for heroism.[58]

Third, the Far East forces were to be significantly reinforced. At the time, the strength of the 18th Corps and the 19th Corps was put at 11,900 and 18,320 combat soldiers, respectively, plus artillery, transport, supply, and other support troops. However, the 18th Corps would soon double in size, and the total forces assigned to the ODVA would grow to over 100,000 soldiers. The 12th Corps with its 26th Division went to Blagoveshchensk and arrayed along the Amur on the Northern Front, allowing the 5th Regiment stationed there to rejoin its parent unit, the 2nd Division, assembling across from the mouth of the Sungari on the Soviet side of the Amur. The 21st Corps was sent to Chita. Its 12th Rifle Division remained at the home garrison of Omsk and would not participate in the war, while the 21st "Perm" Rifle Division was reassigned to the Western Front, becoming the Trans-Baikal Group reserve. As with all the territorial units, the 21st Division and the 26th Division were manned at low levels but welcomed reinforcements.[59]

The Buryat–Mongol Territorial Cavalry Division and the 1st Tank Company, consisting of eleven MS-1 tanks, were also sent to the Western Front. The tank deployment was significant. On 17 July, Triandafillov had ordered the creation of an experimental armored unit whose mission included studying tactical tank coordination with infantry and cavalry units. The CER crisis presented an opportunity to observe that cooperation under combat conditions. The Western Front also witnessed an early attempt at mechanization, as in addition to the tank company, an armored car company was already present; twenty trucks along with three motorcars from the 1st Moscow Transport Unit were assigned to "motorize" a battalion from the 36th Division's 106th Regiment. Additional units augmented the ODVA. Three heavy artillery and two engineer battalions were added, along with a Headquarters Signals Battalion and the 4th Separate Radio Battalion.[60]

Air forces were strengthened. The five squadrons available in July, numbering under 50 aircraft, were tripled to fifteen squadrons with some 160 aircraft. The deployment was either by rail shipment, as in the case of the 2nd "Lenin" Reconnaissance Squadron, or by cross-country flight, as witnessed by the 26th Bomber Squadron, which flew 4,000 kilometers from European Russia to the Western Front. There, the 26th Squadron joined the 6th Fighter and 25th Bomber squadrons, which formed the 9th Air Group and numbered approximately forty aircraft. The 9th Air Group was combined with the 17th and 19th Fighter squadrons already present, bringing the total air forces in support of the Trans-Baikal Group to five squadrons of approximately sixty-four aircraft. The remaining squadrons were located in the east and contained about ninety-six aircraft, a few of which were sent to Blagoveshchensk to support the Northern Front. It would take until early September to complete the movement of the reinforcements to the fronts.[61]

Not directly commanded by the ODVA were at least three regiments assigned to the GPU Far East Border Guard Region under Mikhail P. Volsky, an old comrade of Blyukher's. Reinforcing Volsky, the 9th GPU Rail Guard Regiment had arrived on the Western Front, and 7,000 additional GPU troops were later sent to the Far East. Simultaneously, the Soviet-controlled Mongolian People's Republic sent two cavalry brigades of the MPRA under RKKA officers to the Mongolian frontier adjacent to the Western Front.[62]

Blyukher went to work on developing a strategy that aligned military pressure with diplomatic efforts to force the Chinese into accepting Soviet demands. The proposed campaign plan was to be carried out in three sequential phases: (1) deployment of the ODVA, with small-scale border raids, and sabotage; followed by (2) larger and deeper raids on the fronts; and culminating in (3) a simultaneous offensive on the Eastern and Western fronts. The key military objectives were linked to the CER Zone as it stood at the time of the 1924 agreements: rail facilities or centers (Suifenho, Manchouli, and Hailar); coal-mining regions that supported CER operations (Dalainor and Mishan); and the Sungari River, where the CER shipping line had operated before the crisis.[63]

While Blyukher planned and Moscow formed the largest field army since the civil war, RKKA units already on the frontier stepped up their activities. The first real test of the modern Red Army was about to commence, but a series of unconventional attacks preceded the conventional military thrusts. Four days after the failure of negotiations at Siding No. 86, the CER became the object of a sabotage campaign orchestrated by the GPU and carried out by secret organizations set up by Soviet CER union leaders. The first attacks erupted during the hours of darkness on 6 August when the Hsienliho rail bridge (40 kilometers west of Suifenho) was bombed. It was an inauspicious beginning, as it caused no real damage. Raids in Harbin yielded better results; rails were removed along a stretch of line that traversed Old Harbin, in Pristan; telephone lines were cut; and the roundhouse at the main rail yards was damaged. On the following evening, the CER locomotive repair shop at Machiho (near the Harbin racetrack) was sabotaged, several trains were damaged, and the shop was out of service for several weeks. A day later, rails were again removed from the tracks about ten kilometers outside Harbin.[64]

Over the next two nights, the raids expanded along the line. At the Manchouli rail yard, two tons of hemp were set ablaze; at Dalainor, there was a failed attempt to flood the coal mines; and telegraph lines were downed at Poketu. Rails were removed at three sites: near the Sungari River bridge, in Old Harbin, and outside Ashibo station forty kilometers east of Harbin. The last act of sabotage resulted in the derailment of a twenty-three-car train that temporarily shut down the line. On 9 August, a police patrol outside Harbin found and defused a dynamite charge placed under the tracks, and the first civilian fatality occurred during another derailment along a spur line serving the Mishan coalfields. Death was no deterrent. On 10 August, police uncovered what was reported to be a saboteur's headquarters in Harbin, which prevented imminent attacks on the CER Sungari River bridge and the Pristan shipyard. While no one was captured, the police confiscated eleven guns and many improvised explosive devices.[65]

Soon Chinese CER train crews were demanding that armed guards be posted and that the Harbin police arrest Pumpiansky, head of propaganda under Melnikov, whom they blamed for inciting sabotage attacks. The authorities were quick to react, and on 10 August, martial law was declared throughout the CER Zone. Tensions were high and tempers short. Fifteen hundred additional police were added to the trains, and foot patrols along the rails began; the increased surveillance caught unawares two Americans crossing a New Town bridge over the CER late in the evening. They were badly beaten before convincing the police they were not Russians. The efforts to ferret out real saboteurs became a nasty business. A former communist helping the police identify suspects was gunned down on a Pristan street on 14 August, and the next day, an ethnic Russian Harbin police officer was shot in the back of the head. The assassin fled in a waiting automobile. The Harbin police announced that in the future, Soviets arrested would be imprisoned, not deported.[66]

The sabotage attacks were coordinated with strikes and work stoppages. The first work stoppage occurred at Changchun in 22 July when Soviet CER engineers and mechanics walked off the job, but the action had no effect on railway operations. A greater effort was made on 6 August, the first night of the sabotage campaign. Posters were pasted on walls and telegraph poles in Harbin directing Soviet CER employees to resign within four days or lose their citizenship. The potential consequences for disobedience were severe; the GPU could execute noncitizens out of hand. Many did quit, while others took "leaves of absence." The Chinese retaliated with the arrest and deportation of 200 Soviet CER workers. Soviet coal workers at Dalainor went out on strike, only to see their leaders arrested by the Chinese police. The mines stayed open. When the strike reached Manchouli on 12 August, it too failed. Another 1,000 arrests were made, and the police brutally suppressed the strikes.[67]

Moscow's attempts to shut down the CER through the CCP proved equally futile. Liu Shao-chi traveled to Harbin to restart organizing efforts among Chinese CER employees. Working against Liu's CCP cadres in Harbin was the legacy of Soviet discrimination. The Soviet Russian rail workers did walk off the job, but the Chinese workers remained. Liu did have some success after he enlisted a small group to sabotage part of the Harbin railway factory, but police retribution was quick, and Liu himself was detained on 21August after a meeting with union leaders in Mukden. The Soviets had also underestimated Chinese competence. Much of the Peking–Mukden railroad had been under Fengtien's control for years and was considered the "most profitable and efficient" in China.[68] The Chinese knew how to run a railway without the Russians, and with large numbers of skilled workers available, the CER Zone authorities were free to resort to large-scale arrests of Soviet employees. The past Soviet failure to support the organization of Chinese CER workers by the CCP now helped ensure that the railway would continue to run despite Moscow's best efforts.[69]

The Fighting Begins

On 7 August, Red Army and Chinese soldiers clashed at Suifenho and Manchouli; some suspected the RKKA—not local saboteurs—of placing the bombs on the railways near Suifenho. However, the real war began on 11 August, before the RKKA reinforcements arrived. During a twelve-day period, the Red Army struck, often repeatedly, at a number of critical points, including Liang's positions on the Western Front and Tungchiang as well as Suifenho, Mishan, and Tungning on the Eastern Front. Raids across the Amur from Blagoveshchensk were directed at Teheiho and Aigun. Tracking the situation on the remote Northern Front had proved difficult to begin with, but became almost impossible after the Amur River was closed. Even attempts by authorized Japanese military observers to visit the Northern Front were thwarted. On the Russian side, no one was allowed near the border region, and Chinese police followed visitors on their side of the Amur, arresting any who violated the restrictions. The war in the far north would remain obscure to outside observers for the duration of the crisis.[70]

The first battle deaths occurred at Suifenho on the Eastern Front. Although there had been a number of incidents, and although both sides had been digging trenches and preparing artillery positions, none of these actions had resulted in fatalities. The Suifenho skirmish changed that after 1st "Pacific" Division troops attacked the Chinese positions, initiating a firefight that began around 11:00 A.M., lasted for over an hour, and resulted in two Chinese soldiers being killed and twenty wounded. The Soviet losses could not be determined but were considered comparable. The crisis became a shooting war. Nanking lodged a formal protest in Berlin with highly respected German foreign minister

Gustav Stresemann for transmission to Moscow, and publicly released the contents of the missive condemning the attack and reaffirming China's commitment to avoid all offensive military acts.[71]

Dalainor and its coal mines were raided late in the afternoon on 17 August by elements of the 5th "Kuban" Cavalry Brigade, opening a battle with the 38th Infantry Regiment that lasted four hours and left twenty Russian dead, followed by a Red Army predawn attack against the 38th Infantry. The first clash appeared unplanned: it began at around 3:00 P.M. when a Soviet cavalry patrol encountered a Chinese patrol somewhere along the poorly marked border and shots were exchanged. More cavalry arrived, and the Soviets soon gained the upper hand, with the Chinese force withdrawing back toward its lines. At that point, the Soviet cavalry apparently overpursued the retreating Chinese and hit the 38th Regiment's main defensive trenches, whose soldiers, supported by artillery from an armored train, made short work of the exposed and unprepared Russian troopers. The RKKA had been given a black eye by the Heilungkiang infantry. Another clash with GPU border guards occurred the next day, and a follow-up Soviet night attack on Chinese positions had negligible results. A relative calm then returned to the Dalainor sector.[72]

On the same day, on the Eastern Front, Soviet cavalry raided the Muleng coalfields near Mishan, while another Soviet cavalry detachment was repulsed during a raid on Tungning; the number of casualties went unreported. On 18 August, the 2nd Regiment of the 1st "Pacific" Division led by L. Shchyogolev entered into a sharp fight at the Poltavka border post south of Tungning. The next day, elements of the 1st Division reattacked Tungning, inflicting heavy Chinese casualties, routing the Kirin troops there, and leaving half of the city engulfed in flames before the Red Army troops retired across the border. Along the Northern Front, an irregular cavalry force landed on the south bank of the Amur near the village of Lopeh and began a long advance inland some 200 kilometers to briefly menace the Koshan coalfields before departing.[73]

In the midst of the fighting, Chiang Kai-shek addressed the Chinese people on the CER crisis. His 19 August speech not only laid down the rationale for wresting control of the railway away from the Soviets—to both recover "our national rights" and advance China's national interests—but also revealed Chiang's deep bitterness toward Moscow. Chiang spoke of how he had trusted Soviet Russia when it renounced imperialist ambitions in China; he had seen it as a good friend and a savior of weak nations. In time, he realized that the real Soviet policy was aggressive imperialism "worse than that of Tsarist Russia." Chiang told the nation that the Red Army reinforcements and military raids taking place on the border were proof of their "sinister and cunning" objectives and declared it was his duty to "first expose the truth of its aggression and then expose the truth of the Soviet Union's brutal invasion." The general finished by urging the people and central leadership to remain calm and be confident that the government's policy would succeed.[74]

The next day, the 108th Rifle Regiment, which had been moved from Borzhya to a forward position near the village of Abagaitevskya, some five kilometers from the frontier, engaged the Dalainor garrison. The regiment, aided by artillery and GPU border guards, engaged a battalion-sized unit of the 38th Infantry that was supported by artillery fire from a Chinese armored train. The fight began with an artillery duel between the two sides that was followed by a successful assault on the first trench line by the 108th Regiment before safely withdrawing back across the border to Russia. A smaller raid by 5th Brigade cavalry supported by artillery fire from an armored train at Siding No. 86 occurred on the same day but had little to show for the effort. On the 22nd, the Soviets were permitted to recover their dead in front of the 38th Regiment's trench lines.[75]

The last major clash occurred when the Soviets launched an attack that evening by sending an armored train across the border toward the defensive works of the 51st Heilungkiang Infantry Regiment entrenched outside Manchouli. By this time, a good degree of standardization had been adopted by the RKKA. Red Army armored trains were divided into three categories: strike, artillery, and heavy artillery. The most common was the strike train with the armored locomotives placed in the center and armored railcars placed to the front and rear. The cars generally carried two or three 76mm guns along with machine guns and were capable of transporting 100 or so infantry or a smaller number of cavalry to conduct dismounted assaults.[76]

While it is known that three armored trains (numbers 65, 66, and 67) were present on the Western Front, it is not known which two trains participated in the night raid on 22 August. As it involved a full battalion of Soviet troops, a transport train would have been following behind to carry some of the infantry. The attack began at 11:00 P.M. and lasted until dawn. The reported fighting was highly exaggerated yet undoubtedly bloody; the Chinese side reported three officers and forty-one soldiers killed along with five officers and twenty-six soldiers wounded, while there were no accurate estimates on Soviet casualties. General Liang was sufficiently impressed by the attack: to prevent another raid, on 26 August, he ordered his troops to the point where the CER crossed the border and had them remove several kilometers of track.[77]

In the following days, both sides traded artillery barrages on the Western Front while night attacks by small units from the 35th and 36th divisions became routine—often targeting Chinese artillery positions. The Chinese quickly adapted to the night raids by assigning troops to patrol their flanks and issuing lights to sweep the front and identify Soviet movements. Liang's soldiers also quickly adapted to the ODVA artillery barrages. Captain Kawamata noted that the soldiers "were not necessarily afraid of being hit by the artillery fire and marveled and bet on the shooting."[78] When the large-scale fighting had ended on 22 August and the front lines settled into a routine of small-scale skirmishes and raids, the two sides assessed their positions. The confidence emanating from Nanking was reflected in its low-key approach to resolving the CER crisis: it would defend the border but not escalate the fighting while pursuing a slow-paced diplomatic policy aimed at a negotiated settlement. Soviet objectives were harder to discern.[79]

Karakhan let it be known in Moscow that the Soviets had "no intention of invading Chinese territory."[80] Given the scale of the recent fighting, why did Karakhan made such an obviously untrue claim? If that answer remains unclear, one truth was evident: there was concerted effort on the part of the Kremlin throughout the war to make contradictory and misleading, even false, statements. In part it was a response to the inflammatory anti-Soviet propaganda campaign conducted by the nationalists, a technique to make the Chinese side appear to be in the wrong and the Soviet Russian side in the right during an age when it was difficult for outside sources to verify the claims. It was equally true that isolated battles in a remote part of the world were hard to cover, either by diplomats or reporters. More to the point, such statements furthered Moscow's aim of blurring the line between war and peace. The ODVA could wage war under a murky cloud that prevented China and the other Powers from making a clear case for invoking the Kellogg–Briand Pact, a more successful twist on Trotsky's World War I "no peace, no war" gambit.

The military rationale behind the August attacks was to both defeat the frontline NEFDF forces and shut down the coal mines at Dalainor and Mishan. As Hanson in Harbin noted, the loss of the coal supplies would have left the Chinese with the undesirable options of purchasing coal from the Japanese Fushun mines or burning wood. Taking away the coal supply was intended to close down the CER, creating an economic disaster for the Mukden regime. If that could be achieved, the Soviets were confident that the Chinese would be forced to accede to their ultimatum. The Red Army failed to achieve either objective, and the CER continued to operate; there was no economic pressure on the Chinese to give in.[81]

Why the August raids were so poorly executed also was not clear, however. If an additional aim was to prove that the local Far East commanders were better suited to defeat the Chinese than the new commanders being forced upon them by Moscow, they could not have made a worse case. What was clear was that Blyukher was the right man for the job. Blyukher was still forming the ODVA and had not arrived at Chita to take command of the Far East forces until 24 August; as a commander who always led from the front line, he had no role in the August raids. Their failure did benefit him indirectly, however. The Red Army in the Far East clearly needed to sharpen its skills, as the mid-August raids suffered from substandard reconnaissance, and the integration of artillery, infantry, and cavalry forces was either absent or uncoordinated, as demonstrated by the ability of the isolated 38th Heilungkiang Infantry Regiment to fend off repeated Soviet attacks at Dalainor.[82]

Of all the senior Red Army commanders, Blyukher was best positioned to assess the scope of the problem; no other officer could so well judge the fighting abilities of both the Chinese and Soviet soldiers. Reflecting on the poor performances of the Red Army units, he moved quickly to dismiss two dozen officers from their posts and shifted the ODVA headquarters from Chita to Khabarovsk on 25 August to be closer to the front. Blyukher pushed aside Feldman, the 19th Corps commander on the Eastern Front, and absorbed his staff. Given that Kuibyshev had taken over the Northern Front in July and Vostretsov had just replaced Graisnov, all the precrisis rifle corps commanders had been removed. Blyukher made it clear to his commanders that he expected war, and the sole mission of the ODVA was to fight and win. Upon his arrival at the 1st "Pacific" Rifle Division headquarters on the Eastern Front, Cherepanov reached a similar conclusion. Knowing that time was short, he moved to improve his subordinates' ability to fight and maneuver their units under combat conditions by launching a program of demanding field exercises. The ODVA was moving in the right direction.[83]

For the Chinese, the August rebuffs created conflicting reactions. On the one hand, they reinforced a sense of overconfidence. An American officer captured the problem: the Chinese military held the Russian soldier "in contempt," and the Red Army was "a thing of slight consequence."[84] The Ta Chung news agency echoed these feelings, declaring that the mid-August raids were unimportant and isolated, while the NEFDF was so large that the smaller ODVA could neither engage it in battle nor hope to match its size in the future. On the other hand, the NEFDF general staff realized that the Soviets were preparing for action. There were a series of meeting with senior NRA officers at the supreme headquarters beginning on 20 August. Two days later, the Young Marshal ordered 60,000 Fengtien troops to the frontier, and nearly 2,000 land mines as well large quantities of hand grenades were shipped from the Mukden arsenal to the Western Front. Chiang Kai-shek alerted Tang Shen-chih's nine divisions in the Peiping–Tientsin area to be prepared to reinforce the NEFDF; these divisions were in a high state of readiness, having been positioned to keep Feng's Kuominchun in check after the close of the Kwangsi rebellion. Mukden and Nanking appeared ready to meet force with force.

8 | Renewed Talks, Fighting, and Frustration

That Chinese military reinforcements were needed in the Northeast revealed how the events of July and August had ended in a crisis that seemed to be moving beyond the control of Chiang and Chang. The international community had not rallied to China's side. Even worse, an attempt at peaceful resolution had failed, and military mobilization with bloody border clashes had ensued. Moscow had acted with force and resolve to undo the hoped-for Chinese fait accompli. As all parties groped fitfully for a solution in the weeks that followed, China and the Soviet Union continued to battle unevenly along a variety of lines, diplomatically, militarily, and with propaganda. It was only along the latter that Nanking and Mukden seemed to have gained ground, but what would happen through renewed efforts at diplomacy or on the battlefield remained to be seen.

The Faltering CCP Propaganda Campaign

A CCP proclamation for a general strike across China issued on 30 July never materialized. The Shanghai police smothered the pro-Soviet protests held during the weekend of 27–28 July, and the police were even more effective in containing the 1 August demonstration. By mid-August, the CCP was urging its youth organizations to stage rallies in support of the Soviets, but the protests ended in a whimper. There were no such problems for the nationalists as they fought back. The KMT expanded their efforts, holding conferences or public meetings in Foochow, Nanking, Peiping, Shanghai, Tientsin, Wuhan, and host of other cities. In addition to KMT party cadres and student organizations, the Federation of Trade Unions and the Hong Kong Federation of Workers also staged protests and issued declarations against Soviet Russia.[1]

The fundamental difficulty with the CCP strategy was the popularity of Nanking's policy. "Rights recovery" resonated across China, while the CCP message, "The victory of the Soviet Union is the victory of the Chinese revolution," fell flat.[2] Ironically, Ch'en Tu-hsiu, the scapegoat for the failure of 1927, led the fight to reformulate the CCP's national response and opposed the Comintern diktats uncritically adopted by the Central Committee. The problem, Ch'en argued, was poor messaging. Defining the crisis in terms of a "gentry bourgeois attack" and similar class-conscious propaganda was "too didactic, too beyond the masses and too monotonous."[3] He argued instead for a message that portrayed the KMT as "traitors" and that exhorted that they destroy their "false mask" as leaders advancing the nation through the recovery of the CER.[4]

While some in the Central Committee did enter into a dialogue with Ch'en, his arguments were condemned and the recommendations rejected. Ch'en vainly urged for better tactics into August, charging the Central Committee with confusing strategy with principles, but his words were ignored while the party's fortunes continued to fall. After the belated attempt to organize the CER workers failed, the CCP efforts in the Northeast were scaled back to distributing pamphlets and carrying out local propaganda activities. On balance, the police were too efficient and the CCP message too convoluted; the past injustices meted out by CER Soviet managers had left the CCP's Northeastern Provinces Branch with no good options. The month of August ended with the arrest of Wang Chen-hsiang and fourteen cadres at the Fushun coalfields, an apropos close to a doomed effort.[5]

Whatever motivations were behind the Soviet decision to escalate the crisis into a war during August, the policy had not succeeded. The CCP had failed to move public support against the railway's seizure either in the Northeast or China in general, or to shut down the CER through Chinese labor strikes. The sabotage campaign initially had no effect; nor did the strike by Soviet rail workers. The unproductive Red Army raids along the frontier had only made China more determined to fight and led to a doubling of the NEFDF troops on the border. Forceful coercion by the Soviets had failed. The negotiation's table again became the focus.

Military Escalation and a New Round of Negotiations

During September, the 1st Fengtien Army under General Wang Shu-chang deployed to the Eastern Front. Wang had been a long-serving subordinate of Chang Tso-lin and a supporter of the Young Marshal; he had been one the cosignatories of the 11 January 1929 circular telegram that condemned Yang Yu-ting and Chang Yin-huai after their liquidation.[6] The army's 1st Cavalry Division went to the border east of Lake Khanka, while his three mixed brigades straddled the CER behind the front line at Suifenho and Tungning. General Hu Yu-kin's 2nd Army moved to the Western Front. Hu was one of the war college–educated young Turks who had caught the Young Marshal's eye during the Northern Expedition. He positioned three mixed brigades and a cavalry brigade at Hailar, where he made his headquarters. He sent his last unit, the 3rd Fengtien Mixed Brigade under General Chang Shu-ko, to Teheiho, where it faced the Soviet 26th Territorial Rifle Division and GPU troops across the Amur at Blagoveshchensk.[7]

Hu reflected the Chinese nonchalance when he did not improve the defenses at Hailar and declined to reinforce Liang with additional artillery and cavalry. None of Hu's Fengtien troops went into the trenches on the Western Front, a decision that captured the lingering warlord rivalries within the NEFDF. The message to General Liang was clear: Hu was there as a show of force for the Russians; fighting was the responsibility of the Heilungkiang troops. The arrival of the 2nd Army did offer one tactical benefit for General Liang: he was able to transfer General Han's 17th Heilungkiang Brigade from Hailar to Dalainor, freeing up the 38th Regiment for the defense of the railway between Dalainor and Manchouli.[8]

The mid-August fighting accomplished little and was dismissed internationally. Once again, the outside world was convinced that a negotiated settlement was at hand. The halt of RKKA attacks seemed a good omen. Chang's advisor, Donald, wrote on 29 August, "Raids have stopped ever since the pow-pow has been going on in Berlin, and that seems significant."[9] Publicly, Soviet remarks became conciliatory. In New York City, an official named Bladmetev addressed a special session on the CER crisis at the Institute of International Relations and conceded that some of the published documents captured at the Harbin consulate "indicated subversive intentions, but urged, however, that a distinction be drawn between words and actions"; he defended steps taken to protect Soviet rights in China by arguing that the CER was Russia's critical outlet to the Pacific.[10]

There was truth in Bladmetev's words; the CER was critical to the Russian Soviet Far East economy. Tokyo saw the problem immediately;

a foreign ministry spokesman stated on 18 July, "We do not exclude all chance of war between the two as the loss of the Chinese Eastern Railway must be a question of life or death for Vladivostok."[11] In Manchuria, collaborationists hoping to keep trade with Vladivostok alive faced severe penalties. A Chinese merchant, Shuang Ho-sheng, was found guilty of selling 200 carloads of flour to the Soviets. He was shot and his business confiscated. Many regional companies felt the pinch once the borders closed as 18,000 tons of goods piled up at the Harbin rail yards. Even minor businesses, like the local green tea merchants, were badly hurt. Fortunately, the cargo was soon on the move—but only to the Japanese port at Dairen while ships sat with empty holds in Vladivostok. The crisis created a financial windfall for the SMR and the Japanese leasehold. The issue of the CER's disappearing revenues also came to a head.[12]

On 2 August, the Young Marshal initiated an investigation of CER finances, and Nanking sent John J. Mantell, an American advisor with the ministry of railways, to direct the audit. A few weeks later, John Stevens, former RRSC and CER head and a colleague of Mantell's, added fuel to the fire by calling the railway a "gold mine" while blaming Chinese mismanagement for the lack of profits; the British consul in Mukden, B. G. Tours, blamed it on the corruption of CER *tupan* Lu. A month later, Mantell released his findings. By his analysis, Stevens was correct: the railway should have been very profitable—but the fault did not lie with the Chinese.[13] Mantell found that the Soviets had "what amounts to absolute control" and were responsible for missing profits that he put at $45 million. The Soviets overstated the CER value by two times (400 million gold rubles versus 200 million gold rubles), and the books were kept in such a way that it was "practically impossible to tell the real situation."[14] Mantell closed by concluding that the railroad, facilities, and equipment were in a good state. The Kremlin roundly condemned the report, while Mukden enjoyed a reversal of fortunes. The CER was running at a profit while the Soviets were reeling from "the commercial extinction of Vladivostok," as Lampson put it.[15] The bad economic news helped push Moscow toward renewed negotiations.[16]

Nanking was also eager to restart the talks. Having successfully weathered the first month of the crisis, the Chinese military was still being told that the Red Army could not fight, this time by their German military advisors, who declared that it was "absurd to think the Soviets can carry out an offensive in China."[17] The nationalists were convinced they held the upper hand in their dealings with the Soviets. The German officers' dismissive attitude toward the Red Army was surprising. Given the extensive covert military training conducted between the two countries, it appears that the Germans could not shake their World War I image of the Russian army—a prejudice that blinded them to tangible progress made by the Red Army. It was a disservice to their Chinese counterparts.[18]

Nanking took over the diplomatic lead from Mukden and opened a second round of negotiations. The posturing at Siding No. 86 was to be forgotten. A repeat was avoided by conducting the talks through the good offices of Germany; these began shortly after the collapse of the Manchouli negotiations. Germany was an ideal conduit, as both sides had gone to Berlin to look after their respective interests in Russia and China after Sino-Soviet diplomatic relations had been severed. The key go-betweens were General Chiang Tso-ping, the Chinese minister in Berlin, and German ambassador Herbert von Dirksen in Moscow, together with acting Soviet foreign minister Litvinov. By 28 August, the Germans had formulated a joint declaration agreeable to both sides, which American ambassador Jacob G. Schurman in Berlin characterized as "embodying an essential surrender" by the Chinese.[19]

The official joint declaration, issued as a *note verbale,* directed both parties to "immediately release all persons arrested in connection with this incident, or after May 1, 1929," making it retroactive to before the Harbin consulate raid. The Chinese side also caved on the legitimacy of the CER seizure by stating that only the framework outlined in the 1924 agreements could be used to settle disputes. The Chinese also met the Soviet demand to reinstate the status quo ante by acknowledging that any changes related to the CER could only be implemented during a future conference, nullifying the Chinese actions of 10 July. In short, the Chinese side again met all three points of the 13 July Soviet ultimatum while making feeble points in an attempt to save face. Nanking requested that Moscow instruct Soviet railway employees to observe the antipropaganda clauses in the 1924 agreements. Both sides moved to strictly adhere to the status quo ante language. Nanking watered down Mukden's demand for the removal of Emshanov and Eismont by instead asking the Soviet government "to recommend a new Director and a new Vice Director," and in return, the Soviets withdrew the order for the removal of the CER *tupan.*[20]

News of a peaceful resolution was eagerly received around the world. In the days that followed, the German foreign ministry expressed confidence that a path to a peaceful solution had been opened, while Japanese ambassador Debuchi Kastuji told Secretary Stimson in Washington that Tokyo felt that the situation was improving. On 9 September, *Time* optimistically opined that a deal had been reached based on the points in the Berlin-brokered *note verbale*. What the outside world had missed was that the negotiations had fallen apart as soon as the Soviet response to the Chinese "surrender" had been presented to Dirksen. The reason was simple: Stalin had no interest in the solution.[21]

Stalin's principal aim was not to resolve the crisis but to "use our tough position to . . . completely undermine the authority of Chiang Kai-shek's government."[22] When he saw the contents of the *note verbale*, he flew into a rage, writing to Molotov that he had lost his nerve by "letting the Chinese put one over on you" and that a beaten foe [China] had been given "the fruits of our victory." He went on to ridicule the "wisdom" of Bukharin and Litvinov.[23] Despite the disconnection between reality and Stalin's perceptions (the Chinese had not been beaten militarily, and the declaration equated to a humiliating acceptance of the Soviet ultimatum on the part of China), Stalin's strong displeasure quickly reached the foreign affairs commissariat. Litvinov met Dirksen in Moscow on the evening of 29 August and began by inoffensively reconfirming that the Soviet side had accepted the joint declaration. Then the other shoe dropped: Litvinov added that Russia "saw no reason to appoint" new CER managers, and the demand for the resignation of the Chinese CER *tupan* was reintroduced.[24]

Stalin's rationale offered a sobering insight into his method of rule. He wrote that responding to the two Chinese points regarding propaganda and the CER managers was a matter of right and wrong. It seems improbable that Stalin actually believed that consular officers in Harbin along with Soviet CER officials Emshinov and Eismont had not been interfering in Chinese internal affairs and violating the 1924 agreements. They had clearly done so. Attempts to overthrow both the Young Marshal's regime and the nationalist government under Chiang Kai-shek had been a goal of the Kremlin and the Comintern since 1927, and Stalin had personally directed such steps on a number of occasions. It was apparent that he simply could not accept victory on any terms but his own. The "right" facts were what Stalin declared them to be, and he would crush those who opposed him, even if it meant war.

Nanking reacted angrily. Foreign Minister Wang stated on 2 September that the new Soviet demand "was impossible to accept."[25] Unaware of Stalin's intentions, Nanking and Mukden could not make sense of the sudden change; nor did they realize that the negotiations were over. They saw it as at most a temporary setback. In Tokyo, Vice Foreign Minister Yoshizawa Kenkichi noted that Mukden was uninterested in scoring propaganda points and more than ready to settle on almost any terms. Lampson in Peiping wrote that a frustrated Foreign Minister Wang confided to him, "There had been a hitch somewhere and that Russia, who had virtually agreed to China's terms, was now raising difficulties."[26]

Nanking attempted to restart the talks by directing Chiang Tso-ping to depart Berlin for Geneva on 5 September and meet with Ambassador C. C. Wu, who had arrived from Washington to attend the tenth session of the assembly of the League of Nations.[27] The Chinese diplomats then sought out Litvinov, who had also arrived in Switzerland. It was not a good outing for Wu. He stated to the press, "Without declaring war, the Soviets seem to be committing acts of war."[28] This vague description played into the Soviet strategy of ambiguity that allowed Moscow to aver that there was no war, no violation of the peace pact, and no role for third parties. The situation further deteriorated when Wu delivered a letter to the League that reiterated Chinese justifications for the replacement of Emshanov and Eismont—a move bound to pique the Soviets. An angry Karakhan and Litvinov brushed aside Chinese overtures to resume negotiations. For China, Geneva diplomacy had misfired. The Soviets evoked the now-familiar ploy of decrying so-called White raids to justify fresh ODVA attacks along the border.

Renewed Red Army Attacks

Once it became clear that the Berlin talks were at an impasse and that the League of Nations would take no action, a major escalation of Russian military force was applied in a pattern that little resembled the mid-August fighting. Blyukher's efforts to mold the ODVA into a combat-ready army had begun to show results. While the negotiations were underway, there was little activity; on 27 August, the day after the *note verbale* had arrived in Moscow, Tungning was again raided by cavalry supported by aircraft, and on the Western Front, Chinese troops in the trenches before Manchouli experienced three raids that morning, followed by a second wave of three attacks on the next day. On 28 August, Soviet cavalry raided a Chinese toll station on the Argun River, leaving six dead. Stalin had concluded that the sword could be mightier than the pen.[29]

These raids culminated in a large show of force near Dalainor on 29 August that combined a cavalry regiment from the 5th Kuban Brigade with the 1st Tank Company in a short night raid, the first example of a combined mechanized force being employed in the conflict. After the tank–cavalry demonstration, a brief calm returned to the western front lines. Reported attacks on the Northern Front consisted of small-scale cross-river raids by the Red Army. A successful rescue mission was launched across the Amur to free several Soviet prisoners held in the small town of Wangtsing near Teheiho, and on 30 August, a Chinese magistrate was taken prisoner during an assault on the river town of Chikan. As September arrived, there was an uptick in activity on the Western Front; a large body of Soviet troops crossed the border near Manchouli on 3 September and briefly engaged soldiers of the 15th Brigade. An uneasy peace settled over the Western Front. There were no armed clashes, and only Red Army observation flights were noted. Gone were the hit-and-miss August raids. The ODVA was conducting the well-coordinated attacks needed for a successful offensive.[30]

The September Battle at Suifenho

The fighting was not limited to the Western Front. The Amur River Flotilla carried out an amphibious operation on the north shore of Lake Khanka on 24 August. Once ashore, the battalion-strong landing force raided toward Mishan. The primary Soviet objective on the Eastern Front, however, was the CER rail hub at Suifenho, which was situated at a natural pass between China and Russia and named for the river that flowed to the town's south. It was also home to important rail shops and yards, storehouses, a customhouse, and foreign consulates. That Suifenho was a key ODVA target was no secret. The first armed clash of the war took place there in July, and the nearby rail lines had been subjected to numerous sabotage attacks. The town was also the frequent scene of aerial, cavalry, and even searchlight demonstrations. It had been under martial law since 7 August. By September, the Red Army was familiar with the ground, in addition to the ongoing small-scale fighting at Suifenho and Tungning to the south. A successful if costly mid-August cavalry raid hit the Hsilinho rail station to the west of Suifenho and thirty-five kilometers inland from the border. The Chinese also recognized the town's value. General Wang, the 1st Fengtien Army commander, visited its front lines on 4 September, and the Kirin regiment that arrived in July had been strongly reinforced.[31]

Suifenho was defended by the 21st Kirin Mixed Brigade under General Ting Chao and lay less than five kilometers to the west of the border, well within striking range for the Red Army. Nearness to the border was the only tactical advantage for Blyukher. As on the Western Front, to advance directly on Suifenho, the ODVA would have to work through several lines of NEFDF trenches. Unlike the more open Western Front, at the Suifenho pass, there was only a five-kilometer-wide front to assault the trenches before rolling hills to the north and forests to the south restricted freedom of movement for an attacker. The hills, rising 100 meters or more, also protected the town from attack in any other direction. The Chinese used the terrain to organize tough defenses that necessitated a skilled approach. Was the Red Army prepared to pay the price necessary to break through, seize the town, and eliminate Suifenho as a military target?[32]

Subtle proof that the ODVA had the will occurred on Friday, 6 September; on that day, aircraft from the 2nd "Lenin" Reconnaissance Squadron was spotted over the city. The ODVA was carefully preparing for action, and preparatory raids began on the evening of the next day. The night attacks on 7 September had one purpose—to isolate Suifenho and its defenders—and began with an attack on the CER line heading toward Harbin. Just as a passenger train was a few minutes from arrival at the Suifenho station, demolition charges blew away a section of track, derailing the engine and several cars. Two people were killed and a number wounded; the rail connection to Suifenho was severed. The telegraph lines were cut at the same time, interrupting outside communications—with the exception of the NEFDF and CER radio stations. On Sunday morning, an artillery barrage preceded 1st "Pacific" Division attacks on the Chinese trench lines at both Suifenho and Tungning. Neither assault succeeded in breaching the 21st Brigade's defenses, and the fighting raged throughout the day. The most significant attack, however, came from the air.[33]

The buildup of airpower before the Suifenho battle was impressive. In July, only eight RKKA airplanes from the 7th and 13th Air Squadrons were known to be operating on the Eastern Front. As fresh fighter and bomber squadrons arrived from across Russia, the picture changed. By late August, as many as thirty-eight aircraft were spotted over Suifenho on a single day. Beginning on the afternoon of 8 September, the Red Army air force struck Suifenho in strength. Instead of playing a ground support role, as seen on the Western Front, the aircraft bypassed the Chinese defensive works and struck directly at the town's railroad facilities. In a series of air raids, the station and rail yards were destroyed. Predictably, among the wreckage of buildings, trains, and cars lay many dead and wounded CER workers and their Chinese soldier guards.[34]

Major Kanda of the IJA admitted that ODVA artillery fire hit the Chinese for eight consecutive days in September, but the combat was dominated by three days of air attacks. The destruction was extensive. By Monday, the rail station and CER telegraph and radio stations were destroyed, but Soviet success was not universal. A late-night sabotage raid on 8 September was discovered and beaten off by heavy Chinese fire. Battling along the trenches was heard all day that Monday and lasted until midday on 10 September, but the Chinese lines held. One 21st Brigade battalion commander was killed in action, along with twenty-nine soldiers, and another hundred were treated at the Suifenho hospital. An additional forty soldiers were reported to have died in the bombings. Panicked customs and CER railway officials fled the city by any means possible.[35]

The rudimentary bomber guidance systems and close proximity of civilian structures—the train station was located in the city center—led to widespread damage beyond the military targets, as well as a large number of civilian casualties. The bombs also ignited numerous fires that became uncontrolled and led to a breakdown of order and looting within the town. The number of CER workers who perished in the rail station bombings was put at twenty. Frightened Japanese residents resorted to flying national flags from the buildings, but it did not prevent the death of one Japanese resident, who was killed when the Hotel Europe was bombed. After three days of air raids, much of the city had been burned to the ground. Its residents were living out of cellars or had fled into the hills. Suifenho became a ghost town as surviving businesses shuttered their storefronts.[36]

The final count of civilian deaths from the air attacks was put at 117; the number injured went unreported. With their targets destroyed, and likely unaware of the civilian toll, the Red Army squadrons opted not to attack the city again. On 10 September, they dropped leaflets that carried the traditional Russian greeting of "bread and salt" and added, "We shall not bombard again."[37] The town was slow to recover. Many people did not immediately return, and most shops and businesses had not reopened a month later. Militarily, the ODVA's results were satisfactory, if unexpected. After conventional ground assaults stalled, it was airpower that obtained the objective of the attack: the elimination of Suifenho as a railhead. Regardless of who accomplished the mission, the job was over, and there was no need for further Red Army attacks.[38]

The question was, what did it all mean? That the soldiers of the ODVA and NEFDF were in a war was unequivocal. What was not clear was for how long and at what cost, but the events of September cast little light on the answer. Tactically, the ODVA had succeeded. Strategically, the Red Army had accomplished little. What message was the Kremlin sending? The Young Marshal's confusion over the Western Front and Suifenho battles was apparent. In a telegram sent to his commanders, he wrote that the reasons behind the attacks were undetermined. They might be an attempt to change China's negotiation's stance or a prelude to an invasion and a major war. On 10 September, the ODVA paper *Alarm* carried a message from Blyukher urging the "greatest vigilance" in the face of the recent battles.[39] More fighting was to be expected. The diplomatic fallout in Nanking was immediate. The next day, Foreign Minister Wang responded to the attacks by discarding the Berlin joint declaration and again refused to accept the 13 July Soviet ultimatum. A fortnight later, Marshal Chang sent Tsai to Nanking in hopes of clarifying the situation. By the end of the month, it was clear that China was in a serious conflict with Soviet Russia, but where it would go no one in Nanking or Mukden knew.[40]

The White Russian Threat

During this period, a great deal of "claim and counterclaim" over border raids was traded between the two sides in the form of diplomatic démarches and propaganda campaigns. That the Soviet side had launched sizable military forays into China was not in dispute; attesting to the veracity of Soviet claims against military raids into Russian territory was more problematic. It was true that small groups of militant Russian émigrés were foes of the Soviet Union and the Soviets often used them as a "scapegoat" or "specter."[41] The Soviets had blamed the Whites almost from the outset for starting hostilities between the two sides; the first

Pravda stories were picked up in the West on 21 July. TASS also adopted the White terrorism theme, and hardly a week went by when additional claims were made. Yet there was never a credible independent report proving them true.[42]

During a trip by the press to the Western Front, reporters searched for White Russian troops and concluded that there were none. Mukden rejected the claims of White terrorism. Dr. Y. D. Chen, chairman of the Committee for Public Enlightenment, stated that, excluding Russians who had become Chinese citizens, "There were less than 10,000 White Russians, most of whom were engaged in honest work or business, and all of whom were unarmed."[43] The Young Marshal had also rejected a September offer of service from Semenov and Dog Meat Chang's former White Russian mercenaries in Shantung.[44]

The British dismissed the White movement in Manchuria as having no military capability, revisited the issue monthly during the crisis, and always reached the same conclusion. As far as they were concerned, "the white boogey created by Soviet propaganda does not exist."[45] American intelligence officers had reached the same judgment a year earlier, reporting that the four major White organizations had a combined membership of less than 700, and although professed to be secret, the names of the organizations' officers were easily obtained. Their only value lay as conduits to CER employees and Russians living in the Soviet Far East, a portal to hard-to-gain information welcomed by the Harbin police. The Whites were toothless; Nanking saw to this by directing Mukden to suppress their activities in August, and the Young Marshal considered White offers of assistance as "valueless."[46] The timing of the White terrorism claims was also suspect, as they arose to suit Soviet propaganda needs. When a settlement appeared close, there was silence in Moscow. After a setback, such as the failure of the Berlin talks, claims of "unceasing attacks of the White Guard," denunciations of the documents seized in Harbin as "illiterate and false fabrications by Whites," and bogus accusations of White Russian raids became grist for the Soviet press.[47]

Was the entire issue a sham, concocted by the propagandists in Moscow? There was no evidence that the NEFDF ever conducted raids into the Soviet Union, and ample evidence that the contrary was true: the NEFDF maintained a completely passive defense throughout the crisis. A more nuanced explanation comes closer to the truth. The former White military organizations did engage in anti-Soviet propaganda—albeit in an ineffective manner—and there had long been problems along the border. Japanese sources estimated that 58,000 bandits were active in Manchuria in 1929, and Chinese *hunghutzu* had operated in the sparsely populated regions of the Russian Far East since before World War I. These gangs were a military threat; they could number in the hundreds. As discussed previously, one of the Young Marshal's first combat experiences occurred during a bandit suppression campaign carried out by his brigade in Kirin. The multiethnic makeup of gangs would also lead the Soviets to blame these activities on Whites, as some former White soldiers had turned bandit after their defeat.[48]

The border was easy to cross—as well as a route for illegal trafficking of all kinds. Most of the Amur gold mined in the Soviet Union made its way into Manchuria, and some opium made its way into Russia. Suifenho lay near the poppy-growing region; the border town was a center for smuggling opium, silk, and vodka; the end of the New Economic Policy in 1928 put more mundane items such as farming equipment in demand—a boon for smugglers. Another difficulty was illegal immigration. As the League of Militant Atheists cracked down on Christians inside the Soviet Union, a number fled to Manchuria. Earlier, in November 1927, the GPU guards at Blagoveshchensk had to be reinforced by additional cavalry and infantry to try to cut down on the smuggling and refugee traffic crossing the Amur. Illegal cross-border violations did not cease during the crisis; indeed, the importance of these illicit operations only increased when the legal border crossings closed.[49]

It was inevitable that as thousands of ODVA and fresh GPU soldiers arrived on the frontier, they would run into the worst of these gangs, presenting Moscow with proof that hostile armed groups were crossing into Soviet territory. In reality, it was nothing new, as any veteran GPU border guard could have attested. What was new was the CER crisis, and absent a real White threat, the Kremlin had to manufacture one. The illegal border activities became the perfect tool. The bandit activities allowed Moscow to create an ingenious propaganda program that excited its own population, vilified the Chinese government, and built up a false case that Whites attacked across the frontier, turning the Soviets into victims. The White issue would not go away; it had become the centerpiece of Soviet justifications for military action. The Kremlin had repeatedly affirmed that Russia would not attack China directly, and it never backed off that claim. Without the White boogeyman, there could be no ODVA response—and without military action, no solution acceptable to Stalin. The vilification of White provocateurs became a permanent feature of the war.[50]

Chinese Patriotism, the Sabotage Campaign, and Stalled Negotiations

That the CER recovery was popular in China was an understatement, and the Young Marshal found the people rallying to his side. When the 1st Army entrained for the Eastern Front, the Mukden chamber of commerce organized a rally to see the troops off. One estimate put the size of the crowd at 100,000—an unprecedented show of support for the former warlord army. The escalation of hostilities also stirred up support for the war in Harbin. By the end of August, the Northeast Merchant Marine School, the Engineering High School, and the elite First and Third middle schools all had active student defense associations with the shared goal of sending volunteers to serve on the Western Front. Encouraged to support the war effort by education director Chang Kuo-chen, student activism continued to explode, with 1,000 students joining and their representatives holding a coordination conference on the evening of 10 September. The conference ended with the formation of the Harbin Student Corps. Chang Hsueh-liang was forced to intercede.[51]

While the support was welcomed, having the province's most promising youths volunteering to go to the war front without training was unacceptable to the authorities. On the day after the student conference, the Young Marshal telegraphed the education director and ordered him to reverse his policy. Chang Kuo-chen was to direct the school administrators to meet with the students by 2:00 P.M. on 13 September and inform the students that their duty lay in their studies and that two recently formed associations were to be banned. The Young Marshal made his argument public, stating, "It is good to know about the student's firm intentions, but the NEFDF is well trained and unrivaled. . . . There is no need for the student corps." He added, "It was not beneficial for the students to give up their academic studies."[52] To placate the students, the Feng Yung Student Corps was allowed to continue, and a detachment of volunteers left for the Western Front after a rousing send-off. A few weeks later, Chang issued the National Volunteers Organization Ordnance to regain control over the student movements. Chinese resolve was stronger than ever. So was that of the Soviets.[53]

Unlike the ODVA military raids that were directly tied to the negotiations efforts, the sabotage campaign never ended. Throughout August and into September, the attacks continued. On 19 August, a mail train was bombed near Suifenho, and on the following day, near the same location, the locomotive of a passenger train was derailed, injuring the crew. After martial law was imposed, Chinese troops and police shot on sight anyone found within 200 feet of the rails after darkness. The saboteurs were undeterred. Two bombs placed underneath a rail bridge near Dalainor were spotted and disarmed on 24 August. At the close of the month, Suifenho remained the center of activity; on 29 August, Chinese troops entered into a firefight along the rail and uncovered two dynamite charges with an electronic detonator. In the days that followed, a buried charge successfully derailed a passenger train, killing three and wounding twenty. A similar attack on the Muleng coal mine rail spur killed three and wounded several others.[54]

CER police authorities announced that the death penalty would be meted out to saboteurs. More arrests were made, including that of the manager of the Grand Hotel in Harbin. On 4 September, they conducted an important raid that captured the radio set used for clandestine communication with Blagoveshchensk, the center for GPU operations. Arrested were M. Zharbulinsky, the CER telegraph services director, along with the CER telephone services chief. Severing the radio link and regaining complete control over the CER telegraph and telephone systems badly hurt the saboteurs' ability to coordinate and direct their efforts. The last major attack, conducted in the hours of darkness on 17 September, was a second attempt on the Sungari CER bridge. As the raiders drew near, a sharp firefight ensued, and among the casualties were Chu Ke-wen, the local rail guard company commander, who was killed, and Sergeant Chao Yoh-wen, who was badly injured. Their sacrifice was not in vain; the attack failed. Although the sabotage assaults waned, the Chinese had been forced to take drastic measures and commit large numbers of police and soldiers to secure the railway—troops better used on the front lines. Action on the front again heated up as talks stalled.[55]

The Berlin negotiations remained at an impasse, and fruitless debates over terms such as "the appointment" versus "the immediate appointment" of new Soviet CER managers went nowhere.[56] On 13 September, Moscow received (via Dirksen) Nanking's response to the Soviet demand for the removal of the Chinese CER *tupan*: a proposal for a new two-party conference in Berlin to address remaining differences over a joint settlement. There was no urgency to act as far as Nanking was concerned. In Tokyo, Soviet ambassador Aleksandr A. Troyanovsky informed Foreign Minister Shidehara on 16 September, "The Soviets are in a position to obtain the ultimatum as they are prepared to accept the risk of following a hardline policy."[57] The next day, the Soviets publicly replied to the Chinese proposal for another Berlin conference: there would be no such meeting until the Chinese unconditionally accepted the July ultimatum and agreed to remove the CER *tupan*. The statement concluded ominously, "The responsibility for the further development of the conflict devolves fully upon the Nanking government."[58] The negotiations were dead. Stalin had made up his mind and would force a resolution on the battlefield.[59]

The October Night Fights on the Western Front

The first indication that the ODVA was astir again on the Western Front occurred on 29 September with an overflight of Chinese positions by three Soviet aircraft. Nothing happened the next day, but on 1 October, a similar reconnaissance flight was observed, and the pace of activity picked up. During the afternoon, RKKA artillery shelled Chinese trenches near Manchouli for thirty minutes, and raiders cut the telegraph lines between Manchouli and the rest of Manchuria that evening. Also that night, a battalion of Trans-Baikal Group soldiers supported by two field guns attacked the Chinese trenches north of Manchouli for about twenty minutes. The attack was a diversion from the main assault, which commenced at 6 A.M. on 2 October. Over the next five hours, Russian artillery shelled a wide swath of the Chinese defensive works. The air attacks began thirty minutes later, at 11:30 A.M., when three aircraft began bombing and strafing runs along the Manchouli trench lines while two other aircraft went after targets at Dalainor. After ninety minutes, the aircraft returned to their bases, initiating a brief lull in the fighting.[60]

The peace was broken at 5:00 P.M. when the bombardment cycle began again. The shelling from the Russian guns lasted an hour, followed by attacks by six aircraft that lasted an hour, until darkness fell. All told, the aircraft alone had killed at least forty Chinese soldiers and damaged the Manchouli rail station. At 8:00 P.M., a night artillery barrage kicked off but ended after only thirty minutes. That was when Russian infantry struck north of Manchouli—a brief attack lasting only twenty minutes, and then nothing. The uneasy silence that had settled over the Chinese trench lines near Manchouli was broken over two hours later, when a battalion of the 21st Division's 61st Rifle Regiment hit the trench lines held by 38th Heilungkiang Infantry near the Abugatai Siding, located midway between Manchouli and Dalainor. By 1:00 A.M., the first line of Chinese trenches was in Russian hands.[61]

An hour later, the second major Russian assault began close to the site of the earlier northern raid. A battalion of infantry from the 36th Division's 108th Rifle Regiment under Commander Alekseev, along with a troop of cavalry, advanced across the border in three groups from their position near Siding No. 86. One company occupied a small hill not far from the main Chinese defenses. The remainder of the force fell on the Chinese and engaged in hand-to-hand combat using grenades to clear the trenches. In time, the Soviet troops penetrated all three trench lines, along with a number of bunkers and communication trenches. The fighting was intense. Leszczynsky, one of the assault company commanders, was wounded. He refused evacuation until his soldiers were safely out of the trenches. An ethnic Korean platoon leader named Kim Yu-gen spoke Chinese and was able to trick the defenders of a fortified blockhouse into opening the bulletproof door to let him in. Kim was killed in the fighting, but the position was successfully stormed. Political commissar K. D. Zaparina also died heroically in the fighting, and several soldiers were later decorated for exceptional bravery.[62]

Chinese artillery began to shell the captured lines, and soldiers of the 15th Brigade mounted counterattacks. It was at that time that the raids drew to a close. By 3:00 A.M., the Russian soldiers had withdrawn from both Chinese trench lines. By 6:00 A.M., the last of the fighting between Liang's troops and the Soviet rear guard ended, and an hour later, all the ODVA raiders were across the border. Both sides incurred heavy casualties. In the fighting around the Abugatai Siding, one American intelligence report put the 38th Infantry's casualties at 314 wounded and killed, with the 61st Rifle Regiment suffering 183 casualties. There was no report of the losses for the smaller yet bloody fight between elements of the 15th Brigade and the 108th Rifle Regiment, but given the losses in RKKA officers, the total casualties for both sides certainly exceeded 200.[63]

A similar Russian attack was made on the evening on 4 October. By then, the 15th Brigade was on high alert, and it met with little success. Trench warfare proved a bloody business, and Chinese resolve proved unwavering. Hanson, the American consul at Harbin, was present at the battle and noted that the "Chinese troops displayed remarkable fighting ability in defending their positions and certainly emerged victorious."[64] A day after the last Soviet night attack, several hundred "Daredevil" cadets from the Mukden military academy arrived at the Western Front, providing a boost to morale as well as an infusion of green but disciplined and enthusiastic small unit leaders.[65]

The fighting on the Western Front had just calmed down when the Northern Front heated up. By early October, Kuibyshev's 12th Corps had grown to over 12,000 troops with as many as sixty artillery pieces. On 7 October, Chinese authorities, somehow alerted to trouble, ordered the evacuation of the civilian population in and around Teheiho, and beginning the next day, the city came under bombardment from Russian artillery positions at Blagoveshchensk that lasted for four days. No sooner had the barrages ended than ODVA aircraft launched air raids on 11 October. With the sudden onslaught, and with the Amur beginning to ice over, fear of a cross-river attack became a reality for General Chang Shu-ko and his 3rd Brigade. Then, as suddenly as the attacks began, they ended. The Young Marshal was left to guess where the next ODVA strike would land, but the NEFDF stood firm. The attacks did nothing to drive either Mukden or Nanking into accepting Moscow's demands.[66]

After the early October battles, an aroused Stalin wanted to "stir up rebellion" and declare Chang Hsueh-liang "overthrown."[67] While that demand proved as infeasible as his 1 June 1927 overreach with the KMT-Left, Stalin did have a success. Since 1923, the Soviets had been courting Feng Yu-hsiang—with some effect, as by 1926 the British War Office accurately considered Feng the leader of the Red forces in Northern China and the Soviets had sent arms and large quantities of ammunition to his forces at Kalgan from Soviet bases in Outer Mongolia as recently as May 1929. That effort was about to pay off.[68]

As early as September, it became apparent that Feng was in Moscow's good graces; in Ichang, troops under Chang Fa-kuei, former commander of the 4th NRA "Ironsides" Corps, rebelled against Nanking, using the slogan, "Down with Chiang Kai-shek, up with Wang Ching-wei, long live Feng Yu-hsiang, cooperation with Soviet Russia."[69] Feng took the cue. On the Double Tenth, his officers threatened to march on Nanking, and Chiang Kai-shek ordered an immediate attack on the Kuominchun. The betrayal was not surprising, even if Feng was a less than reliable ally of the Russians; US military attaché Joseph Stilwell had stated years earlier, "He [Feng] double crosses everybody—is strictly for himself."[70] On 14 October, Chiang publicly denounced Feng and his generals, calling them rebels and traitors. The NRA was soon fighting the Kuominchun in Honan and northern Hupeh, and the 1st Army Group divisions that Chiang had assigned to support the Young Marshal were gone. The NEFDF stood alone, and the timing was critical: the first major ODVA offensive had begun two days earlier.[71]

9 | The Decisive ODVA Offensive

Final Plans

The ODVA campaign developed in August by Blyukher was proceeding but had yet to realize its purpose. Phase 1 (deployment, border raids, and sabotage) had been completed by September and had yielded many positive results. Phase 2 was not yet completed; the larger attacks at Suifenho and on the Western Front, although not perfect, had succeeded, but without the approval of Stalin and Voroshilov, the deep raids and the phase 3 offensive would remain unfinished business. Blyukher was eager for the final offensive—for the ODVA to "smash both enemy groups with a simultaneous blow" and end the war.[1] Convincing Voroshilov proved easy; he had secretly met with Blyukher at Chita on 24 August, and both were convinced the ODVA would prevail.[2]

Stalin was the obstacle. Failed negotiations helped Blyukher's cause, but a primary reason for Stalin's hesitancy was out of Blyukher's hands: uncertainty remained over how Japan would react to a Soviet invasion of Manchuria, despite Tokyo's July declarations that it would not intervene. A solution arose in September. The Soviet embassy in Tokyo was able to ascertain (according Litvinov, through former Home Secretary Suzuki Kisaburo) that the Kwantung Army would not act if Soviet forces did not go beyond the old tsarist sphere of interest and if the Western Front offensive did not advance more that fifty kilometers east of Hailar. Both restrictions were acceptable to Stalin. With fears over military intervention by Japan removed, he approved the execution of the last phases of the war plan.[3]

In late September, Voroshilov departed for Chita with Stalin's authority to commence the final offensive at a time of Voroshilov's choosing. In reality, weather determined the pace of operations. The proposed deep raids up the Sungari had to begin before the river iced up, while a two-front final offensive had its best chance of success after the marshes froze in November but before the bitter winter cold set in. The ODVA gained a further advantage when Chinese generals drew the opposite conclusion: they saw the onset of the cold weather as the end of the campaign and had begun the transition into winter quarters. As the early October fighting on the Western and Northern fronts drew to a close, the first major ODVA offensive of the war was about to commence: deep raids up the Sungari River.[4]

The Sungari River Operation (12 October–2 November)

From his headquarters at Khabarovsk, Blyukher directed a successive series of attacks to penetrate the river and threaten Harbin. ODVA deputy commander Lapin was placed in overall command. The operation had three objectives: defeat the Sungari River Flotilla, launch an amphibious raid on Tungchiang, and close with a second amphibious raid on Fuchin. The 2nd Division, the Amur River Flotilla, and an aviation group were assigned to the operation. The 2nd Battalion, 4th Regiment's, amphibious experts trained other 2nd Division units in river-crossing operations in the weeks that preceded the attacks. That battalion, along with two battalions each from the 5th "Blagoveshchensk" and 6th "Khabarovsk" Rifle regiments, formed the division's assault group. Final preparations began on 7 October and included detailed aerial photography missions. The window to conduct the attack was closing; temperatures had already reached freezing, and ice was forming on the Sungari. John B. Powell, an American newspaper correspondent who covered the Sungari operations, noted that at the time of the Tungchiang attack, movement on the Sungari was possible, "but with the paddle-wheel and rudder of our steamer so covered with ice that we had difficulty in moving against the current."[5]

Tungchiang was on the Sungari's eastern bank, five kilometers from the confluence of the Amur River, where the muddy alluvial waters of the Sungari mingled with the clear, flowing Amur. The Chinese defenses were imposing. Kirin governor-general Chang Tso-hsiang, the Eastern Front commander, had been preparing for weeks and had constructed a series of trench and pillbox defensive works in an L shape that lined ten kilometers of the Amur's southern bank and seven kilometers of the Sungari's eastern bank from the river mouth to Tungchiang. The terrain favored the defenders; the Sungari's western bank was swampland crisscrossed with streams, making it unsuitable for infantry operations or as a base for artillery; the Chinese had also mined the river entrance.

The 9th Kirin Mixed Brigade's 3rd and 35th Infantry regiments of two battalions each manned the main defenses. The 3rd Regiment held most of the Amur River line, with the northernmost positions held by the 3rd Battalion while the 2nd Battalion held a five-kilometer stretch to the south. There it met the 1st Battalion, 35th Infantry, dug in approximately five kilometers north of Tungchiang. Adjacent to the 1st Battalion at the small coastal village of Mogonho were the main artillery positions comprising two 76mm gun batteries that covered the entrance to the Sungari as well as Tungchiang.[6]

The southernmost Chinese positions were in and around the city where the 35th Regiment's headquarters, its 3rd Battalion, and several naval infantry companies were located. Finally, beginning at the batteries and ending in a taiga, a secondary defensive trench line stretched inland for six kilometers before Tungchiang. The Chinese Sungari River Flotilla, under the command of Captain Yi Kiang-tsu, was anchored near the eastern shore, just north of the city and south of the batteries. It comprised four gunboats and seven patrol craft. Yi made the gunboat *Kiang-heng*, under Captain Chang Lih-sen, his flagship. Both were seasoned veterans who had risen from the ranks after beginning their careers as common sailors in the Imperial Chinese Navy during the Sino-Japanese War of 1894–1895. As a final defensive measure, Yi hid a river barge, the *East B*, with two heavy 4.7-inch deck guns mounted, in the coastal reeds to provide added firepower to the flotilla's guns.[7]

The ODVA plan was to soften up the Chinese positions by air attack and fire from both land-based artillery on the Russian bank of the Amur and the Amur Flotilla's naval guns. The 2nd Division's headquarters would be located with the southernmost batteries. The Chinese batteries would be eliminated, while the 2nd Battalion, 3rd Infantry's, lines would be worked over by the northern Soviet batteries. After minesweepers cleared a channel, the Amur River Flotilla, led by the monitor division, would enter the Sungari and engage the Chinese flotilla. A river crossing on the Amur aimed at the 2nd Battalion would follow, and the troops in the landing barges would be under the protection of the Soviet gunboat and fast patrol boat divisions. The lone Chinese battalion would face the 1st Battalion, 6th Regiment, to the north, the 2nd Battalion, 5th Regiment, in the center, and 1st Battalion, 5th Regiment, to the south. It was a textbook application of the military dictum of mass.[8]

The looming naval engagement was unique in the interwar years.

While gunboats had long been a common sight on China's broad, long rivers, a clash between these warships was unusual, and a battle between two massed flotillas unprecedented. The modernity of the coming battle was also remarkable; the use of mines by the NEFDF, countered by Soviet minesweepers and the integrated use of ODVA aircraft and ships, added a high degree of complexity to the naval operation. Finally, the presence of the monitors introduced a quantum leap in firepower. The four Chinese gunboats carried a total of eighteen guns with a combined caliber of 50.3 inches. They outgunned the four Russian gunboats, which carried a total of eleven guns with a combined caliber of only 41.8 inches.[9]

The addition of the Soviet monitors, originally built with a main battery of four turrets, each housing one six-inch gun, dramatically changed the balance of power. By 1929, all but one, the *Sverdlov,* had their older 6-inch gun turrets replaced by two twin and two single 4.7-inch gun turrets, while carrying a secondary battery of two or three deck guns, giving the monitor division a total of thirty-two guns with a combined caliber of 130.2 inches, dwarfing the firepower of any gunboat flotilla that plied China's waters. The monitor's advantages did not end with it naval batteries; as with all monitors, its decks were clean to allow the maximum freedom of fire for its guns, and its turrets and upper hulls armored. The ship's ability to draw ballast to reduce its freeboard offered a minimal target for opposing gunners. These were deadly fighting ships.[10]

During the late evening of 11 October, the Soviet warships began to sail up the Amur from their anchorage near Khabarovsk toward the mouth of the Sungari. At 5:30 A.M. the next morning, the battle began with a naval and artillery bombardment accompanied by air attacks—the opening rounds of what became the largest naval engagement up to that time since the end of World War I. While the shelling was underway, Russian minesweepers *T-3-1* and *T-3-2* opened a lane to the port of Tungchiang. Once past the mines, the Sungari River was broadly welcoming, being anywhere from one to two kilometers in width, but as the river neared Tungchiang, it quickly narrowed to only a few hundred meters. When the Russian monitors approached the anchored Sungari Flotilla thirty minutes later and opened fire, these point-blank ranges made for a fearsome battle, as their 6-inch and 4.7-inch main guns were designed to effectively engage targets at a range of 10,000 meters. The two sides engaged at perilously close range. It was virtually impossible to miss.[11]

The lead armored monitor, *Sverdlov*, under the command of Captain A. I. Traynin, sank the Chinese patrol craft *Kiang-tai*, armed with two 2-inch deck guns, and the *Kiang-an*, armed with one 2-incher, before engaging Captain Mok Yiu-ming's more heavily armed gunboat *Li-shui*, mounting one 3.5-incher, two 3-inchers, and two 2-inch deck guns. The *Li-shui* suffered under Soviet fire, with three fourths of the crew becoming casualties and Captain Mok killed. The Chinese responded in kind; the 4.7-inch guns on the *East B* scored a direct hit on *Sverdlov*. The flagship lost all power, and the commander of the Amur River Flotilla was reportedly killed on his bridge. The loss of power threw the ship's gunners into complete darkness, but in the no. 3 turret, and despite the limited visibility and noxious gases, the lead petty officer, Fedor Vulahov, continued to manually operate the turret and fire his gun. His actions in suppressing the Chinese gunners may well have saved the ship.[12]

Moving to take the place in the battle line of the dead-in-the-water *Sverdlov*, the monitor *Red East*, commanded by R. I. Yuanzem, continued the fight by silencing a shore battery and sinking the badly outgunned patrol craft *Kiang-ping* in a heated ten-minute duel. When the action began, the Soviet armored monitors flooded their ballast tanks to reduce the ship's silhouette to the Chinese gunners. As they settled into the water, their decks "almost awash," the Chinese crews mistakenly assumed that the Soviet ships were sinking—an observation that both encouraged the Chinese sailors and later led to erroneous reporting after the battle of Soviet ship losses.[13] Despite the confusion, the fight drew to a close with renewed intensity as the Soviet monitor *Sun Yat-sen*, helmed by Captain I. I. Nikitin, engaged and destroyed the armed barge *East B*, taking its lethal 4.7-inch guns out of the fight. Before succumbing, the Chinese gunners gave their best, hitting the *Sun Yat-sen* three times and inflicting many casualties. The gunboat *Lu-chi*, with two 3.5-inch and one 2-inch deck guns, was also pummeled and abandoned; it became a Russian prize, along with the patrol craft *Tsen-I*. The cannonade of the Amur River Flotilla proved overwhelming. Within an hour, the Sungari Flotilla had suffered enough as the surviving vessels fled upriver to the port of Fuchin. The flagship *Kiang-heng* was able to lead the escape, but both Yi and Chang died during the fighting. In addition to the gunboat *Lu-chi*, seven former CER barges and an NEFDF transport ship were captured. The river fight was over, and the ground battle was about to begin.[14]

At 6:27 A.M., less than an hour after the naval battle began, the first of the ODVA assault battalions landed on the Chinese banks of the Amur. Twenty minutes later, I. A. Onufriev, the commander of the 2nd "Amur" Rifle Division, landed with his command group. He would lead the daylong fighting as the Chinese mounted a strong defense. It took the Soviet assault battalions six hours to advance the six kilometers to Tungchiang. The Russians pressed hard against the last line of defense. By late afternoon, the Kirin units began a withdrawal. The pursuing ODVA troops turned the retreat into a rout, inflicting a number of casualties. Chinese losses were estimated at nearly 1,000 killed and wounded, including 148 sailors and 225 naval infantry, along with 98 taken prisoner. The ODVA lost 172 killed and another 100 wounded. The Chinese also reported that among the dead were 30 officers, including the leader of the naval infantry and a senior colonel, probably a regimental commander. A subsequent air raid at Fuchin on 19 October by the Amur River Flotilla's 68th Seaplane Squadron put the already damaged *Li-shui* out of commission. Admiral Shen shut down all downriver traffic, confiscated sixteen steamers anchored at Fuchin, and directed that an army steamer and three barges be sunk downstream. All remaining mines were laid in an attempt to block the river and protect the town from attack by the Amur River Flotilla.[15]

Whether intended to further enrage the Soviets or not, on 16 October, the thirty-seven nondiplomat Soviets arrested during the May raid at the Harbin consulate were found guilty and sentenced to prison terms ranging from a maximum of nine years for the men to two years each for the four women prisoners. Faced with a significant defeat on the Sungari and a politically angered Soviet Russia, four days later, the Young Marshal held a war council at Mukden. Present were over fifty of his officers, along with General Chang Chun, former KMT vice war minister and close confidant of Chiang Kai-shek, and senior representatives from the NRA. Although little was disclosed, it was announced that armed resistance would continue, that the NEFDF had been ordered by Nanking to "stop the Russian incursions," and that reinforcements were being sent to the Sungari area.[16]

As the Young Marshal's generals attempted to reorganize the Sungari River defenses, the ODVA Amur River Flotilla and the 2nd "Amur" Rifle Division regrouped and prepared for the final phase of their operation. In the meantime, GPU units quickly replaced the ODVA forces at Tungchiang, reportedly from the 49th and 51st Regiments of the 17th GPU Brigade, which had the responsibility of collecting NEFDF weapons and munitions and eventually confiscated enough foodstuff to fill eight river barges. To their credit, the ODVA soldiers treated the Chinese civilians with respect and paid the laborers who helped load the captured supplies. The weapons collected included one 152mm and six 88mm artillery pieces, along with several machine guns and hundreds of Russian-made rifles. The foodstuff included over 2 million pounds of wheat flour along with "large quantities of potatoes, cabbages," and other stocks, giving credibility to claims that food shortages in the Soviet Far East could be blamed on both the loss of access to Manchuria's crops and the continuing problems stemming from dekulakization.[17]

The final phase of Blyukher's Sungari River operation began on 30 October with the raid on Fuchin, an important port on the southwest bank of the Sungari, some fifty kilometers upriver from Tungchiang. With Tungchiang controlled by the ODVA, and aware that a strike on Fuchin would open the river route to Harbin, the Young Marshal moved quickly to shore up the town's defenses with the aim of repelling an expected ground attack. A regiment from the 7th Kirin Mixed Brigade with two squadrons of the 43rd Kirin Cavalry had been rushed to Fuchin from Harbin, where they joined with the remnants of the Tungchiang garrison and the Sungari River Flotilla. The Kirin troops prepared two parallel lines of trenches approximately five kilometers apart just north of city. The lines began on the riverbank, stretched inland for about ten kilometers, and straddled the Fuchin–Tungchiang road. Additionally, a third and final set of entrenchments ringed the walled Old City to the south.[18]

The ODVA plan was simple: a second amphibious assault, not the anticipated overland march toward Fuchin. The Amur Flotilla was divided in two. A strike group, led by the minesweepers and monitors *Sun Yat-sen* and *Red East*, was tasked to clear the river of mines and engage what remained of the Sungari River Flotilla. The second group escorted the transports with the monitor *Sverdlov*, and the *Lenin* (commanded by Captain S. P. Byrny and armed similarly to the *Red East*) was to provide supporting fires during the landing. The landing force, consisting of two battalions of the 5th Regiment, intended to come ashore between the two Chinese trench lines to split their defenses, and aircraft would support the ships and landing force. The attack began at dawn on 30 October. The naval engagement was brief as the Chinese ships fled from the approaching monitors. The greatest Russian naval success occurred when pilot D. I. Borovikov from the 68th Seaplane Squadron hit and sank the gunboat *Kiang-heng*, the Chinese flagship.[19]

The landing proved more difficult, as the Chinese directed their fire at the minesweepers. It was late morning before the waters were cleared, and Aleksandr Musatov, commanding the *T-3-1*, was awarded the Order of the Red Banner for his leadership in sweeping the lanes clear of mines. The landing did not begin until 11:00 A.M. Once ashore, the 3rd Battalion turned north to attack the front line from the rear and soon routed the Chinese, but the 1st Battalion was forced to attack the second trench line frontally and was repulsed. Fortunately for the Soviets, the fleeing Chinese troops from the front line disorganized the defense in the second line. The 3rd Battalion took advantage of the momentary confusion and was able to occupy a small group of hills in front of the second line of trenches and then broke through. After four hours of fighting, both Chinese lines had been breached. At 6:00 P.M., the telegraph lines between Fuchin and Harbin went dead. The two Russian battalions regrouped and pushed on to the final defensive works at the Old City. After breaching the trenches, the Chinese quit the field and retreated west along the Sungari. By 8:00 P.M., the 5th Regiment held Fuchin with the Amur Flotilla anchored offshore. After gathering up stores and foodstuffs, the force withdrew unmolested three days later on 2 November and returned to Khabarovsk. As was the military custom of the day, the ODVA dead were interned in a mass grave at the Vladivostok naval cemetery, where a monument to their sacrifice was later erected.[20]

In the course of twenty days, the NEFDF's Sungari River Flotilla had been annihilated, while two Chinese regiments had been badly bloodied at Tungchiang and another at Fuchin. The best Admiral Shen could do to prevent the ODVA from sailing on to Harbin was to order the sinking of more ships to block their passage and hope for winter to freeze the river over. The residents of Harbin were "depressed," even "panicky," but the war against the Soviets was still popular in many quarters, as witnessed by the warm reception at the Harbin station given to the Feng Yung Student Corps detachment upon their return from the Western Front and the departure of a replacement group of student volunteers.[21] Nanking remained defiant, refusing to accede to the new Soviet ultimatum and still insisting on the replacement of the Soviet CER managers. The Soviets were equally unwavering in their resolve to end the crisis on their terms, and the preparations for the final ODVA offensive were completed over the next few weeks. Blyukher stood at the ready and awaited the order to attack from Voroshilov at Chita and Stalin in the Kremlin.

The October Massacres

While the ODVA's operations were progressing, a darker side of the conflict reared its head. Ordinarily the end of the harvest season in October was a time of gladness for the small, close-knit ethnic Russian Starovary farming communities in the far west of Manchuria, but the unresolved CER crisis in 1929 proved an exception. There is no record of which villager first spotted the armed and mounted band that approached Tineho in the Trekhreche District on the morning of 1 October. What happened immediately afterward was: The Soviet riders, later said to have numbered as many as 250 (as if numbers mattered when attacking defenseless civilians), quickly rounded up every male over the age of twelve and led them out of the village to a field where two machine guns stood at the ready. The brutally efficient modern weapons made quick work of most of the farmers—a pitiful collection of boys, men, and their elders. Bayonets and pistols shots finished the task as the blood of sixty-odd bodies drained into the rich, black Manchurian soil. As the day was young, and looting the farmers' meager possessions while burning their homes did not take long, there was time to duplicate the bloodbath at the smaller village of Tsangkir before the brigands headed back across the border. The dead were overwhelmingly Starovary, devout Christians who had fled European Russia to escape tsarist persecution and a people who cared about their dairy cows but not a whit about who ruled in Moscow. Moscow, however, "cared" about them; the madness that was Stalin's Russia had arrived in full bloody force.[22]

Since August, the GPU had been orchestrating acts of sabotage intended to shut down the CER and unconventional raids across the border designed to eliminate the perceived White threat. To facilitate the anti-White operations, the GPU recruited a 2,000-man "Brantia" force of "bandits and irregulars" on the Eastern Front, and a Mongol and Cossack unit formed into several independent detachments on the Western Front, some reportedly recruited from the Young Mongolia Party (formally the Inner Mongolian People's Revolutionary Party). The GPU on the Western Front had been operating on both sides of the border since the illegal 1928 Buryat crossings and were still very active in Manchouli as late as June 1929. The onset of the July CER crisis only increased the GPU's operational tempo; it was a detachment from the Western Front irregulars that carried out the massacres at Tineho and Tsangkir.[23]

The depredations piled up—eight more villages were raided in the days that followed—and soon fully half the Russian farmers abandoned their life's work. Hundreds of families desperately fled eastward toward the CER, carrying whatever belongings they could save. The financial losses for these impoverished wretches exceed $3 million (in 1929 dollars). Even some of the escape efforts were in vain, Powell later wrote:

> Fearing for the safety of their families, the White Russians sent their wives and children and all elderly males across country in a long wagon train to the railway at the town of Hailar, about 500 miles west of Harbin. The caravan, accompanied by a Russian Orthodox priest, had reached a point about fifty miles north of the railway when it was attacked by a force of Red Mongolian cavalry, allegedly led by Red army officers.
>
> The woman and boy to whom I talked and who claimed to be the only survivors of this caravan, having escaped into the forest, told me that the Mongols had slaughtered every other member of the caravan. They then built a vast funeral pyre of the wagons and their contents, consisting of firkins of butter and large fifty-pound cheeses. Upon this pyre they piled the bodies of their victims, with that of the priest at the apex. They ignited the pyre and, yelling and shooting their rifles, rode their ponies in a wide circle about it as it burned.[24]

By 18 October, reports of the massacres began to leak out. The tales of torture and murder appalled the international community. The onset of cold weather only worsened the plight of the survivors, but nothing of any import was done; they were just the newest and poorest band of stateless Russian refugees in the Northeast.[25]

Why the massacre of the Russian Christians? Religion played a role. The GPU was engaged in a purge of practitioners within the Soviet Union, and religiosity by Russians along the Northeastern frontier must have been an irritant. However, the Old Orthodox Believers were not missionaries; they had always kept to themselves, and they posed no threat to Soviet Russia. It was also true that such distinctions or subtleties did not enter into the calculation at the time of the CER crisis. By 1929, persecution was not simply acceptable but demanded of those in the Communist Party rank and file; the antireligious campaign directed by the unambiguously named League of Militant Atheists was peaking, and half measures were not tolerated. Nonetheless, the violence of the Three Rivers massacres was exceptional and communist intolerance of religion alone an insufficient motive.[26]

Collectivization proved the more compelling reason: ridding the border region of successful Russian private farmers had became essential, especially in light of the 1928 Buryat exodus after Moscow's collectivization in Central Siberia. The idea of Soviet farmers along the frontier picking up stakes and moving to the open farmlands in Heilungkiang was troublesome to the Soviet authorities, but what was unacceptable was risking an internal rebellion. Allowing a condition to fester where successful Starovary farms could become the cause of unrest among Soviet farmers—a danger recognized by local British officials at the time—could never be tolerated. Further, the violence of war gave cover to extreme solutions, and Stalin had always been exceptionally harsh on anyone suspected of being a "whiteguarist."[27] The 1929 CER conflict presented Moscow with the opportunity to rid itself of the problem, and the presence of the GPU-controlled irregulars provided the tool needed for a solution. The massacres, rather than an aberration, became unavoidable. The oft-unreported political retributions of Stalin's secret police never ceased.[28]

Did the ODVA play a role in the atrocities? Blyukher never sanctioned unlawful bloodletting during the civil war or in China, and there is no evidence that he deviated from that policy in 1929. During the civil war, Blyukher often took the opposite line of encouraging Whites to join the revolution and opposed collectivization in the Far East, seeing the mistreatment of the peasants as counterproductive. That was a shared conclusion. Revulsion at the violence resulting from dekulakization combined with a rejection of the rapid implementation of the collectivization policy also reflected the position of Litvinov and Bukharin in 1929. There is no reason to believe that Blyukher and the ODVA were behind the killings; this was a GPU operation and likely launched from Outer Mongolia, akin to the earlier Russian-sponsored cross-border attacks on the Hailar region in June 1912 and August 1928. The actions of the Red Army did much to undo the political damage caused by the massacres by sending a far different signal to the world: the RKKA was a foe not only to be feared but respected.[29]

The Continued Illusion of Peace and Hope for a Negotiated Settlement

The fighting was not limited to the Sungari River. On the Western Front, the periodic artillery duels and infantry skirmishing that had been going on since August had taken a toll on the Soviet farmers living on the Argun River. For the Trans-Baikal Group commander, Vostretsov, it was a problem that needed resolution. On 30 October, he informed Blyukher of the situation, then decided to eliminate an offending 17th Heilungkiang Brigade strongpoint across the river from the small Russian village of Olochinskaya. During a cold, rainy week in early November, the 5th Brigade's 73rd Cavalry Regiment, supported by Gregory I. Khetagurov's horse artillery battery, left their camp near Abagaitevskya and rode out into the night. Khetagurov's unit was part of the brigade's artillery battalion commanded by Ivan P. Kamera, one of the Red Army's best artillery officers. In darkness, Khetagurov moved his battery into place on high ground overlooking the Chinese position and was joined by Brigade Commander Rokossovsky, who had arrived to direct the assault. Rokossovsky had served in Blyukher's campaign against Kolchak and was the same cavalry officer who had helped defeat the Mad Baron in 1921. At first light, the Chinese discovered the cavalry and opened fire. In return, Rokossovsky ordered Khetagurov's artillery to engage the Chinese. His gunners soon scored a number of hits, knocking out mortars and setting the blockhouse afire. Two Russian cavalry squadrons then charged across the waters of the Argun. The Chinese were quickly overrun, with nearly eighty killed. Captured weapons included two artillery pieces and six mortars.[30]

While the Sungari River operation and the strike on the Western Front were wrapping up, hope that a resolution to the crisis was at hand rose anew in diplomatic circles. The Germans were still engaged, and they attempted to jump-start the talks by promoting an act of good faith: the mutual exchange of civilian prisoners held by the Chinese and Soviet authorities. Stimson anxiously contacted the other Powers, asking them to help push the talks forward. Only the British remained openly aloof. When approached by the Americans, they declined on the basis of severed diplomatic relations with the Soviet Union and the ongoing efforts of Germany. It proved a wise move, as neither Berlin nor Washington's efforts gained any traction in Nanking or Moscow.[31]

One illuminating exchange that revealed what the United States and Japan were thinking took place in Washington on 31 October. During a meeting between Stimson and Debuchi, Stimson sought out the ambassador's advice on how to resolve the differences between two seemingly contradictory reports. The first dealt with the battle at Tungchiang and the second emanated from Myrl S. Myers, the American consul in Mukden. The former indicated a marked escalation in the war. The latter was a report stating that Chiang Kai-shek had reached his end in negotiating a settlement and was passing the lead back to the Young Marshal, who appeared eager to accept the Soviet demands. Myers concluded that the chance of a peaceful solution "seems brighter than ever before."[32] Which was correct? Were the two parties on the road to war or peace? Debuchi assured Stimson that Tokyo was of a like mind with Myers. For Stimson to embrace such optimism made little sense, as a day earlier, Minister Wu had made clear that China understood Stalin's real intent. The sticking point was not about railway managers or board presidents; the conflict centered on "the maintenance of the existing government in China" and Stalin's effort "in every way to undermine the government."[33] The impasse was unbridgeable, and no pacific solution was possible.[34]

Why would Tokyo and Washington seemingly accept such an unrealistic outcome? A few days earlier, Debuchi had also downplayed the military action in the Northeast, stating that "there was no fighting, only 'clashes.'"[35] This flew in the face of actions on the ground and the declaration of the Young Marshal, who reaffirmed on 20 October the NEFDF's resolve in repelling ODVA attacks. The discussion then went to the heart of the Kellogg–Briand Pact: what would constitute a war? Stimson and Debuchi agreed that a Soviet thrust to seize the CER and Harbin would mean war. Such a high bar was attractively self-serving. On the basis of the understanding reached between Moscow and Tokyo in September, the ODVA offensive approved by Stalin did not envision taking the whole of the CER or seizing Harbin, placating the Kwantung Army hotheads and allowing Tokyo to permit a Soviet military offensive while supporting the Kellogg–Briand Pact.[36]

For Washington, the need to preserve the concept of the Kellogg–Briand Pact overwhelmed any sense of objective judgment. On 4 November, the press reported the destruction of the Teheiho electric power station's central dynamo by explosives planted by Red Army raiders. After the lights went out, the town was shelled by Soviet artillery. The report changed nothing. In tandem, the diplomats in Tokyo and Washington were more than content to accept that the war raging in the Northeast was no war at all. Outside of China, the rest of the world was only too willing to agree. As mid-November approached, the Young Marshal saw things much differently and connected his plight to Feng's rebellion. Mukden believed Moscow would not negotiate until the outcome of that conflict was determined; he feared the ODVA "intends in the meantime to invade and occupy Chinese territory."[37] It was a fatefully prescient insight.[38]

Unleashing the Red Army Onslaught

When the Chinese failed to capitulate after the Sungari River operation, Stalin approved the ODVA's final offensive. On 15 November, Blyukher, along with operations chief Chuikov and other key staff officers, departed Khabarovsk for Dauria to oversee the Trans-Baikal Group's offensive on the Western Front. Blyukher directed the ODVA deputy commander Lapin to remain behind and take charge of the Eastern Front with Cherepanov as the tactical commander. In Moscow, Stalin chose this moment to move against his last major opponent: Nikolai Bukharin. The once close ally turned rival, opponent of immediate collectivization, and advocate for a peaceful settlement of the CER crisis was ousted from the Politburo on the day the offensive began.[39]

The CCP Central Committee also used this period to clean house. As Blyukher rode on a military train heading west, Ch'en Tu-hsiu was expelled from the party he had helped create, another casualty of the CER crisis. Mao later wrote a rare letter of support to Li Li-san that lauded the expulsion and condemned Ch'en's stance against the Central Committee's pro-Soviet CER policy, characterizing his actions as "truly outrageous."[40] Mao stood firmly in the Soviet camp, writing two months later that the Soviet Union was China's "elder brother" while Chiang Kai-shek was an imperialist lackey who "created the agitation of these last several months regarding the Chinese Eastern Railway."[41] The time for the final ODVA offensive had arrived.

The Mishan Operation (17–18 November)

The destruction of Suifenho in September left only one major target for the Soviets on the Eastern Front: the city of Mishan and the nearby Muleng coalfields. The attack, launched on 17 November, was a division-size operation that was the smallest of the major Soviet offenses, but it was also one of the best planned and executed. Mishan lay just south of the Muleng River and some forty kilometers northwest of the border. Since the opening of the mines in 1924, the area had become an important coal-mining center used to supply the CER. For the operation, Cherepanov had the 9th Cavalry Brigade under D. A. Vaynerh attached to his division. An air group commanded by E. P. Karklin, composed of the 5th and 19th Fighter and 40th Bomber squadrons, was to provide air support. Cherepanov's force would face the 1st Mukden Cavalry Division to the east and its 1st Independent Cavalry Brigade to the west. The Chinese cavalry were stretched across a sixty-kilometer front. There was also a squadron of five observation aircraft at Mishan to help coordinate Chinese actions. The 1st Mukden Mixed Brigade could also reinforce the cavalry units; the brigade's 42nd Regiment was located at Pantahsai, about twenty-five kilometers to the southwest.[42]

The Soviet attack was punitive: the 1st "Pacific" Division was to rapidly seize Mishan, render the coal mines unusable, and withdraw back across the border. Cherepanov divided his forces into three columns. The main attack consisted of the bulk of the division, built around the 2nd "Nerchinsk" and 3rd "Verkhneudinsk" regiments that assembled near Turi Rog, a scene of border clashes since July. Their mission was to drive north and capture Mishan by following a roadless route covered with iced-over swamps and thickly forested hills. The second column was also located in the vicinity of Turi Rog and consisted of Vaynerh's brigade reinforced by three horse-drawn batteries of three 76mm mountain guns each and the 3rd Battalion, 3rd Regiment, transported in horse-drawn carts. Vaynerh's mobile group was to be the vanguard and operate on the left flank of the main body. It was designed for speed, and its mission was to either meet and defeat or bypass Chinese forces until it reached Mishan, embodying the fast-paced task-organized forces advocated in the *1929 Regulations*. Once there, it was to isolate the city and prevent the escape of the Chinese defenders. The third column consisted of the 1st "Chita" Rifle Regiment under I. F. Kunitzsky, which had been assembled in the vicinity of the small village of Krayny, some fifteen kilometers to the west of Turi Rog and four kilometers from the Manchurian border to the northwest. Its mission was to seize the town of Taipinchien, located ten kilometers from the border and defended by elements of the 1st Mukden Cavalry Brigade. Once there, the regiment was to prepare defensive positions to block the road from the west and prevent any advance by the 1st Mixed Brigade.[43]

At 6:00 A.M. on Sunday, 17 November, Russian cavalry and infantry, pushing aside surprisingly effective barriers of soybean cakes, crossed the border in the face of stiff Chinese resistance.[44] Small detachments fanned out across the area to cut telegraph lines and scout out Chinese positions. At 6:40 A.M., aircraft from the 19th Fighter Squadron attacked the Chinese airfield at Motaishih near Mishan, destroying the observation aircraft on the ground. Lapin also launched an attack at Suifenho, which served as a diversion to pin down the Chinese forces there while the main body of the 9th Brigade moved quickly on Mishan. Shortly before 10:00 A.M., and alerted by aircraft, the brigade was able to defeat a Chinese cavalry regiment that had advanced on it from Miaoling. The Soviet drive was relentless. By 2:00 P.M., they were nearing the outskirts of Mishan from the west. Meanwhile, Kunitzsky's regiment to the west had also seized Taipinchien, pushing back the troopers of the 1st Cavalry Brigade.[45]

The 9th Brigade had advanced over forty kilometers in half a day. At 3:00 P.M., the 87th Cavalry, led by F. A. Parkhomenko, began to encircle Mishan despite counterattacks by the defending Chinese cavalry. The deputy regimental commander, Ivan Chebotar, was killed during this action. By 4:00 P.M., the 3rd Battalion, in carts and accompanied by horse artillery, had arrived and began a coordinated assault on Mishan's defensive works. The Russian infantry breached the trenches; the Chinese cavalry units remounted and fell back to the north. The Chinese cavalry broke through the encirclement but suffered heavy casualties from artillery fire and air attack as they retreated across the icy Muleng River. By evening, Cherepanov's division held Mishan.[46]

The Chinese were not ready to give up, however. At dawn on 18 November, the remnants of two cavalry regiments from the 1st Cavalry Brigade, along with the 42nd Infantry Regiment, attempted to dislodge Kunitzsky's "Chita" Rifle Regiment at Taipinchien. Intense small arms and artillery fire, reinforced by air strikes, beat back the attacking Chinese. Kunitzsky then counterattacked and pursued the retreating Chinese until darkness forced a halt. The fighting was over, and the Russians returned across the border a few days later. The Soviets reported that the Chinese suffered nearly 1,500 killed, mostly during the breakout at the Muleng River, and lost large amounts of equipment as well as several regimental colors. The ODVA fallen were brought back to Ussuriysk and buried with honors in a mass grave. After Cherepanov's strike, the Eastern Front remained quiet, with the exception of a few air strikes, including a second attack at the Motaishih airfield that resulted in the destruction of three more NEFDF aircraft on 29 November.[47]

The Dalainor–Manchouli–Hailar Operation (16–25 November)

The simultaneous Western Front offensive constituted the largest operation of the war and began on the evening of 16 November, when Rokossovsky's Cavalry Group, consisting of the 5th Cavalry Brigade plus two battalions from the 35th Division's 107th Regiment and the Buryat–Mongol Cavalry Division, began to move across the border in the dark, bitter cold, and shortly all the Trans-Baikal Group assault units were underway. Earlier in the day, the senior commanders had conducted their last reconnaissance of the Chinese positions, and the division commanders briefed Blyukher that evening. Everything was at the ready. Thick fog aided the Trans-Baikal Group as they advanced along concealed "pre-designated" routes. The soldiers carried their weapons with a full load of ammunition, and most importantly, they had been issued winter clothing.[48] A few kilometers from the border, a rest was ordered, and horse hooves and wheels were wrapped in cloth to deaden the sounds of movement. Blyukher and his ODVA command team moved close to Abagaitevskya, one kilometer from the border. The maneuver was a deep envelopment around the rear of General Han's 17th Brigade, covering over 100 kilometers and designed to isolate both Dalainor and Manchouli from General Hu's 2nd Fengtien Army at Hailar. Rokossovsky sent the 73rd Cavalry Regiment with an attached horse artillery battery to seize Hill 1005, the dominating ground between Manchouli and Dalainor.[49]

The 36th Division's 106th Regiment then moved to cut Dalainor off from Manchouli by capturing Hill 810, which was across from Hill 1005 and adjacent to the CER, while the regiment's 6th Company moved to sever a nearby section of the CER railway, along with the field phone and telegraph lines that connected Liang with Dalainor and Hailar and guarded by a small unit of the 38th Infantry. The Chinese detachment was caught by surprise and fled. The soldiers of the 6th Company quickly went to work cutting the lines and disabling the rails, but before they could begin, the signal lamps lit up and an express train from Manchouli sped by. Their frustration was momentary, as the train was spotted by some of Rokossovsky's cavalry, and Khetagurov's horse artillery hit the engine on the second round. The train ground to a tumultuous halt, and the passengers, mainly Chinese soldiers, were surrounded and captured, including a senior officer found grasping a leather case full of military documents.[50]

The 6th Company succeeded in breaking the line and severing the telephone and telegraph communications, but the Chinese quickly mounted counterattacks. As soon as there was light, the 106th Regiment came under fire from other 38th Infantry units; the 17th Brigade's 13th Infantry Regiment tried to dislodge the Soviets on Hill 1005 but was beaten back. A larger battle developed when the Chinese 3rd Cavalry from Dalainor attacked the 75th Cavalry, led by Makar Yakimov. A vicious saber fight ensued. The timely arrival of the horse artillery from Hill 1005, with their grapeshot and canister salvos, sealed the Soviet victory. The 75th Cavalry suffered over 70 killed, including a highly decorated squadron commander, F. I. Pilipenko. The 3rd Cavalry left over 200 dead on the field, half of its strength. Vostretsov was in the thick of the fight and directed an assault on the 38th Infantry to stabilize the situation around Hill 1005 before moving on to the next hot spot. The Russian encirclement held.[51]

The primary objective was Dalainor, defended by Han's reinforced 17th Brigade. The 36th Division's assault group, which consisted of the 107th and 108th Rifle regiments, 1st Tank Company, conducted the attack. The 21st Division, supported by the armored trains, tied up the 15th Brigade at Manchouli, and its 63rd Regiment linked up with the 106th Regiment at midday, preventing the 15th Brigade from coming to Han's aid, while the 35th Division conducted a diversionary attack against the 14th Infantry manning the southeastern Dalainor defenses. At 7:00 A.M., the artillery opened fire, signaling a two-hour-long bombardment of the Chinese positions. According to Captain Kawamata, the Japanese military observer, the intensity of fire "wilted" the stunned Chinese.[52] The assault group then began a daylong fight with the entrenched 6th Infantry. At 11:30 A.M., sixteen Soviet aircraft in two formations began attacking. Shortly afterward, the power went out when the Dalainor generator plant was put out of action. For the rest of the day, aircraft were constantly overhead, inflicting casualties on the Chinese. By nightfall, Rokossovsky's Cavalry Group had isolated the two cities, seized Hill 1005, and defeated several counterattacks. To deter any relief column, the nearest NEFDF garrison, a battalion at the Tsagan train station (20 kilometers east of Dalainor) was bombed. Hailar was also bombed, resulting in damage to the rail station there. The 21st Division had pinned the 15th Brigade at Manchouli and the 35th Division gained some ground against the 14th Infantry at Dalainor, but the Soviet attack was not meeting its objectives.[53]

While these successes meant that General Liang's forces had been cut off from General's Hu's forces at Hailar and Liang's connection to General Han's 17th Brigade in Dalainor had been cut, the 36th Division's assault group had failed to break the 17th Brigade's defenses, the principal goal of attack. That was not the only difficulty as Soviet tank deployment proved uncoordinated. Two tanks missed their attack position north of Dalainor and wandered into the 106th Regiment's zone. Although lost, they were put to use in dislodging some dug-in troops of the 38th Regiment before finding their way back to the tank company. The remainder of the tank company fared only a little better; while effectively engaging the Chinese bunkers, the Red Army soldiers failed to exploit the advantage. Chuikov later wrote that the Chinese and Russian soldiers were so amazed by the sight of the tanks that they froze in wonder.[54] Adding to the problems at Dalainor, the bulk of the Trans-Baikal's artillery group, located near Manchouli, was out of range and could not support the attack, forcing part the assault group to make a frontal attack on the well-prepared and largely intact trench lines.[55]

The Chinese defenses were formidable. In addition to several lines of trenches and barbwire entanglements, the front was further broken up with minefields and antitank ditches measuring thirteen feet in depth. There was one glaring weakness: smoking chimneys gave away the location of many of the Chinese blockhouses, and the Russian troops assaulted them in close combat by dropping grenades down the pipes. While the Soviets' progress was slow but steady, the Chinese continuously counterattacked to try to regain lost ground. The 51st Infantry from Manchouli attacked a machine gun company from the 106th Regiment near Hill 810. When the Russians ran low on ammunition and were in danger of being overrun, the commander, I. G. Tozov, ordered a withdrawal and stayed back with a small group to slow down the Chinese. Tozov and the others were killed, but the rest of the company escaped. During the morning, General Liang's staff met and recommended a 1:00 P.M. attack on the ODVA artillery positions in and around Siding No. 86 to disrupt the Red Army offensive. Liang turned down the proposal. It was the only known instance when the Chinese considered taking the war into Soviet territory.[56]

As evening fell, Voroshilov in Chita contacted Blyukher at the front informing him that he was prepared to halt the offensive and order the Trans-Baikal Group back across the border. Voroshilov had reason to be worried. Moscow was anxious: artillery ammunition was running low, the attacking troops had suffered hundreds of casualties, and they had failed to breach the defenses—and the weather was turning worse. A snowstorm was approaching; the high temperature had only reached –11°C and would soon fall to –20°C, making life almost unbearable for the exposed Russian frontline troops. As one participant described it, the soldiers were too far forward to deliver hot food, and the loaves of bread brought up to augment the field rations were frozen solid by the time they arrived and had be cut into pieces with hatchets. Setting warming fires in the darkness proved impossible, as they immediately drew accurate Chinese artillery and mortar fire. Blyukher knew the conditions, having visited the frontline units throughout the day. Despite the hardships brought on by the weather and combat, the Trans-Baikal Group was fighting well. At 5:00 P.M., Blyukher called his officers together and announced the attack would resume the next morning.[57]

The night would be a busy one for both sides. The Chinese were fighting hard; the 51st Regiment launched a night attack on Hill 810. From his position on the hill, Ivan I. Fedyuninsky commanded both his 6th Rifle Company and Tozov's machine gun company. As the sixteen machine guns opened fire at a range of only 400 meters, a "sea of lead" ripped into the Chinese ranks. Their screams could be heard over the sounds of the guns. The 51st Infantry continued to advance until beaten back by a Russian bayonet charge.[58] The bravery of the Chinese troops was frequently acknowledged; Fedyuninsky later remarked that they never lacked courage and often fought to the last bullet without retreating. Blyukher was able to convince Voroshilov to allow the offensive to continue while Vostretsov organized a new attack on Dalainor, this time by the 35th Division. Voroshilov ordered further reinforcements east from the Moscow Military District. Chuikov spent a sleepless night overseeing the redeployment of artillery batteries and redistributing ammunition to ensure that the assault units would get needed supporting fire before moving south of Dalainor to brief Rokossovsky at his headquarters on the attack plan. The night's efforts worked: the attack on 18 November quickly gained momentum.[59]

As the day dawned, a strong wind had arisen that only served to make the hardships of the exposed troops more difficult. At 7:00 A.M., the Chinese defenses at Dalainor came under a continuous barrage by the Soviet artillery. Adding to the defenders' misery, ODVA aircraft began to hit their lines at 8:30 A.M. Finally, after a two-and-a-half-hour bombardment, the 35th Division advanced on the trench lines held by the Chinese 14th Infantry Regiment while the 6th Infantry was fully engaged with the 108th Rifle Regiment's diversionary attack. Soon one regiment from the 35th Division broke through, then another. By 11:00 A.M., the Dalainor barracks fell, and a company from the 104th Rifle Regiment was moving toward the rail station—a new focal point of fighting. When the company commander was killed during an attempt to capture a key bridge, the commissar, A. P. Beloborodov, took over and led the charge that took the bridge. The Russian advance seemed unstoppable. During the morning's fighting, General Han was killed; by that time, two of his three regimental commanders had also lost their lives in battle. The 17th Brigade, which had fought so well, began to collapse. Isolated Chinese units surrendered, and the fighting became disorganized.[60]

One group of Chinese soldiers attempted to break out near the hamlet of Nos, but the Buryat–Mongol Cavalry Division quickly closed in on them. Ignoring the subzero temperatures, the division commander, Bulgakov, ordered his cavalrymen to remove their coats to free their saber arms before charging. Rokossovsky, who had not fought with the Buryats before, was enraged, exclaiming, "What is he doing? Freezing his people!" Bulgakov, referring to the Chinese soldiers, replied, "How, Comrade Brigade Commander, should we be cutting the sheepskins? We shear them with our blades."[61] A free saber arm was essential, even if it meant stripping down in the frigid weather. The response brought a hint of a smile to Rokossovsky's face, and the charge proceeded. The Chinese were routed after suffering 400 casualties.[62]

At Manchouli, the 15th Brigade's deputy commander, Wei Changlin, was also killed in action; the ODVA attacks were proving fiercer than the day before. Liang realized that the end had come for the 17th Brigade when the Chinese artillery at Dalainor fell silent shortly after noon. By 1:30 P.M., the 18th Corps had overrun the Chinese defenses, although pockets of resistance in the town and coal mines held on until darkness fell before being overwhelmed. Of the over 6,000 Chinese defenders, only the remaining troopers of the 3rd Cavalry escaped as unit. Approximately 1,500 NEFDF soldiers had become casualties and some 3,000 surrendered; a rabble numbering perhaps 800 skirted both sides of Hill 1005 and fled in panic toward Manchouli. The horse artillery on the hill took the soldiers under fire, but Blyukher ordered them to cease. "Enough of blood," he stated flatly. "Let them tell the others that it is impossible to stop a Soviet attack."[63]

Mercifully for both sides, there was a pause in the fighting as day broke on 19 November. After the fall of Dalainor, the Trans-Baikal Group needed several hours to shift men and guns to tighten the noose around Manchouli. It was still a raw environment for the soldiers; the temperature was –14°C at 4:00 A.M., and snow had begun to fall. The poor weather only added to gloom that had settled over the Chinese headquarters. General Liang knew he had to retake the southern high ground if Manchouli was to hold out, but he failed to grasp the magnitude of the ODVA offensive, instead assuming that there was only a small Red Army force on the hill.[64]

He picked his best regiment, the 38th Heilungkiang Infantry—the unit that had bested the Soviets during the August Dalainor attack—to lead an attack against Hill 810 that evening. The tactics followed the standard at the time; multiple single-file columns approached the hill in darkness. The assault began at 7:00 P.M. when the 38th Regiment passed through the lines of the 51st Infantry, advanced some 2,000 meters, and attacked up the hill. The battle raged for more than an hour as the Chinese pushed the Buryat–Mongol troopers back on the left flank. Eventually the Russians were able to mount a counterattack that broke the 38th Infantry, and a battalion from the 107th Rifle Regiment was quickly dispatched to steady the Russian line.[65]

The Red Army had taken its revenge on the 38th Infantry, but more importantly, with the failure to retake the commanding hills to the south, the Chinese forces in the Manchouli basin were in a hopeless position and further defense was futile. Without an alternative, the 15th Brigade attempted to breakout through the hills to the southeast, but Rokossovsky's cavalry thwarted the effort. Freed from their nighttime trenches and back in the saddle, his horsemen from the Buryat–Mongol Cavalry Division moved to the left flank of the leading unit of the retreating brigade and charged directly into the ranks of the Chinese with their sabers slashing, spreading panic among the riflemen. Ground markings visible from the air were placed at the forward ODVA positions, allowing aircraft to bomb and strafe Chinese troops at close range. The final blow came when Khetagurov's artillery, backed by machine guns, tore into the Chinese ranks. Casualties mounted as the 15th Brigade's soldiers fell "in rows," with no end in sight to the slaughter.[66]

Finally the line broke; the Chinese fell back toward Manchouli. There was no escaping the trap for the 15th Brigade.[67]

Later in the morning of 20 November, General Liang met for the last time with his staff, made the decision to surrender, and asked for the good offices of the Japanese in conducting the formalities. The timing undoubtedly saved many lives, as the ODVA assault on Manchouli was scheduled to begin at 11:00 A.M. At 1:00 P.M., Consul Fujino, in a sedan flying the Japanese flag, escorted the Manchouli district governor and several NEFDF officers to a waiting group of ODVA officers at a small wooden shack adjacent to the tracks at Siding No. 86. Chuikov, representing Blyukher, presented the terms: the NEFDF troops were to lay down their arms where they were, end further violence and looting, and assemble at the military barracks on the eastern outskirts of Manchouli with the officers confined to separate barracks.[68]

General Liang was conspicuously absent. Blyukher instructed Chuikov to demand a meeting in person with Liang before any terms would be accepted. Informed that he was at the Japanese consulate, both groups departed by automobile for the city. Once there, Liang pleaded for twenty-four hours to effect the surrender, but Chuikov gave him two. There was nothing for Liang to do but submit. Vostretsov arrived at 3:00 P.M. to formally accept the surrender. In return, the ODVA promised to guarantee the life and property of the surrendered Chinese soldiers and the town's residents. The town had been badly damaged and looted before the Soviets arrived. Hundreds of Chinese soldiers had deserted and had ransacked every building they encountered in the city, destroying nearly 400 homes in the process. ODVA troops occupied Manchouli that afternoon, began arresting the deserters, and quickly restored a good semblance of order.[69]

The actions of the deserters dishonored the considerable sacrifice and discipline displayed by the majority of the NEFDF on the Western Front. The fighting had exacted a heavy cost: the Chinese brigades had been destroyed in three days of severe fighting; the 17th Brigade suffered approximately 1,000 killed and 1,500 wounded, and the 15th Brigade lost just under 700 killed and slightly over 700 wounded. Over 9,000 Chinese soldiers had been captured, while the Russians suffered over 1,000 casualties.[70]

The Final Fighting, Occupation, and Aftermath

After destroying Liang's forces, the Trans-Baikal Group did not rest. An advance on Hailar, 150 kilometers to the east, was underway by 23 November. The 21st Division under P. I. Ashahmanov, having participated in the attacks on Manchouli, was directed to relieve the 18th Corps of occupation duties so its two divisions could move on Hailar. Remaining behind with the 21st Division was the 73rd Cavalry, and some Buryat-Mongol troopers tracked down the scattered remains of Liang's cavalry. The Chinese horsemen fled across the Mongolian frontier, were disarmed by RKKA-led MPRA cavalry, and interned for the rest of the fighting. With the last threat to Dalainor and Manchouli removed, the drive on Hailar intensified.[71]

Rokossovsky's Cavalry Group screened ahead of the advancing 106th Rifle Regiment. The rest of the 36th Division departed a short time later as the 35th Division made its final preparations for the march east. The reinforced 9th Air Group conducted scouting missions and continued to bomb Hailar. Panic reigned in the town. Fortunately an exodus of the civilian population had begun on 19 November, as soon as the news arrived of the attack on Dalainor. Train tickets were quickly sold out for five days in advance, but additional trains were ordered by the CER, allowing many to escape the bombing raids. The distance from the airfields to Hailar meant the Soviets could only attack from the west, allowing the Chinese to concentrate their fire. Hailar gunners were able to claim three Soviet aircraft, but the raids broke the morale of the Chinese garrison.[72]

General Hu Yu-kun had never prepared the 2nd Mukden Army for a fight, and the Dalainor–Manchouli defeat and the news that Tsagan had fallen to Red Army cavalry, coupled with the air raids, were all that was needed for him to call a hasty retreat on 23 November. As the troops departed, there was a breakdown in discipline. The Hailar rear guard, the 55th Fengtien Regiment, turned into an unruly mob, and the police deserted their posts. Later in the day, the power went out and hundreds of buildings were burned. Arsonist's fires, not electric lights, lit the city that night. Hu's performance was as disgraceful as the Trans-Baikal Group was relentless. After advancing day and night over difficult and often roadless terrain, the Red Army reached Hailar on 25 November. The march proved the most difficult task, as the town was taken without firing a shot, and the Red Army troops soon restored order. The Soviets kept their promise to the Japanese and did not advance far past Hailar, but that did not prevent them from ordering several squadrons of aircraft forward to bombard the retreating 2nd Army.[73]

At 1:00 P.M. on 28 November, planes from the 9th Air Group struck the Poketu rail station (215 kilometers east of Hailar) in two waves. The first, composed of three aircraft, dropped twelve bombs before the main strike of thirteen planes arrived, dropping another fifty-two bombs that resulted in severe damage to the rail station, locomotive shed, and an awaiting passenger train, as well as CER employee quarters and the hospital. The attacks resumed the next day. For two hours beginning at 11:00 A.M., nineteen aircraft reattacked the railway station. During the raid, the ammunition dump was struck, resulting in a terrific explosion; by luck, a train loaded with refugees had left the station just twenty minutes before the attack began. The railroad staff had had enough and deserted. Hu's forces quickly followed their lead. Once again, the poorly led troops fled after looting the place. Pictures of one CER employee's house told the story: all that was left was ashes, the foundation, and two chimneys. The worst of Hu's soldiers were not brought to heel until fired upon by Heilungkiang troops led by Governor-General Wan Fu-lin after the rabble attempted to force its way across the Nonni River bridge outside Tsitsihar. They were lives wasted; the Red Army air raid on 29 November was the last engagement. The war was over.[74]

The ODVA occupation was in full swing by then. In addition to dismantling the extensive NEFDF defensive works and military facilities, Ashahmanov had been able to clear the streets and restore basic public services in Manchouli by 25 November. His troops had also conducted surveys to locate available food and fuel stocks, and had completed a census to determine the needs of the civilian population. Ashahmanov directed that those without would have rations and fuel delivered to their homes. Unable to let the opportunity pass, the populace was subjected to propaganda praising the Soviets while denigrating the imperialist warlord rulers in Mukden and Nanking. Adding to the humiliation, a film of several Chinese deserters who sought to escape detention by dressing in women's clothing was made and shown to crowds in Manchouli. To help maintain order, drinking by ODVA soldiers was prohibited after two soldiers went on a drunken rampage; outside of some municipal government officials, no civilians were allowed to leave the area, and the telegraph office remained closed. An exception was made on 26 November, when each member of the foreign community was allowed to send a one-sentence telegram.[75]

Prisoners of the NEFDF had to be looked after as well. The Red Army immediately began to politically educate the captured soldiers. The proselytization effort, combined with fair treatment, paid off: a number of prisoners moved to join the Young Communist League. The Red Army had not lost its revolutionary zeal. One distressing area of concern was the plight of the wounded Chinese soldiers. With the presence of the CER and municipal hospitals, as well as a small medical staff assigned to the bomb-damaged Plague Prevention Clinic and Laboratory augmenting the NEFDF medical personnel, treatment was lavish by warlord-era standards, but the numbers requiring medical treatment were still overwhelming. There were over 200 severely wounded and over 500 with lesser injuries that required hospitalization. Under Ashahmanov's orders, ODVA doctors soon began to care for the casualties; they organized a unified medical agency to improve treatment. The aid was possible because of a Red Army casualty treatment system characterized by rapid evacuation. As ODVA soldiers were wounded, they were first sent to the field hospital at Dauria, and those requiring extended care were sent to nearby hospital trains. Once there, they could be further evacuated to Chita or elsewhere as needed. In short order, ODVA troops requiring hospitalization were quickly out of the combat zone, freeing up the medical staffs to help with the wounded Chinese soldiers.[76]

Elements of the 36th Division remained to occupy Hailar. The first order of business was to get fresh water after marauding Chinese soldiers destroyed the existing supply. Food and fuel were again shared with the civilian population, and disciplined ODVA troops restored order, although there was minor looting until the end of the month. Foreign residents were kept safe; they welcomed the arrival of the Trans-Baikal Group after two days of lawlessness. The behavior of the troops as they interacted with the town's inhabitants mimicked that at Dalainor–Manchouli; the troops' fondness for fresh ramen noodles delighted the local vendors, although the wrapping paper was changed from white to black to avoid giving offense. Because each ODVA rifle company was responsible for providing its soldiers with soup and boiled water (often for hot tea), the noodles were a welcome addition to their rations. Both the soldiers and the remaining civilians were satisfied with the occupation, but the Soviets did not leave empty-handed; on the afternoon of 27 November, they seized Hailar's gasoline and kerosene stocks, and shipped twenty fully loaded cars by special train back to Russia.[77]

As was the case in the October massacres, there was a darker side to the occupation when the GPU entered the scene at Manchouli on 24 November. They too conducted a census, but this one focused on the Russian male population. Once completed, it was quickly followed by orders to have hundreds of the men report to the GPU occupation authorities, where they were detained. Those failing to appear were sought out and arrested. The secret police swept up a total of 317 men in Manchouli and another 129 at Dalainor. Most were CER or government employees or police officers; women and children were not arrested. Soon the only remaining Russian men were Soviet citizens and those identified by the GPU as Soviet sympathizers. The imprisoned Russians, whom supporters described as having "lived in China for several years, being engaged in peaceful occupations and taking no part in politics," were shipped under guard to the Soviet Union. The GPU euphemistically described it as a voluntary repatriation. Despite pleas from the families and their representatives, neither the Chinese government nor the diplomats in Peking did anything about "these unfortunate people."[78] As stateless exiles, they were of no political value and not worth the effort. The arrested men were never heard from again.[79]

War's End

The international community reacted to the ODVA offensive. On 26 November, Stimson attempted to invoke the Paris Pact, but it was too late. In Moscow, American UPI newspaper reporter Eugene Lyons considered the effort a "fiasco." He wrote with the typical hard-nosed cynicism of that era's press, "Stimson in Washington decided to invoke the Kellogg Pact to prevent the war that had already been fought to a finish," adding that the Kremlin enjoyed the folly of Stimson's proposal for a "belated and uncalled-for intervention."[80] The outlawry of war had met harsh reality. Even before the fall of Hailar, on 24 November, Chang Hsueh-liang had notified the Soviets of his complete acceptance of the 13 July ultimatum and the immediate removal of the CER *tupan*. Hundreds of Mukden university students protested in vain while the *North China Daily News* proclaimed Blyukher the "Red Napoleon."[81]

Chiang Kai-shek in Nanking could only fume over the outcome, but a disjointed effort had become apparent in July. Throughout the crisis, Chiang and the Young Marshal had followed paths of convergence toward rights recovery, but they diverged in how to achieve that goal.

Chiang had been unable to assist the NEFDF militarily, his attempts at negotiations were easily foiled by Moscow, and he was never able to control the discussions between Mukden and Moscow. The two men had never formed an effective team. Defeat on the battlefield brought their differences to the fore, and after the crushing military defeat, the Young Marshal acted quickly to end the crisis.[82]

On 30 November, Tsai Yun-sheng departed Harbin for Suifenho and then across the border to Nikolsk–Ussuriysk. There he met with A. Simanovsky, the senior Soviet foreign affairs official in the Far East. After hurried negotiations to cement the peace, Tsai signed the humiliating Nikolsk Protocol on 3 December. The Young Marshal initially balked at the terms of the agreement, insisting on the removal of the Soviet managers, but the threat of a renewed ODVA offensive overcame his objections. Two days later, the Kremlin received a telegraph from Chang Hsueh-liang that reconfirmed the protocol, and Stalin wrote to Molotov that ODVA troops were not to be withdrawn until the "conditions are guaranteed" by the Chinese.[83] Tsai's actions at Nikolsk and Chang's message were a good start, but until the Soviets imprisoned during the May consulate raid and those arrested during the crisis were released, Stalin would keep the occupation in place.[84]

The status quo ante was officially restored on 31 December 1929. The Soviet prisoners were released in Harbin. Then at 2:00 P.M., the CER board of directors met; after deliberating a little over an hour, announced that general manager I. V. Rudi had taken over the CER. The point of honor that justified the war, the return of Emshanov, was of no importance in the end, and the object of the war, the CER, had become a secondary issue. As Litvinov remarked, the war provided the opportunity to "rap Chang's knuckles."[85] Stalin's goal was to humiliate and embarrass Nanking and Mukden—to let Chiang and Chang know who held the real power over the CER—and he succeeded. Later, Stalin succinctly summed up the war: "The ODVA gave them a good scare."[86]

Yet for Stalin, hostile emotions almost always meant blood, and in this case, "a good scare" meant thousands of Chinese and Russian casualties. However, he had failed in his prime objective: Chiang would rule China for another two decades, and both Chiang and Chang would long outlive the Soviet dictator. Many among the Powers lauded the rigorous Soviet defense of foreign rights in China, and Britain's minister in Peiping, Miles Lampson, was unstinting in his praise, declaring the outcome a "triumph of Soviet diplomacy," although he added that such diplomacy was "incompatible with . . . our hopes for world peace."[87] The *New York Times* opined on 8 December 1929 that while other Powers "argued, protested, but . . . submitted" when China abrogated their rights, Soviet Russia responded with "an ultimatum backed by military force."[88] At the dawn of the era of perpetual peace, war won.[89]

The end of the occupation began before the 31 December ceremonies in Harbin and continued into the new year. The last soldiers from the 36th Division withdrew from Hailar on 25 December, and the 5th Kuban Cavalry Brigade left the Manchouli–Dalainor area on 10 January 1930. The departure from Hailar was accompanied by music from the military band and a crowd of "well-wishers," while a similar crowd saw off Rokossovsky's cavalry. The Soviet occupation had been a success.[90]

Blyukher awaited the soldiers as they arrived at Dauria. His appreciation was palpable; the army had endured harsh conditions and bloody combat. Fourteen soldiers of the Trans-Baikal Group were awarded the Order of the Red Banner, the highest RKKA decoration, and the Buryat–Mongol Cavalry Division was honored with the Red Flag of the Revolution. Stalin conferred the Order of the Red Banner on the GPU Far East Border Guard Region and the entire ODVA on 2 January, changing the title to OKDVA, or Special Red Banner Far Eastern Army.[91] The army's newspaper *Alert* was renamed *Rebuff* in honor of the victory, and each veteran had the OKDVA badge pinned to his chest. Those of the Trans-Baikal Group killed in action had been buried in mass graves near Siding No. 86; before returning to their peacetime garrisons, the departing units paid their respects by putting up a red flag with a black border, to which Blyukher attached the Order of the Red Banner. After giving honors to the fallen in the biting cold, Khetagurov later wrote that the soldiers' spirits were festive nonetheless. Having emerged victorious, they were on their way home.[92]

10 | The 1929 Conflict and Interwar Warfare

From a military history standpoint, the 1929 Sino-Soviet conflict is significant for two reasons. First, the conflict provides an important glimpse into the Red Army during the interwar period. Second, the war offers insights into the integration of evolving technological and doctrinal advances made since the end of World War I—a snapshot of the transitional employment of aircraft, tanks, and other motorized vehicles into armies that still defined combat by foot-mobile infantry and saber-armed cavalry. To attempt to capture that information, the analysis that follows addresses six areas. Military strategy will be covered first, followed by wartime leadership, technology, unconventional warfare, and tactics. The chapter will close with a discussion on Red Army operational art.

Military Strategy

China's military strategy for the 1929 Sino-Soviet war strayed far from any ideal. Having obtained their political objective (control of the CER) almost immediately, Chiang and Chang assumed that a negotiated settlement would quickly be reached. In contrast to the thoroughly planned seizure of the railroad, Chang Hsueh-liang only began to develop a military strategy after the Soviet Union unexpectedly and forcefully countered with a status quo ante ultimatum. This created an immediate dilemma for Nanking. With Feng Yu-hsiang and Yen Hsi-shan still in command of their armies and Mao's guerrillas slowly rising from the ashes in the Chingkang Mountains, there was no possibility of a united military front, ruling out even the threat of a full-scale conflict with the Soviet Union.

China had to fight a limited war, and a strategic defense by NEFDF in Manchuria was the best solution; it would safeguard CER control, and a "no military aggression" policy placed Mukden and Nanking in a favorable diplomatic position. The NEFDF leadership also correctly assessed that the Red Army would focus its operations along the lines of the CER. The military strategy only began to unravel when the Young Marshal also adopted a rigidly passive tactical defense. This allowed the Red Army to seize the initiative, and once this initiative was gained, Blyukher never looked back. With its hands tied, the NEFDF was forced to react to the ODVA's actions from the beginning of the conflict to its finish—a poor method to conduct a war, and arguably no method at all. While the NEFDF was thrown off balance by the Red Army time and time again, its passivity failed to divert the ODVA from its aims, compounding the failure.

It was only after the RKKA's Far East mobilization began that the first of the Kirin and Heilungkiang regiments started their movement to the frontier. When the sabotage campaign was launched—an unpredicted event—Mukden reacted by shifting forces to the internal railway zone instead of the frontier. After the frontier heated up during the August and September ODVA raids, the NEFDF pivoted again to refocus on the border regions. The Young Marshal and his generals were frequently and belatedly adjusting to Soviet initiatives. Mukden could have avoided the fiasco, but only by positioning its armies to forcefully counterattack ODVA strikes into Manchuria—something neither Chang nor his army commanders ever attempted. Why this happened is more troubling in light of the generalship of Liang Chung-chia, who met the Trans-Baikal Group's offensive with a series of counterattacks and almost succeeded in weathering the Soviet onslaught. Why did his superiors not emulate his strategy?

Chang Hsueh-liang and Hu Yu-kun were veteran officers and war college graduates. They were taught the tenets of both Clausewitz and Sun Tzu: to balance the defense with the offense. For Clausewitz, defense was "the stronger form of war," but he argued that it was "absurd" to defend without the "intention to counterattack."[1] Sun Tzu held that a general had to be expert in defense and offense, or to be "capable both of protecting themselves and of gaining a complete victory."[2] This tactical balance was never reached in the 1929 conflict, where a passive defense dominated the thinking of the NEFDF's senior generals. The best explanation for the failure was residual warlordism. Warlord culture was impervious to military doctrine when the two clashed. For rising generals like Liang, success on the battlefield was the route to advancement; for senior generals like Chang and Hu, preserving the army superseded all other considerations. Liang fought to win, while Chang and Hu wanted no part of a pitched battle. Fortune, however, initially favored the NEFDF, as the flaws in its strategy were not immediately evident to the Soviets.

Clausewitz described military strategy as "the use of an engagement for the purpose of war," with war being "an act of force to compel our enemy to do our will."[3] For the Soviet Union, no better definition was possible. Its military strategy, like its political objectives, followed the will of Stalin, and nothing else mattered. Stalin's decisions were influenced by the fact that the senior RKKA leadership had become convinced that they faced considerable external dangers. Looking to the east, Stalin had witnessed the loss of hard-earned gains in China; to the west were revived concerns of an imperialist war against the Soviet Union. Stalin had even spoken of an "actual threat of a new war," with an attack from Poland posing the most peril.[4] Adding to his unease about a war with China, there was not much in the way of outside military assistance, only the small MPRA. The bulk of it was duly sent to the Manchurian border after the CER crisis began, but it was an inadequate force and did not participate in the war beyond interning scattered and defeated Chinese cavalry who fled across the border.

Despite their obvious strengths, the Soviets felt militarily exposed and alone. Overestimating both military strength and will to use it by the other Powers (with the exception of Japan) was an error shared by both Nanking and Moscow, and by 1929, the Kremlin was taking counsel of its own fears, while Stalin had never needed much prompting to see enemies where none existed. Russia's fear worked to China's advantage. Fear drove the Military–Industrial Directorate to object to any major commitment of RKKA resources to the Far East; when the decision to form the ODVA was made in early August, it came with the caveat that the transfer of European forces to the Far East would be kept to a minimum.[5] Like China, the Soviets were only willing to wage a limited war.

Aside from his late August outburst, Stalin did not interfere with the strategic details. The ODVA campaign remained true to the plan drafted by Blyukher—one that resembled in key ways General Grodekov's 1900 plan of attacks down the Sungari River combined with those from the west at Manchouli and east at Suifenho. Once the plans were completed, only the timing of events were controlled by Stalin, and he cleverly delegated that authority to Voroshilov when he allowed him to move his headquarters to Chita. Litvinov saw great subtlety in the creation of the Stalin–Voroshilov–Blyukher chain of command. Blyukher complained of what he saw as onerous oversight—a reaction that reportedly delighted both Voroshilov and Stalin—but the process had more serious undertones.[6] If things went badly for Blyukher during the November offensive, Voroshilov would also take the blame, shielding Stalin from responsibility; otherwise, it became an example of Stalin's strategic brilliance. Litvinov termed it "Koba's Machiavellianism."[7]

Wartime Leadership

The interactions between Chiang Kai-shek, Feng Yu-hsiang, Chang Hsueh-liang, and Hu Yu-kun, the 2nd Fengtien Army commander, revealed both the strengths and weaknesses of China's military leaders. Taken separately, the most damaging relationship was that of Feng and Chiang, as it represented the rivalries of high warlordism that kept China weak, divided, and vulnerable to the outside Powers—a rift that Moscow exploited. The October uprising by Feng left the Young Marshal alone on the field of battle at its most critical juncture. It was a tragic turn of events. The relationship between Chang and Chiang was different. Unlike Feng, who sought ultimate leadership and saw no leader as his equal, let alone superior, the Young Marshal repeatedly expressed a willingness to subordinate himself to a higher national purpose, but only to a degree.

China came first, but absent a strong unified state, Chang Hsueh-liang's loyalty to the KMT and Chiang Kai-shek only went as far as to not threaten his rule over Manchuria. Chiang also had reservations about the Young Marshal. During the crisis, Wellington Koo noted that Nanking thought that the Young Marshal "did not listen to orders," and there was a real fear that his inexperience would permit him to be "lured into a trap" by the Soviet diplomats.[8] Moscow did attempt to take advantage of the disunity between Chiang and Chang, but Chang Hsueh-liang's patriotism thwarted this effort. He was not fooled by the Soviet's diplomatic stratagems and held firm against the Soviets until the November defeats left him no choice. The Young Marshal's real weakness was as a military strategist, not as a political leader.

Last, there was Hu Yu-kun, on whose shoulders most of the blame for the NEFDF defeat must rest. Hu proved to be a poor general. In addition to witnessing the defeats at Dalainor and Manchouli without launching a relief operation, Hu must also take the blame for abandoning Hailar without a fight. The latter was a stunning lapse in leadership, as he had three mixed and one cavalry brigade at his disposal and the town was ringed by half a dozen hills—a defensive position superior to that held by either of General Liang's brigades at Dalainor and Manchouli. In August 1945, it took two weeks for the Soviet 86th Rifle Corps, manned by veterans of the Eastern Front and reinforced by heavy artillery and a tank brigade, to destroy a single Japanese mixed brigade defending Hailar. Had defenses been prepared, Hailar could have held in 1929. That it did not was due to Hu's failure as a battlefield commander.[9]

The only positive outcome from Hu's leadership was the preservation of the 2nd Army—a quintessential warlord ideal, but a notion completely out of place in a national army defending the country from foreign aggression. Even that success disappointed. Hu deemed it better to suffer the loss of the rear guard (the 55th Mukden Infantry Regiment) through desertion and banditry—another shameful recourse for a warlord army in retreat—than have the brigades at Hailar stand and fight. If preservation of military power was the ultimate objective, then what of the reinforced 15th and 17th Heilungkiang brigades? Kawamata pointed out that Hu should have withdrawn the two isolated brigades to Hailar before the weather turned cold. Once the marshlands froze, the Red Army was able to maneuver rapidly, rendering the passive defense of Manchouli and Dalainor fatal. The NEFDF was simply out-generaled by the ODVA.

Who were the battle captains of the ODVA? The senior leaders and many of the junior officers had risen in ranks based on party loyalty and accomplishment in combat. After the end of civil war, the top performers obtained a sound military education after the establishment of officer academies, staff schools, and war colleges. The worst were dismissed from the service. By 1929, the RKKA possessed a cadre of professional officers dedicated to Soviet Russia, and many of the best served in the war. This gave the ODVA a remarkable degree of cohesion and unity of purpose that was too often lacking in the NEFDF. This superiority manifested itself in a crucial way: leading from the front in battle. The key advantage lay at the level of the senior officer.

From the brigade level down, Chinese officers exhibited every bit as much courage as their Red Army counterparts. During the battle of Suifenho, a Chinese battalion commander fell. During the naval engagement at Tungchiang, captains died while fighting for their ships, and the commander of the naval infantry was killed at the front of his troops. At Dalainor, the brigade commander, two regimental commanders, and a large number of other officers fought to the death. The actions of the 15th Brigade chief of staff at Manchouli were so distinguished that a monument was later erected in his honor. What made the Red Army different was the leadership of its top commanders. While the Young Marshal was safely ensconced in Mukden, so far removed from the action as to play no role, and while Hu sat satisfied in his unpreparedness at Hailar, Blyukher and his top commanders were positioned to influence the action whenever and wherever needed.

Rokossovsky, who had been elevated from a brigade to a cavalry group commander, was repeatedly sighted at decisive scenes of combat. His superior and General Hu's counterpart, Corps Commander Vostretsov, visited the front when it was most dangerous and stayed the course. In his memoirs, Fedyuninsky remembered seeing Vostretsov directing the battle under fire on at least four occasions, and Chuikov described Blyukher as man in perpetual motion once battle was joined—a leader adroit at dealing with any problem, whether raised by small unit leaders or RKKA chief Voroshilov. No other attribute was more important or responsible for the ODVA victory.

Technology

Aviation

The warplane came into its own during World War I and remained an important emerging technology. Not having participated in the war put China at a disadvantage. As in artillery (discussed below), NEFDF air forces held a significant edge over other Chinese armies, but they lagged behind the other Powers and again dealt with the deficiency by creating smaller units—squadrons of five to nine aircraft, compared to eight to twelve fighters or fifteen to eighteen bombers in Red Army squadrons. Nonetheless, they were a source of pride for the Young Marshal. His squadrons were sent to the front several weeks after the seizure of the CER, beginning with the arrival of a five-plane squadron at Manchouli shortly before the Dalainor fighting broke out in August. There was no indication of how the aircraft were used, and reports of NEFDF warplanes arriving in the war zone without any indication of follow-up activity became routine.[10]

A week after the squadron reached the Western Front, a shipment of twenty-eight new French Breguet 19s arrived at Mukden. They were unloaded and prepped, and in a break with tradition, they were then hastily formed into two large fourteen-plane bomber squadrons that were on their way to the front before the end of the month. By September, Mukden boasted eighty aircraft near the frontier, with an additional 100 personnel en route to the forward air bases. On the Western Front, nine bombers were sighted at Manchouli in early October. A few weeks later, five of the nine NEFDF aircraft stationed at Hailar flew to Manchouli, but outside a few courier shuttles, there were no reports of active air operations. No aerial combat with the ODVA took place, and the prohibition against border crossings ruled out reconnaissance missions or bombing raids, the two areas where the Fengtien pilots had gained some combat experience during the tuchun wars and the Northern Expedition. That left the NEFDF air force without a mission, and it played no role in the war. Combat losses came not in the air but during ODVA air raids on NEFDF squadrons sitting uselessly on the ground.[11]

Red Army squadrons, on the other hand, went into action early and demonstrated marked superiority over its tsarist predecessor of World War I. The advances could be seen in three areas: the ability to concentrate aircraft in the Far East, mission assignments, and aerial tactics. Within two months of the seizure of the CER, the RKKA was able to transfer twelve squadrons from European Russia and western Siberia to the Manchurian frontier. In comparison, US Army aviation, which was created in 1926 and was comparable in size to the RKKA air arm, had thirty-eight combat squadrons in 1929. The methods of deployment were noteworthy. While many aircraft were shipped by rail, requiring both disassembly at the point of entrainment followed by reassembly upon arrival, the more impressive method was flying the squadrons from the home bases directly to advanced airfields at the front. This technique had been tested during the July 1925 flight of R-1s from Moscow to Peking, led by pioneering Soviet aviator Mikhail M. Gromov. Using that experience to subsequently transfer a large number of aircraft thousands of kilometers in wartime was a signal achievement. By September, the previously outnumbered Red Army squadrons had gained an insurmountable advantage over their NEFDF opponents.[12]

Red Army aviation, operating without the restrictions placed on the Chinese squadrons, carried out a wide range of missions. In addition to mainstay fighter-bomber assignments, dedicated reconnaissance units, like the 2nd "Lenin" Squadron, allowed the ODVA to use aerial photography in the planning of the Sungari and Mishan operations. Vaynerh's cavalry group drive on Mishan proved exceptionally successful. The continuous use of air support, both through ground attacks and observation flights that provided timely information to his ground commanders, helped them develop the tactical situation to their advantage and ensure victory.

The ODVA also excelled in the use of aircraft during riverine operations, where the 68th Seaplane Squadron proved invaluable. Although the military seaplane was a technological advance of transient value, its utility in riverine environments was peaking in the 1920s, when the aircraft roamed free, untethered to airfields, and their speed and maneuverability lagged only a bit behind ground-based warplanes. When teamed with the tender *Amur*, which possessed fuel and munitions along with shipboard repair and maintenance spaces, the 68th Squadron could operate almost anywhere along the Amur, Sungari, and Ussuri rivers. Its expertise in striking ships culminated in the sinking of the gunboat *Kiang-heng* during the Fuchin landings—one the earliest instances of a warship being sunk by aircraft in combat.

The 17 November dawn air raids on Chinese airfields during the Mishan operation proved that the RKKA had grasped the importance of gaining air superiority, a new concept first addressed by Italian air warfare theorist Giulio Douhet in 1921 and developed more fully in 1925 by the British Royal Air Force under Hugh Trenchard, another air warfare visionary. Unlike Douhet, who saw the bomber as the ultimate arbitrator in war, RKKA ground forces were always paired with aviation units, and the aircrews supported army operations. The Western Front offensive demonstrated planning techniques that allowed the 9th Air Group to maintain aircraft over the battlefield during daylight hours throughout the operation, although an inability to establish reliable real-time air–ground communications kept the strikes clear of the RKKA ground forces. Attacks against fixed targets of importance to the enemy and away from friendly forces became the focus.[13]

Physical destruction was not the only advantage of using warplanes; bombing missions directed against the rail yards and facilities at Suifenho and Manchouli as well as the electrical generation plant at Dalainor also proved effective as a shock weapon, resulting in panicked evacuations of the civil population. As Douhet correctly predicted, air bombardment directed at civilians would "reach the heights of atrocity" and came close to but failed in reaching his goal of "a complete breakdown of the social structure" in the 1929 war. In the case of Suifenho, the heavy air raids within the confines of a populated town was a new precedent for East Asia and predated the German bombing of Guernica by almost eight years. However, it was not an early example of terror bombing, as the targets were railroad facilities, not unprotected inhabitants. They were, to use modern terminology, collateral damage, although from a humanitarian standpoint, the civilian losses were shocking. The raids also revealed an expanded scope of targeting that moved beyond the World War I preoccupation with aerial observation, dogfighting, and attacking enemy ground forces and toward the type broadly defined as tactical bombardments, which became the norm in World War II.[14]

Finally, RKKA air tactics displayed an ability to quickly adapt to local combat conditions. While the NEFDF aircraft never challenged the Red Army to aerial battle during the war, Chinese antiaircraft fire was a threat. During early demonstrations, RKKA squadrons often flew in disciplined formations over Chinese positions, but once the shooting war began, more sophisticated schemes of attack were used, no doubt possible as a result of the experience of the pilots. As the fighting on the Western Front evolved, Red Army pilots developed tactics of attacking a target singularly from multiple directions while varying their altitude—methods still used today—and dive-bombing runs were common. The performance of ODVA air squadrons embodied a fundamental application of the *1929 Regulation*'s air–ground battle concepts. Taken together, a proven competence in deploying air forces over great distances, executing a variety of operational missions, and rapidly adopting effective air tactics showed that the RKKA had developed a culture of innovation and experimentation that put it at the forefront of modern aerial warfare.[15]

Communications

The 1929 war revealed an appreciation of multifront strategy by the Red Army that grew out of experiences from World War I and the Russian civil war. Specifically, the RKKA had improved its ability to command and control widely disbursed forces. The early dispatch of the Headquarters Signals and 4th Separate Radio Battalions gave the ODVA the ability to coordinate operations, epitomized by the simultaneous November offensives over two fronts separated by 1,150 kilometers. This ability had been detected earlier, during the Northern Expedition, although the value of radio transmissions was downplayed. Major Magruder reported in early May 1927 that the "synchronization of the movements of three individual army groups over five hundred miles of front, at a time when communications were in a most defective state, was a clear indication of the excellence of the Russian staff work."[16]

Magruder underestimated the role of communications, as Blyukher's RKKA advisors with the NRA in 1927 relied on radio transmissions. A radio school had opened at Whampoa in early 1926, and the NRA Communications Battalion facilitated radio signals between corps and army headquarters. The message traffic was of such importance that in March 1927, the Chinese protested the interference with their communications by the radio transmissions from the American gunboat *Isabel* at Hankow. The advantage of the radio was not a new idea in China. Sun Yat-sen had recognized its importance in 1920, asking the Soviets to establish a transmitter in Vladivostok or Manchuria to communicate with Canton; he made his first broadcast from Shanghai on 26 January 1923. The Powers were in stiff competition to gain radio contracts, as firms like Marconi, RCA, and GE engaged in bidding wars to gain Chinese customers. The Japanese entered the market in 1926. In that sense, the NRA was at the forefront of radio communications, as the concept was not appreciated within all military circles. Some disdained the new technology. Radio communication had been of limited value during the static warfare on the Western Front in World War I, and during World War II, when the battle of France began in 1940, the headquarters of General Maurice Gamelin, the supreme Allied military commander, did not possess a single radio.[17]

The Red Army had taken the same road as China and had advanced even further. Blyukher was able to communicate freely with subordinate commanders regardless of distance, as well as with Voroshilov at Chita and Stalin in Moscow. The network also allowed Blyukher to move to the center of the action on either front and still maintain a high degree of connectivity. The NEFDF did not benefit from as rich a system; it relied overwhelmingly on telegraphic communiqués. Once those lines were severed, as happened during the outset of the November offenses on both fronts, beyond hand-carried messages, the only remaining conduits consisted of a handful of radios at sedentary senior command posts, augmented by aerial couriers when flying was possible. During the 1929 war, the advanced capabilities of RKKA communication systems provided the ODVA with a dynamic asset in the conduct of the operations across the far-flung Manchurian fronts.

Tanks and Mechanization

One of the more disheartening aspects of the way in which the NEFDF fought the war was its failure to use its armored force. On the day the CER was seized, Chang Hsueh-liang had at his disposal thirty or more FT-17 tanks, roughly equal to the Soviet MS-1, while the Red Army had not assigned a single tank to the Far East. The advantage was squandered. Mukden's focus was on possessing the technology, not on developing tactics to exploit its advantages. This created a gap between procurement and application—or to put it another way, a damning disconnect between possessing a weapon and effectively using it. The NEFDF had a meaningful quantity of tanks, enough to influence the outcome of the war, but they were ill prepared to face their Red Army opponents in combat. That proved nearly as useless as not having the weapons to begin with. The Young Marshal, unwilling to risk such a valuable asset, never sent them to the front—a move more akin to that of a calculating warlord than a commander at the head of a national army.

The RKKA did ensure that the tank was on the battlefield, but the lone company did not play a decisive role in the fighting on the Western Front. This is not to argue that they failed. The limited Red Army tank operations influenced the battle in favor of the Trans-Baikal Group during both days of the fighting at Dalainor. Even the two "lost" tanks proved to be of immediate help in the action to cut Liang's two brigades apart on the first day of the offensive, and valuable lessons were learned from the experiences gained through its employment in the November offensive. The successes validated Red Army plans for expanded tank forces.

There was one significant problem: the breakdown in tank–infantry cooperation at Dalainor. Soviet historians G. F. Kuzman and N. F. Polkovyh expanded on the 1929 failure:

> The experience of these battles has shown that the success of joint operations by infantry and tanks depends primarily on organized interaction. According to the requirements of the *1927 RKKA Combat Infantry Charter* (Article 150) and the *1929 Regulations* (Articles 206, 207, 210), this interaction should be organized not only at the tank company–infantry regiment

level but also at a tank platoon–infantry battalion echelon. The last of these goals were not fulfilled at Dalainor.[18]

It was expected that the lessons learned in the 1929 war would be incorporated into Red Army doctrine. They were, but practice never caught up with theory, as witnessed during the Red Army's disappointing experiences in Spain, where no fewer than 731 modern Soviet tanks were delivered in piecemeal fashion during the 1936–1939 war. After suffering a defeat outside Madrid on 29 October 1936, the cause was obvious: "since the infantry could not keep pace the tanks could neither develop the attack nor exploit their success"—the same infantry–tank cooperation failure that occurred at Dalainor seven years earlier.[19] The problems encountered in Spain were so profound that senior Red Army leaders considered abolishing the armored corps formation in the summer of 1939. The RKKA had gained battle experience, but the lesson had not been internalized. Ironically, a major weakness of the Red Army tank forces in the interwar years, infantry–tank coordination, was the only strength of foot soldier–centric militaries like France and the United States—an asset that became a fatal liability during World War II when not combined with advanced motorized maneuver theories such as the RKKA innovations of deep battle and operational art. Fortunately, the United States, unlike France, had time to correct its errors.[20]

Closely related to the introduction of tanks was mechanization. The Soviets had noted the importance of trucks and other vehicles in World War I. The fivefold increase in motorization between 1914 and 1918 had what Soviet military theorist Y. E. Savkin later described as "a serious influence on military art, the term the Red Army used to describe the triad of strategy, operational art and tactics."[21] The RKKA was eager to experiment with mechanized transport, as the effort to motorize the battalion from the 106th Regiment on the Western Front demonstrated, although the battalion was not used as a motorized unit during the November offensive. Similarly, a number of trucks were observed on the Eastern front as early as September but were not used during the Mishan operation. The fragile wheeled vehicles of the 1920s lacked the mobility to be of ready use on the battlefield. Like tank employment, the test under combat conditions was limited, but again, the lack of failure meant that mechanization would progress. The RKKA's bias toward modernization—both technologically and operationally—could only be deterred in the face of convincing setbacks or the orders of Stalin.

Unconventional Warfare

The term "unconventional warfare" comes from World War II and thus is anachronistic when applied to the 1929 conflict, but the term is useful. During the war, actions that were described then as "propaganda" and "sabotage" today would be referred to as "psychological" and "direct action" operations under the overall aegis of unconventional warfare. Their influence on the war was significant, and in the case of sabotage not duplicated in later RKKA conflicts until the rise of the Russian guerrilla bands operating behind Nazi lines during World War II. Regardless of terminology, the role played by sabotage and propaganda during the 1929 Sino-Soviet conflict was an integral part of the war.

The Russian sabotage campaign was unique in its blending of political action and military operations. Soviet CER employees under the direction of the GPU and ODVA units independently carried out attacks on the CER rails, and their objectives also crossed paths. Some were aimed at the disruption of CER services. Others, closely timed to conventional attacks, had the tactical purpose of cutting off lines of communication before assault by ODVA forces. The sabotage attacks in and around Suifenho in September are a case in point: most were designed to impair rail operations as part of a systemwide campaign, while several were specifically conducted to cut the city off from resupply and reinforcement immediately before air and ground attacks. The most intriguing sabotage raid took place at Teheiho in October with the disabling of the electrical dynamos at the city's power station, a strike that accelerated the evacuation of the city. Like most actions on the Northern Front, no details were reported, but the most likely causes were a cross-river commando raid by either ODVA or GPU troops or internal sabotage by those able to access the plant. Either would indicate a sophisticated Soviet direct action capability, but uncovering the full story will be the work of future historians.

The results of the sabotage attacks had mixed results. This was due to two self-imposed constraints set by the Soviets. First, Moscow's strategic objective was a return to the status quo ante, requiring a fully functioning CER under Soviet control. Second, the war was to be limited in nature. The sabotage campaign was never intended to destroy the CER, and that created the nearly impossible task of harming the railway to the point where it was rendered unusable while allowing the damage to be speedily repaired. As Chinese security forces took countermeasures and began making arrests, the shrinking number of saboteurs could not launch a sufficient number of "fixable" attacks to adversely influence CER operations. The capture of the radio set in Harbin also cut off the saboteurs from GPU direction. The primary goal failed, but the secondary benefit of tying down thousands of NEFDF soldiers as guards made the campaign a worthwhile undertaking.[22]

Because the war was limited, propaganda assumed an outsize role during the conflict; its importance to Nanking and Mukden on one side and to Moscow and CCP on the other could be judged on how early it began, its duration, and the many forms it took. Within two weeks of the 10 July CER seizure, there were organized street protests in Moscow and competing CCP and KMT agitation in Shanghai. The KMT campaign soon spread across China, while Soviets made good use of traditional methods along with the new medium of radio. The real question, however, was, did it all work? To try to answer this question, the problem needs to be viewed through a review of CCP, KMT, and Soviet propaganda efforts.

The CCP had the most at stake, and while its campaign met with a singular lack of success during the CER crisis, that short-term failure was eclipsed by what it achieved strategically. With the CCP Red Army in shambles and no overt political power, propaganda was the only tool left. The CCP worked diligently to rally public support to their cause, but little went as planned; in particular, calls for action fell flat. As Ch'en Tu-hsiu's criticisms highlighted, the campaign was misdirected tactically, but it did not matter. How the CER crisis was resolved remained of secondary importance compared to the real prize: the continued support of the Soviet Union. Granted, the wall posters, distribution of handbills, calls for rallies, and strikes failed to stir the Chinese people, yet each action offered affirmative proof of the CCP's unflinching loyalty to the Soviet cause. To keep the Chinese communist revolution alive, the need to prove the party's loyalty to Stalin became imperative, and in that task—the only one that mattered—the CCP succeeded.

The propaganda focus of the KMT was different. The two thrusts of the KMT were to solidify home support and win over foreigners. As described previously, the KMT won the propaganda war with the CCP, which was not difficult. Recovery of rights had long been a plank of Sun Yat-sen's policies, and it was a shared policy of both the KMT and CCP. The CER seizure was too popular to be countered, as seen in the enthusiastic send-off of Fengtien soldiers at Mukden and the Harbin student volunteers. Positive propaganda also boosted the morale of the NEFDF. Soviet sources noted that General Liang regularly issued proclamations and published pamphlets to induce his Western Front troops to fight hard against the Russian enemy, and when ODVA attacks came, Liang's troops stood their ground. The home front propaganda war ended in a KMT victory.[23]

On the international front, the KMT had become so good at propagandizing that there was an expectation that their messaging alone would favorably influence events. Confidence and skill were not always advantages, as propaganda could prove counterproductive and the campaign harmed diplomatic initiatives. At the height of the crucial August negotiations, Japanese vice foreign minister Yoshizawa expressed fears to the British ambassador in Tokyo, John Tilley, that no immediate breakthrough between China and Soviet Russia was expected, as Nanking appeared more interested in winning domestic propaganda points. A Whitehall official added that the Chinese were "obviously disinclined to yield an inch."[24] During a 29 August meeting in Tokyo, Soviet ambassador Troyanovsky rejected Foreign Minister Shidehara's proposed solution to the conflict based on Moscow's "distrust of the Chinese and resentment of their propaganda."[25] Anti-Soviet targeting was clearly a two-edged sword for the KMT, and one edge cut deeper than expected. Had international pressure proven as potent as the Chinese expected, then their campaign may have worked. When events forced a two-party solution, alienation of the Soviets by the KMT worked against Mukden and Nanking.

With pro-Soviet papers in Harbin having been shut down since the May consulate raid, the Soviets were forced to conduct an underground effort in the Northeast. Calls for job resignations, strikes, and protests by Soviet CER workers inside the Northeast led to immediate action, and their effectiveness was seen in demands by Chinese CER workers for the arrest of Pumpiansky, the propaganda director at the Soviet consulate in Harbin. Had it not been for the Chinese railway workers and police, the goal of shutting down the CER might have been achieved. Domestically, as the July Moscow marches demonstrated, support for the government never wavered, allowing the Kremlin to direct its propaganda efforts at the frontline soldiers and the Soviet people living in the Far East. To cheer on the soldiers, the ODVA published a weekly called *Alert* that carried messages from Stalin, Blyukher, and other senior officials, along with news that was carefully edited by the PUR commissars to enhance loyalty and lift morale. It proved popular; the arrival each new edition was eagerly awaited by the troops. In September, Blyukher used the paper to urge for continued vigilance, self-discipline, and self-defense. In the Kuban Cavalry Brigade, patriotic songs cheering the fight against the nationalists were composed and sung. The Red Army also exploited Chinese propaganda to motivate its soldiers against the NEFDF; Fedyuninsky, while omitting specifics of what was said, later referred to "white guard" Chinese newspaper statements against the Soviet Union as "vicious" as well as "thoroughly false and vile."[26] Given his junior status, the Red Army made a conscious effort to translate and disseminate Chinese propaganda to serve the Soviet cause, and tapping that patriotic anger inspired the ODVA soldiers.[27]

In the Far East, Soviet propagandists had moved beyond newspapers, handbills, and posters, making use of radio; the Soviets were fortunate to have the powerful radio station at Khabarovsk whose signal could reach Mukden, over 1,000 kilometers away. Reaching a listening audience was more challenging. Civilian radio sets were not available in numbers in the Northeast, but those who did have them tended to be people of importance and influence. Inside the Soviet Far East, Moscow ensured that Communist Party and Communist Youth League members had access to radio broadcasts that maximized state objectives. The daily programs focused on anti-Nanking and Mukden proclamations and official announcements on the crisis. Reinforcing the egalitarian nature of the RKKA, individual heroics of "righteous soldiers" were reported, such as the story of a young Russian sailor named Pokra who had been called up to active duty and killed in action at Tungchiang.[28] The combination of anti-Chinese and pro-RKKA messages, stiffened by Communist Party edicts from the Kremlin, made for convincing listening.[29]

For outside audiences, the heart of the anti-KMT campaign came during weekly Chinese- and English-language broadcasts. English-language messaging continued into January and ran from 6 to 8 P.M. During a seven-day period, the CER crisis was often mentioned, noting that "the Red Army victory had strengthened the position of Soviet Russia in the eyes of the world."[30] As in the Soviet newscasts, Nanking was blamed for the crisis. The Young Marshal and his generals were tarred as incompetent imperialists who were working against the Chinese worker, while the Soviet Union was presented as the vanguard of the revolution and a nation to be supported by the Chinese people. It was a modified replay of the CCP message. It also failed to resonate, even though Kirin governor-general Chang Tso-hsiang vocally complained about Soviet slander. Recurring themes were threats of Red Army action against China and warnings to White Russians. Broad-brush attacks were not the only Russian tactic. On occasion, messages were directed at specific audiences. In the weeks leading up to the November ODVA offensive, the population in Harbin was twice thrown into a panic after hearing radio broadcasts from Khabarovsk that the Red Army would soon be advancing on the city; one declared that the Soviets would be in the city in time to celebrate the 7 November anniversary of the 1917 October Revolution.[31]

One final lesson of the Soviet campaign deals with understanding the targeted audience. Among the ODVA rank and file, the Soviets actively supported the idea that the real Chinese objective was not simply control over the CER but rather the conquest of the Russian Far East. To the Chinese or an objective outside observer, that concept was absurd—nothing more than fantasy—but it was a believable threat to the Red Army. RKKA soldiers who could remember the foreign invasions of World War I knew their borders were not inviolate; seizing the Russian Far East had been the clear objective of the IJA during the 1918–1922 Siberian intervention, in which China had actively participated. To the Soviet soldiers on the Northeast's frontier, a call to arms to fight and defend their homeland rang true.[32]

Overall, the Soviet campaign met with the greatest degree of success. Its use of radio propaganda raises two points. First, it is one the earliest known examples of that medium being used as a propaganda tool. The second point regards the panic in Harbin. The Khabarovsk radio messages were credible because the ODVA had made them so in battle. This leads to one of the enduring truths of any propaganda war: some of the most effective messages are linked to related actions, whether diplomatically or militarily.

That no one was able to put together a complete program showed the difficulty in waging a comprehensive propaganda war. The CCP aimed its limited resources solely at the Chinese people and failed, but it did reassure its indispensible ally, the Soviet Union. The KMT efforts proved effective, but only to a degree, as they made no attempt to sway the Soviet population or its soldiers, opting instead to steel the NEFDF and solidify domestic support while fighting a messaging war designed to win over the other Powers. The Soviets left no venue unaddressed; they attained the most. However, both China and the Soviet Union's campaigns to influence each other ended in tone-deaf failure. They left the Chinese feeling too confident and Stalin intransigent. These uneven accomplishments in no way diminished the value of modern propaganda. It had become an important political-military tool that would continue to be honed in the years ahead.[33]

Tactics

The tactics used by the two armies were in a state of flux in 1929. Some, like those used by the cavalry, were rooted in the past, while others, like those of the infantry, had not changed much since World War I. Still others were undergoing rapid changes. To better capture the dynamics, this section will explore four areas of tactics used in carrying out military operations during the conflict: artillery, cavalry, infantry, and riverine warfare.

Artillery Tactics

How the two armies utilized their artillery offers an especially good view into the changes taking place in the interwar years. While both nations were making advances, the Red Army was on an unparalleled trajectory. For China, progress was clear when comparing NEFDF performance in 1929 to that of earlier warlord battles. The accuracy of the Chinese night shelling described by Fedyuninsky was a far cry from the simplistic direct-fire barrages used in 1922. The presence of larger-caliber guns to augment mainstay 75–77mm pieces gave the NEFDF the opportunity to lay down truly destructive bombardments—another factor that had been missing earlier in the decade. The Chinese had taken significant strides in directing and concentrating their fire, but there were shortcomings that had not been overcome.[34]

On the Western Front, each mixed brigade was given the equivalent of an artillery regiment, the amount reserved for a full army, yet the level of support proved inadequate when confronting the ODVA. The NEFDF, while holding an ample number of guns compared to its Chinese foes, fell far below the standards used by the other Powers. The shortage was handled by forming battalions of two two-gun batteries, compared to RKKA light artillery battalions of four six-gun batteries or heavy battalions of two six-gun batteries. It was an admission of inferiority. Even more crippling were inadequate munitions stockpiles. While the Soviets prepared for a post–World War I–era battle, the NEFDF amassed shells at levels that would suffice in warlord battles. When the November offensive opened, they were forced to try to counter multidivision ODVA attacks and quickly used up their stores. As Captain Kawamata reported, they expended twenty days of artillery rounds in three days. With their supply nearing exhaustion, Liang's troops were bereft of a critical means of defense while engaged in desperate combat.[35]

The RKKA model was grounded in the experience of World War I: massed guns with extended bombardments. During the 1914–1917 period, the Russians would concentrate twenty guns per kilometer. Although the Russians could not match the density seen during a Western Front offensive (over 100 pieces per kilometer by 1916), they had a different tactical aim: massed fires on specific targets. Meanwhile, in France, entire frontages were shelled. Sticking to that tactic during the 1929 conflict, RKKA artillery was often devastating in its effect. After the war, as the Five-Year Plan kicked in, the lethality of Red Army artillery increased almost exponentially. The Chinese were at a disadvantage from the outset; the NEFDF operated within a different set of realities. Further, China's industrial base could not match that of the Soviet Union, making the Soviet advantage insurmountable.[36]

China's material gap with Russia was too vast to close, an outcome that highlighted the contrasting roles artillery played in Soviet and East Asian armies. Experience and capacity meant everything, and China was not alone in misunderstanding the Soviet way of war. Reflecting on RKKA artillery employment, Kawamata and Major Kanda not only noted the superiority of Russian cannoneers over their Chinese counterparts but also the divergent visions of potential. While Chuikov later wrote that the 1929 Soviet barrages were intense but nothing compared to those of World War II, Kawamata and Kanda, coming from a Japanese military that had to carefully husband its resources, found the RKKA shelling highly effective yet also excessive, even extravagant.[37]

What the 1929 war confirmed was that the Red Army's objective was to surpass World War I standards. Conversely, China struggled to reach even 1914 levels. The Japanese army, although having advanced beyond the 1914 model, would face a similar fate when it confronted the Red Army a decade later in 1939 at Nomonhan (180 kilometers southeast of Manchouli on the Manchurian–Mongolian frontier). In that battle, the IJA massed the greatest concentration of artillery in any battle in its history—more than double that used by the ODVA in 1929—only to be outgunned by the Soviets both in quantity and quality. Russian obsession with artillery would be seen again during the 1945 fighting in Manchuria during Operation August Storm, when the Red Army fielded over 27,000 mortars and artillery pieces. The RKKA had no alternative: it had to prepare to win in a Western-style total war. That was not the case for either China or Japan. Success on the East Asian battlefield during the interwar years was decided by a different set of constraints, most notably a reliance on rifle-armed infantry. Neither China nor Japan had to use the quantities of artillery essential in the West in the years leading up to World War II.[38]

Cavalry Tactics

Surprisingly for 1929, the saber was still the primary weapon for cavalrymen, even though they were armed with rifles for service as dismounted infantry. The saber-armed Soviet cavalry survived during the war as a result of the lack of machine guns on the Chinese side and by restricting attacks to other cavalry units or exposed troops where the shock value of horsemen still counted. Once confronted by infantry in a static defense, the cavalry dismounted and took up their rifles, as seen during the night fighting by the Buryat–Mongol Division on 19 November. Lacking mechanization, the RKKA cavalry was also the only force able to complete the speedy advances over long distances espoused in the *1929 Regulations*. It was the last gasp of an outdated mode of warfare. Saber-armed cavalry never played a major role in a modern war again.

Infantry Tactics

The one area in which the NEFDF continuously earned high praise from all observers was in the toughness of its infantry in defense, including the August rebuff at Dalainor, the steadiness during the Suifenho attacks in September, and the fighting on the Western Front in November. When properly led and supported, Chinese riflemen were as good as any in the world. Since the tactical focus was on the defense, there is a good amount of evidence on how that type of combat was conducted in the Dalainor–Manchouli sector. Russian sources refer to a modern system of defensive works that were more in keeping with later conflicts, such as the 1952–1953 period during the Korean War, than the Western Front trenches of World War I. Terrain played an important role on the Western Front. The lands were open and an international boundary separated the two opponents, creating a security zone between front lines that bristled with outposts and were crisscrossed by mobile patrols.

Artillery and armored trains fired in support of the entrenched Chinese soldiers; the effective Stokes mortar provided close-in indirect fires. The actual trenches were nothing special, usually consisting of three successive defensive lines with firing parapets. Land mines, barbwire, and at points the antitank ditch, a relatively new feature, protected the earthworks. The NEFDF also relied on fortified blockhouses and bunkers that were so impressive that the Soviets believed that they had been designed by the NRA's German military advisors. The Chinese had mastered the art of defensive warfare.[39]

Red Army infantry, like their NEFDF opponents, did not display groundbreaking innovations, but there were three areas that stood out when assessing the ODVA's infantry tactics: planning, preassault attacks, and night attacks. After the poorly executed attacks in mid-August, the ODVA under Blyukher became a model for tactical planning. The Red Army participants frequently referred to the conduct of leader's reconnaissance patrols to augment information obtained by observation aircraft. Sometimes the RKKA leaders were brazen in their efforts; in September, a group of officers, field glasses in hand, spent two days standing out in the open while surveying the Chinese positions on the Western Front. Having gained the best intelligence possible, plans were completed and followed by briefings at each command level that covered every tactical step, from departing the base area through the conclusion of the mission. To ensure ultimate success, commanders readily adjusted their plans to meet the changing tactical situation, as witnessed in the hectic night reorganization during the battle for Dalainor.[40]

Preassault operations were excellent; both the Mishan and Trans-Baikal groups successfully isolated their objectives by severing lines of communication between NEFDF commands before the assaults began. During the Mishan operation, this was accomplished when the 1st Rifle Regiment occupied a blocking position to protect the left flank of the main attack while cavalry detachments cut telegraphic lines connecting the forwardmost Chinese units with their headquarters and rear echelons. When combined with the dawn air raids that destroyed the NEFDF observation aircraft on the ground, the 1st Mukden Cavalry Division commander was isolated and tactically blinded at the critical moment when the assault began. On the Western Front, Rokossovsky's cavalry and the Trans-Baikal air groups met with similar successes.

The tactics used by the Red Army in their night attacks on the Western Front—disciplined silent movement by multiple columns to release points just beyond the enemy lines, followed by a vigorous attack—are still used by many armies in the twenty-first century. Only those who are equipped with the latest night-vision devices have abandoned the tactic. Adding another layer of complexity to the ODVA night operations was the fact that most were raids, requiring strict accountability of personnel under conditions of darkness and minimal verbal communications, along with a carefully thought-out plan of disengagement and withdrawal to friendly lines. The one unique characteristic of the 1929 night fighting was the use of searchlights to detect and foil the raids. In future wars, battlefield illumination came via flares delivered by mortars, artillery, or aircraft, although the Soviets and several other militaries mounted searchlights, especially infrared lights, on their tanks until late in the twentieth century.

Riverine Fighting

If not the largest naval battle (in terms of ship size and projectile throw weight, the 1938 night battle of Cape Polis during the Spanish civil war may win that honor), the 12 October Tungchiang battle was by far the most significant of the interwar era. Had the story ended with the monitor division or the seaplane squadron that sank a warship, or had the success of the operation led to the codification of new sections on joint riverine warfare in the *1936 Field Service Regulations*, the successor to the *1929 Regulations*, the battle still would have been significant, but there was more. What made the battle exceptional was the ODVA's ability to expand the innovative combined-arms Amur River Flotilla concept to execute the large-unit landing operation by the 2nd Division against a defended shore. That required the integration of seaplane-, gunboat-, and shore-based artillery fires and the task organization of the flotilla into separate mine clearing, landing support, and ship-on-ship battle groups. Given its scope and complexity (and the fact that no other battle of that period included a greater number of warships and naval aircraft), the battle may have been the largest, and was certainly the most important, of the interwar era.[41]

Soviet Operational Art

The development of Red Army operational art has been recognized as a major breakthrough in twentieth-century military theory. In 2002, Felix Patrikeeff posited a link between the 1929 Sino-Soviet conflict and military art, writing that the war could be seen as "a major stage in the development of Soviet Operational Art." That raises the question, was operational art present on the 1929 battlefield? The answer is less than straightforward. The actions of the ODVA did indeed resemble operational art, as they contained many of its conceptual facets. Operational art was an evolving concept in the early RKKA that began a few years after the end of the Russian civil war. Glantz defined it as the planning and conduct of independent operations by large forces (armies or fronts) as a bridge linking strategy to tactics, or more succinctly, "Operational art determines methods of preparing for and conducting operations to achieve strategic goals."[42]

To insert the 1929 conflict into this process, a brief review of the historical development of operational art is needed. Amnon Sella held that the "basic tenets" that led to operational art were in place by 1925. Glantz argued that Tukhachevsky's tactical concept of consecutive battles, codified in the *1929 Regulations*, began the lineage that was formalized in 1932 with the *Provisional Instructions on the Organization of Deep Battle*. Afterward, the RKKA reconfigured successive and deep battle tactics into operational formulations first delineated by Triandafillov. Those doctrinal successes provided the Red Army with the tools needed to formalize operational art theory in the *1936 Regulations*, overseen by Tukhachevsky. Svechin, writing in 1939, stressed that operational art "regulated" tactics and characterized battles not as "independent phenomena" but the "essential materials" of operations. In a greater sense, it completed the Red Army's "military art" triad of strategy, operational art, and tactics that rejected the primacy of two well-established martial constructs: the Napoleonic decisive battle and the attrition warfare of World War I.[43]

There are two insurmountable objections against the 1929 conflict being an example of operational art. For one, it is an anachronism, a chronological impossibility. Tukhachevsky did not coin the term for another two years, and then only as an undefined goal, and as noted above, comprehensive operational art doctrine was not completed until the publication of the *1936 Regulations*. Additionally, operational art was inseparable from mechanized warfare, a capability that was only hinted at in 1929. That reality—an absence of any real Red Army mechanized capability—explains Tukhachevsky's 1928 decision to back off deep battle theory, an essential component of operational art, and adopt a more realistic offensive policy based on successive battles. He only revived it after the RKKA began to mechanize.[44]

In support of the argument that operational art fundamentals were present, the search for evidence of Tukhachevsky's successive battles is important in two respects and gets to the center of Patrikeeff's "major stage" thesis. First, it provides evidence for answering the question of why the Soviets decisively defeated the Chinese forces. Second, it provides an opportunity to validate the argument that Red Army doctrinal innovations developed before the war had been institutionally internalized, becoming a combat reality and not simply a theory. To paraphrase Glantz, the question that needs answering is, was a distinctive concept of successive battles readily apparent to Soviet commanders? Were combat operations during the 1929 Sino-Soviet conflict merely an extension of the "maneuver character" of the Russian civil war that stemmed from a limited number of troops being forced to operate over vast areas, or a valid example of the application of successive battle doctrine in combat, the first practical step toward the development of operational art?[45]

The evidence is conclusive. The ODVA, composed of corps-sized operational groups fighting on two fronts separated by over 1,000 kilometers, was able in a seven-week period to synchronize three major operations: successive naval and amphibious engagements on the Sungari River in October, and the simultaneous operations on the Eastern and Western fronts in November. When looking to the Mishan operation on the Eastern Front, we see an advance of 40 kilometers in less than a day, and on the Western Front, the Rokossovsky Cavalry Group covered over 60 kilometers during the evening of 16–17 November and severed Liang's brigades from their logistical rear and reinforcements at Hailar. Beginning on 22 November, during the advance on Hailar, the Trans-Baikal Group advanced nearly 150 kilometers in three days. As the 21st Division commander, P. I. Ashahmanov, put it after the fall of Manchouli, the ODVA had not come "to 'sit on a nest,' but to advance [on Hailar] and not let the Chinese army recover."[46] The Western Front offensive, sequentially aimed at Dalainor, Manchouli, and Hailar, was a clear example of successive battles.

That leads to two final questions. Given the results, did the 1929 advances achieve the depths advocated by the theorists? How closely were the operations related to the future ideals of operational art? The old parameters allowed for infantry–cavalry forces to advance as few as five and as many as ten kilometers per day. Triandafillov advocated offensive drives beginning at twenty to twenty-five kilometers per day for infantry and thirty-five to fifty kilometers per day for cavalry-mechanized forces to encircle and cut off the enemy's main formations. The distances covered by the ODVA were in keeping with his goals, not a linear improvement over past practices. Triandafillov had to have been encouraged by the results of the ODVA offensives, especially Rokossovsky's encirclement of Dalainor and Manchouli. Regarding operational art, the *1936 Regulations* held that deep operations—the heart of operational art—assigned the primary role to the infantry and were characterized by simultaneous preliminary attacks by artillery and aircraft, followed by the "penetration of the tactical zone of the defense by attacking units with widespread use of tank forces."[47] The resultant tactical success was to translate into operation success, "with the aim of the complete encirclement and destruction of the enemy." With the sole exception of the widespread use of tank forces, the November offensive conducted by the Trans-Baikal Group met all the requirements of a 1936 deep operation.

While the 1929 Red Army lacked the mechanization to conduct deep operations, the ODVA's schemes of maneuver and distances covered, coupled with the use of artillery, airpower, and the few tanks available, argue that operational art tenets were present on the 1929 battlefield. Finally, the sine qua non of operational art, the link between tactics and strategy, was present as the ODVA operations achieved the strategic objective of forcing China to unconditionally accede to the Soviet demands. At that time, only the RKKA possessed both a doctrine and the field commanders capable of realizing such a strategic vision. It offers a key reason why Savkin praised Blyukher as having played "a particularly noteworthy role" in the development of Soviet military art. The ODVA battled in a class far above that of the NEFDF.[48]

11 | A War of Consequences

No War at All?

Telling the story of the 1929 Sino-Soviet conflict has always been a difficult task for historians. Writing in 1935, Eugene Lyons, the UPI Moscow correspondent in 1929, described the conflict as "serious enough in terms of casualties and political consequences, it remains to this day the war nobody knew."[1] Eighty years later, unearthing information remains a challenge; English-language documents are limited, necessitating a search for Chinese, Russian, and Japanese sources. Chinese sources have the additional handicap of being few, as the defeated had no interest in writing about their failure and the NEFDF no longer exists. One of the most difficult barriers to break down is the wall of misinformation. Politicizing history, especially twentieth-century Soviet and East Asian military history, is nothing new, as David King and Lyman P. van Slyke pointed out decades ago, and the Soviets almost immediately began to shape the tale of the 1929 war to fit their narrative, writing a victor's history. They largely succeeded.[2]

The Soviets stressed three points: it was not a real war, nothing much happened, and the Red Army scored a quick, relatively bloodless, and overwhelming victory. All three points are inaccurate and hinder the efforts of historians. It was war; the scale was huge, and both sides fought well. A lot happened in 1929 after the seizure of the CER. The war created thorny diplomatic issues in the capital of every major power and was covered by many of the world's leading print publications. There was enduring damage done to the Northeast. Further, the war shook the interwar world order in important ways, discussed below. The Red Army never found a quick and bloodless path to victory. The August and September RKKA attacks were costly and never achieved their political purpose of compelling the Chinese to capitulate. Even when complete success was reached during the October and November offensives, Soviet casualties easily exceeded 1,000 soldiers and sailors, and the Chinese losses were considerably higher. It was a bloody road to victory.

Perhaps the easiest way to deconstruct the Soviet mythology surrounding the war is to use a 13 February 1930 letter by Henry W. Kinney, an American working for the SMR. His letter is particularly insightful not simply because, in the war's immediate aftermath, it captured what became the key Soviet arguments defining the conflict but also because of its lasting influence. Major newspapers of the day quoted Kinney's report, and it entered into both the American and British archives. As such, he introduced the West to the official Soviet line, one that endured throughout the Soviet era; his paper is still cited by twenty-first-century historians.[3] Who Kinney was working for while undertaking his 1929 war project is unclear and raised concerns at the time. He was characterized variously "as a sort of publicity agent" for the SMR and someone "with a strong natural bias in favor of his employers."[4] The British and American recipients noted, however, that it was apparent that the Japanese were not behind it, making the remark of British diplomat Simon Harcourt-Smith that Kinney "had appeared to have garnered his information chiefly from Soviet sources" telling.[5] The combination of Kinney's track record of tilting accounts in favor of his employer, his free access to Soviet officials, and the pro-Moscow flavor of his letter point to a Soviet or pro-Soviet sponsor. Whether in their direct employ or not, the Kinney report proves illuminating, if problematic in that more objective and reliable sources repeatedly contradict the Russian sources he cited.

To downplay the fact that a war had taken place, Kinney always used the word with quotation marks to discount its accuracy. Soviet sources scrupulously avoided the word "war," and even the Japanese went to pains to not use it, as witnessed during the diplomatic discussion over the definition of war with Stimson—although Stimson was more concerned about the use of force, not terminology. Others agreed with Stimson. The Austrian government, when invoking the Paris Pact on 12 December 1929, dispensed with semantics entirely and cut to the heart of the matter when it declared that the war was "the first great international conflict" since the pact had come into force. The war was over by then; however, the advantage gained by the "nonwar" stratagem was not lost on the Soviets. They reapplied it a decade later during the 1939–1940 winter war with Finland. In December 1939, after four Red armies totaling over 400,000 troops had invaded and were fighting in Finland, the Soviets declared to the League of Nations, "The USSR is not at war with Finland and does not threaten the Finnish nation with war."[6] Politically, the ploy failed, as the League expelled Soviet Russia on

14 December, but militarily, as in 1929, diplomatic action did nothing to halt the invasion.[7]

Kinney began the Soviet's "nothing much happened" story line by quoting a White Russian manager who stated that the Dalainor coal mines were back up and running in early 1930. This was false; a Chinese economics publication noted that Dalainor coal mines were still closed in 1931 as a result of the lasting damage incurred by the 1929 fighting.[8] Kinney's reference to a White Russian manager is also suspect. We know from Kawamata and others that the GPU had systematically purged Dalainor of every possible White sympathizer, real or suspected. There were no Whites left for Kinney to interview, let alone one in a management position, and the idea that those arrested "returned [to the Soviet Union] at their own request" is incredulous, as was his notion that there was "no animus against White Russians" on the part of the Soviets. Kinney even blamed White Russian terrorists for the massacre of the Starovary Christians after claiming to have been given access to "pictures" of the guilty pro-tsarist thugs.[9] There is no other record of the alleged pictures, and no independent source has ever supported this novel pro-Soviet claim. The reality was that the thriving farming community never recovered. However, the message was that a massacre had occurred, but it had nothing to do with Soviet actions relating to the 1929 war.[10]

Again downplaying the damage done, neither Kinney nor subsequent Soviet writings make any mention of the sabotage campaign or the Suifenho air attacks. Kinney went so far as to claim that the Chinese, who made continuous efforts to keep the CER running during the war, were responsible for "ever so much greater damage than that done by the Russians" to the railway and its facilities.[11] That assertion is inaccurate. In addressing the economy, the war's ill effects were defined as "temporary" by Kinney.[12] V. Dushenkin echoed the "return to normal" argument in 1969, writing, "On 22 December 1929 in Khabarovsk, a protocol was signed which restored the CER situation that existed before the conflict." Cherepanov made a similar statement in his 1984 autobiography: "After receiving an object lesson, the Chinese government began to seek ways of reconciliation and restoration of normalcy on the CER. Soon after this had been achieved."[13] Taken together, these omissions and assignations lead to a conclusion of a war that had no significant downside—that nothing much happened—yet Patrikeeff in *Russian Politics in Exile* demolished this view, making a compelling argument that things never returned to the status quo ante in his aptly titled chapter, "Decline into Oblivion, 1930–1931."[14] Patrikeeff was correct: the conflict ended in lasting damage to the CER and the economy in the Northeast.

The story of an overwhelming Soviet victory was not as clear-cut as proclaimed. Victory was not clear-cut if for no other reason than Voroshilov's 17 November deliberations over abandoning the Western Front offensive after hitting unexpectedly tough Chinese resistance. While Kinney correctly heaped praise on the Soviet Red Army, Chinese martial valor was wrongly debased. He gave due credit to the Chinese defending Manchouli, but the heavy fighting at Dalainor was discounted entirely, and the story of the handful of Chinese deserters captured in women's dresses made its way into the report.[15] Only the biographies of Soviet military heroes provide insight into the difficulties the ODVA faced and offered praise for the fighting abilities of the Chinese.

The idea that "a relatively small number" of Russians soldiers that never exceeded "three thousand men" fought in the November offensive while facing 60,000 Chinese was sold to and then by Kinney. With it, the legend of the outnumbered RKKA fighting to victory entered the record and continued forward. Three decades later, in Kuzman's 1959 *Defense of Peace,* Chinese strength was put at 300,000 troops plus 70,000 "White Guard" bandits; he averred that "in all places, the enemy forces outnumbered the Soviet troops by 3 to 5 times." G. I. Salminov, in his 1980 *Transbaikal Sky,* lowered the number to 165,000 Chinese troops, and, citing the Central State Archive of the Red Army, reported that Soviet troops were outnumbered 3:1 on the Western Front.[16] The opposite was true. More precise Japanese army reporting tallied the combined Dalainor–Manchouli NEFDF garrison at about 15,000 troops while facing 35,000 Red Army soldiers and GPU troops of the ODVA Trans-Baikal Group.[17]

The number of Soviet casualties was made secret and remains unknown, allowing the idea of a relatively bloodless nonwar to take root. The use of mass graves further muddied the waters; true figures may never be uncovered. Kinney was silent on the subject. In 1993, Soviet colonel-general G. F. Krivosheev issued a declassified report that put the total number of RKKA killed and wounded at 812, with 147 of that number killed during the October and November offensives.[18] Glantz noted that Krivosheev's low numbers for twentieth-century Red Army casualties have been a point of argument among scholars for years, and Krivosheev's 1929 totals do not approach the truth.[19] Contemporaneous firsthand Japanese army and press reports, many backed up by Russian military accounts, listed dozens of engagements that resulted in hundreds—likely thousands—of casualties in the months before the October and November offensives. As for the offensives themselves, the casualties during the Mishan operation, based on the reports of officer deaths, were not insignificant; Kawamata wrote in the immediate aftermath of the November Western Front battles that precise numbers were unclear, but he had seen a Dalainor casualty list that contained the names of approximately 1,000 Red Army soldiers.[20] We know from John J. Stephan that the GPU erected monuments for the border guards who "fell defending the Far Eastern frontiers in 1929," but those numbers have never been reported by any source.[21] We likely will never know the full extent of those who gave their lives or were wounded in the war—and it was a war, in every possible sense.

Red Army invincibility was flaunted in Kinney's commentary while the Chinese armies suffered a "debacle."[22] The ODVA did score a decisive victory, but Kinney took the point to extremes. He proffered a story of Red Army air attacks by "soot" bombs and cabbages that "strove entirely to frighten . . . but avoided . . . serious damage," which was later repeated by *New York Times* correspondent Hallett Abend.[23] The problem with the tale is that it was at odds with the firsthand accounts. No eyewitness noted a shortage of bombs; in fact, Soviet aircraft were still in action at Hailar and Poketu after the ground combat ended. Kawamata attested to the professionalism and deadly efficiency of the Red Army airmen, which was also demonstrated in the earlier bombings at Suifenho and the air attacks during the Sungari River operation that left the Chinese flagship at the river's bottom. Kinney's reporting on harmless soot bombs and cabbages was nonsense.

Later Soviet reporting followed much of this minimalist line. The sources made a short war shorter still by focusing on the Sungari and Western Front operations in October and November. The August and September fighting received scant attention, yet those fights led to large-scale military escalation, while the lack of RKKA success made further bloodshed unavoidable. The only detailed report of the Mishan operation on the Eastern Front occurred in Dushenkin. Kuzman and Salminov covered the August and September fighting with one sentence each, and Dushenkin elected to only refer to Blyukher's position in reacting to Chinese "provocations" but offered no specifics.

N. P. Suntsov and I. M. Tretiak presented the most detailed description in several paragraphs, and V. N. Bagrov and N. F. Sungorkin offered another paragraph on the early incidents, but the impression left was of a conflict that consisted of a few days of fighting. The preceding months of sabotage, raids, bombings, artillery duels, and night attacks, along with the ebb and flow of diplomatic negotiations, were ignored.[24]

When examining the broader record, the inescapable conclusion is that there was war in the Northeast in 1929—a complex, multifaceted, and bloody war. Equally true was the fact that beyond the military clashes, much happened during and after the war, both within the Northeast and internationally. The Red Army achieved an overwhelming victory, but often in the face of stiff resistance, and only after a major multifront offensive was launched in the wake of many weeks of limited or no success against a determined Chinese army.

Consequences: The Broken Illusion of an Orderly and Peaceful World

In truth every war is a war of broken dreams, but the 1929 Sino-Soviet conflict stands out in time and place, a circumstance when idealism came face to face with violent reality. Although the war is frequently ignored and downplayed, it was a watershed that redefined relationships within the community of nations, and not for the better. The war changed the world, subtly in some cases and more profoundly in others. It revealed a breakdown in the postwar world order. The League of Nations proved impotent and the Paris Pact to outlaw war unenforceable. For China, it signaled defeat as it tried to reemerge as a country willing and able to defend what was thought to be in its national and territorial interests against the aggression of a major power. The Red Army victory compelled Japan to reorient its defenses toward Northeastern China and Soviet Russia. For the Soviet Union, it provided evidence that the Stalinist era of Soviet imperialism had begun. The futures of China, Soviet Russia, and Japan were on a less desired path.

After World War I, the dream of creating a stable world through pacific diplomatic means never held greater sway; the problem of maintaining peace seemed manageable because the community of independent nations was small. In East Asia were China, Japan, and Siam (Thailand); in the Pacific, Australia and New Zealand; in South Asia,

Afghanistan, Persia (Iran), Nedj and Hejaz (Saudi Arabia), and Yemen; and in Africa, Egypt (under British occupation), Ethiopia, Liberia, and South Africa. Only Europe and the Americas boasted large numbers of sovereign states. Making the task seemingly easier, international affairs were dominated by six powers: France, the United Kingdom, Italy, Japan, the United States, and Soviet Russia.

In practice, nothing was made easier, as the Powers were a disjointed assemblage and not on an equal footing in 1929. France and the United Kingdom remained global empires—true superpowers. Italy had adopted fascist nationalist socialism under Benito Mussolini and stood apart from the others, while Japan had been set adrift after the collapse of the Anglo-Japanese Alliance in 1923 and was dealing unsuccessfully with its militarists. The influence of the United States was on the decline as its policies became increasingly isolationist, and the Soviet Union followed its own revolutionary path and was still rebuilding after the destructive 1914–1922 conflicts that had convulsed the country. Germany was reemerging as a power but had not regained its lost stature. China too was rising in influence but remained weak. Within that cauldron of uneven strengths and competing interests, the great Power diplomats—supported by a small coterie of international legalists—struggled forward without a unifying aim save a shared sentiment directed toward world peace.

How to achieve peace had become an imperative, and the diplomats seemed to have gotten off to a good start. Beginning with the 1919 Versailles treaty, they attempted to erect an operative framework built around the League of Nations and its attendant Permanent Court of International Justice, which was bolstered by the 1928 Paris Pact. The framework to preserve East Asian peace was more elaborate than that centered on Europe, as it also contained the 1919 China arms embargo and the agreements codified in the 1922 Washington treaty.

It all fell short in 1929. The Versailles treaty had produced a tangled mosaic of unintended consequences, as seen in the May Fourth Movement, a revolutionary rejection of the new world order by millions of Chinese. The international court was ignored by all parties. Despite the embargo, China witnessed nearly endless warfare, and the number of soldiers under arms and casualties exploded during the years it was in effect. It had done nothing to deter a Chinese conflict in 1929. Similarly, the Washington treaty, aimed at securing peace and stability in East Asia, accomplished neither. Beyond an unpopular side agreement with Japan over the return of Shantung, China gained little. Japan left Washington alienated and more isolated than at any time in a generation, and Soviet Russia played no part in the process. That left the League of Nations and the Kellogg–Briand Pact.

The League of Nations proved a poor global caretaker in 1929. China was frustrated from the outset, as Nanking overvalued the League's ability to prevent the dispute from escalating into war and Wu's September plea struck at the heart of the interwar political framework: what was the responsibility of the League? The preamble to the covenant stated its purpose: the League existed to promote international cooperation and achieve international peace under an obligation not to resort to war. Article X went further, stating that "any war or threat of war, whether immediately affecting any of the Members of the League or not, is hereby declared a matter of concern to the whole League." The words were powerful, but the League was more than a bit dysfunctional, and finding a path to preserve world peace had remained elusive. American scholar John Bassett wrote in 1928 that the League relied on an "effective guarantee" by member states, adding that the term had no definition and was nothing short of useless. It was also unwieldy. Structurally, both the assembly and the council had the power to enact laws independently of each other, and by 1929, the governing council had been expanded from an original proposal of five to thirteen members who often worked at cross-purposes.[25]

When the CER crisis arose, the League chose inaction. As Bassett put it, "The League has functioned because the Foreign Secretaries have willed it."[26] Given its charter to prevent war, their decision was craven but not unexpected. The League had no stomach for action; in 1923, it assiduously avoided the Corfu crisis when Italy's navy seized the Greek island in retaliation for the assassination of an Italian official in Greek territory. A year later, the League took up a draft treaty for mutual assistance to any member attacked by an aggressor. Concurrently, the assembly voted to strike Article X, which obligated member states "to respect and preserve as against external aggression the territorial integrity and existing independence of all Members." The draft treaty died through delaying tactics led by Britain, which was unwilling to enter into new military commitments, while only the veto of Persia ensured the continuance of Article X.[27]

Collective military action proved anathema in 1929. Entreated by China in September 1929, the League of Nations pretended that the preamble, along with Article X and Article XI, was of no import. War was unwanted, but for the diplomats in Switzerland, there was no will to do anything other than wash their hands of the matter. The League refused to enter into any deliberations that did not involve member states—a prerequisite that did not even have a technical justification in the convention. As the League dithered and the Soviets declared that only unconditional acceptance of Moscow's ultimatum was acceptable, any resolution through either the Permanent Court of International Justice or The Hague court of arbitration also vanished. The diplomatic postwar safeguards to keep the peace collapsed.

Once tested, the Paris peace pact fell apart in almost every aspect; it went into effect on 24 July, and the first deadly military clash occurred only weeks later on the Manchurian frontier. The inability to identify an aggressor clouded the waters further, as both China and Russia justified their actions under the right of self-defense. The gradual and opaque escalation of hostilities allowed the Soviets to argue that there was no war to renounce until the decisive November offensive rendered the debate moot. By the time Stimson invoked the pact on 22 November, Russia had won the conflict, and the fighting, save a few air raids, was over. Finally, the absence of viable enforcement tools doomed the effort. Kellogg's vision that war could be avoided through an aroused public conscience was manifestly ineffective. The Soviets easily dismantled the threat by refusing to recognize any role for public opinion; Bukharin made it clear that the conflict was to be resolved solely between China and Russia.[28]

Thousands had been killed and wounded and a new era of war ushered in. As the years progressed, the pact to outlaw war became little more than an uncomfortable memory. Stalin's intransience once the crisis arose demonstrated that the postwar order could be undone if one or more of the Powers chose to challenge the status quo. Not simply passive consensus but collective action was required. The war proved beyond doubt that there were limits to diplomacy and the rule of law. War as an instrument of policy was again in the ascendancy. From the Wilsonian idealism of Versailles and the formation of the League of Nations to the Washington treaty and the Kellogg–Briand Pact, in a matter of months, the 1929 Sino-Soviet conflict undermined years of effort. In its aftermath, the dream that the new order would bring peace and prosperity lay shattered and broken. War was here to stay. The pathway to future conflicts, which had been believed shuttered, was instead reopened.

Consequences: China

For Chang Hsueh-liang and Chiang Kai-shek, the war was a painful setback; historian S. C. M. Paine correctly concluded that the 1929 conflict "had serious consequences for the Nationalists."[29] Nanking's rising military stature stemming from the successful Northern Expedition was called into question, and Lattimore wrote in 1931 that the 1929 defeat revealed a nation that was "weak in its external affairs."[30] Internally, the KMT's political divisions came to the fore. While the Young Marshal evinced a remarkable degree of loyalty, Chiang had been unable to support him militarily, and politically, the two were never able to stay on the same page during the Soviet parleys, which exposed a lack of unity and strength in Nanking. Chiang wrote that the Young Marshal's negotiations with the Soviets had "driven a wedge" between them, and the November defeat, followed by the Young Marshal's quick agreement to the Soviet ultimatum in December, further strained their relationship.[31] Lampson judged the war a "debacle" and Nanking's efforts to prevent it as "belated and futile." Chiang Kai-shek found himself forced onto a less desired road. He never again attempted to unilaterally abolish an unequal treaty through the threat of armed confrontation; protracted, if peaceful, negotiations took its place.[32]

The wrongly assessed war cast a long shadow over the Chinese military. The November defeats and Feng's mutiny exposed its weaknesses, as the other Powers were quick to note. In its wake, Chiang Kai-shek adopted a military policy of nonresistance if confronted by the other regional Powers. The Young Marshal willingly concurred. During the CER crisis, he had been convinced that the NEFDF, supported by the rest of the NRA, was more than ready to face the Red Army, but when the time for battle came, the NEFDF fought alone and ultimately failed. He later recounted that in light of the difficulties encountered with the RKKA, "I knew that China had no power to fight with Japan."[33] The perception that the NRA, to include the NEFDF, had made notable strides in closing the gap with those of the other Powers appeared mistaken, but they judged the Chinese army too harshly. Most observers failed to appreciate the strengths displayed by NEFDF. This was the first true national battle for the Fengtien troops. Before 1929, it had been a warlord army with the trappings of Chinese nationalism, but the war with the Soviets was a true fight for China. The cheering of the troops as they marched off to war and the emergence of student movements were unprecedented in the Northeast, while the arrival of the military cadets at the front lines echoed the revolutionary spirit of the Whampoa academy in 1926. Progress had been made.

That the NEFDF was unprepared to fight either the RKKA or IJA was unmistakably true. The performance of the senior commanders, especially Hu on the Western Front, spotlighted a glaring weakness in combat generalship, and the technological proficiency of the Soviet Red Army was enough to give any objective observer reason for sober reflection. However, the toughness of the Chinese line units, the companies and battalions, was glossed over by too many observers. The Chinese infantrymen took the best the Russians could throw at them, and in the face of many disadvantages, they fought with courage. The stoic acceptance of Russian artillery barrages, seen in their gallows humor as they wagered on where the shells would land, as well as the patriotic enthusiasm of the student volunteers showed a determination to stick it out and not run or break. While these factors did not translate into immediate battlefield success, they captured the rising nationalism essential to transition from a mercenary to a professional army, one that could in time face the Powers militarily—a transformative process that Japan in particular underestimated. That truth goes far in explaining how just a few years later the NRA turned what was supposed to be a quick, clean, and victorious invasion of China by Japan in 1937 into a hopeless, never-ending quagmire for the IJA.[34]

The conflict did nothing to unify the nation. Sun Yat-sen's dream of a constitutional democratic republic remained unrealized. Rule by authoritarian warlords had finally receded, only to be replaced by an authoritarian one-party state. The only question to be resolved was whose ideology would prevail, that of the KMT or the CCP. Even Chang Hsueh-liang, a man of unquestioned patriotism, never championed democracy and was acceptingly ambivalent toward what form of socialist totalitarian rule was acceptable, telling British reporters in 1933 that China should adopt "an organisation similar to fascism or communism; I don't know which I would prefer."[35] Of the two revolutionary movements, the war benefited the CCP the most. The fact that the CCP struggled and failed to convince the Chinese people to support the Soviet Union offered an important lesson even if the messenger, Ch'en Tu-hsiu, suffered a harsh fate. The failure was not simply the victory of Chinese nationalism over political ideology; it reflected the inauthentic voice of the CCP then under the direction of the Comintern, which meant Stalin. The 1929 failure was an example of a broader problem of cultural bias that helped lead to the KMT–CCP split and later the ousting of the Moscow-educated CCP cadres and their replacement by Mao Tse-tung.

The Soviets, while sensitive to societal nuances, found it difficult to compromise on the primacy of their political philosophies. It was taken as a given that the arguments of Marx, Engels, and Lenin were superior to anything espoused by Sun Yat-sen. That was a costly mistake. The Chinese revolution only could succeed under the direction of Chinese revolutionaries. If in conflict, Sun Yat-senism would always defeat communism unless and until an authentic Chinese communist leader arose, and in 1929, no such person held the reins of power in the CCP. That left the field to Chiang Kai-shek. It was not until the rise of Mao and his adherents—leaders who placed China before the Soviet Union—that the CCP found the Chinese voices that it needed. The CCP moved ahead while the KMT struggled to regain what had been lost. The dream that China would soon reunify and foreign encroachments quickly rolled back or eliminated died on the 1929 battlefields. The nation seemed trapped in a cycle of military conflict that stretched back to 1911 and had no apparent end in sight.

Consequences: Japan

Historian Shuji Taneine used the word "shock" to describe the reaction of the IJA officers to the resounding ODVA November victory. It was no overstatement. Manchuria was not simply central to Japan's East Asian policy; to the IJA, it defined Japan's place in the world. A decade earlier, Japan had declined to take Germany's place within the East Asian economic-financial consortium because it would not agree to open up the Northeast to the other Powers. After the seizure of the CER, Moscow, respectful of Japan's position, had sought an understanding with Tokyo before approving military action against the NEFDF. Reviewed internally during the 1921 and 1927 Eastern Region conferences, Japan's leaders reconfirmed their commitment to remain the paramount power in the Northeast and had no intention of relinquishing it. The ODVA victory shook that policy to the core and reopened the Manchurian "problem" to a degree not seen since the Russo-Japanese War.

The IJA came to the realization that they faced a "transformed"

RKKA, and the Soviet Five-Year Plan would only make it stronger. A Kwantung Army officer stated that after the 1929 Sino-Soviet conflict, "We had a sense of mission that emerged rapidly with the unexpected need to somehow solve the Manchuria problem."[36] Colonel Ishihara, embracing the 1928 goals of Komoto, had begun to plan an intervention in July and completed his work by year's end, when he submitted the ambitiously titled, "A Plan for the Solution of the Manchurian and Mongolian Problem as a Basic Policy to Change Our Country's Destiny."[37] Fellow Kwantung Army officers drew a number of lessons from the war. The overriding fear was that if Nanking would act to abrogate Russia's CER rights unilaterally, the SMR faced the same danger. The Chinese defeat loomed equally large. Historians Chen Tsung-yan and Wang Chien-hsueh argued that the 1929 Sino-Soviet war "had a profound impact on the Mukden Incident" and sped up the pace of Japanese aggression against China.[38]

Everything the Japanese militarists needed to seize the Northeast was now in place. Soviet Russia, through its successful exploitation of the Kellogg–Briand Pact, provided them with a framework that, if not legitimizing the use of force, allowed for its application without fear of meaningful consequences. As long as the pact remained the accepted international policy for dealing with armed conflict, the Kwantung Army knew it could seize Manchuria without the risk of military action by the other Powers. The army also learned that defeating the NEFDF would not be a formidable task, but Japan had to act while it possessed undisputed military superiority. The die was cast, and any dream for a peaceful future in the Northeast ended with the 1929 Sino-Soviet conflict. When the Kwantung Army struck on 18 September 1931, Chang adhered to the nonresistance policy as the NEFDF again stood alone. While the IJA had stood by idly in 1929, it was now the OKDVA's turn to watch while the Kwantung Army marched across Manchuria, although the Soviets were quick to let Japan know that they did not see any parallels between the limited 1929 conflict and those of 1931. After initially putting up a limited defense in Mukden, the Young Marshal withdrew his forces behind the Great Wall in December. Only isolated formations, primarily in Heilungkiang and Kirin, continued to battle the IJA until overwhelmed. The Northeast fell completely under Japan's sway. Chang Hsueh-liang expressed no lingering sense of guilt over the loss; he was unwilling to fall into the 1929 trap a second time. The one gain for China was a quick repair of relations with the Soviets, which had been ruptured during the 1929 conflict under circumstances similar to those that led to Chinese acquiescence in creating the CER in 1896: mutual fear of further Japanese aggression in East Asia.[39]

Strategically, the Red Army victory forced Japan to realign its defense policy. After the collapse of tsarist Russia and the massive naval expansion undertaken by the United States during World War I, the Japanese military had replaced Russia with the United States as its primary hypothetical foe in 1923.[40] The 1929 Sino-Soviet conflict changed that assessment, and after 1930, the IJA pivoted away from the United States, making Soviet Russia the main potential foe, while the Imperial Japanese Navy insisted that the United States remain the prime threat.[41] Japan's divided military was forced into an irresolvable dilemma. If the Soviet Union was the main enemy, then priorities had to shift toward the army, but if the United States was the likely enemy, the focus had to remain on the navy. Japan did not possess the resources to do both, and when it tried the impossible, it opened up vulnerabilities in both. If the navy was to get new aircraft carriers like the *Soryu* and superdreadnoughts like the *Yamato*, the army could not field the first-rate mechanized forces needed to keep pace with the RKKA, and taking half steps by diverting some monies and materials away from the navy to expand the number of tank and motorized units led to an inflated sense of strength.

Japan's defense problems led to another unintended consequence of no small significance, and the beneficiary was the United States. In addition to operational art, another of the great military innovations of the interwar era was the development of amphibious warfare. With the United States perceived as the likely foe and the Pacific Ocean the battlefield, the Japanese military had become the world's leader in amphibious operations by 1923. Beyond Japan, only the US Marine Corps seriously studied amphibious operations, but by early 1929, all three of its brigades were overseas and progress in amphibious warfare had stalled. The 1929 conflict changed that dynamic. As the IJA focused on Soviet Russia, advances in landing operations stagnated, and by the mid-1930s, the US Marines had taken the lead. The United States entered World War II as the world's most advanced practitioner of amphibious warfare—a capability that showed itself to be critical to the Allied victory.[42]

Both the drive to militarily conquer Manchuria and the shift in military strategy were symptoms of a more profound broken dream: that of a multiparty constitutional form of imperial government. When the advocates of moderation and reasoned peaceful coexistence fail and are discredited, the appeal of more extreme arguments are legitimized, and this is what happened in Japan. In the years following the 1929 conflict and the onset of the Great Depression, IJA extremists vied for control of the country. The suppression of the 26 February 1936 military coup by a radical army faction was nothing more than a chimera for the advocates of democracy, as the imperial government almost immediately came to be dominated by army officers. They became a cancer that ate at the body politic and almost destroyed the nation.

Consequences: The Soviet Union

Soviet Imperialism

If the July 1919 Karakhan manifesto captured the idealism of a new postimperialist future, then by 1924, the year that the CER condominium began, that view was dead. The transition was driven in part by the political changes in China but more by the Kremlin's adoption of realpolitik. Stalin's shift toward building socialism in one country legitimized imperialist aspirations as reasoned defensive steps, the need for buffer regions, and the high value placed on the CER as a strategic line of communication. This put the Republic of China and the Soviet Union on a collision course. Liang Chi-chao, a reformer whose writings influenced Sun Yat-sen, reflected on the Soviet's relationship with China and concluded that even before the 1929 war, the Soviet Union was an imperialist power. Afterward, the other Powers recognized it as such, and some leaders, such as Lampson, actually welcomed the return to the fold. Being condemned by Chinese revolutionaries and praised by British diplomats was proof that Soviet imperialism had taken root.[43]

Empty Victory

The consequences were unexpected, as the victory did not make Soviet Russia more secure. British diplomat John Pratt observed in 1932 that the CER had become a "running sore" for the Soviets, a *damnosa hereditas*—a damned inheritance.[44] The conflict ended in a Pyrrhic victory, and Soviet influence in the Northeast never recovered.[45] Despite the signing of the Soviet ultimatum, the status quo ante never returned.

CER profitability sputtered as the Great Depression took hold, and in September 1931, the Japanese seized Manchuria, reducing Russian influence to almost nothing. Finally, in 1935, the Soviets rid themselves of the "blister" by selling the CER to the puppet Manchukuo regime. The conflict also sowed some of the earliest seeds of the future Sino-Soviet split, as the 1929 seizure of a number of Amur and Ussuri river islands offended Chinese nationalism. They became a battlefield again forty years later, in 1969, when the People's Liberation Army moved to recapture Chenpao Island from the Soviets (on the Ussuri approximately halfway between Lake Khanka and Khabarovsk); the island issue would not be resolved until 2011.[46]

Josef Stalin as Dictator

A clenched fist accurately describes Stalin's method of rule, and the 1929 war accentuated the hazards of the unrestrained exercise of power in someone whose behavior was violent and at times erratic. Stalin's thirst for retribution—a foreshadowing of the horrors to come—was on full display in the massacre of the Starovary Christians at Trekreche and the GPU's arrest and annihilation of hundreds of White Russians in Manchouli and Dalainor after the fighting. He had yet to reach such extremes in his dealing with fellow Communist Party members—even Trotsky was only expelled to Turkey in 1929—but suppression of Politburo dissent in July and the November purge of Bukharin raised the prospect of worse to come. The 7 October letter to Molotov was an example of Stalin's ability to suspend reality when enraged. The order that fell to the crippled CCP northeastern branch to "declare Chang Hsueh-liang overthrown" and form a multibrigade Chinese Red Army in Manchuria just a week before the beginning of the ODVA Sungari River operation showed an inability to distinguish impossible ambition from concrete action.

The intensity of Stalin as dictator also was disclosed in the rejection of the Chinese diplomatic "surrender" in late August. Everything Stalin wanted from the July ultimatum and what he actually settled for in December had been conceded by both Mukden and Nanking by the end of August. The 29 August letter to Molotov was equally insightful.[47] It exposed how Stalin could become abusive by a cursory review—a misreading of the facts—and it revealed how quickly he attacked those with whom he disagreed. As historian Robert Service observed, Stalin could not settle for simply defeating his opponents, as he often needed to degrade, even physically punish, them.[48] By late August, the man of steel had moved on; humiliation was now the object. Stalin ordered an unnecessary military offensive that resulted in thousands of casualties. He had no regrets. That chain of logic exemplified the rationale that would underlie the great famine in Ukraine, the Great Terror, and the infamous 1939 nonaggression pact with Adolf Hitler that presented Stalin with the opportunity to crush the Baltic states, regain territories in Poland and Romania, and ushered in World War II. He also had gained confidence in fighting in the Northeast. In later years, Stalin had no fear of taking on the IJA at Lake Kashan in 1938 and Nomonhan in 1939, or in the full-scale invasion of Manchukuo and Korea in August 1945. In the aftermath of the 1945 offensive, he did not hesitate to dictate to Chiang Kai-shek and the KMT his terms for the military occupation of the Northeast. The conclusion that must be drawn after assessing Stalin's conduct in 1929 is that nothing that happened afterward was terribly unexpected or new, only increasingly dreadful. Had the Soviet system not enabled Stalin to amass such extraordinary powers, a different and more peaceful outcome in 1929, and likely afterward, almost certainly would have occurred.[49]

Conclusions

The crisis over the CER escalated into the tragedy that became the 1929 Sino-Soviet conflict. While the major fighting was of short duration and the objectives limited, the war was one of the largest and most significant of the interwar period. The prize was the CER, which was of great political, economic, and military value. China wrongly perceived Soviet Russia as vulnerable; there was an almost universal assumption that the Red Army was not a threat, and China trusted the international community to enforce the Paris Pact, precluding the possibility of war. Nanking and Mukden entered into talks with Moscow thinking they were negotiating from a position of strength, but the reality could not have been more different.

The Soviet decision to go to war rested with one man, Stalin, and the key to understanding Moscow's aims was one that Soviet leaders continuously struggled to find, solving the "puzzle of what Stalin had in mind."[50] The solution was easy to uncover. The formation of the ODVA meant war was an option; the parleys were only a venue for Chinese capitulation. The Chinese were to be humbled. Stalin would achieve that goal either at the negotiation table or on the battlefield, while weather—the coming winter—forced the pace of events. Miscalculation again crippled the Chinese strategy as the NEFDF generals assumed it was too late in the season for major fighting. Conversely, the Soviets knew there was a window to attack before winter took hold. When China refused to submit to Stalin in October, a military solution was inevitable.

The Red Army won in short order for a number of reasons. For China, residual warlordism was the crucial weakness; it had a disunited army. Feng Yu-hsiang's rebellion drew off needed NRA reinforcements, and Chang Hsueh-liang's distrust of the NRA generals dissipated a unified effort against the ODVA. Tactically, General Hu reflected much of what was wrong with warlord-era officers: Hu was more concerned with preserving his Fengtien army than fighting the Russians. Because the Manchouli–Dalainor defenders were from Heilungkiang, he never gave them his full support. These competing loyalties and divisions among the generals wasted the sacrifices made by the frontline soldiers and paved the way for defeat.

For the Soviets, the ODVA benefited from handpicked leaders, superior training, and discipline as well as a marked advantage in artillery and airpower, but the deciding factor was the application of superior doctrine, and that put the RKKA on a revolutionary path. That Blyukher was able to launch the integrated sea–air–land Sungari River operation followed by simultaneous multidivision offensives on two fronts separated by over 1,100 kilometers was a realization of that vision. While not an example of operational art, the employment of tanks, attempt at motorization, and combined use of cavalry, artillery, and infantry battle groups with airpower during the November offensive were further evidence of Soviet commanders who had internalized the philosophy of successive battle. This edge allowed the ODVA to defeat the larger NEFDF.

The Soviet victory reverberated across the globe as the closely aligned diplomatic and military strategy nullified both the League of Nations and the Paris Pact to outlaw war. The Kellogg–Briand Pact was a failure. Once again, might made right. Japan reoriented its military policy away from the United States. The officers of the IJA were convinced that the future of Japan rested in controlling the Northeast. The Soviet Red Army now was its most powerful opponent, ensuring that the region would remain the flash point of the Far East. Chang Hsueh-liang and Chang Kai-shek both emerged as weakened leaders and were forced to adopt a passive defense policy in the face of foreign military threats, while Stalin wielded more power both internally and internationally than he had before the war and Russia was confident in waging a land war against either China or Japan. Stalin's Soviet Union had reentered the East Asian arena in dramatic fashion. The 1929 war was the cause.

Appendix A | Orders of Battle

Table 1. Chinese Northeast Frontier Defense Force (NEFDF)

Senior NEFDF Command

Rank	Name
Commander	Chang Hsueh-liang
Vice Commander—Kirin	Chang Tso-hsiang
Vice Commander—Heilungkiang	Wan Fu-lin
Commander, Harbin Special District	Chang Ching-hui

Sungari River Defense Units

Ground Forces	Place
2nd Kirin Mixed Brigade	Tungchiang
U/I Regiment/7th Kirin Mixed Brigade	Fuchin
9th Kirin Mixed Brigade	Tungchiang/Fuchin
2 Squadrons, 43rd Cavalry Regiment	Fuchin
Several Naval Infantry Battalions	Tungchiang

SUNGARI RIVER FLOTILLA UNDER CAPTAIN YIN SHUO

Boat	Armament
Gunboat	
Kiang-heng	
(Captain Mok Yui-ming)	1 × 4.7in, 1 × 3.5in, 1 × 2in, 1 × 40mm
Lu-chi	2 × 3.5in, 1 × 2in
Li-chieh	4 × 3in, 2 × 2in
Li-shui	1 × 3.5in, 2 × 3in, 2 × 2in
River patrol craft	
Kiang-ping	2 × 2in
Kiang-tai	2 × 2in
Kiang-nan	2 × 2in

(continued on next page)

Boat	**Armament**
River patrol craft	
Kiang-tung	1 × 2in
Kiang-an	1 × 2in
Ch'in-han	1 × 2in
Tsen-I	4 × 2in
Armed Barge	
East B	2 × 4.7in

Eastern Front

Unit	**Commander**	**Place**
First Fengtien Army	General Wang Shu-chang	
4th Mixed Brigade		
12th Mixed Brigade	General Chang	Southeast of Harbin on CER
19th Mixed Brigade		
1st Cavalry Division		Mishan
2nd Artillery Regiment		
Communications Company		
18th Kirin Mixed Brigade		
21st Kirin Mixed Brigade	Suifenho	
25th Kirin Mixed Brigade		

Western Front

Unit	**Commander**	**Place**
Second Fengtien Army	General Hu Yu-kun (Je-yu)	Hailar
3rd Mixed Brigade	General Chang Shu-ko	Teheiho
5th Infantry Brigade		Hailar
14th Infantry Brigade (-)	General Tsu Yeng-ho	Tsitsihar
24th Infantry Brigade		Hailar
3rd Cavalry Brigade (-)		Hailar
9th Cavalry Regiment		Hailar
5th (3rd?) Artillery Regiment	Colonel Huang Yeng-an	Hailar–Dalainor
1st (7th?) Engineer Battalion		Manchouli–Dalainor

Unit	Commander	Place
Communications Company	Wang Ju-mei	
15th Heilungkiang Brigade	General Liang Chung-chia	Manchouli
38th Infantry Regiment		
43rd Infantry Regiment		
51st Infantry Regiment		
10th Cavalry Regiment/ 3rd Cavalry Brigade		
9th Artillery Regiment (- 3rd Battalion)		
1st Company, 7th Engineer Battalion		
17th Heilungkiang Brigade	General Han Kuang-ti	Dalainor
6th Infantry Regiment		
13th Infantry Regiment		
14th Infantry Regiment		
3rd Cavalry Regiment/ 3rd Cavalry Brigade		
2nd Battalion 3rd Artillery Regiment		
3rd Battalion, 9th Artillery Regiment		
7th Engineer Battalion (- 1st Company)		

Table 2. Soviet Special Far East Army (ODVA)

Senior ODVA Command

Rank	Name
Commander	V. K. Blyukher
Deputy Commander	A. R. Lapin
Commissar	A. A. Gusev
Chief of Operations	V. I. Chuikov
Chief of Communications	C. Gulin

(continued on next page)

Army Reserve

12th "Omsk" Territorial Rifle Division
  34th Rifle Regiment
  35th Rifle Regiment
  36th Rifle Regiment
  12th Artillery Regiment

Northern Front

Unit	Commander	Place
26th "Zlatousk" Rifle Division	N. V. Kuibyshev	Blagoveschensk
76th Rifle Regiment		
77th Rifle Regiment		
78th Rifle Regiment		
26th Artillery Regiment		

Transbaikal Group (Western Front)

Rank	Name
Commander	Griasnov, then S. S. Vostretsov in August
Chief of Staff	Ermakov
Commissar	Skovorodnikov
Artillery Chief	Sivkov

18th Rifle Corps

Unit	Commander
35th Rifle Division	V. P. Ivanov
103rd Rifle Regiment	
104th Rifle Regiment	
105th Rifle Regiment	
35th Artillery Regiment	
36th Rifle "Zlatoust" Division	E. V. Baranovich
106th "Sakhalin" Rifle Regiment	M. I. Puzyrev
107th Rifle Regiment	
108th "Belorechensk" Rifle Regiment	
36th Artillery Regiment	
36th Engineering Batallion	

1st Tank Company	
Detachment, 1st Moscow Transport Unit	
5th "Kuban" Cavalry Brigade	K. K. Rokossovsky
Armored Car Company	
Heavy Artillery Battalion	
Heavy Howitzer Battalion	

Other Group Forces

Unit	**Commander**
1st/45th Buryat-Mongol Cavalry Division	
"Tersk" Cossack Cavalry Regiment	
21st "Perm" Rifle Division	P. I. Ashahmanov
61st Rifle Regiment	
62nd Rifle Regiment	
63rd "M. V. Frunze" Rifle Regiment	
21st Artillery Regiment	
Armored Train Nos. 65, 66, 67	

Pacific Group (Eastern Front)

Unit	**Name**
19th Rifle Corps	
Commander	Feldman
Chief of Staff	Smirnov
Artillery Chief	Kozerovsky
1st "Pacific" Rifle Division	A. I. Cherepanov
Commissar I. A. Svinkin	
1st "Chita" Rifle Regiment	Kunitsky
2nd Rifle Regiment	Chyobolev
3rd Rifle Regiment	
1st Independent Cavalry Battalion	
1st Artillery Regiment	
2nd "Amur" Rifle Division	I. A. Onufriev
4th "Insk" Rifle Regiment	
5th Rifle Regiment	
6th Rifle Regiment	
2nd Independent Cavalry Battalion	

(continued on next page)

Unit	Name
2nd Artillery Regiment	
9th Cavalry Brigade	D. A. Vaynerh
85th Cavalry Regiment	
86th Cavalry Regiment	
87th Cavalry Regiment	Porkhomenko
Mountain Light Artillery Battalion	
58th Communications Company	
59th Communications Company	
19th Mortar Artillery Battalion	
Other Group Forces	
Armored Train No. 13, I/U	
Coastal Artillery Division	

22 November Reinforcements from Moscow (arrived after hostilities ended)

Unit	Name
1st "Proletariat" Rifle Division	N. Kamenev
1st Tank Regiment	
1st Heavy Tank Company	
2nd Heavy Tank Company	
7th Light Tank Company	
19th Light Tank Company	
3rd Tank Regiment (1st Battalion?)	
30th Light Tank Company	
31st Light Tank Company	
33rd Heavy Tank Company	
1st Fighter Squadron	
2nd Fighter Squadron	
7th Fighter Squadron	
8th Fighter Squadron	
10th Fighter Squadron	
11th Fighter Squadron	

Amur River Flotilla (Commanders Y. I. Ozolin and Pstozhekov)

DIVISIONS AND ARMAMENT

Division	Ship	Armament
Monitor	*Sverdlov*	4 × 6in, 2 × 3in, 1 × 40mm
	Lenin	6 × 4.7in, 2 × 40mm
	Red East	6 × 4.7in, 2 × 3in, 1 × 40mm
	Sun Yat-sen	6 × 4.7in, 2 × 40mm
Gunboat	*Peasants*	2 × 4.7in, 1 × 3in
	Proletariat	2 × 4.7in, 1 × 40mm
	Red Star	2 × 4.7in, 1 × 3in
	Buryat	2 × 3in
Fast patrol	*Peak*	1 × 4.7in
	Konye	1 × 4.7in
	Leopard	1 × 37mm
Minelayer	*Strong*	2 × 40mm
Minesweeper	*T-3-1*	
	T-3-2	

OTHER AMUR RIVER FLOTILLA MEMBERS

Unit	Commander
2nd Battalion, 4th "Insk" Rifle Regiment	
68th River Seaplane Squadron	E. M. Mutha and Lucht
Seaplane Tender *Amur*	

GPU Units (identified)

Unit	Location
17th GPU Brigade	Eastern Front
49th GPU Regiment	
51st GPU Regiment	
"Brantia" Irregulars	Eastern Front
33rd GPU Regiment	Western Front
Cossack–Mongol Irregulars	Western Front

(continued on next page)

Air Forces

EASTERN FRONT (COMMANDER E. P. KARKLIN)

Squadrons	No. of Aircraft
2nd "Lenin" Reconnaissance Squadron	8
5th Fighter Squadron (Commander I. I. Kaplina)	10
6th Fighter Squadron	
40th Bomber Squadron	15
41st Bomber Squadron	15
42nd Bomber Squadron	15
43rd Bomber Squadron	15
Detachments 7th/13th Air Squadrons	8

WESTERN FRONT (COMMANDER KUSH)

Squadrons	No. of Aircraft
17th Air Squadron	8
19th Air Squadron	8
6th Fighter Squadron, 9th Air Group	12
25th Bomber Squadron, 9th Air Group	18
26th Bomber Squadron, 9th Air Group	18

Note: 9th Air Group led by Commander I. R. Seitzinger

Appendix B | Location Names

Most locations below are in China, and the Wade-Giles form has been applied for transliteration, as it was used during this period in Chinese history and in the English-language primary sources. For ease of transition, the second column uses current location Chinese names in pinyin form. Commonly used alternative names are also provided.

Place Name	Modern Name	Alternate Name or Names	Comments
Barga	Baerhu	Bargut	
Canton	Guangzhou		
Dalainor	Zhalainuo'er	Chalainor, Chzhlaynora Jalainor	
Fengtien province	Liaoning province	Fengtian province	
Fushin	Fujin	Fugden	
Hailar	Hulunbur		
Harbin	Haerbin		
Heilungkiang	Heilongjiang	Amur River, Black Dragon River	
Kalgan	Zhangjiakuo		
Kirin	Jilin		
Kyakhta	Kyakhta	Troitsosavsk or Troitze-Casavsk (merged with Kyakhta during the Soviet Era)	Sometimes confused with the Chinese trading town of Maimaicheng located across the border from Kyakhta

(continued on next page)

Place Name	Modern Name	Alternate Name or Names	Comments
Maimaicheng	Altanbulag	Maimachen, Maimaichin	Maimaicheng was the name used for any Chinese trading town in Mongolia
Manchouli	Manzhouli	Manchuria Station Manchuria	
Mishan	Mishan		
Mukden	Shenyang	Fengtien	
Muleng	Muling		
Poketu	Boketu	Pokotu, Puhetu	
Suifenho	Suifenhe	Pogranichnaya	
Sungari	Songhua		
Taipinchien	Banzhiang	Panchienho	
Barga Three Rivers Region		Trekhreche	
Teheiho	Heihe	Heiho	
Tsagan	Cagan	Tsokang	
Tungchiang	Tongjiang	Lahasusu	Shores and waters around Tungchiang were referred to as Sankiangkuo
Tungning	Dongning		
Ude	Sainshand	Buyant Uhaa	
Urga	Ulan Bator		
Verkhneudinsk	Ulan Ude	Verkne-Oudinsk, Verkne-Udinsk Verchniudinsk	
Yungting River	Yongding River	Kuan Ting or Hun or Yun River	

Notes

Introduction

1. Primary sources used Union of Soviet Socialists Republics, Soviet Union, Soviet Russia, and Russia interchangeably and referred to its citizens as Soviets or Russians. The same convention is followed here.

2. Waldron, *From War to Nationalism*, 95; Foreign Relations of the United States (hereafter FRUS) 1929, II, 352. See Appendix A for Chinese and Soviet forces. The Soviet total includes border guard brigades and regiments. A comparable force was sent to the 1939 Khalkhin-Gol/Nomonhan battlefront, where the Red Army fielded two rifle divisions and the 36th Motorized Rifle Division (a modernized version of the 1929 division) along with seven brigades (two tank, three motorized rifle, one machine gun, and one paratroop), two small Mongol cavalry divisions, and numerous supporting units; see Coox, *Nomonhan*, 587–589.

3. Sheridan, *China in Disintegration*; Sheridan, *Chinese Warlord*.

4. Cooling, "Towards a More Usable Past," 29.

5. Patrikeeff, *Russian Politics*, xii.

Chapter 1. The Troubled Frontier

1. Saga, *Confessions of a Yakuza*, 122.

2. Gottschang and Lary, *Swallows and Settlers*, 133; Suleski, *Civil Government*, 2–3; SMR, *Manchuria*, vi, 28. Manchuria was the term widely used in 1929 and was the homeland of the Manchu people. The region was also known as the Northeast and the Three Northeastern Provinces.

3. Lee, *Revolutionary Struggle*, 73; Nobuo and Trewartha, "Land Utilization Maps," 480; Gottschang and Lary, *Swallows and Settlers*, 173; SMR, *Manchuria*, 3. There were no census data available, only estimates. Gottschang and Lary, *Swallows and Settlers*, put the figure at 32.67 million in 1924 and 36.47 million in 1929; Murakoshi and Trewartha, "Land Utilization Maps," used 30.69 million; and SMR, *Manchuria*, put the number much lower, at 25 million in 1924.

4. Jin, "Nature of Tsarist Russia's Inroads," 76–77. Dairen had been called Dalny during Russian rule and Lüshun by the Chinese. See Appendix B for current and alternative place-names used in this text.

5. Patrikeeff, *Russian Politics*, 31; Stephan, *Russian Far East*, 67.

6. Powell, *My Twenty-Five Years,* 177.

7. SMR, *Manchuria,* 24, 67; Crossley, *Manchus,* 200; Lee, *Revolutionary Struggle,* 24; Patrikeeff, *Russian Politics,* 30.

8. Murakoshi and Trewartha, "Land Utilization Maps," 482–483, 487, 489–490, 492; Suleski, *Civil Government,* 109; SMR, *Manchuria,* chap. 2.

9. Sun, *Economic Development,* 69–71; Hsieh and Chu, *Foreign Interests,* 19–20, 48.

10. Sun, *Economic Development,* 70, 73–74; Hsieh and Chu, *Foreign Interests,* 21–22, 25, 50.

11. Sun, *Economic Development,* 94; Suleski, *Civil Government,* 108–109, 122–123; United States Office of Naval Intelligence (ONI) Report, Serial 399, 14 December 1927.

12. Wolff, *Harbin Station,* 38; Powell, *My Twenty-Five Years,* 181; Lattimore, *Manchuria,* 192; Lee, *Revolutionary Struggle,* 54; United States Military Attaché (hereafter MA) Report 7208, 11 February 1928.

13. Tang, *Russian and Soviet Policy,* 433, 436–438; Gottschang and Lary, *Swallows and Settlers,* 178; SMR, *Manchuria,* 49; Bisher, *White Terror,* 16. Dollar figures are based on a 1929 exchange rate of US$1.12 = 1.00 1913 Haikuan tael. Over time, the silver Haikuan tael was reduced in size, depreciating its value, as the 1924 tael was only worth US$0.74.

14. Nathan, *Plague Prevention,* 2.

15. Tang, *Russian and Soviet Policy,* 172–174, appx. on 433–455; Nathan, *Plague Prevention,* 56; Glantz, *August Storm: Soviet 1945 Strategic Offensive,* photo on 23.

16. Tang, *Russian and Soviet Policy,* 47–49; Cheng, *Sino-Russian Relations,* 59; Carnegie Endowment for International Peace, *Manchuria,* 13–14; see 17–27 for a copy of the bank's charter.

17. Cheng, *Sino-Russian Relations,* 59; Tang, *Russian and Soviet Policy,* 50; Clubb, *China and Russia,* 123–124; Carnegie Endowment for International Peace, *Manchuria,* 46–49.

18. Carnegie Endowment for International Peace, *Manchuria,* 15.

19. Cheng, *Sino-Russian Relations,* 59; Tang, *Russian and Soviet Policy,* 50; Carnegie Endowment for International Peace, *Manchuria,* 46–49.

20. Tang, *Russian and Soviet Policy,* 39.

21. Duus, *Abacus,* 64.

22. Cheng, *Sino-Russian Relations,* 58–59; Tang, *Russian and Soviet Policy,* 51, 55–56; Carnegie Endowment for International Peace, *Manchuria,* 17–18, 28–30, 41, 46. The operative phrase for permitting Russian control was, "The Company will have the absolute and exclusive right of administration of its land." Russia, France, and Germany united against Japan in the Triple Intervention.

23. FRUS 1920, I, 686, 689; Duus, *Abacus,* 64; Tang, *Russian and Soviet Policy,* 39, 55–56; Carnegie Endowment for International Peace, *Manchuria,* 17–18, 28–30, 41, 46.

24. Esherick, *Origins*, 97; Lattimore, *Manchuria*, vii; Lensen, *Russo-Chinese War*, 5–6; Sawyer, "Martial Prognostications," 45, 48–49; Elleman, *Modern Chinese Warfare*, 119.

25. Hu, *Opium War*, 197; Preston, *Boxer Rebellion*, 32; Rhoads, *Manchus and Han*, 71; Elleman, *Modern Chinese Warfare*, 120.

26. Elleman and Kotkin, *Manchurian Railways*, 22.

27. Li, *Political History*, 185–186; Hu, *Opium War*, 191–192; Preston, *Boxer Rebellion*, 92, 97. The term "Powers" evolved over time. Before World War I, it meant the major European states along with Japan and the United States. After the war, it generally meant the victors—France, Italy, Japan, the United Kingdom, and the United States—although other European nations with interests in China were sometimes included.

28. Guo, "Russian Railway Guard," 8; Preston, *Boxer Rebellion*, 107–108, 123; Rhoads, *Manchus and Han*, 72; Worthing, *Military History*, 77. The eight powers were Austro-Hungary, France, Germany, Italy, Japan, Russia, the United Kingdom, and the United States.

29. Hu, *Opium War*, 261; Preston, *Boxer Rebellion*, 30; Gottschang and Lary, *Swallows and Settlers*, 39.

30. Asada, *Railway Management*, 313; Guo, "Russian Railway Guard," 5–6; Lensen, *Russo-Chinese War*, 7–8; Nish, *Origins*, 83, 93; Esherick, *Origins*, 305.

31. Lensen, *Russo-Chinese War*, 11–12; Guo, "Russian Railway Guard," 7, 12.

32. Hu, *Opium War*, 220, 236, 237; Lensen, *Russo-Chinese War*, 42, 53, 58; Worthing, *Military History*, 76; Preston, *Boxer Rebellion*, 32, 39.

33. Hu, *Opium War*, 220, 237; Lensen, *Russo-Chinese War*, 42, 53, 58; Worthing, *Military History*, 76; Guo, "Russian Railway Guard," 7; Asada, *Railway Management*, 315.

34. Dmitriev-Mamonov and Zdziarski, *Siberian Railway*, 408–409; Nathan, *Plague Prevention*, 58; Asada, *Railway Management*, 316; Lensen, *Russo-Chinese War*, 82, 110, 58, 75–76, 84.

35. Lensen, *Russo-Chinese War*, 103.

36. Stephan, *Russian Far East*, 60; Lensen, *Russo-Chinese War*, chap. 8, "The Massacre"; Asada, *Railway Management*, 316; Hu, *Opium War*, 263.

37. Lensen, *Russo-Chinese War*, 146; Hu, *Opium War*, 262; Guo, "Russian Railway Guard," 8; Asada, *Railway Management*, 316; Wolff, *Harbin Station*, 65.

38. Wolff, *Harbin Station*, 33, 35; Asada, *Railway Management*, 316; Lensen, *Russo-Chinese War*, 146–147. Fortunately the destruction order never had to be issued, but Red Guards later destroyed the cathedral in 1966 during the Cultural Revolution.

39. Lensen, *Russo-Chinese War*, 160–161; Guo, "Russian Railway Guard," 8; Asada, *Railway Management*, 317.

40. Lensen, *Russo-Chinese War*, 117–118, 121, 123; Guo, "Russian Railway Guard," 9. Russian troop strengths during the Boxer Uprising presented here

reflect combat troops only (infantry, cavalry artillery, and sappers), not logistics or other support troops. Also excluded are garrison and occupation soldiers.

41. Guo, "Russian Railway Guard," 8; Asada, *Railway Management*, 316–317; Lensen, *Russo-Chinese War*, 151–152, 194.

42. United States War Department, *Military Operations in China*, 12–13, 179–180.

43. Lensen, *Russo-Chinese War*, 197, 203–205; Guo, "Russian Railway Guard," 9.

44. Lensen, *Russo-Chinese War*, 211–212, 229, 232; Guo, "Russian Railway Guard," 9.

45. Lensen, *Russo-Chinese War*, 253–254, 278; Stephan, *Russian Far East*, 60; Nish, *Origins*, 111; Preston, *Boxer Rebellion*, 310; FRUS 1921, I, 402. The Boxer Indemnity totaled US$333,900,000 in 1900 dollars plus a 4 percent per annum interest charge for forty years.

46. Asada, *Railway Management*, 319–320; Hsieh and Chu, *Foreign Interests*, 3; Nish, *Origins*, 91–92; Guo, "Russian Railway Guard," 14; Asada, "China–Russia–Japan Military Balance," 1286.

47. Guo, "Russian Railway Guard," 11; Carnegie Endowment for International Peace, *Manchuria*, 61–62, 69; Lukoianov, "Russian Imperialism," 238; Nish, *Origins*, 150.

48. Zhang, *Warlord Chang Tso-lin*, 464–465; McCormack, *Chang Tso-lin*, 17; Elleman, *Modern Chinese Warfare*, 82, 83–86; Worthing, *Military History*, 61–62.

49. Stephan, *Russian Far East*, 60–61.

50. Nish, *Origins*, 159; Tyler, *Japan–Russian War*, 26; Paret, *Makers of Modern Strategy*, 320.

51. Evans and Peattie, *Kaigun*, 60, 90; Drea, *In the Service of the Emperor*, 78, 81, 93, 99; Nish, *Origins*, 169, 179, 197, 202–203, 210, 256–257.

52. Drea, *In the Service of the Emperor*, 103–104; Tyler, *Japan–Russian War*, 169; Nish, *Origins*, 241; Sun, *Economic Development*, 62. The Dalainor coal mine had been opened in 1902 but was unable to meet wartime demand.

53. Drea, *In the Service of the Emperor*, 106, 119; Tyler, *Japan–Russian War*, 397, 491–492, 521.

54. Carnegie Endowment for International Peace, *Manchuria*, 30–31; Hu, *Opium War*, 287–288.

55. Sakurai, *Human Bullets*, 54–55.

56. Tyler, *Japan–Russian War*, 427–428; Echevarria, *After Clausewitz*, 2. Orlov led a division, while Fleisher, Gergross, and Rennenkampf became corps commanders.

57. Asada, "China–Russia–Japan Military Balance," 1295; Nish, *Origins*, 187; Carnegie Endowment for International Peace, *Manchuria*, 108, 116–117.

58. Sheridan, *Chinese Warlord*, 47–48; McCormack, *Chang Tso-lin*, 19, 24–25; Hu, *Opium War*, 458; Young, *Presidency of Yuan Shih-kai*, 71. The three divisions were the 3rd, 20th, and 23rd along with the 2nd Mixed Separate Brigade. At

that time, a Chinese division was approximately a 10,000-man-strong force, and a mixed brigade was half that size. The brigade was so named because it contained a mixture of infantry, cavalry, artillery or machine gun units, and sappers, allowing it to operate independently in battle like a division. Mixed brigades unattached to a division often had the name "separate" added.

59. Young, *Presidency of Yuan Shih-kai*, 30–31; Hu, *Opium War*, 303, 403, 462. Under the New Army plan, four divisions were to be based in Peking, three each in Kiangsu and Szechwan, two each in Hupeh, Chihli, Kwangtung, Yunnan, and Kansu, and one division in each of the fifteen remaining provinces along with the Jehol Mongol region to the north of Peking.

60. Sheridan, *Chinese Warlord*, 47–48; McCormack, *Chang Tso-lin*, 19, 24–25; Asada, "China–Russia–Japan Military Balance," 1292; Hu, *Opium War*, 458; Li, *Political History*, 195.

Chapter 2. The Northeast Evolving: The 1911 Revolution and the Great War

1. Sun Yat-sen, *Memoirs*, 202; Sharman, *Sun Yat-sen*, 123; *Who's Who in China, 1925*, 771–772. The Revolutionary Alliance was also known as the United Alliance. Wang Ching-hui was the pen name of Wang Chao-ming. He was also referred to as Henry Waung. Educated in the law in Japan, his anti-Ch'ing writings made him a national figure.

2. Sun Yat-sen, *Memoirs*, 216–217; Dingle, *China's Revolution*, 35, 45, 49, 54–55; Elleman, *Modern Chinese Warfare*, 143; FRUS 1912, 48; Elleman, *Modern Chinese Warfare*, 142. The first rebels came from the engineer battalion of General Chang's 8th Division. There were two brigades in Hankow on 10 October, and both rebelled, the 8th Division's 15th Brigade (the division's other brigade [16th] was away in Szechuan) and Li's 21st Brigade (of the still-forming 11th Division). The bulk of Chang's troops were banner men from the 15th Brigade's 30th Regiment.

3. Dingle, *China's Revolution*, 62, 67; Hu, *Opium War*, 485–486; Rhoads, *Manchus and Han*, 175–176; Sharman, *Sun Yat-sen*, 125; *Who's Who in China, 1925*, 494. The Peiyang Army expanded to seven divisions, with the 20th added in 1910. The armies were as follows: 1st Army—4th Division, 3rd Brigade/2nd Division, and 11th Brigade/6th Division; 2nd Army—3rd and 5th Divisions, 39th Brigade/20th Division; 3rd Army—1st Division and the Imperial Guards. The 3rd Army, with the remainder of the 2nd, 6th, and 20th Divisions, was in North China. Li had gone from colonel to full general by November 1912.

4. FRUS 1912, 49; Young, *Presidency of Yuan Shih-kai*, 50, 56; Dingle, *China's Revolution*, 67; Hu, *Opium War*, 486; Rhoads, *Manchus and Han*, 181–182; "Imperial Edict" (Wellington, New Zealand) *Evening Post*, 1 November 1911.

5. Hu, *Opium War,* 480, 487, 498, 500, 502; Rhoads, *Manchus and Han,* 177–178; Dingle, *China's Revolution,* 70, 73, 79, 94, 96, 101, 106, 114–115, 126, 129, 136–139; "Two-Thirds of Hankou Destroyed," *Evening Post,* 10 November 1911; "Sack of Hanyang" and "Terms Rebels Will Accept," *Evening Post,* 30 November 1911; "The Chinese Civil War," *Evening Post,* 1 December 1911; Elleman, *Modern Chinese Warfare,* 144. Some estimates put the Hankow homeless figure in the hundreds of thousands. The key armistice terms were continuation of the Ch'ing dynasty; final parliamentary authority over drafting and ratifying changes to the constitution; death penalty cases solely under the purview of parliament; and military control under the emperor except when used during domestic disturbances, in which case the military would answer to parliament.

6. Hu, *Opium War,* 508; Spence, *In Search of Modern China,* map on 251; Rhoads, *Manchus and Han,* 180; Lary, *Region and Nation,* 38. In Changsha, it was the 25th Brigade/13th Division and the10th Division in Fukien. In the north, Chang Shao-feng led the 20th Division and Lan the 2nd Separate Brigade.

7. Sheridan, *Chinese Warlord,* 47–48; Taylor, *Generalissimo,* 21, 23; Furuya, *Chiang Kai-shek,* 15, 31–32; *Who's Who in China,* 1925, 43; Tien, *Government and Politics,* 116; Fenby, *Chiang Kai-shek,* 32; Ch'en, "Defining Chinese Warlords," 592; Young, *Presidency of Yuan Shih-kai,* 33, 60–61; "Taiyuen-Fu in Ruins," *Evening Post,* 22 November 1911; "Fighting at Nankin," *Evening Post,* 30 November 1911. Feng's battalion was from the 80th Regiment/20th Division; he was reinstated after the Revolution. Chu led a 21st Division regiment and Chiang the 83rd Republican Brigade.

8. Chen Kuiyuan, "Revolution of 1911"; Young, *Presidency of Yuan Shih-kai,* 32–33; Dingle, *China's Revolution,* 152–153, 156.

9. McCormack, *Chang Tso-lin,* 15, 24–25; Rhoads, *Manchus and Han,* 23; "Manchurians and a Russian Loan," *Evening Post,* 13 November 1911.

10. Zhang, *Warlord Chang Tso-lin,* 86; McCormack, *Chang Tso-lin,* 15, 24–25, 27, 120ff.; Rhoads, *Manchus and Han,* 23; Ch'en, "Defining Chinese Warlords," 589; "Chinese Terror Stricken," *Evening Post,* 31 January 1912.

11. Ven, "Public Finances," 832; Young, *Presidency of Yuan Shih-kai,* 101; Ch'en, "Defining Chinese Warlords," 566, 587–589; Hu, *Opium War,* 575–576; FRUS 1912, 101–102; "Poorly Armed," *Evening Post,* 3 December 1911; "Move to End Hostilities," *Evening Post,* 19 December 1911; "Trouble in Tibet," *Evening Post,* 21 December 1911; "Who Will Be President!," *Evening Post,* 2 January 1912; "No Pay for Soldiery," *Evening Post,* 21 January 1912; Li, *Political History,* 261.

12. Spence, *In Search of Modern China,* 267; Dingle, *China's Revolution,* 33, 43; "Sun Yat-Sen Interviewed," *Evening Post,* 25 November 1911; "Chinese Revolution: Extraordinary Meeting in Tokio," *Evening Post,* 26 December 1911; FRUS 1928, II, 154; Gao, *Historical Dictionary,* 285. Sun was elected by a 16–1 vote. No delegations came from the Tibetan, Muslim, Mongol, or Manchu lands.

13. Dingle, *China's Revolution,* 33, 43; FRUS 1912, 66; "Chinese Rebellion," *Evening Post,* 21 December 1911. The 1912 Constitution can be found at http://www.gongfa.com/linshiyuefa.htm (in Chinese).

14. Young, *Presidency of Yuan Shih-kai,* 117, 130; Li, *Political History,* 286–287; Chiu, "Constitutional Development," 5–6; Sun Yat-sen, *Memoirs,* 125; *Who's Who in China,* 1925, 114.

15. Young, *Presidency of Yuan Shih-kai,* 66, 131–132, 151–152, 157; Sharman, *Sun Yat-sen,* 218–219; Gillin, "Portrait of a Warlord," 290; see also Sze and Lo, *Constitutional Compact*; and Nathan, *Peking Politics,* 61. Per Article 40, the eight ministries were Foreign Affairs, War and Navy, Interior, Agriculture and Commerce, Communications, Education, Finance, and Justice. (War and Navy later became separate ministries.) The premier was also referred to as the prime minister and chief of staff. Yuan had also lost tariff revenues.

16. Meyer and Brysac, *Tournament of Shadows,* 434; FRUS 1912, 75, 86; Hopkirk, *Great Game,* 1–2; Asada, "China–Russia–Japan Military Balance," 1299, 1301; "If There is a Republic," *Evening Post,* 3 January 1912; "Independence of Mongolia," *Evening Post,* 9 January 1912; "Russian Mongolian Note," *Evening Post,* 12 January 1912; "Millard's Review No. 14," *China Monthly Review,* October 1920, 215.

17. Meyer and Brysac, *Tournament of Shadows,* 434; FRUS 1912, 75, 86; Hopkirk, *Great Game,* 1–2; Asada, "China–Russia–Japan Military Balance," 1299, 1301; "If There Is a Republic," *Evening Post,* 3 January 1912; "Independence of Mongolia," *Evening Post,* 9 January 1912; "Russian Mongolian Note," *Evening Post,* 12 January 1912.

18. McCormack, *Chang Tso-lin,* 26.

19. Drea, *In the Service of the Emperor,* 137.

20. Wilbur and How, *Documents,* 43; Sun, *Economic Development,* 29; Young, *Japan's Total Empire,* 32; Chou, "Railway Development," 60.

21. Matsusaka, *Making,* 191, 204–205; Bland, "Manchuria," 839.

22. Chou, "Railway Development," 81–82.

23. Xu, *China and the Great War,* 66; FRUS 1919, I, 415; Sun, *Economic Development,* 28, 62, 70, 7; Asada, *Railway Management,* 237; Hsieh and Chu, *Foreign Interests,* table I-B: Sino-Foreign Mines under Special Organized Agreement.

24. Suleski, *Civil Government,* 38–39, 47; McCormack, *Chang Tso-lin,* 27.

25. Dickenson, *War and National Reinvention,* 91, 115; FRUS 1915, 99–105, 127, 144–145; Carnegie Endowment for International Peace, *Manchuria,* 164–170; for details on the 1915 Sino-Russian Outer Mongolian agreement, see Carnegie Endowment for International Peace, *Outer Mongolia,* 18–23 and 32–39.

26. Lary, *Region and Nation,* 28–29; Hu, *Opium War,* 641–641.

27. *Who's Who in China,* 1936, 283.

28. Waldron, *From War to Nationalism,* 36–37; Twitchett and Fairbank, *Cambridge History of China,* 275; "Political Crisis in China: President Dismisses the

Premier," *Evening Post,* 25 May 1917; "Trouble in China," *Evening Post,* 19 July 1920; Pye, *Warlord Politics,* 18; Sharman, *Sun Yat-sen,* 207–208; "Political Crisis in China: President Dismisses the Premier," *Evening Post,* 25 May 1917; Rider, *Information,* 440; Ch'i, *Warlord Politics,* 246; Young, *Presidency of Yuan Shih-kai,* 122. "Anfu" in this case is said to be a contraction of Anhwei and Fukien. Some sources use "Anhwei" in place of "Anfu."

29. Ch'i, *Warlord Politics,* 49ff.; "Fighting Round Pekin: Mediation Fails," *Evening Post,* 19 July 1920.

30. Asada, *Railway Management,* 333; Lary, *Region and Nation,* 31; McCormack, *Chang Tso-lin,* 31, 34–35, 46; Asada, "China–Russia–Japan Military Balance," 1306; Hu, *Opium War,* 651; Ch'i, *Warlord Politics,* 246. According to Asada, at the outbreak of World War I, Chang commanded 38,300 troops in Fengtien while 15,000 troops were available in Kirin and 14,600 in Heilungkiang.

31. Xu, *Strangers on the Western Front,* 4.

32. Bergère, *Sun Yat-sen,* 272; Xu, *China and the Great War,* 203; Treadgold, *Twentieth Century Russia,* 119; Maddox, *Unknown War,* 6. The United States did not sign the treaty as a show of independence and was technically an associated, not allied, power during World War I. In 1914, St. Petersburg was renamed Petrograd.

33. Ironically, Lenin had been a boyhood friend of Kerensky.

34. FRUS 1918, Russia III, 206; FRUS 1920, 437; White, "American Role," 30.

35. Chou, "Railway Development," 75–76.

36. Kennan, *Russia and the West,* 93; Morley, *Japanese Thrust,* 38; Dunscomb, *Japan's Siberian Intervention,* 35; Faulstich, *Siberian Sojourn,* vol. 2, chap. 21.

37. White, "American Role," 30–31; FRUS 1919, Russia, Chapter 2: Siberia (hereafter FRUS 1919, Siberia), 392. The RRSC was to staff fourteen divisions to cover the Trans-Siberian Railway and CER, which oversaw long-haul rail transportation of supplies, matériel, and equipment.

38. Jones, "Diary"; Morley, *Japanese Thrust,* 177.

39. Morley, *Japanese Thrust,* 31, 50–51, 233, and appx. A; Gilbert, *First World War,* 425; Kennan, *Russia and the West,* 44.

40. Asada, *Railway Management,* 333; Chen Zhixin, "Establishment," 16; Morley, *Japanese Thrust,* 110; FRUS, 1918, Russia II, 5; FRUS 1919, Paris I, 241, 242. Beginning in late November 1918, China was represented during Supreme War Council meetings when matters concerning the Far East arose.

41. Chen Zhixin, "Establishment," 17. The Harbin CER Soviet guard consisted of two understrength battalions from the 618th Tomsk Rifle Regiment.

42. Asada, *Railway Management,* 334; McCormack, *Chang Tso-lin,* 40; Bisher, *White Terror,* 45.

43. Jennings, "Mad Baron's March," 7, 9.

44. McCormack, *Chang Tso-lin,* 35; Morley, *Japanese Thrust,* 110–112; Dun-

scomb, *Japan's Siberian Intervention*, 46–47; Asada, "China–Russia–Japan Military Balance," 1305, 1307. Lin's brigade was composed of some of Tao's railway guards along with 9th Heilungkiang Brigade troops.

45. Ch'i, *Warlord Politics*, 19, 246; Sheridan, *Chinese Warlord*, 68; Ch'i, *Chinese Warlord System*, 27. Disobeying Tuan came with a price: Feng Yu-hsiang's mentor, General Lu Cheng-wu, was assassinated by Little Tsu in 1918 over his opposition to the war in the south.

46. Bland, *China, Japan, and Korea*, 101; FRUS 1919, I, 318–319; Ch'i, *Warlord Politics*, 22.

47. Ch'i, *Warlord Politics*, 24–25; McCormack, *Chang Tso-lin*, 47; *Who's Who in China*, 1925, 349.

48. FRUS 1919, I, 596; Morley, *Japanese Thrust*, 189–191, 207. Kolchak led the Black Sea Fleet until the February Revolution and duty in the Provisional Government's Navy Ministry.

49. Worthing, *Military History*, 89; FRUS 1920, I, 417. Besides Sun and his protector turned rival, Lu, the council included Admiral Lin Pao-yi, General Tsen Chun-hsuan, and General Tang Chi-yao, along with Tang Shao-yi and Dr. Wu Ting-feng, father of Dr. C. C. Wu.

50. FRUS 1918, Russia II, 34.

51. Wheeler-Bennett, *Brest-Litovsk*, 226; Trotsky, *My Life*, chap. 32, "Peace."

52. Ulam, *Expansion and Coexistence*, 71; Chi, *Warlord System: 1916–1928*, 27–28. RKKA stands for Raboche-krest'yanskaya Krasnaya armiya (Workers' and Peasants' Red Army).

53. Gilbert, *First World War*, 401; Carr, *Russian Revolution*, 10; Service, *Stalin*, 160; Kotkin, *Stalin*, 255–256.

54. Kotkin, *Stalin*, 250, 260–261; Wheeler-Bennett, *Brest-Litovsk*, 304; Kennan, *Decision to Intervene*, 138; Wollenberg, *Red Army*, appx. 1. Lenin failed to gain a peace vote in January, with Josef Stalin, an up-and-coming if ruthless leader, the only prominent Bolshevik to take his side.

55. Watt, *Dare Call It Treason*, 283.

56. United States Government, "Roumanian Peace," in *Proceedings of the Brest-Litovsk Peace Conference*; Gilbert, *First World War*, 398, 425, 430; Churchill, *World Crisis*, 2:963. Although no war indemnity was imposed, territory was taken, Germany and Austro-Hungary took control of the oil fields, and all surplus foodstuffs and textiles were to be sold at prices set by the victors.

57. FRUS 1918, Russia II, 27; Morley, *Japanese Thrust*, 146, 236–237, 255; Kennan, *Decision to Intervene*, 97; Kennan, *Russia and the West*, 95–96; Durvov, *Russian and Soviet Orders*, 29; Graves, *America's Siberian Adventure*, 49.

58. FRUS 1918, Russia II, 287–290; Maddox, *Unknown War*, 50; Morley, *Japanese Thrust*, 251; Bisher, *White Terror*, 93; "Ex-Czar of Russia Killed by Order of Ural Soviet," *New York Times*, 22 July 1918.

59. Kennan, *Russia and the West*, 91.

60. MacMillan, *Paris*, 71; Graves, *America's Siberian Adventure*, 4, 51; Maddox, *Unknown War*, 77. Wilson's Fourteen Points, 8 January 1918, are available at http://avalon.law.yale.edu/.

61. Dunscomb, *Japan's Siberian Intervention*, 38.

62. Xu, *Strangers on the Western Front*, 4, 93–94, 97, 100; Xu, *China and the Great War*, 114–115, 153–154; Bland, *China, Japan, and Korea*, 101.

63. Richard, *When the United States Invaded Russia*, 35; Graves, *America's Siberian Adventure*, 82–83; Maddox, *Unknown War*, 16; Carnegie Endowment for International Peace, *Manchuria*, 142–143, 183–184; Morley, *Japanese Thrust*, 102, 124; Dunscomb, *Japan's Siberian Intervention*, 35–38.

64. The formations were simply numbered the 1st, 2nd, and 3rd War Participation Divisions, with a similar numbering system used for the first four mixed brigades.

65. McCormack, *Chang Tso-lin*, 49n, 50, 53; FRUS 1919, I, 276, 300. Some WPA units were still not ready in early 1919.

66. Morley, "Russian Revolution," 454–455; Stephan, *Russian Far East*, 119; Morley, *Japanese Thrust*, 80, 255, 334–335, 341, 355; Jennings, "Mad Baron's March," 10; Dunscomb, *Japan's Siberian Intervention*, 68. The 7th and 12th Divisions and 40th Mixed Brigade were assigned. The Japanese provided the Czech Legion with large quantities of ammunition as well as twenty machine guns and a battery of mountain guns.

67. Bisher, *White Terror*, 165; FRUS 1918, Russia II, 330, 349; Morley, *Japanese Thrust*, 3; Stephan, *Russian Far East*, 129, 132; Graves, *America's Siberian Adventure*, 84; Kedzior, *Evolution and Endurance*, 10. Ward was joined by the 9th Battalion, Hampshire Regiment. The French battalion was an ad hoc formation of eight companies, three from the 3rd Tonkinese Rifle Regiment, two each from the 9th and 16th Colonial Infantry Regiments, and one from the 3rd Zouaves Regiment. A Colonial artillery battery arrived in October, completing the battalion. The 31st US Infantry joined the 27th Infantry a few days later, which was then joined by troops from the 8th Division stationed in California, whose soldiers were used to bring the two regiments up to wartime strength of 3,650 men each. Yu Yu-ssu's name is also recorded as Yuyousi.

68. Stephan, *Russian Far East*, 121–122, 124, 130; Morley, *Japanese Thrust*, 71, 235–236; Graves, *America's Siberian Adventure*, 63, 66; Drea, *In the Service of the Emperor*, 75; Richard, *When the United States Invaded Russia*, 58–59; Bisher, *White Terror*, 99; King, *King's Complete History*, 457, 483; United States Government, *Proceedings of the Brest-Litovsk Peace Conference*, appx. 25, "Status of the Russian Fleet, 14 September 1918"; FRUS 1918, Russia II, 26; see also Poznansky, *Siberian Red General*. Oi arrived with the 14th Infantry Regiment. Bela Kun formed the Internationalists when he was head of the Soviet All-Russian Prisoner of War Committee. Kun failed to win over the Czech Legion. By August 1918, the units in the Far East were the Vladivostok International Battalion,

Mate Zalka's Hungarian "Revolutionary" Regiment, Avgust Goldfinger's Hungarian cavalry detachment, and Erno Svetets's brigade. In May 1919, Bela Kun with his Hungarian Internationalists established a Soviet regime in their homeland, only to be overthrown by a French-aided Romanian army. Returning to Russia, he was executed in 1938 during the Great Terror. Mate Zalka later joined the Red Army and was sent to Spain during its civil war; he was killed there in 1937. Taube, a veteran of the Russo-Japanese War, was a former tsarist general who was in the Far East recuperating from wounds suffered on the Eastern Front.

69. Graves, *America's Siberian Adventure*, 67; King, *King's Complete History*, 484; Gilbert, *First World War*, 479; Bisher, *White Terror*, 170; FRUS 1920, Russia III, 566; FRUS 1921, I, 570. Besides the POW legion, the Italian contingent consisted of a battalion from the 85th Infantry Regiment, a machine gun company, a mountain artillery battery, and a Carabinieri detachment totaling about 1,600 troops. The 4,200-strong Canadian force was built around the 16th Infantry Brigade. For a detailed history of the Canadian expedition, see Moffat, "Forgotten Battlefields."

70. Graves, *America's Siberian Adventure*, 130; Maddox, *Unknown War*, 63; Wright, *Chinese Steam Navy*, 140–141; FRUS 1920, Russia III, 510; FRUS 1917, I, 291; FRUS 1918, Russia II, 334–335; Morley, *Japanese Thrust*, 363–364; Jones, "Diary," part 1, news clipping, 8 September 1918.

71. FRUS 1919, I, 387; FRUS 1919, Paris II, 466; FRUS 1920, I, 758.

72. ONI Report, "Japanese Aviators in Siberia," 31 December 1919; Dunscomb, *Japan's Siberian Intervention*, 122. The Japanese used a few Sopwith and Nieuport fighters, carried out scouting missions, and conducted tests on their airworthiness in extreme cold during the winter of 1919–1920, but the role of the airplane was negligible.

73. Efimov, Manzhosov, and Sidorov, *Armored Trains*, 7–9; Trotsky, *My Life*, chap. 34, "The Train"; Bisher, *White Terror*, 177–180; US National Archives, photo 111-SC-75877, depicting an early Czech Legion armored train, http://www.archives.gov/; Kennan, *Russia and the West*, 115; Hosek, "Hailar Incident," 107. For a photo of Kalmykov's train with his name on the side, see "General Ivan Kalmykov's Armored Train in Vladivostok," http://digitallibrary.usc.edu/.

74. Ch'i, *Warlord Politics*, 27; Twitchett and Fairbank, *Cambridge History of China*, 276–277; Nathan, *Peking Politics*, 96–97, 107n33, 123–124. *Anfu* meant "peace and happiness" and was named for the Peking street where the organization's headquarters was located—and, of course, it matched the name of Tuan's Anfu Clique.

75. McCormack, *Chang Tso-lin*, 48; Zhang, *Warlord Chang Tso-lin*, chap. 9, pt. 2; Sheridan, *Chinese Warlord*, 72–73; FRUS 1919, I, 311, 322; FRUS 1919, I, 270–271, 277, 345; Young, *Presidency of Yuan Shih-kai*, 66; Bunn, "Military Events of the World," 220.

76. FRUS 1919, 615; Suleski, *Civil Government*, 54; McCormack, *Chang Tso-lin*, 32.

Chapter 3. Talks, Wars, and Railroads (1919–1924)

1. FRUS 1919, Paris II, 498.

2. Most contemporary sources, such as US diplomatic communications, usually referred to the foreign minister as Lu Cheng-hsiang; however, he preferred Lou Tseng-Tsiang.

3. FRUS 1919, Paris II, 157; FRUS 1919, Paris III, 491–492.

4. FRUS 1919, Paris III, 756–757.

5. FRUS 1919, Paris III, 740; Sharman, *Sun Yat-sen*, 224; MacMillan, *Paris*, 459; Hu, *Opium War*, 673; Bruce A. Elleman, *Wilson and China*, 64, 93, 98. An undercurrent to the whole Shantung question was the Asian concept of face. At Versailles, Japan sought to regain its national pride by humiliating Germany over the Shantung, just as Germany had humiliated Japan during the Triple Intervention after the First Sino-Japanese War. Similarly, China was loath to seek Japan's approval to recover its own sovereign territory.

6. Wilbur and How, *Documents*, 43.

7. FRUS 1919, I, 367–368; FRUS 1919, Paris III, 383–384; Hu, *Opium War*, 676–677.

8. FRUS 1919, I, 710, 714–715; FRUS 1920, I, 405; MacMillan, *Paris*, 476; Elleman, *Diplomacy and Deception*, 16.

9. FRUS 1919, I, 292, 311, 316; Willoughby, *China at the Conference*, 245.

10. Bland, *China, Japan, and Korea*, 102; FRUS 1919, I, 299–300, 304–305, 317, 381, 492. The four were Britain, France, Japan, and the United States. Getting the Allies to agree to the embargo was difficult. Italy excluded armament contracts signed before the embargo took effect, and Japan remained committed to its agreement to equip Tuan's WPA. Japan later agreed to halt shipments by March 1919. By early 1920, the NWDFA consisted of the 1st to 3rd FD Divisions (with the 4th FD Division being formed in Outer Mongolia from 1st and 23rd FD Mixed Brigades), along with the 2nd FD Mixed Brigade in Suiyuan, another mixed brigade in Inner Mongolia, and four located near Peking.

11. FRUS 1919, I, 315, 322, 329, 341–341, 353–355, 491, 670; FRUS 1921, I, 537; Lary and MacKinnon, *Scars of War*, 36.

12. Kennan, *Russia and the West*, 114; Graves, *America's Siberian Adventure*, 113–116; FRUS 1919, Paris II, 466; FRUS 1919, Siberia, 278. The Czech Legion was reemployed as follows: Corps Headquarters at Vladivostok, 1st Division at Irkutsk, 2nd Division at Tomsk, and 3rd Division at Krasnoyarsk.

13. Graves, *America's Siberian Adventure*, 342–343; FRUS 1919, Siberia, 298, 303–304; FRUS 1920, Russia III, 567; Bisher, *White Terror*, 239; Jones, "Diary,"

12 June 1919. By February 1920, the CER Defense Corps consisted of three brigades, one each in Kirin and Heilungkiang in addition to the brigade protecting the Ussuri Line. The United States funded the repatriation of the Polish, Latvian, Yugoslavian, and Romanian troops.

14. FRUS 1920, Russia III, 488, 569; FRUS 1921, II, 707; Dunscomb, *Japan's Siberian Intervention,* 198–199; Lensen, *Japanese Recognition,* 16; Euden and North, *Soviet Russia,* 66, 80; Graves, *America's Siberian Adventure,* 328; Moffat, "Forgotten Battlefields," 82. Transport ships for the Czech Legion had been arranged through the International Red Cross with United States funding.

15. FRUS, 1919, Siberia, 236–237, 239. The IARC was composed of one member each from Britain, China, France, Japan, the United States, the Czechoslovaks, and the Omsk Regime, and it supervised three subordinate agencies: the Technical Board under Stevens to operate the railways; the Transportation Board to process Allied rail usage requests; and the Military Board, responsible for joint defense of the rails.

16. FRUS 1919, I, 334.

17. FRUS 1919, I, 279, 595–97; FRUS 1919, Siberia, 239; Graves, *America's Siberian Adventure,* 181–182; FRUS 1919, I, 590, 613–614; FRUS, 1919, Siberia, 240–241, 256, 258; Asada, *Railway Management,* 336.

18. Graves, *America's Siberian Adventure,* 103; Stephan, *Russian Far East,* 138; King, *King's Complete History,* 593; Voroshilov, *Stalin and the Red Army,* 22; Erickson, *Soviet High Command,* 58–59, 61, 64; Service, *Stalin,* 172; Treadgold, *Twentieth Century Russia,* 180, 184–185; MacMillan, *Paris,* 74, 77, 81; FRUS 1919, Siberia, 202, 205, 209, 213, 222, 227, 229. A Red "army" at this time was actually little more than a division, numbering around 13,000 soldiers.

19. FRUS 1919, I, 385; Carnegie Endowment for International Peace, *Manchuria,* 107–108; McCormack, *Chang Tso-lin,* 39. The overlapping rail lines were directed in a 1907 Russo-Japanese Convention.

20. FRUS 1919, I, 385.

21. FRUS 1919, I, 379–380, 385; McCormack, *Chang Tso-lin,* 39–40.

22. Hosek, "Hailar Incident," 110.

23. FRUS 1919, I, 610; McCormack, *Chang Tso-lin,* 102; Zhang, *Warlord Chang Tso-lin,* chap. 9, pt. 2.

24. *Who's Who in China,* 1925, 37, 66; Zhang, *Warlord Chang Tso-lin,* 471; *Who's Who in China,* 1936, 8.

25. FRUS 1919, I, 331; Ch'i, *Warlord Politics,* 31; Pye, *Warlord Politics,* 20–21. By the time of his death, Feng's forces had withered to the 1st Division at Peking and the 16th Division in Chahar, and numbered no more than 20,000 troops, compared to Tuan's estimated 212,000 troops or Tsao and Wu who together commanded 114,000 soldiers.

26. FRUS 1920, I, 461; Ch'i, *Warlord Politics,* 32; McCormack, *Chang Tso-lin,* 50.

27. FRUS 1920, I, 462–464, *Who's Who in China,* 1925, 24, 66; "The Military

Position" and "Chinese Unrest," *Evening Post,* 12 July 1920; "No Serious Clash Yet" and "War at Door of Pekin, Tuan Chi-Jui's Ambitions," *Evening Post,* 13 July 1920; FRUS 1920, I, 442.

28. FRUS 1920, I, 467; McCormack, *Chang Tso-lin,* 71. The 16th Division was of questionable reliability, having been loyal to Feng Kuo-chang before his death.

29. FRUS 1920, I, 457; McCormack, *Chang Tso-lin,* 53; Lau, *China, Britain, and Hong Kong,* 142–143.

30. FRUS 1920, I, 441, 445, 453, 460; *Annual Register,* 278; "Outbreak of Fighting," *Evening Post,* 14 July 1920; "Moral Suasion," *Evening Post,* 15 July 1920; "Fighting Round Pekin: Mediation Fails" and "Chinese Struggle," *Evening Post,* 19 July 1920; "China's Civil War: Severe Anfu Defeat," *Evening Post,* 23 July 1920; *Who's Who in China,* 1925, 22, 776–777, 808; McCormack, *Chang Tso-lin,* 50. Wang subsequently joined a number of the NWFDA soldiers with his brigade, reforming the 23rd Division after the 1920 war. Kaopeitien is almost midway between Peking and Paoting.

31. FRUS 1920, I, 465; United States War Department, *Military Operations in China,* 43–44; McCormack, *Chang Tso-lin,* 52–53; "Chinese Struggle," *Evening Post,* 19 July 1920; "A Dramatic Turn: Tuan Chi-Jui Offers Peace," *Evening Post,* 21 July 1920; "China's Civil War: Severe Anfu Defeat," *Evening Post,* 22 July 1920; *Who's Who in China,* 1925, 38. Hsiao-Chan had been one of Yuan's training centers for the Peiyang army.

32. Zhang, *Warlord Chang Tso-lin,* chap. 9, pt. 2; McCormack, *Chang Tso-lin,* 53.

33. FRUS 1920, I, 418, 424; Bland, *China, Japan, and Korea,* 111; Dunscomb, *Japan's Siberian Intervention,* 137.

34. Chen Zhixin, "Establishment," 19; Elleman, *Diplomacy and Deception,* 24—see 25 for a reproduction of the telegram in its original French.

35. Whiting, "Soviet Offer," 356, 363. The text was also published in a 1919 Moscow pamphlet entitled "China and Soviet Russia"; the French-language text reproduced by Elleman, *Diplomacy and Deception,* was retransmitted to Peking by the Soviets six months later, on 26 March 1920.

36. Chen Zhixin, "Establishment," 20; FRUS 1920, I, 679–682; FRUS 1920, III, 527–528. Verkhniudinsk (Ulan Ude) was a major trading town along the Trans-Siberian Railway about 100 kilometers east of Lake Baikal.

37. FRUS 1920, I, 791–792.

38. McCormack, *Chang Tso-lin,* 112; FRUS 1920, I, 682–683; *Who's Who in China,* 1925, 38; Zhang, *Warlord Chang Tso-lin,* chap. 9, pt. 2; Bisher, *White Terror,* 286.

39. Hosek, "Hailar Incident," 117, 121; Bisher, *White Terror,* 254; FRUS 1920, I, 695, 705, 778, 780.

40. FRUS 1920, III, 546–547.

41. Euden and North, *Soviet Russia*, 133. The FER's capital was at Chita and encompassed the Priamur region, Trans-Baikal, and Sakhalin.

42. Euden and North, *Soviet Russia*, 132, 208–209; FRUS 1920, III, 549–550; Stephan, *Russian Far East*, 146; FRUS 1921, II, 721, 727.

43. Euden and North, *Soviet Russia*, 199.

44. Euden and North, *Soviet Russia*, 200. Urga is now Ulan Bator.

45. FRUS 1919, I, 380–381, 399–400, 756–757; FRUS 1920, I, 756–757; Bisher, *White Terror*, 268; Jennings, "Mad Baron's March," 14; Bulstrode, *Tour in Mongolia*, chap. 8. Maimaicheng, roughly meaning "buy–sell city," was a name used to describe any Chinese trading town in Mongolia. Kobdo, now Khovd (Hovd), is in far western Mongolia near the Atlai Mountains.

46. FRUS 1919, I, 380; FRUS 1920, I, 426, 757; Elleman, *Diplomacy and Deception*, 87; Bisher, *White Terror*, 330; Jennings, "Mad Baron's March," 5–6. Bulstrode, *Tour in Mongolia*, chaps. 11 and 12. For a 1912 panoramic map of Urga, see "Niislel Khuree," *Virtual Collection of Asian Masterpieces*, http://masterpieces.asemus.museum/. Urga was a city of several tens of thousands, stretching a few kilometers along the Tuul River's north bank and centered on a walled monastery complex dominated by the Great White Temple, one of the city's three main temples. Adjoining it was the bustling market that dealt in camels and sturdy Mongol horses. To the south of the complex lay the Khan's palace, and a short distance to the east was the governmental compound. Further east stood the Russian consulate with a guard barracks, the Church of the Holy Trinity, and the imposing headquarters for the Russian-controlled Mongol Ore Company, all surrounded by foreign residences with stores and shops. On the eastern outskirts sat the Chinese Maimaicheng quarter, whose merchants controlled the local economy.

47. FRUS 1920, III, 544; Jennings, "Mad Baron's March," 4–5, 14; Bulstrode, introduction to *Tour in Mongolia*.

48. FRUS 1919, I, 380; FRUS 1920, I, 491–492; FRUS 1920, III, 537; Clubb, *China and Russia*, 176; *Who's Who in China*, 1925, 22; Bland, "Mongolia," 974; United States War Department, *FM 2-15, Cavalry Field Manual*, 152. By Western military standards, a cavalry force conducting a sustained march would have taken three weeks to travel from Kalgan to Urga.

49. FRUS 1920, III, 538, 544; Hopkirk, *Setting the East Ablaze*, 127–130; Stewart, *White Armies*, 403; Bland, "Mongolia," 975; Cheng, *Sino-Russian Relations*, 105; Jennings, "Mad Baron's March," 14, 16–17, 20, 22. Aksha was on the Onon River, ninety kilometers north of the border and 170 kilometers south of Chita.

50. Bisher, *White Terror*, 331; Hopkirk, *Setting the East Ablaze*, 130, 132, 134; Erickson, *Soviet High Command*, 223; Jennings, "Mad Baron's March," 23; Bland, "Mongolia," 975; *Who's Who in China*, 1925, 22.

51. Euden and North, *Soviet Russia*, 201; Elleman, *Diplomacy and Deception*,

87; Stephan, *Russian Far East,* 147; Bisher, *White Terror,* 283; Bulstrode, *Tour in Mongolia,* chap. 8; Salminov and Velikanovm, *Order of Lenin Transbaikal Sky,* 54; FRUS 1921, I, 580; *Who's Who in China,* 1925, 67; Hopkirk, *Setting the East Ablaze,* 135; McCormack, *Chang Tso-lin,* 54–55. The PRA was built around the battle-hardened but exhausted 5th Red Army.

52. Hopkirk, *Setting the East Ablaze,* 137, 146; Jennings, "Mad Baron's March," 24; Euden and North, *Soviet Russia,* 124–125; Bisher, *White Terror,* 280; Khetagurov, *Performance of Duty,* chap. 1; Fedyuninsky, *In the East,* 19–20.

53. FRUS 1921, II, 745; Clubb, *China and Russia,* 180; Bisher, *White Terror,* 280; Forsyth, *History,* 274; Dmitriev-Mamonov and Zdziarski, *Siberian Railway,* 354. *Gusinoe* means "goose."

54. Bisher, *White Terror,* 280.

55. ONI Report, "Japanese Troops in Siberia," 27 December 1919, and "The Nikolaevsk Massacre," 14 June 1920; Stephan, *Russian Far East,* 144–146; Dunscomb, *Japan's Siberian Intervention,* 119–120; Euden and North, *Soviet Russia,* 132; Bisher, *White Terror,* 259.

56. Dunscomb, *Japan's Siberian Intervention,* 122.

57. Dunscomb, *Japan's Siberian Intervention,* 122; Stephan, *Russian Far East,* 147; FRUS 1922, II, 721, 727; FRUS 1919, Russia, 272; ONI Report, "Japanese Troops in Siberia," 27 December 1919. In 1919, the Japanese army suffered slightly over 1,000 killed and wounded in combat, compared to eighty-nine casualties for the 31st US Infantry during the entire 1918–1920 expedition. The real threat was the flu; nearly 56,000 Japanese soldiers fell ill in Siberia from the global influenza pandemic. Of the eight derelict armored monitors captured in 1918, Japan retained one, *Thunder,* while the *Blizzard, Hurricane Squall, Storm, Tornado, Typhoon,* and *Whirlwind* were returned.

58. FRUS 1921, II, 713, 715; Lensen, *Japanese Recognition,* 16, 50; Euden and North, *Soviet Russia,* 214.

59. Erickson, *Soviet High Command,* 224–225; Stewart, *White Armies,* 410; Stephan, *Russian Far East,* 151–152, 327, 333; Lensen, *Japanese Recognition,* 31; Bisher, *White Terror,* 234, 263, 286–282. Semenov departed Vladivostok in September 1921 for an eventual life of exile in Japanese-controlled Dairen before capture and execution by the Soviets in 1945. Molchanov survived the war, immigrated to the United States in 1923, and ran a successful chicken ranch in California until his death in 1975.

60. Asada, *Railway Management,* 336; FRUS 1922, I, 917; FRUS 1921, II, 717. ONI Report, "Japanese Troops in Siberia," 22 June 1922; Dunscomb, *Japan's Siberian Intervention,* 204; Erickson, *Soviet High Command,* 836; FRUS 1922, I, 905. At the time, the IJA 9th Division was relieving the 11th Division, leading to a temporary surge in troops. Petrograd was renamed Leningrad after Lenin's death in 1924.

61. Willoughby, *China at the Conference,* 25–26. The 1904–1905 Portsmouth

negotiations were mediated bilateral talks. This was the first American-hosted international conference.

62. FRUS 1922, I, 949. The full text of the treaty is provided on 948–960.

63. *China Monthly Review*, 8 April 1922, 214.

64. FRUS 1921, I, 613; FRUS 1922, I, 878–879; Willoughby, *China at the Conference*, 29, 229; MacMillan, *Paris*, 67, 69.

65. FRUS 1922, I, 297–298; see Resolution 12.

66. FRUS 1921, I, 876; FRUS 1922, I, 293–294. See Resolution 8, Section 3.

67. FRUS 1920, I, 468.

68. FRUS 1921, I, 327–328; McCormack, *Chang Tso-lin*, 54, 63; FRUS 1922, I, 888–889; Y. S. Yu, "Chihli-Fengtien Fighting Unavoidable," *China Monthly Review*, 6 May 1922, 369. The Central Plains referred to southern Shansi, Honan, and Hupeh. Bisected by the Yellow River, Loyang in Honan was considered the region's most important city.

69. McCormack, *Chang Tso-lin*, 69; *Who's Who in China*, 1925, 114; Lary, *Region and Nation*, 47; Y. S. Yu, "Chihli-Fengtien Fight Imminent," *China Monthly Review*, 22 April 1922, 283; "Wu Is a Patriot," *Evening Post*, 5 May 1922.

70. McCormack, *Chang Tso-lin*, 70; FRUS 1922, I, 690; *China Monthly Review*, 22 April 1922, 294.

71. FRUS 1922, I, 695–696; Zhang, *Warlord Chang Tso-lin*, chap. 9, pt. 2; "Fighting Near Tientsin," *Evening Post*, 27 April 1922; "Hostilities Begun," *Evening Post*, 1 May 1922; "Wu's Forces Heavily Shelled," *Evening Post*, 4 May 1922; *China Monthly Review*, 8 April 1922, 213, and 6 May 1922, 372, 374, 376. Macheng was the site of the famous sixth-century B.C. Battle of Pochu.

72. Sheridan, *Chinese Warlord*, 109; Y. S. Yu, "Chihli-Fengtien Fighting Unavoidable," *China Monthly Review*, 6 May 1922, 368; Boorman and Howard, *Biographical Dictionary*, 1:40; "Railway Traffic Blocked," *Evening Post*, 2 May 1922; Sheridan, *Chinese Warlord*, 109; FRUS 1922, I, 699.

73. FRUS 1922, I, 709, 711; McCormack, *Chang Tso-lin*, 72; Sheridan, *Chinese Warlord*, 110–111, 113; Boorman and Howard, *Biographical Dictionary*, 1:123; Nathan, *Peking Politics*, 60; *China Monthly Review*, 13 May 1922, 420, and 20 May, 466; Lin, "Dog-Meat General," 786–787.

74. Euden and North, *Soviet Russia*, 218; Fenby, *Chiang Kai-shek*, 54–55; *Who's Who in China*, 1925, 114; FRUS 1922, I, 723–724; *China Monthly Review*, 15 April 1922, 254, and 6 May 1922, 396; "Wu Is a Patriot," *Evening Post*, 5 May 1922; McCormack, *Chang Tso-lin*, 69. Sun returned to Canton in February 1923.

75. FRUS 1922, I, 700, 704; McCormack, *Chang Tso-lin*, 70–71; "Gen. Wu's Forces Rout Manchurians in Fighting for Peking," *New York Times*, 5 May 1922; Kuhn, "What War Is Like in China," 824, 826; *Who's Who in China*, 1925, 67; "Battle Round Pekin," *Evening Post*, 2 May 1922; "Pekin Surrounded by Wu's Army," *Evening Post*, 5 May 1922; "Temporary Dictatorship," *Evening Post*, 8 May 1922; *China Monthly Review*, 13 May 1922, 420.

76. FRUS 1922, I, 698, 700, 704, 708, 718–720; McCormack, *Chang Tso-lin,* 72, 76; *China Monthly Review,* 13 May 1922, 419, and 20 May 1922, 462, 464.

77. "Temporary Dictatorship," *Evening Post,* 8 May 1922; FRUS 1921, I, 364; FRUS 1922, I, 711, 804; Sharman, *Sun Yat-sen,* 214; *Who's Who in China,* 1925, 495–496; "Momentous Days in China," 721.

78. Lenin, *Collected Works,* 44:139–140, "Telegrams to A. K. Paikes"; Lenin, "Underlinings on a Telegram from A. K. Paikes and a Note to the Organising Bureau of the CC, RCP(B)," https://www.marxists.org/.

79. Elleman, *Diplomacy and Deception,* 92.

80. Elleman and Kotkin, *Manchurian Railways,* 62, 65; Elleman, *Diplomacy and Deception,* 85, 90–92; Euden and North, *Soviet Russia,* 126, 128, 130.

81. FRUS 1922, I, 930–931. Chang applied Section 3 of Resolution 8.

82. FRUS 1922, I, 915, 917; FRUS 1923, I, 778, 782.

83. FRUS 1922, I, 932.

84. FRUS 1922, I, 934–934.

85. Hu, *Opium War,* 669, 677–678; Schwartz, *Chinese Communism,* 17; Wilbur and How, *Documents,* 39, 55–56; Euden and North, *Soviet Russia,* 138–140.

86. Lee, *Revolutionary Struggle,* 36, 37, 39; Sheng, "Analysis of the Differences," 304; Schwartz, *Chinese Communism,* 47; Wilbur and How, *Documents,* 45.

87. Gottschang and Lary, *Swallows and Settlers,* 44, 47, 49; Lee, *Revolutionary Struggle,* 18–19, 34, 68; Silberman and Harootunian, *Japan in Crisis,* 222; FRUS 1921, I, 706. The Japanese smashed the Communist Party of China, especially after the enactment of the 1925 Peace Preservation Law in Tokyo that criminalized membership in a communist organization.

88. Euden and North, *Soviet Russia,* 141–142, 219; Lensen, *Japanese Recognition,* 87. Communication in 1918 was nearly impossible, as Soviet Russia was not recognized internationally and the Canton regime was not recognized by Peking. Chicherin responded to Sun that August, but the letter never got through, and when Chicherin sent a second letter offering to expand relations on 31 October 1920, it took nearly ten months of circuitous handling to arrive and was not acted on. The Comintern, formed in 1919, was a congress of various communist parties located around the world under the control of the Communist Party of the Soviet Union, the purpose of which was to promote world socialist revolution. It was led by the Executive Committee of the Communist International in Moscow and coordinated the efforts of the national communist parties on a global basis. Maring was the cover name for Hendricus Sneevliet, a Dutch communist loyal to Moscow.

89. Wilbur and How, *Missionaries,* 6–7, 93, 117; Liu, *Military History,* 7, 9, 25; Wilbur and How, *Documents,* 41; Erickson, *Soviet High Command,* 227. Borodin was the Comintern alias for Mikhail Gruzenberg. A lifelong follower of Lenin, Borodin's career followed an eclectic path. After leaving for the United States after the failed 1905 revolution, he became active in the American Socialist

Party before returning to Russia in 1918. Lenin later sent him to the United Kingdom to help form the British Communist Party, but he was arrested and was only released from jail a few months before his arrival in Canton. "Galen" was a name play on Galena, Blyukher's wife.

90. Asada, *Railway Management*, 60. Lev B. Kamenev and Grigory Y. Zinoviev were executed on 25 August 1936.

91. Elleman, *Diplomacy and Deception*, 98; Euden and North, *Soviet Russia*, 245.

92. FRUS 1923, I, 518.

93. FRUS 1919, I, 605; FRUS 1924, I, 479; Euden and North, *Soviet Russia*, 101; *Who's Who in China*, 1925, 780; Vul, "He, Who Has Sown the Wind," 4.

94. Tang, *Russian and Soviet Policy*, 151; Elleman, *Diplomacy and Deception*, 72, 122; *Who's Who in China*, 1925, 780; FRUS 1924, I, 479–481; Whiting, "Soviet Offer," 358. In 1924, US$1 = 2 rubles. The outstanding debt owed to French bondholders was approximately $100 million.

95. FRUS 1924, I, 497; Kuo and Bennett, "Poet with the Northern Expedition," 362. Article 6 dealt with propaganda and Article 9 with the CER. For a complete English-language copy of both documents, see FRUS 1924 I, 495–501. The Soviets had no intention of setting a date for the withdrawal of RKKA troops in Outer Mongolia, as they were in the final stages of establishing the puppet Mongolian People's Republic.

96. *Who's Who in China*, 1936, 44; FRUS 1927, II, 151; Euden and North, *Soviet Russia*, 118; Cooke, "Propaganda as a Weapon?" British operations run out of London's Wellington House provide the best example of efforts to influence the international community during World War I.

97. FRUS 1924, I, 500–501.

98. FRUS 1924, I, 462.

99. Vul, "He, Who Has Sown the Wind," 17–18.

100. FRUS 1924, I, 366; Vul, "He, Who Has Sown the Wind," 4; Lee, *Revolutionary Struggle*, 11; Liu, *Military History*, 30; McCormack, *Chang Tso-lin*, 217–218. By 1924, Chang Tso-lin's Manchuria army was referred to as the Tung-pei-chun, or Eastern Army. Antonov-Ovseyenko was a revolutionary hero who led the 1917 assault on the Winter Palace.

101. For the full text of the accords, see Young, *International Relations*, 295–300, and Elleman, *Diplomacy and Deception*, 127–129.

102. For a comprehensive treatment of the 1924 wars, see Waldron, *From War to Nationalism*.

103. FRUS 1924, I, 361, 371–372, 381–382; "Wicked Pekin," *Evening Post*, 9 September 1924; "Fighting Near Shanghai," *Evening Post*, 8 October 1924; "China's Plight," *Evening Post*, 18 October 1924; "Almighty Dollar," *Evening Post*, 20 October 1924; *Who's Who in China*, 1925, 350. Marshal Chi agreed to pay Lu's troops $20 apiece and transportation home to Chekiang.

104. Waldron, *From War to Nationalism,* 93, 199; Sheridan, *Chinese Warlord,* 132. The walled city of Chengte was home to the Ch'ing summer palace and possessed an arsenal. It was ideal for the Chihli defenders as even if the wall and river could be breached, they could then gradually withdraw down the narrow passes back to the Great Wall.

105. FRUS 1924, I, 368, 376, 379; "Chang in the Field," *Evening Post,* 15 September 1924; "Fengtien Operations," *Evening Post,* 17 September 1924; "War against Chang," *Evening Post,* 19 September 1924; "Position Near Shanghai," *Evening Post,* 21 September 1924; "Chang's Campaign," *Evening Post,* 22 September 1924; "Control of China," *Evening Post,* 6 October 1924; "Civil War in China," *Evening Post,* 9 October 1924; Zhang, *Warlord Chang Tso-lin,* 475; Waldron, *From War to Nationalism,* 99, 115–116.

106. FRUS 1924, I, 382; McCormack, *Chang Tso-lin,* 130; "The Main Battle," *Evening Post,* 11 October 1924.

107. Zhang, *Warlord Chang Tso-lin,* 477; Waldron, *From War to Nationalism,* 116–117, 185; McCormack, *Chang Tso-lin,* 103.

108. FRUS 1924, I, 383; "Mystery of Pekin," *Evening Post,* 25 October 1924; "Chinese Drama," *Evening Post,* 27 October 1924.

109. "Civil War in China," *Evening Post,* 9 October 1924; Pye, *Warlord Politics,* 30; Waldron, *From War to Nationalism,* 195–196; Sheridan, *Chinese Warlord,* 186n, 132–133; McCormack, *Chang Tso-lin,* 141–142. Chang's trusted Japanese army advisor, Machino, helped get the funds to Feng.

110. FRUS 1924, I, 388; "Chinese Affairs," *Evening Post,* 4 November 1924; Sheridan, *Chinese Warlord,* 135; Waldron, *From War to Nationalism,* 183, 185.

111. FRUS 1924, I, 395, 389; FRUS 1925, I, 588–589; Waldron, *From War to Nationalism,* 93, 183; Sheridan, *Chinese Warlord,* 188; "Chinese Proclamation," *Evening Post,* 29 October 1924.

Chapter 4. Warlordism in Decay, CER Troubles, and the Northern Expedition

1. Sharman, *Sun Yat-sen,* 303–304.

2. Waldron, *From War to Nationalism,* 212; Sheridan, *Chinese Warlord,* 149; Waldron, "Warlord," 1075, 1081; FRUS 1925, I, 400, 416. For the Six Articles, see FRUS 1924, I, 399–400.

3. FRUS 1924, I, 403–404.

4. FRUS 1925, I, 589.

5. Sharman, *Sun Yat-sen,* 303–304; FRUS 1925, I, 605.

6. McCormack, *Chang Tso-lin,* 144, 153; FRUS 1924, I, 408; FRUS 1925, I, 598, 601, 610; Nathan, *Peking Politics,* 234.

7. Pye, *Warlord Politics,* 66–67; McCormack, *Chang Tso-lin,* 144; Wilbur and

How, *Missionaries*, 88; Vul, "He, Who Has Sown the Wind," 12; Sheridan, *Chinese Warlord*, 149–150; Vishniakova-Akimova, *Two Years in Revolutionary China*, 100. Feng commanded the 1st Army in Chahar; his loyalists, Chang Chih-chiang and Li Ming-chung, led the 5th Army in northern Jehol and the 6th Army in Suiyuan, respectively. This offset the power of his less dedicated subordinates in western Honan, Hu Ching-i of the 2nd Army and Sun Yueh of the 3rd Army. With the exception of the 1st Army, the units were initially armies in name only, as the 5th Army held the 7th Mixed Brigade, while the 6th Army was composed of the 8th Mixed Brigade.

8. Pye, *Warlord Politics*, 32–33; Erickson, *Soviet High Command*, 397; Wilbur and How, *Documents*, 321, 322; Vishniakova-Akimova, *Two Years in Revolutionary China*, 90–91; Wilbur and How, *Missionaries*, 15, 717. Vera Vishniakova-Akimova was a twenty-two-year-old translator sent up from Canton who excelled in her duties. Putna, like Blyukher, was a highly regarded officer who had served as a division commander (the 27th) in the 5th Red Army during the campaign against Kolchak. I. A. Lapin had served under Blyukher during the campaigns against Kolchak and the Mad Baron. Korneev and Putna were executed in 1937.

9. Vul, "He, Who Has Sown the Wind," 13; Wilbur and How, *Documents*, 337.

10. Sheridan, *Chinese Warlord*, 166ff., 167; Vul, "He, Who Has Sown the Wind," 14, 16; Vishniakova-Akimova, *Two Years in Revolutionary China*, 84, 93–95; Wilbur and How, *Documents*, 355; FRUS 1925, I, 609; Wilbur and How, *Missionaries*, 315, 345; Erickson, *Soviet High Command*, 200. Ironically, the overland supply line began at Verkhneudinsk and ended at depots in Urga before being distributed to Feng's troops in China, a near reverse of the route followed by Ungern, the Mad Baron, in 1921.

11. Vishniakova-Akimova, *Two Years in Revolutionary China*, 85, 87; Wilbur and How, *Missionaries*, 717; Erickson, *Soviet High Command*, 397; Wilbur and How, *Documents*, 321.

12. FRUS 1925, I, 647, 663–664; Bickers, *Empire Made Me*, 163–165, 169; Lescot, *Before Mao*, 50; Wilbur and How, *Missionaries*, 149. Located in an alley off Nanking Road, one of the International Settlement's major thoroughfares, twelve Chinese, eleven Sikh, and one British officer under Inspector Edward Everson, also an Englishman, staffed the station. The exact numbers of the killed and wounded are still in dispute.

13. FRUS 1925, I, 648.

14. Bickers, *Empire Made Me*, 170; Harrison, "Li Li-san Line," 181; FRUS 1925, I, 648, 652, 662, 742. The Canton fighting was between Kuomintang supporters accompanied by armed National Revolutionary Army (NRA) troops and British soldiers defending the Shameen District near the Bund. Reinforcing Chang Hsueh-liang were 2,000 troops of General Hsing Shih-lien's 24th Fengtien Mixed Brigade.

15. FRUS 1925, I, 735–736; Lescot, *Before Mao*, 57; Wilbur and How, *Documents*, 324; McCormack, *Chang Tso-lin*, 144, 150.

16. FRUS 1925, I, 590, 743; Liu, *Military History*, 15; Wilbur and How, *Missionaries*, 119, 143–144, 480.

17. Bickers, *Empire Made Me*, 172; Liu, *Military History*, 25; Wilbur and How, *Missionaries*, 154–155, 566.

18. FRUS 1925, I, 612.

19. Wilbur and How, *Missionaries*, 565.

20. "Trouble of China," *Evening Post*, 8 April 1925.

21. United Kingdom War Office, "Note on the Situation in China," 30 June 1925; Vul, "He, Who Has Sown the Wind," 21; Pye, *Warlord Politics*, 69; FRUS 1925, I, 735–736; Lescot, *Before Mao*, 57; Wilbur and How, *Documents*, 324; McCormack, *Chang Tso-lin*, 144, 150.

22. FRUS 1925, I, 616–617; McCormack, *Chang Tso-lin*, 161. Chiang had led the 1st Eastern Army in the 1924 war. By mid-1925, the 1st Kuominchun had grown to three divisions and two mixed brigades. Sun's domain was Fukien, Kiangsi, Chekiang, Anhwei, and Kiangsu. Hsuchow was the important junction city of the Lunghia and Tsinpu railways.

23. FRUS 1925, I, 619; Vishniakova-Akimova, *Two Years in Revolutionary China*, 109; McCormack, *Chang Tso-lin*, 163, 166; "A Serious Revolt," *Evening Post*, 27 November 1925.

24. Zhang, *Warlord Chang Tso-lin*, chap. 9, sec. 3; Sheridan, *Chinese Warlord*, 182.

25. McCormack, *Chang Tso-lin*, 164, 172, 178; Zhang, *Warlord Chang Tso-lin*, chap. 9, sec. 3; Vishniakova-Akimova, *Two Years in Revolutionary China*, 107; "To Seize Mukden," *Evening Post*, 27 November 1925. Historian Zhang Xueji characterized Kuo as Chang Hsueh-liang's "soul," and his rebellion was the ultimate betrayal. Chinwangtao was the site of Kuo's shared 1924 victory with Chang Hsueh-liang.

26. FRUS 1925, I, 620; Vishniakova-Akimova, *Two Years in Revolutionary China*, 107, 109; McCormack, *Chang Tso-lin*, 166, 182; Sheridan, *Chinese Warlord*, 182; "Enter Li Ching-Lin," *Evening Post*, 8 December 1925; "Kaleidoscopic China," *Evening Post*, 9 December 1925; "Clash in Manchuria," *Evening Post*, 10 December 1925; "Feeling in Japan," *Evening Post*, 11 December 1925.

27. FRUS 1925, I, 620–622, 626; Sheridan, *Chinese Warlord*, 184; Wilbur and How, *Documents*, 262, 327; McCormack, *Chang Tso-lin*, 182–183; "Fighting in China," *Evening Post*, 14 December 1925; "Chinese Warfare," *Evening Post*, 17 December 1925; "Japanese Action," *Evening Post*, 18 December 1925; "Japan and Manchuria," *Evening Post*, 23 December 1925; "Chinese Imbroglio," *Evening Post*, 22 December 1925; "Storm in Japan," *Evening Post*, 24 December 1925. Macheng and Yangtsun had been battlefields during the 1922 First Feng-

tien-Chihli War. The RKKA Kaifeng Group, dismayed by the Kuominchun defeat at Macheng, contemplated returning to Russia because their advice had been ignored.

28. McCormack, *Chang Tso-lin,* 183.

29. Zhang, *Warlord Chang Tso-lin,* chap. 9, sec. 3.

30. Ibid.

31. Wilbur and How, *Missionaries,* 262; Sheridan, *Chinese Warlord,* 188; FRUS 1926, I, 493, 664–666, 958; "Chang's Victory," *Evening Post,* 26 December 1925; Zhang, *Warlord Chang Tso-lin,* chap. 9, sec. 4. Ironically, it was the hated Boxer Protocol that created the sanctuary that protected Li from Feng's vengeance.

32. FRUS 1926, I, 494, 609, 612–613; Hornbeck, *Situation in China,* 4–5; Sheridan, *Chinese Warlord,* 189–190, 198–199.

33. FRUS 1924, I, 499–500; FRUS 1929, II, 315; Vul, "He, Who Has Sown the Wind," 8–9.

34. Tang, *Russian and Soviet Policy,* 153. This was similar to the CER administration created under the 2 October 1920 supplementary agreement between China and the Russo-Asiatic bank that was condemned by the Soviets.

35. Vul, "He, Who Has Sown the Wind," 21, 24.

36. Tang, *Russian and Soviet Policy,* 182–183. C. C. Wang was China's premier railway expert and is not to be confused with noted diplomats C. T. Wang or C. C. Wu.

37. Asada, *Railway Management,* 60. The "commercial" clause is found in Article 9 of the General Agreement and Article 1 of the Mukden agreement.

38. Hsu, *Chou En-lai,* 48.

39. McCormack, *Chang Tso-lin,* 218; FRUS 1924, I, 512; Vul, "He, Who Has Sown the Wind," 9.

40. Tang, *Russian and Soviet Policy,* 183–184; FRUS 1924, I, 369; FRUS 1925, I, 609.

41. Vul, "He, Who Has Sown the Wind," 11; ONI File 103-100, "China—Military–Political Conditions," 15 February 1926; Asada, *Railway Management,* 63; Tang, *Russian and Soviet Policy,* 189.

42. United Kingdom War Office, "General Staff Report on China," 26 October 1926.

43. Asada, *Railway Management,* 62.

44. Vul, "He, Who Has Sown the Wind," 19.

45. Vishniakova-Akimova, *Two Years in Revolutionary China,* 117.

46. Leon Trotsky, "The Sino-Soviet Conflict and the Opposition" (New York) *Militant,* 15 September 1929.

47. Lih, Naumov, and Khlevniuk, *Stalin's Letters to Molotov,* 118ff.

48. McCormack, *Chang Tso-lin,* 221; Tang, *Russian and Soviet Policy,* 194; Haywood, *Engineer of Revolutionary Russia,* 210.

49. FRUS 1926, I, 1097.

50. FRUS 1926, I, 1099; Lih, Naumov, and Khlevniuk, *Stalin's Letters to Molotov*, 117, 118ff.

51. Liu, *Military History*, 27; Wilbur and How, *Documents*, 367; Wilbur and How, *Missionaries*, 318.

52. Liu, *Military History*, 37; Jordan, *Northern Expedition*, 58; Wilbur and How, *Missionaries*, 286; *Who's Who in China*, 1925, 86–87. The plan was written by Chiang and Pia Chung-his and critiqued by Blyukher. The NRA sent the 10th and 12th Divisions from Li Chi-shen's 4th NRA "Ironsides" Corps to help Tang. Tang's army became the 8th NRA Corps. Once a Kuomintang general, Chao had been imprisoned by Tuan but broke with Sun Yat-sen in 1923, becoming an adherent of Wu. In an example of the era's switching loyalties, it was then fellow Kuomintang member General Tan Yan-kai who obtained his release and later led the Kuomintang force that attempted to oust Chao.

53. Liu, *Military History*, 34, 37; Wilbur and How, *Missionaries*, 218, 315, 318; Solecki and Wilbur, "Blücher's 'Grand Plan,'" 23–24. The Northern Expedition order of battle was as follows: Center Army (4th and 7th Corps or Right Route Army and 8th Corps or Left Route Army), Chu's Right Army (2nd, 3rd and 5th Corps with the 1st Independent Division), and the Left Army (9th and 10th Corps). The NRA Reserve consisted of the 1st and 2nd Divisions of the 1st Corps, two 6th Corps divisions, and the artillery regiment. The 1st Corps consisted of the 3rd, 14th, and 20th Divisions.

54. Wilbur and How, *Missionaries*, 315, 317, 319–320; FRUS 1926, I, 620, 622–623, 625, 640, 646–647; Sheridan, *Chinese Warlord*, 193; Kuo and Bennett, "Poet with the Northern Expedition," 372.

55. FRUS 1926, I, 620; Liu, *Military History*, 38; Wilbur and How, *Missionaries*, 321, 323–324, 326; Jordan, *Northern Expedition*, 85; United Kingdom War Office Report, "China: Prepared for the Meeting between CIGS and Dominion Representatives—Imperial Conference, 1926"; US Marine Detachment Peking, Intelligence Summary Report 54, 30 November 1926, and Report 55, 31 December 1926 (hereafter Marine Report). Major Charles F. B. Price, a seasoned officer who led a battalion in France in 1918, who later commanded the 2nd Marine Division during World War II, and who retired as a lieutenant general, wrote the reports.

56. Marine Report 54, 30 November 1926; Sheridan, *Chinese Warlord*, 204, 207; Wilbur and How, *Documents*, 334. The Chihli garrison at Lungchow in Kansu held out until November. The 2nd and 3rd Kuominchun Armies were in Sian. The 1st Kuominchun Army fought Liu's 7th and 35th Chihli Divisions in Shensi. The 7th Division conducted the Sian siege.

57. Marine Report 54, 30 November 1926; Marine Report 55, 31 December 1926; Wilbur and How, *Missionaries*, 345, 366. Tungkuan Pass was the site of the famous third-century battle won by Han general Tsao Tsao.

58. Marine Report 55, 31 December 1926. The 6th Honan Division reinforced Liu.

59. Marine Report 55, 31 December 1926; Wilbur and How, *Missionaries*, 391.

60. Marine Report 55, 31 December 1926; Marine Report 31 January 1927; McCormack, *Chang Tso-lin*, 209–210.

61. Wilbur and How, *Missionaries*, 375, 610.

62. Vogel, *Deng Xiaoping*, chap. 1, "Resisting the Guomindang, 1927–1930." One of Feng's new political officers was a young Moscow-trained cadre named Teng Hsiao-ping (Deng Xiaoping), the future leader of the People's Republic. The second phase was in essence an expanded version of that used successfully by Tsao and Wu during the 1922 Fengtien-Chihli War.

63. FRUS 1927, II, 68–69, 236–237, 257–258. Antiforeign violence and fear of violence led to evacuation orders for non-Chinese in Hankow, Nanking, Ichang, Chungking, and Changsha during January and February 1927. The United States, representative of most powers, settled for nonrecognition relations with Chiang and Chang while officials in Shanghai worked behind the scenes with Sun.

64. Kuo and Bennett, "Poet with the Northern Expedition," 364; Fitzgerald, "Misconceived Revolution," 332; Waldron, "Warlord," 1081.

65. Sheridan, *Chinese Warlord*, 14–15; Schwartz, *Chinese Communism*, 75.

66. MA Report 6036, 21 January 1927.

67. MA Report 6036, 21 January 1927.

68. Marine Report 31 January 1927; FRUS 1927, II, 2–3.

69. FRUS 1927, II, 166.

70. FRUS 1927, II, 7–8, 99, 146–147, 149–150; 158, 164, 222, 292; Fenby, *Chiang Kai-shek*, 143; Liu, *Military History*, 45; Marine Report, 30 April 1927; Wilbur and How, *Missionaries*, 400. Those trapped in Nanking were protected by small landing parties and gunfire from the newly commissioned British light cruiser *Emerald* and the American destroyers *Noa* and *Preston*. The British brought their number of troops in Shanghai to 10,000. The United Stated activated War Plan Yellow, an updated version of the 1900 campaign, designed to evacuate Americans from China and effect a relief expedition to the Peking legations from Tientsin if necessary. The 15th US Infantry Regiment, already at Tientsin, was reinforced by the 31st Infantry from the Philippines, and the 3rd US Marine Brigade departed California for Tientsin with its 4th Marine Regiment going to Shanghai. George C. Marshall commanded the 15th Infantry, and Smedley D. Butler, who twice had been awarded the Medal of Honor for gallantry, led the 3rd Marine Brigade.

71. Liu, *Military History*, 39.

72. Wilbur and How, *Missionaries*, 398; Wu, Tien-wei, "Chiang Kai-shek's March Twentieth Coup d'Etat of 1926," 596. The KMT-CCP split almost oc-

curred on 20 March 1926 when the CCP activist Li Chih-lung sent the armed and ready gunboat *Chung-shan* to Whampoa in an apparent attempt to remove Chiang Kai-shek by force of arms. It was a foolishly reckless plot. Chiang struck first by seizing the *Chung-shan*, arresting Li, and temporarily placing the Soviet advisors under armed guard, an act for which Chiang later apologized. There was no evidence that Li acted as part of greater CCP scheme, and a general reconciliation between all parties was reached with the "Readjustment of the KMT-CCP Relations" in late April. Even Li was rehabilitated.

73. Liu, *Military History*, 41, 45.

74. So, "Western Hills Group," 197, 202–203.

75. FRUS 1927, II, 6, 10, 14, 269; Liu, *Military History*, 40, 48; Fenby, *Chiang Kai-shek*, 127; Wilbur and How, *Documents*, 9–10, 406. Dalbank (Far East Bank) was headquartered in Harbin and kept CER monies.

76. Marine Report, 30 April 1927; Tuchman, *Stilwell*, 116; "Peking Gives Wu Pei-fu, China's Honest War Lord, a Fine Princely Funeral," *Life*, 4 March 1940. Wu first moved to a Buddhist monastery and then Peking, devoting his time to writing poetry.

77. Euden and North, *Soviet Russia*, 303–304; Hsu, *Chou En-lai*, 64–66; Wu, "Review of the Wuhan Debacle," 134–135; Schwartz, *Chinese Communism*, 102. The Red Army was to be formed around 20,000 communists and 50,000 revolutionary workers. The Chinese Red Army later became the People's Liberation Army. The Chingkang Mountains sit astride southwestern Kiangsi and Hunan.

78. Ulam, *Expansion and Coexistence*, 179.

79. Vishniakova-Akimova, *Two Years in Revolutionary China*, 115; Taylor, *Generalissimo*, 72; Wilbur and How, *Missionaries*, 423; Liu, *Military History*, 61–62. Feng was not completely forgiving and expelled his Communist Party of China political officers, forcing Teng Hsiao-ping to secretly escape first to Wuhan and then Shanghai. The beleaguered Borodin party finally made it to Moscow on 6 October. Chiang replaced his RKKA advisors with Germans under retired colonel Max Bauer in November 1927.

80. FRUS 1927, II, 22; Liu, *Military History*, 49–50; Wilbur and How, *Documents*, 416.

81. FRUS 1928, II 23–24, 26, 43, 122; Liu, *Military History*, 50; Sheridan, *Chinese Warlord*, 235. Longtan was defended by the 1st NRA Army's 22nd Division, veterans of the 1926 Fukien–Chekiang campaign and the 1927 drive on Shanghai.

82. FRUS 1928, II 123, 133; Liu, *Military History*, 50. During World War II, Magruder would become a senior officer in the Office of Strategic Services, the precursor of the Central Intelligence Agency, and retire as a major general.

83. FRUS 1928, II 43, 125; Sheridan, *Chinese Warlord*, 236–237; Liu, *Military History*, 47, 51; Jordan, *Northern Expedition*, 161–162. Li was Chiang's former chief of staff and leader of the 4th NRA Army.

84. Zhang, *Warlord Chang Tso-lin*, chap. 9, sec. 5; FRUS 1928, II, 143, 155; Jordan, *Northern Expedition*, 164; "Shantung Battle," *Evening Post*, 20 April 1928.

85. FRUS 1928, II, 136, 149, 266–267, 282; United Kingdom War Office, "Rate of Dispatch of Japanese Troops to China," 1928. The Japanese brigade came from the 6th Division. The NRA troops were from the 40th Army.

86. Taylor, *Generalissimo*, 79.

87. Jordan, *Northern Expedition*, 163.

88. Zhang, *Warlord Chang Tso-lin*, chap. 9, sec. 5; Jordan, *Northern Expedition*, 162, 165; "Chinese Marshal Assassinated by Woman," *Sydney Morning Herald*, 14 November 1935; "War Lord Who Took Harem to Battle Is Slain," *Chicago Tribune*, 4 September 1932. Having forfeited his domain and army, Sun Chuan-fang fled to Manchuria. Years later, in a form of rough justice, Sun was assassinated in Tientsin on 13 November 1935 by Shih Chien-chiao, the daughter of a general he had executed in 1925. Another infamous tuchun had also lost everything: Chang "Dog Meat" Tsung-chang. Like Sun, he fled to Manchuria, but he did not live as long, suffering the same fate—assassination—in 1932.

89. FRUS 1928, II, 154–156. Zhang, *Warlord Chang Tso-lin*, chap. 9, sec. 5; Gillin, "Portrait of a Warlord," 293; Peiping means "northern peace."

Chapter 5. The Rise of Chang Hsueh-liang and the Coming CER Crisis

1. FRUS 1928, II, 150; Yoshihashi, *Conspiracy*, 42.

2. Coox, *Nomonhan*, 16; Yoshihashi, *Conspiracy*, 42. Komoto is sometimes translated as Kawamoto.

3. Dull, "Assassination," 456; Zhang, *Warlord Chang Tso-lin*, pt. 2, chap. 9, sec. 5; Suleski, *Civil Government*, 180–181; McCormack, *Chang Tso-lin*, 189, 214, 251–252.

4. Yoshihashi, *Conspiracy*, 50; Dull, "Assassination," 457.

5. Yoshihashi, *Conspiracy*, 47–48, 50; Furuya, *Chiang Kai-shek*, 254. Komoto used a *ronin* named Adachi Takamori for the task, and he went to former Kuo subordinate Liu Tsai-ming to recruit the Chinese "attackers."

6. Iriye, "Chang Hsueh-Liang," Yoshihashi, *Conspiracy*, 53; MA Peking Report 7309, 8 August 1928; FRUS 1928, II, 155; Zhang, *Warlord Chang Tso-lin*, pt. 2, chap. 9, sec. 5; Suleski, *Civil Government*, 181.

7. Marine Report 55, 31 December 1926; Zhang, *Warlord Chang Tso-lin*, pt. 2, chap. 9, sec. 4.

8. Iriye, "Chang Hsueh-Liang," 36; Zhang, *Warlord Chang Tso-lin*, pt. 2, chap. 9, sec. 6; Yoshihashi, *Conspiracy*, 51, 53, 55.

9. Yoshihashi, *Conspiracy*, 126.

10. Dull, "Assassination," 454; Yoshihashi, *Conspiracy*, 57; Furuya, *Chiang Kai-shek*, 261. Hisajiro is sometimes translated as Kujiro.

11. FRUS 1928, II, 155.

12. McCormack, *Chang Tso-lin*, 88, 98ff.

13. FRUS 1928, II, 166; Zhang, *Warlord Chang Tso-lin*, pt. 2, chap. 9, sec. 7; Iriye, "Chang Hsueh-Liang," 35, 37.

14. MA Peking Report 7309, 8 August 1928.

15. Iriye, "Chang Hsueh-Liang," 36, 40; MA Peking Report 7309, 8 August 1928; Furuya, *Chiang Kai-shek*, 262.

16. Furuya, *Chiang Kai-shek*, 263.

17. Zhang, *Warlord Chang Tso-lin*, pt. 2, chap. 9, sec. 7.

18. FRUS 1928, II, 166.

19. FRUS 1928, II, 172; Phillips, "Picturesque but Hopeless Resistance," 736; Yoshihashi, *Conspiracy*, 53; Iriye, "Chang Hsueh-Liang," 37, 43.

20. Marine Report 31 January 1927; United Kingdom, Foreign Office (hereafter FO) Report F 241/7/10 Peking, 9 November 1928; Euden and North, *Soviet Russia*, 18.

21. FO Report F 241/7/10 Peking, 9 November 1928; Euden and North, *Soviet Russia*, 125, 200; FRUS 1928, I, 166. This area would be the scene of the 1939 battle between the Soviet and Japanese armies.

22. FRUS 1929, II, 187.

23. Ibid., 178.

24. FO Reports F 271/7/10 Harbin, 31 December 1928 and F 2262/7/10 Mukden, 31 March 1929; McCormack, *Chang Tso-lin*, 166.

25. FRUS 1929, II, 123–124, 128; Iriye, "Chang Hsueh-Liang," 40; "Shot at a Party," *Evening Post*, 14 January 1929.

26. Stoner, *Levinson*, 11, 26; Ferrell, *Peace in Their Time*, 260–261.

27. Ferrell, *Peace in Their Time*, 33; Stoner, *Levinson*, 95; Jacob Heilbrunn, "War Torn," *New York Times*, 25 July 2013. Borah infamously remarked in 1939, "There is not going to be any war in Europe this year."

28. Ferrell, *Peace in Their Time*, 44; Stoner, *Levinson*, 133–134, 161–163, 198.

29. Stoner, *Levinson*, 182–183; Ferrell, *Peace in Their Time*, 22–23, 100.

30. FRUS 1927, II, 612.

31. Ibid., 613, 616.

32. Ferrell, *Peace in Their Time*, 35, 62.

33. Stoner, *Levinson*, 247, 250.

34. FRUS 1927, II, 627.

35. FRUS 1928, I, 27, 65, and for the full text see 153–157; Ferrell, *Peace in Their Time*, 169.

36. Kellogg, "War Prevention Policy," 261.

37. Stoner, *Levinson*, ix.

38. FRUS 1928, I, 154–156; Ferrell, *Peace in Their Time*, 192–193.

39. FRUS 1928, I, 173.

40. FRUS 1928, I, 157, 172–174, 212–214.

41. United Kingdom War Office, Peking Attaché, Military Report 8, 18 August 1929; FRUS 1921, I, 315. Chang Tso-lin had turned his Northeast Bureau of Foreign Affairs, created on 1 November 1921, into a de facto foreign ministry on 12 May 1922 after his defeat in the First Fengtien-Chihli War, and afterward envoys in the Northeast had to work through its offices if they expected his cooperation.

42. Service, *Stalin*, 258, 260; Kropkin, *Stalin*, 670, 672, 675.

43. Duranty, *I Write as I Please*, 286.

44. Forsyth, *History*, 271, 275, 330–331.

45. FO Report F 2380/7/10 Harbin, 31 March 1929; Forsyth, *History*, 292; Stephan, *Russian Far East*, 191.

46. Yueng, "Chang Hsueh-liang," 123–124; Elleman, *Diplomacy and Deception*, 131; 1924 FRUS 1924, I, 501; FRUS 1929, II, 188; Christopher, *Conflict*, 75.

47. MA Peking Report 7565, 26 July 1929, 6; FRUS 1929, II, 190; Tang, *Russian and Soviet Policy*, 189, 454–455; Chou, "Railway Development," 67–68.

48. Sheridan, *Chinese Warlord*, 252.

49. Sheridan, *Chinese Warlord*, 253; Lary, *Region and Nation*, 139–141.

50. Sheridan, *Chinese Warlord*, 252, 260.

51. United Kingdom War Office, "Note on the Military Situation in China," 20 June 1929.

52. Lary, *Region and Nation*, 144.

53. Cheng, *Sino-Russian Relations*, 150; Mosher, *Japanese Post Offices*, 113; Tian, "Chang," 136. Powell, *My Twenty-Five Years*, 180; Wolff, *Harbin Station*, 18–19.

54. Government of Japan, Ministry of Foreign Affairs, "Sino-Soviet Conflict" (hereafter JMFA I.3.3), 4 June 1929, message from Counsel General Yagi to Foreign Minister Shidehara; Conquest, *Great Terror*, 399–400; "Soviet Counsel Staff Gaoled," *North China Daily News*, 29 May 1929. Captured documents revealed that Feng had been in discussions with the Soviets in late December 1928 and that the Soviet goal was to strengthen the Russian position in China. See "The Russian Communist Documents Seized at Harbin," *North China Daily News*, 10 June 1929.

55. FRUS 1929, II, 192. "Soviet Consulate Raid," *North China Daily News*, 30 May 1929; "Harbin Consulate Raid," *North China Daily News*, 11 June 1929.

56. JMFA I.3.3, Report from Harbin Counsel General Yagi, 4 June 1929; Cheng, *Sino-Russian Relations*, 150.

57. JMFA I.3.3, Report from Harbin Counsel General Yagi, 4 June 1929; International Relations Committee, *Sino-Soviet Crisis*, 16–18; "Soviet Counsel Staff Gaoled," *North China Daily News*, 29 May 1929; "Harbin Consulate Raid," *North China Daily News*, 11 June 1929.

58. JMFA I.3.3, Report from Harbin Counsel General Yagi, 4 June 1929;

"The Soviet Raid at Harbin," *North China Daily News*, 5 June 1929; "Kuznetzoff Allowed to Go to Moscow," *North China Daily News*, 10 June 1929.

59. "Harbin Consulate Raid Sequel," *North China Daily News*, 8 June 1929.

60. Lih, Naumov, and Khlevniuk, *Stalin's Letters to Molotov*, 149.

61. "Sequel to Raid on Consulate," *North China Daily News*, 4 June 1929; "Harbin Consulate Raid," *North China Daily News*, 11 June 1929.

62. International Relations Committee, *Sino-Soviet Crisis*, 61, 69; FRUS 1929, II, 229; "The Sino-Russian Tension," *North China Daily News*, 13 June 1929; Lyons, *Assignment in Utopia*, 250; FO Report F 5146/3568/10 Peking, 2 July 1930; see para. 20.

63. Sheridan, *Chinese Warlord*, 262; ARCOS (All Russian Co-operative Society) had their London offices raided on 12 May 1927, which revealed that a high-level espionage operation being directed against the British government was being conducted there. The disclosure resulted in the severing of diplomatic relations with Soviet Russia. For more on the ARCOS affair, see Andrew, "British Intelligence and the Breach with Russia in 1927," Flory, "ARCOS Raid."

64. FRUS 1929, III, 253.

65. Tian, "Chang," 138–139; Pye, *Warlord Politics*, 116–117.

66. Tian, "Chang," 140; Yueng, "Chang Hsueh-liang," 125; Chang, "CER Event," 234; Kang, "Chang Hsueh-liang and Chiang Kai-shek," 258; United Kingdom War Office, Peking Attaché, Military Report 10, 24 September 1929; McCormack, *Chang Tso-lin*, 211; FO Report F 444/3568/10, 24 August 1929; Wilbur and How, *Missionaries*, 773.

67. Chang, "CER Event," 234, and Kang, "Chang Hsueh-liang and Chiang Kai-shek," 258.

68. Taylor, *Generalissimo*, 85.

69. Kang, "Chang Hsueh-liang and Chiang Kai-shek," 258–259.

Chapter 6. The Chinese and Soviet Russian Forces

1. Tien, *Government and Politics*, 115; McCormack, *Chang Tso-lin*, 102–104. The Poating Staff School became the War College and moved to Peking in 1913. Paoting remained the home of the Military Academy for training junior officers.

2. Ch'en, "Defining Chinese Warlords," 565.

3. Wilbur and How, *Missionaries*, 619.

4. FRUS 1930, II, 2; FO Report F 1282/106/10, 6 March 1930, 186.

5. Ch'i, *Warlord Politics*, 42, 49.

6. Lary, *Warlord Soldiers*, 16; Sheridan, *Chinese Warlord*, 75; McCormack, *Chang Tso-lin*, 118.

7. "Fengtien Troops at Manchouli," *North China Daily News*, 17 July 1929;

Ch'i, *Warlord Politics*, 102, 139; McCormack, *Chang Tso-lin*, 101. Nearly a dozen senior Fengtien commanders were killed or wounded in action in 1924. For more on the traditional texts, see Sawyer, *Seven Military Classics*.

8. Lu, *Re-Understanding Japan*, 38, 201; Sheridan, *Chinese Warlord*, 39–40. The general was also known as Chiang Pai-li. The full title of Yuan's manual was *The Detailed and Illustrated Book of Yuan Shih-kai's Training and Drilling Methods*.

9. Ch'i, *Warlord Politics*, 109, 127; Kuhn, "What War Is Like in China," 832; Waldron, *From War to Nationalism*, 55–56, 82, 105, 108; Jowett, *Armies of Warlord China*, 186–187.

10. McCormack, *Chang Tso-lin*, 104, 120–122; Zhang, *Warlord Chang Tso-lin*, pt. 1, chap. 2, sec. 3.

11. Lary, *Warlord Soldiers*, 129; Ch'i, *Warlord Politics*, 105; McCormack, *Chang Tso-lin*, 101, 102.

12. Zhang, *Warlord Chang Tso-lin*, pt. 2, chap. 9, sec. 2.

13. Wilbur and How, *Missionaries*, 569; Jowett, *Armies of Warlord China*, 186–187. Jowett held they came from the French Colonial Siberian Battalion. Alternatively, Russia ordered FT-17s before the revolution; they may have been part of the Vladivostok supplies or procured from the tanks the French delivered to White forces during the Russian civil war or purchased in violation of the arms embargo.

14. Wilbur and How, *Missionaries*, 569, 619; Ch'i, *Warlord Politics*, 118–120; "Fengtien Troops at Manchouli," *North China Daily News*, 17 July 1929; McCormack, *Chang Tso-lin*, 107. Sutton was a military engineer who was awarded the Military Cross and lost a hand at Gallipoli, earning him the nickname One-Armed Sutton. Chang Tso-lin made him a major general, and he left the arsenal after the Marshal's death.

15. Ch'i, *Warlord Politics*, 118, 119; ONI Report, Serial 399, "The Three Eastern Provinces," 14 December 1927. The ONI report duplicated MA Report 4410, 7 December 1927; Waldron, *From War to Nationalism*, 56–57, 65.

16. FRUS 1919, I, 667. The five powers were France, Italy, Japan, the United Kingdom, and the United States.

17. Ibid., 671, 668.

18. FRUS 1919, I, 668, 670–672; Valone, *Policy Calculated to Benefit China*, 119; Ch'i, *Warlord Politics*, 121; Waldron, *From War to Nationalism*, 60, 69.

19. Ch'i, *Warlord Politics*, 121; FRUS 1920, I, 436–437, 465, 539, 559, 583, 745–746, 751. It is possible that this shipment originated in Vladivostok, as Curtiss Model K seaplanes were left unassembled there, Remington provided the Russians with equipment to manufacture the Mosin-Nagant rifle with cartridges that were later produced at the Canton arsenal, and the Dutch merchantman *Woudrichem* had been impressed by the United States for duty during World War I before being returned in 1919.

20. FRUS 1921, I, 534, 560–562, 744.

21. McCormack, *Chang Tso-lin*, 58–59, 64–65; Yoshihashi, *Conspiracy*, 21.

22. Dunscomb, *Japan's Siberian Intervention*, 199.

23. Ibid., 198–201; Scully, *Bargaining with the State*, 153–154; Dunscomb, *Japan's Siberian Intervention*, 198–199.

24. Willoughby, *China at the Conference*, 243; FRUS 1922, I, 727, 729.

25. Willoughby, *China at the Conference*, 244, 248; FRUS 1923, I, 618.

26. Ch'i, *Warlord Politics*, 248; FRUS 1924, I, 530–531, 535; FRUS 1925, I, 645.

27. FRUS 1926, I, 733–734.

28. FRUS 1926, I, 735; FRUS 1928, I, 336; FRUS 1928, II, 131.

29. Isby and Ethell, *Handbook*; see chap. 9, "Weapons," sections 1 and 2.

30. Sheridan, *Chinese Warlord*, 242ff.; FRUS 1929 II, 161, 178.

31. McCormack, *Chang Tso-lin*, 101; Government of Japan, "Declassified Observations," 220; Liaoning Provincial Archives, *Selected Historical Materials of Liaoning Province*, 50–51.

32. Crossley, *Manchus*, 103–104; McCormack, *Chang Tso-lin*, 107–108; FO Report F 5297/3568/10, 22 August 1929; Bagrov and Sungorkin, *Red Banner*, 92; Wright, *Chinese Steam Navy*, 139–141. For a list of the Chinese warships, see Appendix A.

33. Government of Japan, "Declassified Observations," 220; Liaoning Provincial Archives, *Selected Historical Materials of Liaoning Province*, 50–51.

34. Carr, *Russian Revolution*, 172.

35. Kotkin, *Stalin*, 687; Trotsky, *Revolution Betrayed*, chap. 8, "From 'World Revolution' to Status Quo." For a discussion on the distinction between authoritarian and totalitarian rule, see Kirkpatrick, "Dictatorships and Double Standards," 34–45.

36. Kipp, "Lenin and Clausewitz," 186; Ree, "Socialism in One Country," 89.

37. Wollenberg, *Red Army*, appx. 1.

38. White, "Soviet Philosophy," 338; White, *Growth of the Red Army*, 236; Wilbur and How, *Missionaries*, 216–217. The other two members of the anti-Trotsky triumvirate or troika were Kamenev and Zinoviev. In 1926, Bubnov led a commission to inspect Soviet activities in China.

39. Kotkin, *Stalin*, 619.

40. Stone, *Hammer and Rifle*, 15; Erickson, *Soviet High Command*, 168, 171.

41. Carr, *Russian Revolution*, 73–74; White, "Soviet Philosophy," 340; Erickson, *Soviet High Command*, 189; Seaton, *Stalin as Military Commander*, 28, 35, 68. Trotsky was removed from the Executive Committee of the Communist International in September 1927, the Politburo in October, and the Communist Party in November and exiled in January 1928. At the 1918 Battle of Tsarytsin during the Russian civil war, Stalin had served as senior commander. The bulk of the fighting was borne by the First Cavalry Army, led by Budyonny with Voroshilov as political commissar, E. A. Shchadenko as his deputy, and Kulik in charge of

artillery. Budyonny, Voroshilov, and Kulik obtained the rank of marshal, and all failed as senior commanders during World War II. Kulik was executed after World War II. E. A. Shchadenko later became a colonel general, RKKA chief of staff, and head of the Red Army. Not everyone who served Stalin at Tsarytsin went on to success; one notable exception was Sergei K. Minin, who sided with Trotsky in 1925 and who committed suicide in 1926; see Service, *Stalin,* 225. Tsarytsin was later renamed Stalingrad, then Volgograd.

42. Erickson, *Soviet High Command,* 174–175.

43. Stone, *Hammer and Rifle,* 14, 18.

44. Litvinov, *Notes,* 128.

45. Rapoport and Alexeev, *Essays,* 156–157. Todorsky was imprisoned by Stalin during the Great Terror but was released and fought with distinction in World War II.

46. White, *Growth of the Red Army,* 260; Reese, *Stalin's Reluctant Soldiers,* 12.

47. White, *Growth of the Red Army,* 197–198; Efimov, Manzhosov, and Sidorov, *Armored Trains,* 13. The GPU was also referred to as the OGPU (Joint State Political Directorate) by 1929.

48. Sella, "Red Army Doctrine," 246; United States Foreign Broadcast Information Service, *Field Regulations,* 41.

49. Reese, *Stalin's Reluctant Soldiers,* 22; White, *Growth of the Red Army,* 234, 265, 267.

50. Reese, *Stalin's Reluctant Soldiers,* 12.

51. Bagrov and Sungorkin, *Red Banner,* 87.

52. Rapoport and Alexeev, *Essays,* 163, 174.

53. Glantz, *Soviet Military Operational Art,* 10, 19, 21, 23; White, *Growth of the Red Army,* 171–172; Sella, "Red Army Doctrine," 246; Erickson, *Soviet High Command,* 316, 318, 717ff.

54. See United States Foreign Broadcast Information Service, *Field Regulations,* Articles 25, 167; for encirclement and mobile envelopment, see Article 115; for sequential or successive operations, see Articles 8 and 25; and for pursuit and annihilation offensives, see Article 165.

55. United States Foreign Broadcast Information Service, *Field Regulations,* Article 213.

56. Glantz, "Observing the Soviets," 158. Gatzke, "Russo-German Military, Collaboration," 578, 586. In the regulations, eight articles were devoted exclusively to tanks, and they were referred to in three others.

57. United States Foreign Broadcast Information Service, *Field Regulations,* Articles 208, 209, 213.

58. United States Foreign Broadcast Information Service, *Field Regulations,* Articles 9, 169, 208.

59. For tank–cavalry cooperation, see United States Foreign Broadcast Information Service, *Field Regulations,* Articles 9, 58, 164, 206; for long-range eche-

lons and deep strikes, see Articles 208, 209, 213; for tanks as help for infantry and cavalry, see Articles 9, 169, 208; for a limited role in the offensive, see Articles 116, 164, 206, 209; United States Army General Services School, *Tactics and Technique of Cavalry*, 865–879.

60. Gatzke, "Russo-German Military Collaboration," 572, 576; Mets, "Origins," 40–41; Kainikara, *Red Air*, 133; Erickson, *Soviet High Command*, 382. Rozengolts was arrested with Bukharin on 27 February 1937; both were shot on 15 March 1938. Lapchinsky was also executed during the Great Terror.

61. Gatzke, "Russo-German Military Collaboration," 578; Erickson, *Soviet High Command*, 264–265; Guderian, *Panzer Leader*, 13.

62. Stone, *Hammer and Rifle*, 26–30, 88; see also table 1 on 35; Government of Japan, "Declassified Observations," 202. After his death from heart failure in 1926, Dzerzhinsky was replaced by Vyacheslav Menzhinsky.

63. Stone, *Hammer and Rifle*, 30, 193; Sella, "Red Army Doctrine," 248; Rohwer and Monakov, "Soviet Union's Ocean-Going Fleet," 847; Mets, "Origins," 42; Gatzke, "Russo-German Military Collaboration," 580; Stone, *Hammer and Rifle*, 14. Christie could promote his tank even though there were no diplomatic relations between the Soviet Union and the United States, as commercial dealings were permitted through the American Trade Corporation, headquartered in New York City.

64. Glantz, "Observing the Soviets," 156, 163; Stone, *Hammer and Rifle*, 35; see table 1; Koyrev, Orekhov, and Fomin, *Tanks*, 27–28; Jones, Rarey, and Icks, *Fighting Tanks*, 148.

65. Only a handful of TB-1s had been built, and none served in the 1929 war.

66. Glantz, *Soviet Military Operational Art*, 67; Reese, *Stalin's Reluctant Soldiers*, 27–28; Erickson, *Soviet High Command*, 181, 183.

67. Erickson, *Soviet High Command*, 221; FRUS 1929, II, 352. That the 1st and 2nd Rifle Divisions began as part of the Far East Republic's People's Revolutionary Army accounts for the numerical duplication with the 1st "Proletariat" and 2nd "Moscow" Rifle Divisions in European Russia. Later the two Far East divisions were redesignated the 39th and 66th Rifle Divisions, respectively.

68. Efimov, Manzhosov, and Sidorov, *Armored Trains*, 12.

69. MA Peking Report, "Disposition of Soviet Troops in Siberia," 1 August 1929; Erickson, *Soviet High Command*, 176; Stone, *Hammer and Rifle*, 53; Bagrov and Sungorkin, *Red Banner*, 90.

70. Bagrov and Sungorkin, *Red Banner*, 91.

71. White, *Growth of the Red Army*, 242; Wollenberg, *Red Army*, chap. 8.

72. Documentary film, *Modern Warfare in China in 1924–1925*.

Chapter 7. The CER Incident and War

1. FO Report F 4671/3568/10 Peking, 19 July 1929; FRUS 1929, II, 199; FRUS 1929, II, 198.

2. FO Report F 4671/3568/10 Peking, 19 July 1929; FRUS 1929, II, 201; Christopher, *Conflict*, 79.

3. FO Report F 5487/3568/10 Peking, 11 September 1929.

4. FO Report F 4671/3568/10 Peking, 19 July 1929; Tang, *Russian and Soviet Policy*, 182; FRUS 1929, II, 198.

5. Elleman and Kotkin, *Manchurian Railways*, 83; FO Report F 4671/3568/10 Peking, 19 July 1929; FRUS 1929, II, 201; Tang, *Russian and Soviet Policy*, 200; "Chinese Purging Harbin," *North China Daily News*, 12 July 1929; "The Seizure of the CER," *North China Daily News*, 13 July 1929.

6. FO Report F 5146/3568/10 Peking, 2 July 1930.

7. MA Tokyo Report 4079, 13 July 1929; Government of Japan, "Declassified Observations," 201; Kuzman and Polkovyh, *On Guard for Peace*, 125; "Americans Seized by Reds on Amur," *New York Times*, 23 July 1929.

8. Suntsov and Tretiak, *Red Banner*, 91; Government of Japan, "Declassified Observations," 200.

9. As a comparison, the Western Front during World War I, stretching from the Alps to the English Channel, was slightly over 700 kilometers in length.

10. Caufield, "Upstream Slowly"; Government of Japan, "Declassified Observations," 215; Block, *Escape Siberia*, chap. 7.

11. Patrikeeff, *Russian Politics*, 31; Bisher, *White Terror*, 43; Stephan, *Russian Far East*, 67.

12. Fedyuninsky, *In the East*, 7; Government of Japan, "Declassified Observations," 207. Other sources refer to Hill 1005 as Hill 100 or 101.

13. Government of Japan, "Declassified Observations," 203; Graves, America's Siberian Adventure, 210.

14. Uchida, *Brokers of Empire*, 310–311.

15. "China Willing to Parley," *North China Daily News*, 17 July 1929.

16. "Dr. Wang Going to Peking," *North China Daily News*, 9 July 1929; "China Willing to Parley," *North China Daily News*, 17 July 1929; Lensen, *Damned Inheritance*, 174–176. The short Soviet silent film, *Kuomintang on the March*, showing the Moscow protest, can be viewed at http://www.soviethistory.org/.

17. FO Report F 5232/3568/10 Peking, 18 August 1929; "Chiang on Red Imperialism," *North China Daily News*, 18 July 1929.

18. FO Report F 4011/3568/10 Oslo, 30 July 1929; FO Report F 4874/3568/10 Mukden, 24 July 1929; "China Willing to Parley," *North China Daily News*, 17 July 1929. The seized islands remained trouble spots for decades. See Goldstein, "Return to Zhenbao Island."

19. Government of Japan, "Declassified Observations," 215; FO Report F

4874/3568/10, 24 July 1929; "World's New Powder Magazine," *North China Daily News*, 13 August 1929.

20. Wang, "Zhongdong Railway Incident," 51; Harrison, "Li Li-san Line," 182. Also see Mao, *Selected Military Writings*.

21. Lee, *Revolutionary Struggle*, 65.

22. Ibid., 66.

23. Lee, *Revolutionary Struggle*, 63, 68–69; Schwartz, *Chinese Communism*, 129.

24. Wang, "Zhongdong Railway Incident," 49; Morley, *Japan Erupts*, 152; Sheng, "Analysis of the Differences," 304; Lee, *Revolutionary Struggle*, 102.

25. MA Report 7573, "Pro and Anti-Russian Agitation in Shanghai," 8 August 1929; "Nanking's Reply Held Up," *North China Daily News*, 20 July 1929.

26. FO Reports F 4011/3568/10, F 5232/3568/10 Peking, 18 August 1929, and F 5274/3566/10, 19 August 1929; Tang, *Russian and Soviet Policy*, 208, 230. Tang noted that in addition to the *Ilan*, the steamers S.S. *Haichen, Ishing, Aigun, Shengyang, Haichong, Weitung*, and *Tungfeng* as well as the towboat *Hwakan* were seized, along with the detention of 1,182 men, women, and children. Mukden had been using electronic mines since the Second Fengtien-Chihli War; see FRUS 1926, I, 593.

27. "Complete Deadlock in Discussions with Russia," *North China Daily News*, 7 August 1929.

28. FO Report F 4011/3568/10, 30 July 1929.

29. FRUS 1929, II, 212.

30. Davis and Trani, *Distorted Mirrors*, 34.

31. MA London Report 25517, 22 July 1929; MA Riga Report 23 July 1929; MA Peking Report 7574, 12 August 1929; "Moscow Closes the Door," *North China Daily News*, 19 July 1929. Tatekawa later played a role in the 1931 Mukden incident.

32. FRUS 1929, II, 240. Smirnov and Brukhanov died during the Great Terror, and Sofia Smidovitch died of natural causes in the early 1930s.

33. "Reds Renew Pledge to Kellogg Pact," *New York Times*, 20 July 1929.

34. Kotkin, *Stalin*, 700, 709.

35. Reiman, *Birth of Stalinism*, 108–109, 176n24; Service, *Stalin*, 255. Antonov-Ovseyenko was executed in 1938 during the Great Terror.

36. FRUS 1929, II, 240.

37. MA London Report 25553, 18 July 1929.

38. FRUS 1929, II, 210; Tsuchida Tetsuro, "Japan and the Sino-Soviet Conflict," 27.

39. FRUS, 1918, Russia II, 5.

40. Trotsky, "Sino-Soviet Conflict."

41. FO Report F 4671/3568/10 Peking, 19 July 1929.

42. Clubb, *China and Russia*, 260; FO Reports F 4874/3568/10 Peking,

28 July 1929, and F 51452/3568/10 Peking, 17 August 1929; Yueng, "Chang Hsueh-liang," 127.

43. Stoner, *Levinson*, 209; FRUS 1929, II, 268. For a copy of the text, see FRUS 1929, II, 242–243.

44. Ferrell, *Peace in Their Time*, 9.

45. FO Report F 4110/3568/10 Peking, 10 August 1929.

46. FRUS 1929, II, 187, 207.

47. FO Report F 4501/3568/10 Peking, 1 August 1929.

48. Morley, *Japan Erupts*, 148–149.

49. FRUS 1929, II, 231, 257; FO Reports F 4043/3568/10 Washington, 7 August 1929, and F 4182/3568/10 Washington, 14 August 1929; FRUS 1929, II, 241, 257. The French effort was rejected by 24 July, and the Japanese offer was declined by the 27th.

50. Fedyuninsky, *In the East*, 12; FRUS 1929, II, 272.

51. FO Reports F 4057/3568/10, 8 August, and F 5232/3568/10 Peking, 18 August 1929; Morley, *Japanese Thrust*, 111–112.

52. FRUS 1929, II, 276; Cheng, *Sino-Russian Relations*, 153.

53. FRUS 1929, II, 276.

54. Stone, *Hammer and Rifle*, 124; Suntsov and Tretiak, *Red Banner*, 90.

55. Cherepanov, *Field of My Martial Feats*, 176. Among those present were V. P. Rogachev (NRA Chief of Staff 1926) and I. Zilbert (Senior Advisor, NRA 2nd Corps). ODVA stood for Osobaya Daln'ne-vostochnaya armiya (Special Far East Army). Zilbert perished in the Great Terror.

56. Wilbur and How, *Missionaries*, 11; Rapoport and Alexeev, *Essays*, 160; Kotkin, *Stalin*, 693; Erickson, *Soviet High Command*, 261, 266.

57. Erickson, *Soviet High Command*, 232; Cherepanov, *Field of My Martial Feats*, 177; Wilbur and How, *Missionaries*, 428; Chuikov, *Mission to China*, 25. Andrei Bubnov was executed on 1 August 1938.

58. Salminov and Velikanovm, *Order of Lenin Transbaikal Sky*, 54; FO Report F 6195/3568/10 Berlin, 1 November 1929; Erickson, *Soviet High Command*, 240–241; Fedyuninsky, *In the East*, 27. During World War II, Chuikov led the heroic defense of Stalingrad and was promoted to marshal.

59. MA Peking Report, "Disposition of Soviet Troops in Siberia," 1 August 1929. These units were undermanned by as much as half. For a compilation of the Chinese Northeast Frontier Defense Force (NEFDF) and ODVA Orders of Battle, see Appendix A.

60. Suntsov and Tretiak, *Red Banner*, 99; Sella, "Red Army Doctrine," 253–254; Kuzman and Polkovyh, *On Guard for Peace*, 124; Koyrev, Orekhov, and Fomin, *Tanks*, 29. The tank company was probably detached from the 1st Tank Regiment assigned to the Moscow Military District.

61. Khetagurov, *Performance of Duty*, chap. 1.

62. FRUS 1929, II, 352; Stephan, *Russian Far East,* 160; "Chiang on Red Imperialism," *North China Daily News,* 18 July 1929; "Russians Reported to Be Rousing Outer Mongolia," *North China Daily News,* 29 July 1929; "China's Last Notes Rejected," *North China Daily News,* 19 September 1929; "Renewed Scare of Mongols," *North China Daily News,* 20 September 1929. A July 1930 intelligence report showed RKKA control at every level of the Mongolian People's Revolutionary Army; see MA Peking Report 7777, 23 July 1930.

63. FO Report F 6195/3568/10 Berlin, 11 September 1929.

64. Government of Japan, "Declassified Observations," 204; FRUS 1929, II, 275; Tang, *Russian and Soviet Policy,* 207; F 4056/3568/10, 7 August 1929.

65. Tang, *Russian and Soviet Policy,* 208; FO Report F 4056/3568/10, 7 August 1929; "Plot to Destroy Sungari Bridge," *North China Daily News,* 17 August 1929; "Sabotage in Railway Works at Harbin," *North China Daily News,* 9 September 1929.

66. FO Reports F 5232/3568/10 Peking, 18 August 1929, and F 5297/3568/10 Peking, 31 August 1929; "Police Brutality in Harbin," *North China Daily News,* 7 August 1929; "Martial Law Declared on CER," *North China Daily News,* 12 August 1929; "Reports of Russian Offensive Considered Doubtful," *North China Daily News,* 16 August 1929; Government of Japan, "Declassified Observations," 204. Melnikov was executed on 28 July 1938.

67. FO Reports F 4874/3568/10, 28 July 1929, F 4056/3568/10, 7 August 1929, and F 4252/3568/10, 16 August 1929; "Martial Law Declared on CER," *North China Daily News,* 12 August 1929; "General of Red Army in Far East Said to Be Galens," *North China Daily News,* 14 August 1929.

68. FRUS 1930, II, 38.

69. Sheng, "Analysis of the Differences," 306; McCormack, *Chang Tso-lin,* 90; Lee, *Revolutionary Struggle,* 107–108.

70. "China Appeals to Powers in the Kellogg Briand Pact," *North China Daily News,* 8 August 1929; Government of Japan, "Declassified Observations," 212.

71. "General of Red Army in Far East Said to Be Galens," *North China Daily News,* 14 August 1929; "Typical Communist Touch," *North China Daily News,* 15 August 1929.

72. FRUS 1929, II, 293; FO Report F 6159/3568/10, 24 September 1929; Fedyuninsky, *In the East,* 8.

73. Cheng, *Sino-Russian Relations,* 154; Suntsov and Tretiak, *Red Banner,* 90; FO Report F 5274/3568/10, 19 August 1929; FRUS 1929, II, 298.

74. Chiang, *Report.*

75. FO Report F 5297/3568/10, 21 October 1929.

76. Efimov, Manzhosov, and Sidorov, *Armored Trains,* 13.

77. "Lull in Manchurian Crisis," *North China Daily News,* 26 August 1929; "Russia Rejects All Mediation," *North China Daily News,* 27 August 1929.

78. Government of Japan, "Declassified Observations," 213.

79. Ibid., 202.
80. FRUS 1929, II, 299. Karakhan was executed on 20 September 1937.
81. Ibid., 298.
82. "Lull in Manchurian Crisis," *North China Daily News*, 6 August 1929.
83. "Russia Rejects All Mediation," *North China Daily News*, 27 August 1929; "Russia Makes Another Move," *North China Daily News*, 28 August 1929; Cherepanov, *Field of My Martial Feats*, 178.
84. MA Peking Report 7584 30 August 1929.

Chapter 8. Renewed Talks, Fighting, and Frustration

1. He, "1929 Chinese Eastern Railroad Incident," 192; MA Report 7573, 8 August 1929; "Communist Plans for 1 August," *North China Daily News*, 25 July 1929; "Communists Quiet over the Weekend," *North China Daily News*, 29 July 1929; "'Red Thursday' a Very Gentle Pink," *North China Daily News*, 2 August 1929; "Sabre Rattling on the Border," *North China Daily News*, 10 August 1929.
2. Sheng, "Analysis of the Differences," 298.
3. Ibid., 298, 301.
4. Lee, *Revolutionary Struggle*, 97; Wang, "Zhongdong Railway Incident," 52; Sheng, "Analysis of the Differences," 301–302.
5. Morley, *Japan Erupts*, 152; Sheng, "Analysis of the Differences," 306; Wang, "Zhongdong Railway Incident," 53–54; Lee, *Revolutionary Struggle*, 98.
6. FRUS 1929, II, 124; Liaoning Provincial Archives, *Selected Historical Materials of Liaoning Province*, 50–51.
7. Liaoning Provincial Archives, *Selected Historical Materials of Liaoning Province*, 50–51; Zhang, *Warlord Chang Tso-lin*, chap. 9, sec. 4.
8. Government of Japan, "Declassified Observations," 206 (pt. 1, Report 2), and 215 (pt. 4, Report 2).
9. MA Peking Report 7586, 6 September 1929.
10. "Marking Time in Siberia," *North China Daily News*, 29 August 1929.
11. "Moscow Closes the Door," *North China Daily News*, 17 July 1929.
12. FO Report F 5297/3568/10, 21 October 1929; FRUS 1929, II, 257; Zhang Hongjun, "Japan and the CER," 341; "Dairen May Benefit by Manchurian Dispute," *New York Times*, 5 August 1929; "America Moves for Mediation," *North China Daily News*, 22 July 1929; "Mediation Declined by Soviet," *North China Daily News*, 24 July 1929; "CER Crisis Abating," *North China Daily News*, 25 July 1929.
13. "World's New Powder Keg," *North China Daily News*, 13 August 1929; "Alleged Thieving on CER," *North China Daily News*, 13 September 1929; FO Report F 4982/3568/10 Peking, 10 August 1929.
14. "Alleged Thieving on CER," *North China Daily News*, 13 September 1929.

15. FO Report F 168/106/10, 20 November 1929.

16. "Alleged Thieving on CER," *North China Daily News,* 13 September 1929; "Mr. Mantell and the CER," *North China Daily News,* 18 September 1929.

17. FO Report F 4361/3568/10, 25 August 1929.

18. Regarding interwar Soviet–German military cooperation, see Erickson, *Soviet High Command,* chap. 6; Stein, "Russo-German Military Collaboration"; Gatzke, "Russo-German Military Collaboration."

19. FRUS 1929, II, 307–308; FO Report F 4361/3568/10, 25 August 1929.

20. For a transcript of the *Note Verbale,* see FRUS 1929, II, 309–310.

21. "Peace," *Time Magazine,* 9 September 1929; FRUS 1929, II, 313. Debuchi is sometimes translated as Izabuchi.

22. Lih, Naumov, and Khlevniuk, *Stalin's Letters to Molotov,* 174.

23. Ibid., 175.

24. FRUS 1929, II, 310–311.

25. Ibid., 312.

26. FO Report F 4576/3568/10 Peking, 5 September 1929.

27. FO Report F 4447/3568/10 Tokyo, 30 August 1929.

28. "Fresh Attacks on Pogranichnaya," *North China Daily News,* 13 September 1929.

29. "Will the Agreement with Russia Be Held Up?," *North China Daily News,* 2 September 1929.

30. Khetagurov, *Performance of Duty,* chap. 1; FRUS 1929, II, 313; "Raid on Jalainor," *North China Daily News,* 3 September 1929; "Fresh Attacks on Pogranichnaya," *North China Daily News,* 13 September 1929.

31. FRUS 1929, II, 219, 232; FO Report F 4874/3568/10 Peking, 28 July 1929; Dmitriev-Mamonov and Zdziarski, *Siberian Railway,* 19; "Chinese Organize Defense," *New York Times,* 22 July 1929; "Soviet Denies All Notes," *North China Daily News,* 27 July 1929; "Martial Law Declared on CER," *North China Daily News,* 12 August 1929; "Lull in Manchurian Crisis," *North China Daily News,* 26 August 1929; "Lull on the Siberian Frontier," *North China Daily News,* 6 September 1929.

32. "General of Red Army in Far East Said to Be Galens," *North China Daily News,* 14 August 1929. For a presentation of the terrain surrounding Suifenho, see Glantz, *August Storm: Tactical and Operational Combat,* maps 1–3.

33. "Russians Attack Pogranichnaya," *North China Daily News,* 10 September 1929.

34. FRUS 1929, II, 219, 315, 316; MA Peking Report, 1 August 1929; "Sabre Rattling on Soviet Border," *North China Daily News,* 9 August 1929; "'Active Warfare' Reported by Moscow," *North China Daily News,* 10 September 1929.

35. Government of Japan, "Declassified Observations," 201, 202; FRUS 1929, II, 316; "'Active Warfare' Reported by Moscow," *North China Daily News,* 10 September 1929; "Is Russia Seeking an Excuse?," *North China Daily News,* 12

September 1929; "Fresh Attacks on Pogranichnaya," *North China Daily News*, 13 September 1929.

36. FRUS 1929, II, 316; Government of Japan, "Declassified Observations," 201; "'Active Warfare' Reported by Moscow," *North China Daily News*, 10 September 1929; "Is Russia Seeking an Excuse?," *North China Daily News*, 12 September 1929.

37. "Fresh Attacks on Pogranichnaya," *North China Daily News*, 13 September 1929.

38. Government of Japan, "Declassified Observations," 201; "Four New Battles on Chinese Border," *New York Times*, 8 September 1929.

39. Fedyuninsky, *In the East*, 9.

40. FRUS 1929, II, 316–317; "Meaning of Soviet Raids," *North China Daily News*, 14 September 1929.

41. Patrikeeff, *Russian Politics*, 34–35.

42. FRUS 1929, II, 296–297; "Moscow and the White Congress," *North China Daily News*, 22 July 1929; "Renewed Scare of Mongols," *North China Daily News*, 20 September 1929.

43. "China Rejects Russia's Demands," *North China Daily News*, 16 September 1929.

44. United Kingdom War Office, Peking Attaché, Military Report 10, 24 September 1929; FRUS 1929, II, 311; "Raid on Jalainor," *North China Daily News*, 3 September 1929.

45. United Kingdom War Office, Peking Attaché, Military Report 10, 24 September 1929.

46. United Kingdom War Office, Peking Attaché, Military Report 8, 13 August 1929; FO Report F 4112/3568/10 Peking, 11 August 1929.

47. ONI File 104-100, "Activities of Local 'White' Organizations," 10 April 1928; FO Report F 5232/3568/10 Peking, 18 August 1929; "Moscow Returns to White Russian Charge," *North China Daily News*, 26 July 1929; "Litvinoff's Reply to Dr. C. C. Wu," *North China Daily News*, 7 September 1929.

48. Government of Japan, "Declassified Observations," 216; Lee, *Revolutionary Struggle*, 24; Bisher, *White Terror*, 263; Smith, *Vladivostok*, 81, 125.

49. Stephan, *Russian Far East*, 162; Jones, "Diary"; Block, *Escape Siberia*; Stephan, *Russian Far East*, 162; ONI File 102-100, serial 406, 20 November 1927.

50. ONI File 102-100, "Report of White Agents to Head of Grand Duke Nikolai Nikolaievich's Organizations in Harbin," 17 December 1927; Christopher, *Conflict*, 116.

51. JMFA I.3.3, Report 756, "Ban on Harbin Student Corps by Chang Hsueh-liang," Harbin, 18 September 1929; United Kingdom War Office, Peking Attaché, Military Report 10, 24 September 1929; FO Report F 6159/3588/10, 5 October 1929; "Lull in Manchurian Crisis," *North China Daily News*, 26 August

1929; "Will the Agreement with Russia Be Held Up?," *North China Daily News*, 2 September 1929.

52. JMFA I.3.3, Report 756, "Ban on Harbin Student Corps by Chang Hsueh-liang," 18 September 1929.

53. Ibid.; FO Report F 151/106/10 Peking, 15 November 1929; Chang, "CER Event," 243.

54. FRUS 1929, II, 265; FO Report F 5297/106/10, 21 October 1929; "Will the Agreement with Russia Be Held Up?," *North China Daily News*, 2 September 1929.

55. "Will the Agreement with Russia Be Held Up?," *North China Daily News*, 2 September 1929; "Lull on the Siberian Frontier," *North China Daily News*, 6 September 1929; "Moscow's Latest Proposal," *North China Daily News*, 17 September 1929.

56. JMFA I.3.3, Report 128, "CER Negotiations: Chinese Response to Soviet Amendment," Berlin, 11 September 1929; FRUS 1929, II, 319.

57. JMFA I.3.3, Conference between Shidehara and Troyanovsky, "Chinese Refused Soviet Amendment," Tokyo, 16 September 1929.

58. FRUS 1929, II, 321.

59. Ibid., 317.

60. FRUS 1929, II, 323; "The Soviet Attack on Manchuli," *North China Daily News*, 5 October 1929; "Manchurian Troubles," *New York Times*, 3 October 1929; ONI File 103-100, "Soviet Activities," Harbin, 4 October 1929.

61. FRUS 1929, II, 324; "The Soviet Attack on Manchuli," *North China Daily News*, 5 October 1929; ONI File 103-100, "Soviet Activities," Harbin, 4 October 1929.

62. Fedyuninsky, *In the East*, 10–12.

63. ONI File 103-100, "Soviet Activities," Harbin, 4 October 1929; "The Soviet Attack on Manchuli," *North China Daily News*, 5 October 1929.

64. "Another Manchuli Raid," *North China Daily News*, 7 October 1929.

65. Ibid.; "The Russian Attacks on Oct. 1–2 on Manchuli Were the Most Serious that Had Occurred Up to Then," *North China Daily News*, 8 October 1929; "Desultory Firing at Manchuli," *North China Daily News*, 9 October 1929.

66. Naval Attaché Peking, "Report on Sino-Russian Border Activities," 9 November 1929; "Russians Pushing Up Sungari," *North China Daily News*, 17 October 1929. General Nikolai V. Kuibyshev became one of the courageous few to speak out against the purge of the Red Army. He was arrested and executed on 1 August 1938.

67. Lih, Naumov, and Khlevniuk, *Stalin's Letters to Molotov*, 182.

68. Wilbur and How, *Missionaries*, 366–367; Erickson, *Soviet High Command*, 228, 231; International Relations Committee, *Sino-Soviet Crisis*, 2; ONI File 103-100, 17 July 1929; United Kingdom War Office, General Staff Report on China, 26 October 1926.

69. FRUS 1929, II, 174.
70. Tuchman, *Stilwell*, 110.
71. FRUS 1929, II, 178; McCormack, *Chang Tso-lin*, 263; Yueng, "Chang Hsueh-liang," 131.

Chapter 9. The Decisive ODVA Offensive

1. Suntsov and Tretiak, *Red Banner*, 96.
2. Litvinov, *Notes*, 126; "Lull in Manchurian Crisis," *North China Daily News*, 26 August 1929.
3. FRUS 1929, II, 212; Litvinov, *Notes*, 128. The old spheres of influence had been reestablished with the opening of Soviet–Japanese diplomatic relation in 1925; see Elleman and Kotkin, *Manchurian Railways*, 75.
4. Litvinov, *Notes*, 127; Government of Japan, "Declassified Observations," 216. See pt. 4, Report 2; United Kingdom War Office, Peking Attaché, Military Report 1, 14 January 1930.
5. Powell, *My Twenty-Five Years*, 175; Fedyuninsky, *In the East*, 13; Salminov and Velikanovm, *Order of Lenin Transbaikal Sky*, 55; Kuzman and Polkovyh, *On Guard for Peace*, 127 and map 2.
6. Dmitriev-Mamonov and Zdziarski, *Siberian Railway*, 417; Bagrov and Sungorkin, *Red Banner*, 92; Fedyuninsky, *In the East*, 13.
7. Yi has also been referred to as Yin.
8. Kuzman and Polkovyh, *On Guard for Peace*, 126–127, and map 2.
9. Bagrov and Sungorkin, *Red Banner*, 92.
10. Bagrov and Sungorkin, *Red Banner*, 91; FO Report F 5232/3568/10 Peking, 18 August 1929.
11. For more on the importance of this naval operation, see Chapter 10.
12. Bagrov and Sungorkin, *Red Banner*, 94.
13. FO Report F 5232/3568/10 Peking, 18 August 1929.
14. Bagrov and Sungorkin, *Red Banner*, 93, 95; "Chinese Defense on Sungari," *North China Daily News*, 19 October 1929; Chang, "CER Event," 237. A photograph of the *Tsen-I* in Soviet hands, with a river monitor in the background, can be found at http://f-picture.net/fp/6049d4164c4d40c3b35ac5aa2812d551.
15. FRUS 1929, II, 337–338; FO Report F 151/106/10 Peking, 15 November 1929; ONI Harbin Memorandum, 28 October 1929, 1–2; Bagrov and Sungorkin, *Red Banner*, 94–95; Kuzman and Polkovyh, *On Guard for Peace*, 126–127, and map 2; Chang, "CER Event," 237; Kulagin and Iakovlev, *Special Far Eastern Feat*, 114–115.
16. FRUS 1929, II, 333. Chang Chun and the Young Marshal maintained a cordial relationship for the rest of their lives.
17. ONI Harbin Memorandum, 28 October 1929, 2.

18. Lorge, *War Politics*, 142; Kuzman and Polkovyh, *On Guard for Peace*, 128, and map 3; Bagrov and Sungorkin, *Red Banner*, 94–95, 97; Kulagin and Iakovlev, *Special Far Eastern Feat*, 114–115.

19. Bagrov and Sungorkin, *Red Banner*, 101; Kuzman and Polkovyh, *On Guard for Peace*, 129, 135, and map 3; Kulagin and Iakovlev, *Special Far Eastern Feat*, 115–116; Erickson, *Soviet High Command*, 242.

20. Bagrov and Sungorkin, *Red Banner*, 100; "Fuchin Captured by Soviet," *North China Daily News*, 4 November 1929; FO Report F 150/106/10 Peking, 15 November 1929; Garthoff, *Sino-Soviet Military Relations*, 22. Erickson, *Soviet High Command*, 242; Kuzman and Polkovyh, *On Guard for Peace*, 129, map 3; Chang, "CER Event," 238. D. Kiselev posted a photo of the gravesite on 11 May 2012 at https://commons.wikimedia.org/wiki/File:Vladivostok_mishanfu.jpg.

21. FO Report F 151/106/10 Peking, 15 November 1929; FRUS 1929, II, 342.

22. FO Report F 6192/3568/10 Peking, 30 October 1929; Patrikeeff, *Russian Politics*, 30; Duranty, *I Write as I Please*, 135.

23. MA Peking Report 7613, 4 November 1929, 2; ONI File 103-100, "Soviet Activities," Harbin, 4 October 1929; Naval Attaché Peking, "Report on Sino-Russian Border Activities," 9 November 1929; Lih, Naumov, and Khlevniuk, *Stalin's Letters to Molotov*, 182; "Conflicts Reported on Manchurian Border," *North China Daily News*, 19 August 1929; FO Report F 3474/7/10 Harbin, 29 June 1929.

24. Powell, *My Twenty-Five Years*, 176.

25. Tang, *Russian and Soviet Policy*, 227; Elleman and Kotkin, *Manchurian Railways*, 96; FRUS 1929, II, 330, 335; FO Report F6192/3568/10 Peking, 30 October 1929; "Chinese Defense on Sungari," *North China Daily News*, 19 October 1929.

26. Reese, *Stalin's Reluctant Soldiers*, 82.

27. Voroshilov, *Stalin and the Red Army*, 17.

28. FRUS 1929, II, 330; FO Report F 6192/3568/10 Peking, 30 October 1929; see para. 9.

29. Forsyth, *History*, 323; Stephan, *Russian Far East*, 191; Litvinov, *Notes*, 113.

30. Khetagurov, *Performance of Duty*, chap. 1; Salminov and Velikanovm, *Order of Lenin Transbaikal Sky*, 54. Both Khetagurov and Kamera became generals, and Kamera would later command the artillery under Rokossovsky in World War II. See Rokossovsky, "At the Heights of Yartsevskaya."

31. FRUS 1929, II, 326.

32. Ibid., 339.

33. Ibid., 340.

34. Ibid., 331, 338–339, 341.

35. Ibid., 327.

36. Ibid., 333.

37. Ibid., 343.
38. "Fuchin Captured by Soviet," *North China Daily News*, 4 November 1929.
39. Chuikov, *Mission to China*, 29; Service, *Stalin*, 266.
40. Schram, *Mao's Road*, 192–193.
41. Ibid., 248–249.
42. Chuikov, *Mission to China*, 31; Dushenkin, "Defeat," 123–124; Cherepanov, *Field of My Martial Feats*, 180; Suntsov and Tretiak, *Red Banner*, 96.
43. Cherepanov, *Field of My Martial Feats*, 180; Dushenkin, "Defeat," 123–124; Suntsov and Tretiak, *Red Banner*, 97; Fedyuninsky, *In the East*, 45.
44. The soybean cakes were disc shaped, usually about two feet in diameter, five inches thick, and stacked to form obstacles. Thousands of the cakes were produced and were mainly used as livestock feed. When stacked en masse, they were as effective as sandbag barriers.
45. Clubb, *China and Russia*, 262; Cherepanov, *Field of My Martial Feats*, 180–181; Dushenkin, "Defeat," 123–124; Suntsov and Tretiak, *Red Banner*, 97. Lapin, a three-time recipient of the Order of the Red Banner, was arrested on 11 May 1937 and executed.
46. Dushenkin, "Defeat," 124; Suntsov and Tretiak, *Red Banner*, 97.
47. Cherepanov, *Field of My Martial Feats*, 181; Dushenkin, "Defeat," 123–124; Suntsov and Tretiak, *Red Banner*, 97; Fedyuninsky, *In the East*, 45; United Kingdom War Office, Peking Attaché, Military Report 1, 14 January 1930. A photo of the grave monument was posted by Andshel on 20 September 2011 and is available at http://commons.wikimedia.org/wiki/File:Братская_могила_красноармейцев,_погибших_на_КВЖД,_Уссурийск.JPG.
48. Fedyuninsky, *In the East*, 21.
49. Chuikov, *Mission to China*, 33; Khetagurov, *Performance of Duty*, chap. 1; Ogarkov, "Manchouli-Dalainor Operation, 1929"; Government of Japan, "Declassified Observations," 223, and map 2; Salminov and Velikanovm, *Order of Lenin Transbaikal Sky*, 56. To visually appreciate the contrast between RKKA summer and winter field uniforms worn during the war, see Jowett, *Armies of Warlord China*, 197.
50. Fedyuninsky, *In the East*, 16, 22; Chuikov, *Mission to China*, 34; Khetagurov, *Performance of Duty*, chap. 1.
51. Fedyuninsky, *In the East*, 22; Khetagurov, *Performance of Duty*, chap. 1.
52. Government of Japan, "Declassified Observations," 213, Report 2.
53. Chang, "CER Event," 239; FRUS 1929, II, 344; FO Report F 6144/3568/10 London, 25 November 1929; "Reds Again Launch Attack on Chinese," *New York Times*, 19 November 1929; Erickson, *Soviet High Command*, 242–243; ; Salminov and Velikanovm, *Order of Lenin Transbaikal Sky*, 56; Kuzman and Polkovyh, *On Guard for Peace*, 131 and map 4; Khetagurov, *Performance of Duty*, chap. 1. Government of Japan, "Declassified Observations," 213, Report 2.
54. Chuikov, *Mission to China*, 34.

55. Fedyuninsky, *In the East,* 23; Kuzman and Polkovyh, *On Guard for Peace,* 131, 134.

56. Fedyuninsky, *In the East,* 22–24 and passim; Government of Japan, "Declassified Observations," 216.

57. Government of Japan, "Declassified Observations," 221; Fedyuninsky, *In the East,* 25; Chuikov, *Mission to China,* 35.

58. Fedyuninsky, *In the East,* 23–25.

59. Chuikov, *Mission to China,* 35; Fedyuninsky, *In the East,* 33; ONI File 105-200, 12 December 1929. Elements of the 1st Proletariat Rifle Division, 1st and 3rd Tank Regiments, and six aircraft squadrons began to arrive on 22 November, after the fighting was over.

60. Cheng, *Sino-Russian Relations,* 156; Government of Japan, "Declassified Observations," 208, 221; Chuikov, *Mission to China,* 36; Kuzman and Polkovyh, *On Guard for Peace,* 132. A. P. Belorodov was a senior commander during World War II and retired as a general of the army.

61. Khetagurov, *Performance of Duty,* chap. 1.

62. Erickson, *Soviet High Command,* 244; Salminov and Velikanovm, *Order of Lenin Transbaikal Sky,* 57.

63. Chuikov, *Mission to China,* 36; Government of Japan, "Declassified Observations," 208, 221; Kuzman and Polkovyh, *On Guard for Peace,* 132; Chang, "CER Event," 239.

64. Government of Japan, "Declassified Observations," 208, 221.

65. Fedyuninsky, *In the East,* 34.

66. Salminov and Velikanovm, *Order of Lenin Transbaikal Sky,* 57.

67. Fedyuninsky, *In the East,* 30–31; Government of Japan, "Declassified Observations," 208, 209; Chuikov, *Mission to China,* 36.

68. Chuikov, *Mission to China,* 38; Government of Japan, "Declassified Observations," 209. See Situation Report 4, 20 November 1929; Garthoff, *Sino-Soviet Military Relations,* 23.

69. Chuikov, *Mission to China,* 38–39; Fedyuninsky, *In the East,* 39–40, 42; Government of Japan, "Declassified Observations," 209, 210.

70. Government of Japan, "Declassified Observations," 221; Fedyuninsky, *In the East,* 45.

71. Khetagurov, *Performance of Duty,* chap. 1; Government of Japan, "Declassified Observations," 221; Fedyuninsky, *In the East,* 35; Kuzman and Polkovyh, *On Guard for Peace,* 132; United Kingdom War Office, Peking Attaché, Military Report 1, 14 January 1930.

72. FO Report F 1673/106/10 14 January 1930, 21; Fedyuninsky, *In the East,* 46; Government of Japan, "Declassified Observations," 210; Dushenkin, "Defeat," 126; Ogarkov, "Manchouli-Dalainor Operation, 1929."

73. Fedyuninsky, *In the East,* 45; FRUS 1929, II, 353; FO Report F 1282/106/

10 Dairen, 13 February 1930; MA Peking Report 7670, 27 February 1930; Government of Japan, "Declassified Observations," 211.

74. FRUS 1929, II, 365, 373; United Kingdom War Office, Peking Attaché, Military Report 1, 14 January 1930; FO Report F 501/106/10 Peking, 9 December 1929; film, *Ruins and Bomb Damage at Station Puhetu in Manchuria, China, 1930*, http://www.criticalpast.com/.

75. Elleman and Kotkin, *Manchurian Railways*, 85; FO Report F 2696/106/10 Peking, 12 March 1930; Government of Japan, "Declassified Observations," 211, 214.

76. Government of Japan, "Declassified Observations," 212; Kulagin and Iakovlev, *Special Far Eastern Feat*, 164; Nathan, *Plague Prevention*, 2, 58, 73. The town warranted attention—Manchouli had been the scene of a devastating plague outbreak in 1910.

77. Fedyuninsky, *In the East*, 47; Government of Japan, "Declassified Observations," 212, 214; FO Report F 2796/106/10 Peking, 20 May 1930. Approximately 1,000 fuel "units" were taken with forty-five to fifty units filling a train car.

78. FO Report F 4762/106/10 Peking, 30 May 1930.

79. Ibid.; Elleman and Kotkin, *Manchurian Railways*, 96; Government of Japan, "Declassified Observations," 211. Japanese authorities were able to obtain the names of 192 White Russians arrested at Manchouli.

80. Lyons, *Assignment in Utopia*, 253.

81. FRUS 1929, II, 362; Yueng, "Chang Hsueh-liang," 129; "Blucher the Red Napoleon," *North China Daily News*, 28 November 1929.

82. Kang, "Chang Hsueh-liang and Chiang Kai-shek," 258.

83. Lih, Naumov, and Khlevniuk, *Stalin's Letters to Molotov*, 183.

84. FRUS 1929, II, 362, 374; Elleman and Kotkin, *Manchurian Railways*, 85.

85. Litvinov, *Notes*, 128.

86. Lih, Naumov, and Khlevniuk, *Stalin's Letters to Molotov*, 183. Emshanov was executed in 1937.

87. FO Report F 5146/106/10, 2 July 1930, para. 55.

88. Nathaniel Peffer, "In Manchuria China Again Faces a Crisis," *New York Times*, 8 December 1929.

89. FRUS 1929, II, 432; FO Reports F 279/106/10 and F 1104/106/10, 14 January 1930.

90. Fedyuninsky, *In the East*, 54; Khetagurov, *Performance of Duty*, chap. 1. Rokossovsky barely survived the Great Terror (he was arrested and tortured while his family sent into exile), but he was released in 1940. He became a marshal of the Soviet Union and later served as defense minister for the communist regime in Poland.

91. OKDVA stands for Special Red Banner Far Eastern Army (Osobaya Krasnoznamennaya Dal'ne-vostochaya armiya).

92. Salminov and Velikanovm, *Order of Lenin Transbaikal Sky*, 58, 59; Fedyuninsky, *In the East*, 54, 57; Khetagurov, *Performance of Duty*, chap. 1; Chuikov, *Mission to China*, 40.

Chapter 10. The 1929 Conflict and Interwar Warfare

1. Clausewitz, *On War*, 358.
2. Sun Tzu, *Art of War*, book IV.5, 85.
3. Clausewitz, *On War*, 75, 177.
4. Erickson, *Soviet High Command*, 284.
5. Erickson, *Soviet High Command*, 240, 292.
6. FO Report F 6195/3568/10 Peking, 1 November 1929.
7. Litvinov, *Notes*, 127. Koba was the name for Stalin used by his intimates.
8. Tian, "Chang," 140.
9. Glantz, *August Storm: Soviet 1945 Strategic Offensive*, 86; and Glantz, *August Storm: Tactical and Operational Combat*, 164. The Corps' 94th Division successfully battled the Werhmacht in 1944 as part of the 2nd Ukrainian Front; the 210th Division started World War II as part of the 20th Mechanized Corps and later distinguished itself during the fighting at Rzhev in 1942. See Poirier and Conner, *Red Army Order of Battle*, 298, 344; Glantz, *Battle for the Ukraine*, 30, Glantz, *Barbarossa Derailed*, 278.
10. "World's New Powder Magazine," *North China Daily News*, 13 August 1929.
11. FO Report F 6195/3568/10 Peking, 1 November 1929; "Marking Time in Siberia," *North China Daily News*, 29 August 1929; "The Wrangle with Russia," *North China Daily News*, 24 September 1929; "Soviet Cattle-Raiders," *North China Daily News*, 10 October 1929.
12. Fedchin, *Aircraft Navigation*, xv; Theodore Shabad, "Mikhail Gromov, Air Pioneer, Dies," *New York Times*, 25 January 1985. The arrival of some of the flight at Urga was captured in the short film *Pioneering Russian Flight from Moscow to Peking by Way of Mongolia (Known as the Great Flight)*, filmed in Peking, 13 July 1925, http://www.criticalpast.com/. Clay, "Squadrons."
13. Douhet, *Command*, 20, 24, 36; RAF Timeline, 1918–1929, *Royal Air Force*, http://www.raf.mod.uk/.
14. Douhet, *Command*, 58, 61.
15. United States Foreign Broadcast Information Service, *Field Regulations*, Article 164, dealt with ground support and fighter protection of bombers and observation aircraft. Article 174 addressed reconnaissance and aerial photography.
16. FRUS 1927, II, 13.
17. Kaufmann and Kaufmann, *Hitler's Blitzkrieg Campaigns*, 121; Wilbur and

How, *Missionaries*, 593, 663, 635; FRUS 1927, II, 330; FRUS 1921, I, 834–835; Euden and North, *Soviet Russia*, 281; Junling Cui, "Osborn Radio Station—China's First Radio Station," *Insight*, 29 January 2015, http://insight.amcham-shanghai.org/; "Sharp History: 1925–1930: First Japan-Made Radio," *Sharp*, http://www.sharp-world.com/.

18. Kuzman and Polkovyh, *On Guard for Peace*, 134.

19. Sella, "Red Army Doctrine," 252.

20. Ibid. Glantz, "Observing the Soviets," 157; Parrish, "Formation and Leadership," 63. As a comparison, in October 1936, the US Army, beyond a few failed prototypes, did not possess a single state-of-the-art tank. By 1939, it had fewer than 300 modern light tanks, with none armed with anything heavier than a machine gun. See Cameron, *Mobility, Shock, and Firepower*, 25, 133.

21. Savkin, *Basic Principles*, 40.

22. Looking forward to World War II, the link between military limitations and unconventional warfare becomes clearer. In 1929, Moscow restricted its military options, while after the fall of France in 1940, an isolated Britain had few alternatives in how to strike at the enemy. As a solution, both Russia in 1929 and England in 1940 raised unconventional warfare operations to important levels.

23. Fedyuninsky, *In the East*, 8.

24. FO Report F 4447/3568/10 Tokyo, 28 August 1929.

25. FO Report F 4449/3568/10 Tokyo, 30 August 1929.

26. Fedyuninsky, *In the East*, 8.

27. FO Report F 5297/3568/10 Peking, 31 August 1929; "Soviet Activities on the CER," *North China Daily News*, 11 July 1929; Salminov and Velikanovm, *Order of Lenin Transbaikal Sky*, 54, 56, 59; Lensen, *Damned Inheritance*, 66–67.

28. Government of Japan, "Declassified Observations," 201.

29. Ibid.; FO Report F 168/106/10 Peking, 20 November 1929. An early 1930 report stated that the Khabarovsk broadcasts could even reach Shanghai; see FO Report F 722/106/10 Peking, 1 March 1930.

30. FO Report F 2722/106/10 Peking, 21 March 1930.

31. Government of Japan, "Declassified Observations," 203; FO Reports F 6195/3568/10 Peking, 1 November 1929; F 151/106/10 Peking, 15 November 1929, and F 168/106/10 Peking, 20 November 1929.

32. For examples of claims for the Chinese conquest of the Soviet Far East, see Salminov and Velikanovm, *Order of Lenin Transbaikal Sky*, 55; Fedyuninsky, *In the East*, 6; Cherepanov, *Field of My Martial Feats*, 180.

33. Government of Japan, "Declassified Observations," 203; "Blagoveschensk Chinese Arrested," *North China Daily News*, 6 August 1929; FO Reports F 6195/3568/10 Peking, 1 November 1929, and F 151/106/10 Peking, 15 November 1929.

34. Fedyuninsky, *In the East*, 25.

35. Glantz, *Soviet Military Operational Art*, 67; Government of Japan, "Declassified Observations," 215.

36. Savkin, *Basic Principles*, 210–211; Government of Japan, "Declassified Observations," 213.

37. Chuikov, *Mission to China*, 35; Government of Japan, "Declassified Observations," 202, 216.

38. Savkin, *Basic Principles*, 38; Goldman, *Nomonhan*, 128; Glantz, *August Storm: Soviet 1945 Strategic Offensive*, 42, table 3.

39. Fedyuninsky, *In the East*, 23.

40. "The Wrangle with Russia," *North China Daily News*, 24 September 1929.

41. Kuzman and Polkovyh, *On Guard for Peace*, 135.

42. Patrikeeff, *Russian Politics*, 86; Glantz, *Soviet Military Operational Art*, 10, 24.

43. Sella, "Red Army Doctrine," 245–246; Glantz, "Observing the Soviets," 158–159; Glantz, *Soviet Military Operational Art*; Savkin, *Basic Principles*, 44; United States Foreign Broadcast Information Service, *Field Regulations*, Articles 8 and 25; Erickson, *Soviet High Command*, 318, 717ff., n80.

44. White, "Soviet Philosophy," 344; Glantz, *Soviet Military Operational Art*, 24–25.

45. Glantz, *Soviet Military Operational Art*, 20.

46. Government of Japan, "Declassified Observations," 212, 213; see pt. 3, Reports 2 and 3.

47. Glantz, *Soviet Military Operational Art*, 25.

48. Savkin, *Basic Principles*, 40, 44.

Chapter 11. A War of Consequences

1. Lyons, *Assignment in Utopia*, 251.

2. King, *Commissar Vanishes*, 9–10; Slyke, "Battle of the Hundred Regiments," 1002.

3. The Kinney letter can be found in MA Report 7670, "Mr. Kinney's Article on Manchuria," 27 February 1930, FO Report F 1282/106/10, 6 March 1930, and FO Report F 2696/106/10, 12 March 1930. The first copy was given to the US Military Attaché's office in Peiping, the second to the British Legation in Peiping, and the third to a *Manchester Guardian* reporter, who forwarded it to the British Legation.

4. FO Report F 1282/106/10, 6 March 1930—see handwritten note on top margin of p. 1 of Kinney Report; FO Report F 2696/106/10, 12 March 1930—see p. 3 of Lampson's introductory report.

5. FO Report F 2696/106/10, 12 March 1930—see handwritten note on cover sheet.

6. League of Nations, Document C.375M.288.1939.VII, "Telegram from the Union of Soviet Socialist Republics" (listed at http://biblio-archive.unog.ch/Dateien/CouncilMSD/C-397-M-301-1939_EN.pdf).

7. FRUS 1929, II, 419; Dyke, *Soviet Invasion of Finland*, 39; Garver, *Chinese–Soviet Relations*, 100.

8. Hsieh and Chu, *Foreign Interests*, 27–28.

9. MA Report 7670, 27 February 1930.

10. Patrikeeff, *Russian Politics*, 100–101.

11. MA Report 7670, 27 February 1930.

12. Ibid.

13. Dushenkin, "Defeat," 126; Cherepanov, *Field of My Martial Feats*, 181.

14. Patrikeeff, *Russian Politics*, chap. 7, 104–120.

15. MA Report 7670, 27 February 1930.

16. Kuzman and Polkovyh, *On Guard for Peace*, 124; Salminov and Velikanovm, *Order of Lenin Transbaikal Sky*, 56.

17. Government of Japan, "Declassified Observations"; see troop tables on 217–220.

18. Krivosheev, *Classification Secret Removed*, 66.

19. Glantz, "Red Army at War," 616.

20. Government of Japan, "Declassified Observations," 221.

21. Stephan, *Russian Far East*, 282.

22. MA Report 7670, 27 February 1930.

23. Ibid.; Abend, *My Life in China*, 106.

24. Dushenkin, "Defeat," 122, 123–125; Kuzman and Polkovyh, *On Guard for Peace*, 123; Salminov and Velikanovm, *Order of Lenin Transbaikal Sky*, 55; Suntsov and Tretiak, *Red Banner*, 90, 92; Bagrov and Sungorkin, *Red Banner*, 90. Vasily Blyukher became a marshal of the Soviet Union and was arrested along with his family on 22 October 1938. He reportedly died as his NKVD interrogators attempted to beat out a confession. He never broke. His wife, Galina, died in prison.

25. Covenant of the League of Nations, signed 28 June 1919, http://avalon.law.yale.edu/; Bassett, *League of Nations*, 3, 5; Henig, *Versailles and After*, 67–68.

26. Bassett, *League of Nations*, 378.

27. Houdsen, *League of Nations*, 129; Henig, *Versailles and After*, 46; Bassett, *League of Nations*, 17; Bassett, *League of Nations*, 230; Garver, *Chinese–Soviet Relations*, 100; also see the Covenant of the League of Nations. Ironically, following the 1939 Soviet invasion of Finland, when the League chose to act, China, dependent on Soviet military aid in fighting Japan, had become Russia's ally and was put into a dilemma over whether to support Finland, who, like China in 1929, was a victim of Soviet military aggression, or Soviet Russia. Unable to decide, Wellington Koo in Geneva abstained from voting, allowing the League to expel the Soviets, an act that briefly soured Sino-Soviet relations.

28. Patrikeeff, *Russian Politics*, 87.

29. Paine, *Wars for Asia*, 86.

30. Kang, "Chang Hsueh-liang and Chiang Kai-shek," 261.

31. Lattimore, *Manchuria*, 278.

32. FO Report F 5146/106/10, 2 July 1930, para. 47; Chen and Wang, "CER Crisis," 350.

33. Chen and Wang, "CER Crisis," 346–347.

34. Government of Japan, "Declassified Observations," 213.

35. "Chang Hsueh-liang" [obituary], *Telegraph*, 16 October 2001, http://www.telegraph.co.uk/.

36. Shuji, "Shock," 95.

37. Ienaga, *Pacific War*, 11.

38. Chen and Wang, "CER Crisis," 344.

39. Paine, *Wars for Asia*, 86–87; League of Nations, *Report of the Commission of Enquiry*, maps 2 and 4; Chen and Wang, "CER Crisis," 350; Erickson, *Soviet High Command*, 335–336.

40. Evans and Peattie, *Kaigun*, 200–201.

41. Shuji, "Shock," 95; Drea, *In the Service of the Emperor*, 25; Drea, *Japan's Imperial Army*, 152.

42. Murray and Millett, *Military Innovation*, 2–3, 51, 67–68; Drea, *In the Service of the Emperor*, 24; United States Marine Corps, *Small Wars Manual*, 2. In 1933, the Fleet Marine Force, designed for amphibious operations, was formed, and in 1934, the *Tentative Manual for Landing Operations* was adopted.

43. Vul, "He, Who Has Sown the Wind," 22. For more on Liang, see Tang, *Global Space*, and Kaufmann, "One Nation Among Many."

44. Lensen, *Damned Inheritance*, page facing 1.

45. Patrikeeff, *Russian Politics*, 104.

46. "China and Russia Will Jointly Develop Black Bear Island," *Epoch Times*, 24 February 2011, http://www.epochtimes.com/b5/11/2/24/n3179098p.htm. See also George Washington University National Security Archive, *Sino-Soviet Border Conflict*.

47. Lih, Naumov, and Khlevniuk, *Stalin's Letters to Molotov*, 175.

48. Service, *Stalin*, 27.

49. Even after the immense Soviet victory in 1945, Stalin remained obsessed with exceeding the achievement of the tsars. When complimented over the Red Army's conquest of Berlin by American diplomat W. Averell Harriman at Potsdam, Stalin replied, "Tsar Alexander got to Paris." As the price for invading Manchuria in 1945, Stalin demanded—and got—from the Western Allies all the territories lost in the 1904–1905 Russo-Japanese War plus most of the Kurile Islands. Afterward, he reimposed control over the Kwantung Leasehold, the SMR, and CER, protected by a Red Army military garrison. See Harriman, "Governor W. Averell Harriman Oral History Interview," 19; Dikotter, *Tragedy of Liberation*, 123.

50. Rohwer and Monakov, "Soviet Union's Ocean-Going Fleet," 837.

Bibliography

Serials

Associated Press
Bulletin of International News
Chicago Tribune
China Monthly Review (Shanghai)
Current History: A Monthly Magazine of the New York Times
Epoch Times
Evening Post (Wellington, New Zealand)
Izvestia
Kuo Min (Official News Agency of the Republic of China in 1929)
Life Magazine
Militant (New York)
New York Times
North China Daily News (Shanghai)
Rengo News Agency (Japan)
Reuters
Sydney Morning Herald
TASS
Telegraph
Time Magazine
Times
Tokyo Nichi Nichi Shimbun

Archival Sources

League of Nations. League of Nations Document C.375M.288.1939.VII.

United Kingdom Foreign Office. Political Departments Records (Groups FO 371/13891-638, FO 371/13954-632, FO 371/13955, FO 371/14699, FO 137/14700).

United Kingdom War Office. China (General) File no. 1/2 and Peking Military Attaché Reports, 1929–1930.

United States Marine Corps. Summaries of Intelligence from the Marine Detachment, American Legation, Peking, 1926–1927.

United States Military and Naval Attaché and Office of Naval Intelligence

Reports. National Archives and Records Administration (NARA) Record Groups 38.4.2, 38.4.3, 165.4.1, 165.4.9, 407.2.3, and 457.2.

Photographs (Web-based)

General Ivan Kalmykov's armored train in Vladivostok: http://digitallibrary.usc.edu/cdm/ref/collection/p15799coll46/id/59.

Red Army 5th Fighter Squadron (Eastern Front)

Squadron Fokker D.XI Fighter: http://www.bellabs.ru/Fotab/KVGD/IS-5_01.html.

Squadron Pilots, Eastern Front, 1929: http://www.bellabs.ru/Fotab/KVGD/IS-5_02.html.

Prewar photo of pilots, 5th Fighter Squadron, Smolensk, June 1929: http://www.bellabs.ru/Fotab/KVGD/IS-5_08.html.

Red Army 19th Bomber Squadron (Western Front)

Squadron personnel in front of R-1 Aircraft: http://www.bellabs.ru/Fotab/KVGD/AO-19_004.html.

Squadron R-1 bomber with crew: http://www.bellabs.ru/Fotab/KVGD/AO-19_02.html.

Squadron R-1 bomber with skis in place of landing gear: http://www.bellabs.ru/Fotab/KVGD/AO-19_005.html.

Red Army 40th "Lenin" Bomber Squadron (Eastern Front)

Four R-1 bombers in formation: http://www.bellabs.ru/Fotab/KVGD/AS-40_003.html.

Two squadron R-1 bombers: http://www.bellabs.ru/Fotab/KVGD/AS-40_002.html.

Red Army 68th Seaplane Squadron, Amur River Flotilla

Squadron MR-1 seaplane on the Amur River: http://www.bellabs.ru/Fotab/KVGD/ORchAO-68_01.html.

Seaplane tender *Amur* (former monitor *Whirlwind*): http://www.bellabs.ru/Fotab/KVGD/ORchAO-68_04.html.

Personnel and seaplanes with the *Amur* in the background: http://www.bellabs.ru/Fotab/KVGD/ORchAO-68_11.html.

Squadron commander Edward Martinovich Lucht: http://www.bellabs.ru/Fotab/KVGD/ORchAO-68_05.html.

Crewmembers relax on the *Amur:* http://www.bellabs.ru/Fotab/KVGD/ORchAO-68_08.html.

Squadron personnel with MR-1 seaplanes: http://www.bellabs.ru/Fotab/KVGD/ORchAO-68_09.html.

Battle of Lahasusu

Photo of the captured Chinese patrol craft *Tsen-I* with a Soviet river monitor in the background: http://f-picture.net/fp/6049d4164c4d40c3b35ac5aa2812d551.

Western Front

http://sammler.ru/index.php?s=4f08d9f309682d1061542868 1c300a20&-showtopic=56247&st=0&.

1. Russian officers holding the captured battle colors of the 15th Mixed Brigade, Northeast Frontier Defense Force, and a smaller military gendarme banner.
2. Chinese cavalry troop (possibly from the 15th Mixed Brigade or 10th Cavalry Regiment at the Manchouli railroad station).
3. Chinese cavalry troop seated with officers walking in the background, probably on the Western Front.

Monuments to Fallen Red Army Soldiers

Special Far East Army (ODVA) Monument at Vladivostok Naval Cemetery, photo posted on 11 May 2012: http://commons.wikimedia.org/wiki/File:Vladivostok_mishanfu.JPG.

ODVA Monument at Ussuriysk, photo posted 20 September 2011: http://commons.wikimedia.org/wiki/File:Братская_могила_красноармейцев,_погибших_на_КВЖД,_Уссурийск.JPG.

Works Cited

Abend, Hallet. *My Life in China, 1926–1941*. New York: Harcourt Brace, 1943.

Andrew, Christopher. "British Intelligence and the Breach with Russia in 1927." *Historical Journal* 25, no. 4 (1982): 957–964.

The Annual Register: A Review of Public Events at Home and Abroad for the Year 1920. London: Longmans, Green, 1921.

Asada Masafumi. "The China–Russia–Japan Military Balance in Manchuria, 1906–1918." *Modern Asian Studies* 44, no. 6 (2010): 1283–1311.

———. *History of Russia and the Chinese Eastern Railway Management: "Manchuria," 1896–1935* [in Japanese]. Nagoya: Nagoya University Press, 2012.

Bagrov, V. N., and N. F. Sungorkin. *Red Banner: The Amur River Flotilla* [in Russian]. Moscow: Ministry of Defense Military Press, 1976.

Bassett, John Spencer. *The League of Nations: A Chapter in World Politics.* New York: Longmans, Green, 1928.

Bergère, Marie Claire. *Sun Yat-sen.* Translated by Janet Lloyd. Stanford, CA: Stanford University Press, 1998.

Bickers, Robert. *Empire Made Me: An Englishman Adrift in Shanghai.* New York: Columbia University Press, 2003.

Bisher, Jaime. *White Terror: Cossack Warlords of the Trans-Siberian.* New York: Routledge, 2005.

Bland, John Otway Percy. *China, Japan, and Korea.* New York: Charles Scribner's & Sons, 1921.

———. "Manchuria" and "Mongolia." In *Encyclopaedia Britannica,* vol. 31, edited by Hugh Chisholm. New York: Encyclopaedia Britannica, 1922.

Block, John D. *Escape Siberia to California, the 65 Year Providential Journey of Our Family.* Self-published, 1995.

Boorman, Howard L., and Richard C. Howard, eds. *Biographical Dictionary of Republican China.* New York: Columbia University Press, 1970.

Bulstrode, Beatrix. *A Tour in Mongolia.* London: Methuen, 1920. http://digital.library.upenn.edu/women/bulstrode/mongolia/mongolia.html.

Bunn, Henry W. "Military Events of the World." *National Service* 8, no. 4 (1920): 193–255.

Cameron, Robert S. *Mobility, Shock, and Firepower: The Emergence of the US Army's Armor Branch, 1917–1945.* Washington: US Army Center of Military History, 2008.

Carnegie Endowment for International Peace. *Manchuria: Treaties and Agreements.* Washington, DC: Byron Adams Press, 1921.

———. *Outer Mongolia: Treaties and Agreements, Division of International Law Pamphlet 41.* Washington, DC: Carnegie Endowment, 1921.

Carr, E. H. *The Russian Revolution from Lenin to Stalin, 1917–1929.* New York: Palgrave, 1979.

Caufield, Catherine. "Upstream Slowly: The Amur River, Siberia." *Sierra* 78, no. 3 (1993). http://www.questia.com/library/1G1-13695274/upstream-slowly.

Ch'en, Jerome. "Defining Chinese Warlords and Their Factions." *Bulletin of the School of Oriental and African Studies, University of London* 31, no. 3 (1968): 563–600.

Ch'i, Hsi-sheng. *The Chinese Warlord System: 1916–1928.* Washington DC: American University, 1969.

———. *Warlord Politics in China, 1916–1928.* Stanford, CA: Stanford University Press, 1976.

Chang Te-liang. "The CER Event and Anti-Russian War: The Whole Story" [in Chinese]. In Guo, *Chinese Eastern Railway*, 232–245.

Cheng, Tien-fong. *A History of Sino-Russian Relations*. Washington, DC: Public Affairs Press, 1957.

Chen Kuiyuan. *The Revolution of 1911: Opening the Door to Progress in China*. Qiushi, the Organ of the Central Committee of the Communist Party of China; 2012. http://english.qstheory.cn/culture/ 201204 /t20120401_14 9164 .htm.

Chen Tsung-yan and Wang Chien-hsueh. "The CER Crisis and the Mukden Incident" [in Chinese]. In Guo, *Chinese Eastern Railway*, 344–350.

Chen Zhixin. "Establishment of the CER Guard Command and Eastern Provinces Special Zone" [in Chinese]. In Guo, *Chinese Eastern Railway*, 16–26.

Cherepanov, A. I. *The Field of My Martial Feats* [in Russian]. Moscow: Military Press, 1984. http://militera.lib.ru/memo/russian/cherepanov_ai/index .html.

Chiang Kia-shek. *A Report to the People on the Chinese Eastern Railway Incident* [in Chinese]. Nanking: Government of the Republic of China, 1929. http://blog.sina.com.cn/s/blog_5174f17701oodnj6.html.

Chiu, Hungdah. "Constitutional Development and Reform in the Republic of China on Taiwan." *Occasional Papers/Reprints Series in Contemporary Asian Studies* 2, no. 115 (1993): 2–61.

Chou, Shun-hsin. "Railway Development and Economic Growth in Manchuria." *China Quarterly* 45 (1971): 57–84.

Christopher, James W. *Conflict in the Far East: American Diplomacy in China from 1928–1933*. Leiden, Netherlands: E. J. Brill, 1950.

Chuikov, V. I. *Mission to China* [in Russian]. Moscow: Military Press, 1983. http://militera.lib.ru/memo/russian/chuykov_vi_1/index.html.

Churchill, Winston. *The World Crisis*. Volume 2. London: Thornton Butterworth, 1923.

Clausewitz, Carl von. *On War*. Edited by Michael Howard and Peter Paret. Princeton, NJ: Princeton University Press, 1976.

Clay, Steven E. "Squadrons, Heavier than Air." In *US Army Order of Battle, 1919–1941*, 3:1359–1438. Fort Leavenworth, KS: Combat Studies Institute Press, 2006.

Clubb, O. Edmund. *China and Russia: The "Great Game."* New York: Columbia University Press, 1971.

Conquest, Robert. *The Great Terror: A Reassessment*. New York: Oxford University Press, 1990.

Cooke, Ian. "Propaganda as a Weapon? Influencing International Opinion." British Library. http://www.bl.uk/world-war-one/articles/propaganda-as-a-weapon.

Cooling, Benjamin Franklin. "Towards a More Usable Past: A Modest Plea for a Newer Typology of Military History." *Military Affairs* 52 (1998): 29–31.

Coox, Alvin D. *Nomonhan: Japan against Russia, 1939*. Stanford, CA: Stanford University Press, 1985.

Crossley, Pamela Kyle. *The Manchus*. Boston: Blackwell Publishers, 1997.

Davis, Donald E., and Eugene P. Trani. *Distorted Mirrors: Americans and Their Relations with Russia and China in the Twentieth Century*. Columbia: University of Missouri Press, 2009.

Dickenson, Frederick R. *War and National Reinvention: Japan in the Great War, 1914–1919*. Cambridge, MA: Harvard University Press, 1999.

Dikotter, Frank. *The Tragedy of Liberation: A History of the Chinese Revolution, 1945–1957*. New York: Bloomsbury Press, 2013.

Dingle, John E. *China's Revolution, 1911–1912: A Historical and Political Record of the Civil War*. New York: McBride, Nast, 1912.

Dmitriev-Mamonov, A. I., and A. F. Zdziarski. *Guide to the Great Siberian Railway*. Translated by L. Kukol-Yasnopolsky and John Marshal. St. Petersburg: Ministry of Ways of Communication, 1900.

Douhet, Guilio. *Command of the Air*. Tuscaloosa: University of Alabama Press, 2009.

Drea, Edward J. *In the Service of the Emperor: Essays on the Imperial Japanese Army*. Lincoln: University of Nebraska Press, 1998.

———. *Japan's Imperial Army: Its Rise and Fall, 1853–1945*. Lawrence: University Press of Kansas, 2009.

Dull, Paul S. "The Assassination of Chang Tso-lin." *Far East Quarterly* 11, no. 4 (1952): 453–463.

Dunscomb, Paul E. *Japan's Siberian Intervention, 1918–1922: "A Great Disobedience against the People."* New York: Lexington Books, 2011.

Duranty, Walter. *I Write as I Please*. New York: Simon & Schuster, 1935.

Durov, V. *Russian and Soviet Orders* [in Russian]. Moscow: Lenin History Museum, 1974.

Dushenkin, V., ed. "Defeat of the Chinese Military in the CER Region in 1929" [in Russian]. *Military Encyclopedia*, 11:121–126. Moscow: Military Press, 1969.

Duus, Peter. *The Abacus and the Sword: The Japanese Penetration of Korea, 1895–1910*. Berkeley: University of California Press, 1995.

Dyke, Carl van. *The Soviet Invasion of Finland, 1939–1940*. Portland, OR: Frank Cass, 1997.

Echevarria, Antulio J. *After Clausewitz: German Military Thinkers before the Great War*. Lawrence: University Press of Kansas, 2001.

Efimov, A. V., A. N. Manzhosov, and P. F. Sidorov. *Armored Trains in the Great Patriotic War, 1941–1945* [in Russian]. Moscow: Transport, 1992.

Elleman, Bruce A. *Diplomacy and Deception: The Secret History of Sino-Soviet Diplomatic Relations, 1917–1927*. New York: E. M. Sharpe, 1997.

———. *Modern Chinese Warfare, 1795–1989*. New York: Routledge, 2001.

———. *Wilson and China: A Revised History of the Shandong Question*. New York: Routledge, 2015.

Elleman, Bruce A., and Stephen Kotkin, eds. *Manchurian Railways and the Opening of China: An International History*. New York: E. M. Sharpe, 2010.

Erickson, John. *The Soviet High Command: A Military Political History, 1918–1941*. 3rd ed. New York: Frank Cass, 2001.

Esherick, Joseph W. *The Origins of the Boxer Uprising*. Berkeley: University of California Press, 1987.

Euden, Xenia Joukoff, and Robert C. North. *Soviet Russia and the East, 1920–1927: A Documentary Survey*. Stanford, CA: Stanford University Press, 1957.

Evans, David C., and Mark R. Peattie. *Kaigun: Strategy, Tactics, and Technology in the Imperial Japanese Navy, 1887–1941*. Annapolis, MD: Naval Institute Press, 1997.

Faulstich, Edith M. *The Siberian Sojourn*. Complied posthumously by Fred Faulstich. 1977. https://edithfaulstich.wordpress.com.

Fedchin, S. S. *Aircraft Navigation* [in Russian]. Technical translation by NASA. Moscow: Transport Aircraft Press, 1966.

Fedyuninsky, Ivan I. *In the East* [in Russian]. Moscow: Military Publishing, 1985.

Fenby, Jonathan. *Chiang Kai-shek: China's Generalissimo and the Nation He Lost*. New York: Carroll & Graf, 2003.

Ferrell, Robert H. *Peace in Their Time: The Origins of the Kellogg-Briand Pact*. New Haven, CT: Yale University Press, 1952.

Fitzgerald, John. "The Misconceived Revolution: State and Society in China's Nationalist Revolution, 1923–26." *Journal of Asian Studies* 49, no. 2 (1990): 323–343.

Flory, Harriette. "The ARCOS Raid and the Rupture of Anglo-Soviet Relations, 1927." *Journal of Contemporary History* 12, no. 4 (1977): 707–723.

Forsyth, James. *A History of the Peoples of Siberia: Russia's North Asian Colony, 1581–1990*. Cambridge: Cambridge University Press, 1992.

Furuya, Kenji. *Chiang Kai-shek: His Life and Times*. New York: St. John's University Press, 1981.

Gao, James Z. *Historical Dictionary of Modern China (1800–1949)*. Plymouth, UK: Scarecrow Press, 2009.

Garthoff, Raymond L., ed. *Sino-Soviet Military Relations*. New York: Praeger, 1966.

Garver, John W. *Chinese–Soviet Relations, 1937–1945: The Diplomacy of Chinese Nationalism*. New York: Oxford University Press, 1988.

Gatzke, Hans W. "Russo-German Military Collaboration During the Weimar Republic." *American Historical Review* 63, no. 3 (1958): 565–597.

George Washington University National Security Archive. *The Sino-Soviet Border Conflict, 1969: US Reactions and Diplomatic Maneuvers, National Security*

Electronic Briefing Book 49. Edited by William Burr. 2001. http://www.gwu.edu/~nsarchiv/NSAEBB/NSAEBB49/.

Gilbert, Martin. *The First World War: A Complete History*. New York: Holt, 1994.

Gillin, Donald G. "Portrait of a Warlord: Yen Hsi-shan in Shansi Province, 1911–1930." *Journal of Asian Studies* 19, no. 3 (1960): 289–306.

Glantz, David M. *August Storm: The 1945 Soviet Strategic Offensive in Manchuria*. Leavenworth Paper No. 7. Fort Leavenworth, KS: Combat Studies Institute, 1983.

———. *August Storm: The Soviet Tactical and Operational Combat in Manchuria, 1945*. Leavenworth Paper No. 8. Fort Leavenworth, KS: Combat Studies Institute, 1983.

———. *Barbarossa Derailed: The Battle for Smolensk, 10 July–10 September 1941*. Volume 1. Solihull, UK: Helion, 2010.

———. "Observing the Soviets: US Army Attaches in Eastern Europe During the 1930s." *Journal of Military History* 55, no. 2 (1991): 153–184.

———. "The Red Army at War, 1941–1945: Sources and Interpretations." *Journal of Military History* 62, no. 3 (1998): 595–617.

———. *Soviet Military Operational Art: In Pursuit of Deep Battle*. New York: Frank Cass, 1991.

Glantz, David M., and Harold S. Orenstein, trans. and ed. *The Battle for the Ukraine: The Red Army's Korsun'-Shevchenkovskii Offensive, 1944*. London: Frank Cass, 2003.

Goldman, Stuart D. *Nomonhan, 1939: The Red Army's Victory that Changed World War II*. Annapolis, MD: Naval Institute Press, 2012.

Goldstein, Lyle J. "Return to Zhenbao Island: Who Started Shooting and Why It Matters." *China Quarterly* 168 (2001): 985–997.

Gottschang, Thomas R., and Diana Lary. *Swallows and Settlers: The Great Migration from North China to Manchuria*. Ann Arbor: University of Michigan Press, 2000.

Government of Japan. "Declassified Observations on the Conspiracy Case Concerning the CER and Soviet Union" [in Japanese]. In *The Manchurian Incident, Contemporary Historical Documents, Volume 11*, edited by Kobayashi Tatsuo, Shimada Toshihiko, and Inaba Masao, 200–225. Tokyo: Macmillan, 1965.

Government of Japan, Ministry of Foreign Affairs [JMFA I.3.3]. "The Sino-Soviet Conflict and the Renunciation of War Treaty Relations." In *Documents on Japanese Foreign Policy*. Part 1, volume 3, chapter 3. http://www.mofa.go.jp/mofaj/annai/honsho /shiryo/archives/s21-3.html.

Graves, William S. *America's Siberian Adventure: 1918–1920*. New York: Peter Smith, 1941.

Guderian, Heinz. *Panzer Leader*. New York: Ballantine, 1957.

Guo Shengjun. "The Russian Railway Guard and the Russian Invasion of China" [in Chinese]. In Guo, *Chinese Eastern Railway*, 1–15.

Guo Shengjun, ed. *The Chinese Eastern Railway and the Chinese Eastern Railway*

Crisis—Zhang Research Center [in Chinese]. Shenyang: Liaoning People's Publishing, 2010.

Hard, William. *Raymond Robins' Own Story.* New York: Harper & Brothers, 1920.

Harriman, W. Averell. "Governor W. Averell Harriman Oral History Interview." Conducted by by Bernard W. Poirier, 10 January 1980. Independence, MO: Harry S. Truman Library. http://www.trumanlibrary.org/oralhist/harrima1.htm.

Harrison, James P. "The Li Li-san Line and the CCP in 1930 (Part I)." *China Quarterly*, no. 14 (1963): 178–194.

Haywood, Anthony. *Engineer of Revolutionary Russia: Iurii V. Lomonosov (1876–1952) and the Railways.* Burlington, VT: Ashgate, 2011.

Henig, Ruth. *Versailles and After, 1919–1933.* New York: Routledge, 1995.

He Zhiming. "The 1929 Chinese Eastern Railroad Incident in the Northeast" [in Chinese]. In Guo, *Chinese Eastern Railway*, 172–185.

Hopkirk, Peter. *The Great Game: The Struggle for Empire in Central Asia.* New York: Kodansha International, 1990.

———. *Setting the East Ablaze: Lenin's Dream of an Empire in Asia.* New York: Kodansha International, 1995.

Hornbeck, Stanley K. *The Situation in China.* New York: China Society of America, 1927.

Hosek, Martin. "The Hailar Incident: The Nadir of Troubled Relations between the Czechoslovak Legionnaires and the Japanese Army, April 1920." *Acta Slavica Iaponica* 29 (2011): 103–122.

Houdsen, Martyn. *The League of Nations and the Organization of Peace.* New York: Pearson Education, 2012.

Hsieh, C. Y., and M. C. Chu. *Foreign Interests in the Mining Industry in China.* Shanghai: China Institute of Pacific Relations, 1931.

Hsu, Kai-yu. *Chou En-lai: China's Gray Eminence.* Garden City, NY: Doubleday Anchor, 1969.

Hu Sheng. *From the Opium War to the May the Fourth Movement.* Volume 2. Beijing: Foreign Language Press, 1991.

Ienaga, Saburo. *The Pacific War, 1931–1945.* New York: Pantheon Books, 1978.

International Relations Committee. *The Sino-Soviet Crisis: The Actual Facts Brought to Light.* Nanking: Government of the Republic of China, 1929.

Iriye, Akira. "Chang Hsueh-Liang and the Japanese." *Journal of Asian Studies* 20, no. 1 (1960): 33–43.

Isby, David, and Jeffery Ethell. *Handbook on Japanese Military Forces.* Baton Rouge: Louisiana State University Press, 1991.

Jennings, John M. "The Mad Baron's March: International Rivalries, the Russian Civil War, and Baron Ungern-Sternberg's Invasion of Mongolia, 1920–1921." Unpublished paper, 2014.

Jin Heng. "The Nature of Tsarist Russia's Inroads into China: The Impact of the CER Treaties" [in Chinese]. In Guo, *Chinese Eastern Railway*, 76–83.

Jones, R. E., G. H. Rarey, and R. J. Icks. *The Fighting Tanks since 1916*. Washington, DC: National Service Publishing, 1933.

Jones, William C. "Diary of Lt. William C. Jones, 2nd Lt. US Army." Edited by Dale C. Jones; transcribed by Robb Adams. 2008. http://nortvoods.net/rrs/japan/journal-1.htm.

Jordan, Donald A. *The Northern Expedition: China's National Revolution*. Honolulu: University Press of Hawaii, 1976.

Jowett, Philip. *The Armies of Warlord China, 1911–1928*. Atglen, PA: Schiffer Military History, 2013.

Kainikara, Sanu. *Red Air: Politics in Russian Air Power.* Boca Raton, FL: Universal Publishers, 2007.

Kang Yanhua. "Chang Hsueh-liang and Chiang Kai-shek: Understanding their Tacit Differences during the CER Incident" [in Chinese]. In Guo, *Chinese Eastern Railway*, 256–268.

Kaufmann, Alison Adcock. "One Nation among Many: Foreign Models in the Constitutional Thought of Liang Qichao." PhD diss., University of California, Berkeley, 2007.

Kaufmann, J. E., and H. W. Kaufmann. *Hitler's Blitzkrieg Campaigns: The Invasion and Defense of Western Europe, 1939–1940*. Cambridge, MA: De Capo Press, 1993.

Kedzior, Richard E. *Evolution and Endurance: The US Army Division in the Twentieth Century*. Santa Monica, CA: Rand, 2000.

Kellogg, Frank B. "The War Prevention Policy of the United States." *American Journal of International Law* 22, no. 2 (1928): 253–261.

Kennan, George F. *The Decision to Intervene*. Princeton, NJ: Princeton University Press, 1958.

———. *Russia and the West under Lenin and Stalin*. Boston: Little, Brown, 1961.

Khetagurov, Georgy. *Performance of Duty* [in Russian]. Moscow: Military Publishing, 1977. http://militera.lib.ru/memo/khetagurov_gi.index.html.

King, David. *The Commissar Vanishes: The Falsification of Photographs and Art in Stalin's Russia*. New York: Metropolitan, 1997.

King, William C. *King's Complete History of the World War, 1914–1918*. Springfield, MA: History Associates, 1922.

Kipp, Jacob W. "Lenin and Clausewitz: The Militarization of Marxism, 1914–1921." *Military Affairs* 49, no. 4 (1985): 184–191.

Kirkpatrick, Jean. "Dictatorships and Double Standards." *Commentary Magazine* 68, no. 5 (1979): 34–45.

Kotkin, Stephan. *Stalin: Paradoxes of Power, 1878–1928*. New York: Penguin Press, 2014.

Koyrev, E. A., E. M. Orekhov, and N. N. Fomin. *Tanks* [in Russian]. Moscow: DOSAAF, 1973.

Krivosheev, G. F. *Classification Secret Removed: Soviet Casualties and Combat Losses in Wars and Military Conflicts* [in Russian]. Moscow: Ministry of Defense, Military Press, 1993.

Kuhn, Bert L. "What War Is Like in China." *Current History* 41, no. 4 (1922): 821–829.

Kulagin, V. M., and N. N. Iakovlev. *Special Far Eastern Feat* [in Russian]. Moscow: Young Guard, 1970.

Kuo Mo-Jo and Josiah W. Bennett. "A Poet with the Northern Expedition." *Far Eastern Quarterly* 3, no. 4 (1944): 362–380.

Kuzman, G. F., and N. F. Polkovyh. *On Guard for Peace (1921–1940)* [in Russian]. Moscow: Ministry of Defense Military Press, 1959.

Lary, Diana. *Region and Nation: The Kwangsi Clique in Chinese Politics, 1925–1937*. Cambridge: Cambridge University Press, 1974.

———. *Warlord Soldiers*. New York: Cambridge University Press, 1985.

Lary, Diana, and Stephen MacKinnon, eds. *The Scars of War: The Impact of Warfare on Modern China*. Vancouver: University of British Columbia Press, 2001.

Lattimore, Owen. *Manchuria: Cradle of Conflict*. New York: Macmillan, 1932.

Lau, Kit-ching Chan. *China, Britain, and Hong Kong, 1895–1945*. Hong Kong: China University Press, 1990.

League of Nations. *Report of the Commission of Enquiry of the League of Nations, signed at Peiping, September 4, 1932*. Reprint, Taipei: Ch'eng Wen, 1971.

Lee, Chong-sik. *Revolutionary Struggle in Manchuria: Chinese Communism and Soviet Interests, 1922–1945*. Berkeley: University of California Press, 1983.

Lenin, Vladimir. *Lenin: Collected Works*. Volume 44. Translated by Clemens Dutt. Moscow: Progress Publishers, 1975.

Lensen, George A. *The Damned Inheritance: The Soviet Union and the Manchurian Crises, 1924–1935*. Tallahassee, FL: Diplomatic Press, 1974.

———. *Japanese Recognition of the USSR, Soviet–Japanese Relations, 1921–1930*. Tokyo: Sophia University Press, 1970.

———. *The Russo-Chinese War*. Tallahassee, FL: Diplomatic Press, 1967.

Lescot, Patrick. *Before Mao: The Untold Story of Li Lisan and the Creation of Communist China*. Translated by Steven Rendall. New York: Harper Collins, 2004.

Li, Chien-Nung. *The Political History of China, 1840–1928*. Stanford, CA: Stanford University Press, 1956.

Liaoning Provincial Archives. *Selected Historical Materials of Liaoning Province, No. 21: The 1929 "Anti-Soviet" Frontier Defense Service Participating Units* [in Chinese]. Shenyang: People's Press of Liaoning, 1987.

Lih, Lars T., Oleg V. Naumov, and Oleg V. Khlevniuk. *Stalin's Letters to Molotov*. New Haven, CT: Yale University Press, 1995.

Lin Yutang. "The Dog-Meat General." In *A World of Great Stories*, edited by Hiram Haydn and John Cournos, 786–788. New York: Crown, 1947.

Litvinov, Maxim. *Notes for a Journal*. New York: William Morrow, 1955.

Liu, F. F. *A Military History of Modern China, 1924–1949*. Princeton, NJ: Princeton University Press, 1956.

Lorge, Peter. *War, Politics and Society in Early Modern China 900–1795*. New York: Routledge, 2005.

Lukoianov, Igro V. "Russian Imperialism in the Far East at the Turn of the Twentieth Century: The Collapse of S. Iu. Witte's Program of Economic Expansion." In *Imperiology: From Empirical Knowledge to Discussing the Russian Empire*, edited by Kimitaka Matsuzato, 225–244. Tokyo: Slavic Research Center, 2007.

Lu Yan. *Re-Understanding Japan: Chinese Perspectives, 1895–1945*. Honolulu: University of Hawaii Press, 2004.

Lyons, Eugene. *Assignment in Utopia*. London: Harcourt Brace, 1937.

MacMillan, Margaret. *Paris, 1919: Six Months that Changed the World*. New York: Random House, 2001.

Maddox, Robert J. *The Unknown War with Russia: Wilson's Siberian Intervention*. San Rafael, CA: Presidio Press, 1977.

Mao Tse-tung. *Selected Military Writings of Mao Tse-tung*. Peking: Foreign Languages Press, 1968.

Matsusaka, Yohihisa Tak. *The Making of Japanese Manchuria, 1904–1932*. Cambridge, MA: Harvard University Asia Center, 2001.

McCormack, Gavan. *Chang Tso-lin in Northeast China, 1911–1928: China, Japan, and the Manchurian Idea*. Stanford, CA: Stanford University Press, 1977.

Mets, David R. "The Origins of Soviet Air Theory and Doctrine." *Military Review* 55, no. 8 (1975): 36–49.

Meyer, Karl E., and Shareen Blair Brysac. *Tournament of Shadows: The Great Game and the Race for Empire in Central Asia*. Washington, DC: Counterpoint, 1999.

Modern Warfare in China in 1924–1925: Struggle between Mukden and Peking. Film 2424. London: Imperial War Museum, 1925.

Moffat, Ian C. D. "Forgotten Battlefields—Canadians in Siberia, 1918–1919." *Canadian Military Journal* 8, no. 3 (2007): 73–83.

"Momentous Days in China." *Current History* 16, no. 4 (July 1922): 721.

Morley, James William. *Japan Erupts: The London Naval Conference and the Manchurian Incident, 1928–1932*. New York: Columbia University Press, 1984.

———. *The Japanese Thrust into Siberia 1918*. New York: Columbia University Press, 1957.

———. "The Russian Revolution in the Amur Basin." *American Slavic and East European Review* 16, no. 4 (1957), 450–472.

Mosher, John. *Japanese Post Offices in China and Manchuria*. Lawrence, MA: Quarterman, 1978.

Murakoshi, Nobuo, and Glenn T. Trewartha. "Land Utilization Maps of Manchuria." *Geographical Review* 20, no. 3 (1930): 480–493.

Murray, Williamson, and Allan R. Millett. *Military Innovation in the Interwar Period.* New York: Cambridge University Press, 1996.

Nathan, Andrew J. *Peking Politics, 1918–1923: Factionalism and the Failure of Constitutionalism.* Berkeley: University of California Press, 1976.

Nathan, Carl F. *Plague Prevention and Politics in Manchuria, 1910–1931.* Cambridge, MA: Harvard University Press, 1967.

Nish, Ian. *The Origins of the Russo-Japanese War.* London: Longman Group, 1985.

Ogarkov, N. V., ed. "Manchouli-Dalainor Operation, 1929" [in Russian]. In *Soviet Army Encyclopedia.* Moscow: Military Press, 1978.

Paine, S. C. M. *The Wars for Asia, 1911–1949.* New York: Cambridge University Press, 2012.

Paret, Peter, ed. *Makers of Modern Strategy from Machiavelli to the Nuclear Age.* Princeton, NJ: Princeton University Press, 1986.

Parrish, Michael. "Formation and Leadership of the Soviet Mechanized Corps in 1941." *Military Affairs* 47, no. 2 (1983): 63–66.

Patrikeeff, Felix. *Russian Politics in Exile: The Northeast Balance of Power, 1924–1931.* New York: Palgrave with St. Antony's College, Oxford University, 2002.

Phillips, Richard T. "'A Picturesque but Hopeless Resistance': Rehe in 1933." *Modern Asia Studies* 42, no. 4 (2008): 733–750.

Poirier, Robert G., and Albert Z. Conner. *The Red Army Order of Battle in the Great Patriotic War, Including Data from 1919 to Postwar Years.* Novato, CA: Presidio Press, 1984.

Powell, John B. *My Twenty-Five Years in China.* New York: Macmillan, 1945.

Poznansky, Vladimir S. *Siberian Red General* [in Russian]. Novosiberisk: Nauka Publishing, 1972.

Preston, Diana. *The Boxer Rebellion: The Dramatic Story of China's War on Foreigners that Shook the World in the Summer of 1900.* New York: Berkley Books, 1999.

Pye, Lucien W. *Warlord Politics: Conflict and Coalition in the Modernization of Republican China.* New York: Praeger, 1971.

Rapoport, Vitaly N., and Yuri Alexeev. *Essays on the History of the Red Army, 1918–1938.* Volume 1. Washington, DC: Center for Planning and Research, 1984.

Ree, Erik van. "Socialism in One Country: A Reassessment." *Studies in East European Thought* 50, no 2 (1998): 77–117.

Reese, Roger R. *Stalin's Reluctant Soldiers: A Social History of the Red Army, 1925–1941.* Lawrence: University Press of Kansas, 1996.

Reiman, Michel. *The Birth of Stalinism: The USSR on the Eve of the "Second Revolution."* Translated by Georges Sanders. Bloomington: Indiana University Press, 1987.

Rhoads, Edward J. M. *Manchus and Han: Ethnic Relations and Political Power in*

Late Qing and Early Republican China, 1861–1928. Seattle: University of Washington Press, 2000.

Richard, Carl J. *When the United States Invaded Russia: Woodrow Wilson's Siberian Disaster.* Lanham, MD: Rowman & Littlefield, 2013.

Rider, Freemont, ed. *Information: A Digest of Current Events and World Progress, 1917*. Volume 3. New York: Holt, 1918.

Rohwer, Jürgen, and Mikhail Monakov. "The Soviet Union's Ocean-Going Fleet, 1935–1956." *International History Review* 18, no. 4 (1996): 837–868.

Rokossovsky, Konstantin K. "At the Heights of Yartsevskaya" [in Russian]. In *A Soldier's Duty*. Moscow: Military Publishing, 1988. http://militera.lib.ru/memo/russian/rokossovsky/index.html.

Saga, Junichi. *Confessions of a Yakuza*. New York: Kodansha International, 1991.

Sakurai, Tadayoshi. *Human Bullets: A Soldier's Story of the Russo-Japanese War.* 1907. Reprint, Lincoln: University of Nebraska Press, 1999.

Salminov, G. I., and N. T. Velikanov. *Order of Lenin Transbaikal Sky: History of the Order of Lenin Transbaikal Military District* [in Russian]. Moscow: Military Press, 1980.

Savkin, V. Y. *The Basic Principles of Operational Art and Tactics*. Translated from the Russian by the United States Air Force. Washington, DC: GPO, 1976.

Sawyer, Ralph D. "Martial Prognostications." In *Military Culture of Imperial China*, edited by Nicola Di Cosmo. Cambridge: Harvard University Press, 2009.

———. *The Seven Military Classics of Ancient China*. San Francisco: Westview, 1993.

Schram, Stuart R., ed. *Mao's Road to Power: Revolutionary Writings, 1912–1949*. Volume 3, *From the Jingganshan to the Establishment of the Jiangxi Soviets, July 1927–December 1930*. Armonk, NY: M. E. Sharpe, 1995.

Schwartz, Benjamin I. *Chinese Communism and the Rise of Mao*. Cambridge, MA: Harvard University Press, 1979.

Scully, Eileen P. *Bargaining with the State from Afar: American Citizenship in Treaty Port China, 1844–1942*. New York: Columbia University Press, 2001.

Seaton, Albert. *Stalin as Military Commander.* New York: Praeger, 1976.

Sella, Amnon. "Red Army Doctrine and Training on the Eve of the Second World War." *Soviet Studies* 27, no. 2 (1975): 245–264.

Service, Robert. *Stalin: A Biography*. Cambridge, MA: Belknap Press of Harvard University, 2004.

Sharman, Lyon. *Sun Yat-sen: His Life and Its Meaning—A Critical Biography*. Stanford, CA: Stanford University Press, 1934.

Sheng Gao Yang. "Analysis of the Differences Within the Communist Party of China in Responding to the Chinese Eastern Railroad Incident" [in Chinese]. In Guo, *Chinese Eastern Railway*, 298–307.

Sheridan, James E. *China in Disintegration: The Republican Era in Chinese History, 1912–1949*. New York: New Press, 1974.

———. *Chinese Warlord: The Career of Feng Yu-Hsiang*. Stanford, CA: Stanford University Press, 1966.

Shuji Taneine. "The Shock of the 1929 Sino-Soviet Conflict: Japan's Growing Awareness of the Soviet Union Prior to the Manchurian Incident" [in Japanese]. *Japanese Journal of Military History* 42, no. 1 (2006): 94–116.

Silberman, Bernard S., and H. D. Harootunian. *Japan in Crisis: Essays on Taisho Democracy*. Cambridge, MA: Harvard University Press, 1974.

Slyke, Lyman P., van. "Battle of the Hundred Regiments: Problems of Coordination and Control during the Sino-Japanese War." In "War in Modern China," special issue, *Modern Asian Studies* 30, no. 4 (1996): 979–1005.

Smith, Canfield F. *Vladivostok under Red and White Rule: Revolution and Counterrevolution in the Russian Far East, 1920–1922*. Seattle: University of Washington Press, 1974.

Solecki, Jan J., and C. Martin Wilbur. "Blücher's 'Grand Plan' of 1926." *China Quarterly* 35 (1968): 18–39.

South Manchuria Railway Company (SMR). *Manchuria: Land of Opportunities.* New York: Thomas F. Logan, 1924.

So Wai Chor. "The Western Hills Group in the National Revolution (1924–1928): A Study of Ideology and Politics in the Kuomintang." Master's thesis, University of Hong Kong, 1981.

Spence, Jonathan D. *In Search of Modern China.* New York: Norton, 1990.

Stein, George H. "Russo-German Military Collaboration: The Last Phase, 1933." *Political Science Quarterly* 77, no. 1 (1962): 54–71.

Stephan, John J. *The Russian Far East: A History*. Stanford, CA: Stanford University Press, 1994.

Stewart, George. *The White Armies of Russia: A Chronicle of Counter-Revolution and Allied Intervention.* Uckfield, UK: Naval & Military Press, 2009.

Stone, David R. *Hammer and Rifle: The Militarization of the Soviet Union, 1926–1933*. Lawrence: University Press of Kansas, 2000.

Stoner, John E. *S. O. Levinson and the Pact of Paris: A Study in the Techniques of Influence.* Chicago: University of Chicago Press, 1943.

Suleski, Ronald. *Civil Government in Warlord China: Tradition, Modernization and Manchuria.* New York: Peter Lang, 2002.

Sun, Kungtu C., assisted by Ralph W. Heunemann. *The Economic Development of Manchuria in the First Half of the Twentieth Century*. Cambridge, MA: Harvard University Press, 1973.

Suntsov, N. P., and I. M. Tretiak. *The Red Banner of the Far East: History of the Far Eastern Military District* [in Russian]. Moscow: Military Publishing House, 1985.

Sun Tzu. *The Art of War.* Edited and translated by Samuel B. Griffith. New York: Oxford University Press, 1971.

Sun Yat-sen. *Memoirs of a Chinese Revolutionary*. Philadelphia: David McKay Co., 1922.

Sze, Sao-ke Alfred, and T. Y. Lo, trans. *The Constitutional Compact, i.e. The Amended Provisional Constitution of the Republic of China.* Peking: Peking Daily News, 1914.

Tang, Peter S. H. *Russian and Soviet Policy in Manchuria and Outer Mongolia, 1911–1931.* Durham, NC: Duke University Press, 1959.

Tang, Xaibing. *Global Space and Discourse of Modernity: The Historical Thinking of Liang Qichao.* Stanford, CA: Stanford University Press, 1996.

Taylor, Jay. *The Generalissimo: Chiang Kai-shek and the Struggle for Modern China.* Cambridge, MA: Belknap Press of Harvard University, 2009.

Tian Wenmin. "Chang: Preparations to Recover Sovereignty and the CER Incident" [in Chinese]. In Guo, *Chinese Eastern Railway,* 132–142.

Tien, Hung-mao. *Government and Politics in Kuomintang China, 1927–1937.* Stanford, CA: Stanford University Press, 1972.

Treadgold, Donald W. *Twentieth Century Russia.* Chicago: Rand McNally, 1976.

Trotsky, Leon. *My Life.* New York: Charles Scribner's Sons, 1930.

———. *The Revolution Betrayed: What Is the Soviet Union and Where Is It Going?* Translated by Max Eastman. Reprint, Mineola, NY: Dover, 2004.

Tsuchida Tetsuro. "Japan and the Sino-Soviet Conflict of 1929." *Chuo University Journal* 22, no. 3 (2001): 17–27.

Tuchman, Barbara. *Stilwell and the American Experience in China, 1911–1945.* New York: Macmillan, 1972.

Twitchett, Denis, and John K. Fairbank, eds. *The Cambridge History of China.* Volume 12, *Republican China, 1912–1949, Pt. 1.* Cambridge: Cambridge University Press, 1983.

Tyler, Sydney. *The Japan–Russian War: An illustrated History of the War in the Far East.* Philadelphia: P. W. Zeigler, 1905.

Uchida, Jun. *Brokers of Empire: Japanese Settler Colonialism in Korea, 1876–1945.* Cambridge, MA: Harvard University Asia Center Press, 2011.

Ulam, Adam B. *Expansion and Coexistence: Soviet Foreign Policy, 1917–1973.* New York: Praeger, 1974.

United States Army General Services School. *Tactics and Technique of Cavalry: A Text and Reference Book of Cavalry Training.* Harrisburg, PA: Military Service Publishing, 1939.

United States Department of State [FRUS]. *Papers Relating to the Foreign Relations of the United States, 1912–1930.* Washington: GPO, 1943.

United States Foreign Broadcast Information Service, trans. *Field Regulations of the Red Army, 1929.* Springfield, VA: National Technical Information Service, 1985.

United States Government. *Proceedings of the Brest-Litovsk Peace Conference: The Peace Negotiations between Russia and the Central Powers, 21 November, 1917–3 March, 1918.* Washington, DC: GPO, 1918.

United States Marine Corps. *Small Wars Manual, 1940.* Washington, DC: GPO, 1940.

United States War Department. *FM 2-15, Cavalry Field Manual: Employment of Cavalry.* Washington, DC: GPO, 1941. http://www.ibiblio.org/hyperwar/USA/ref/ FM/PDFs/FM2-15.pdf.

———. *Military Operations in China.* Washington: GPO, 1900.

Valone, Stephen J. *A Policy Calculated to Benefit China: The United States and the China Arms Embargo, 1919–1929.* Westwood, CT: Praeger, 1991.

Ven, Hans J., van de. "Public Finances and the Rise of Warlordism." *Modern Asia Studies* 30, no. 4 (1996): 829–868.

Vishniakova-Akimova, Vera Vladimirovna. *Two Years in Revolutionary China, 1925–1927.* Translated by Steven I. Levine. Cambridge, MA: Harvard University East Asian Research Center Press, 1971.

Vogel, Ezra F. *Deng Xiaoping and the Transformation of China.* Cambridge, MA: Belknap Press of Harvard University, 2011. Kindle edition.

Voroshilov, K. E. *Stalin and the Red Army.* Moscow: Foreign Languages Publishing House, 1941.

Vul, Nikita. "He, Who Has Sown the Wind: Karakhan, the Sino-Soviet Conflict over the Chinese Eastern Railway, 1925–26, and the Failure of Soviet Policy in Northeast China." *Modern Asia Studies* 30, no. 4 (2014): 1–25.

Waldron, Arthur. *From War to Nationalism: China's Turning Point, 1924–1925.* Cambridge: Cambridge University Press, 1995.

———. "The Warlord: Twentieth-Century Chinese Understandings of Violence, Militarism, and Imperialism." *American Historical Review* 96, no. 4 (1991): 1073–1100.

Wang, Lianjie. "Zhongdong Railway Incident and Great Repercussions Caused by Letters from Chen Duxiu." *Asian Culture and History* 2, no. 1 (2010): 48–58.

Watt, Richard M. *Dare Call It Treason.* New York: Simon & Schuster, 1963.

Wheeler-Bennett, John W. *Brest-Litovsk: The Forgotten Peace, March 1918.* New York: Macmillan, 1966.

White, D. Fetotoff. *The Growth of the Red Army.* Princeton, NJ: Princeton University Press, 1944.

———. "Soviet Philosophy of War." *Political Science Quarterly* 51, no. 3 (1936): 321–353.

White, John Albert. "The American Role in the Siberian Intervention." *Russian Review* 10, no. 1 (1951): 26–36.

Whiting, Allen S. "The Soviet Offer to China of 1919." *Far Eastern Quarterly* 10, no. 4 (1951): 355–364.

Who's Who in China. Edited by M. C. Powell. Shanghai: China Weekly Review, 1925.

Who's Who in China: Biographies of Chinese Leaders. Shanghai: China Weekly Review, 1936.

Wilbur, C. Martin, and Julie Lien-ying How. *Documents on Communism, Nationalism, and Soviet Advisors in China, 1918–1927*. New York: Octagon Books, 1972.

———. *Missionaries of Revolution: Soviet Advisors and Nationalist China, 1920–1927*. Cambridge, MA: Harvard University Press, 1989.

Willoughby, Westel Woodbury. *China at the Conference—A Report*. Baltimore: Johns Hopkins Press, 1922.

Wolff, David. *To the Harbin Station: The Liberal Alternative in Russian Manchuria, 1898–1914*. Stanford, CA: Stanford University Press, 1999.

Wollenberg, Erich. *The Red Army*. London: New Park Publications, 1978. http://www/marxist.org/.

Worthing, Peter. *A Military History of Modern China: From the Manchu Conquest to Tian'anmen Square*. Westport, CT: Praeger Security International, 2007.

Wright, Richard K. J. *The Chinese Steam Navy, 1862–1945*. London: Chatham, 2000.

Wu, Tien-wei. "Chiang Kai-shek's March Twentieth Coup d'Etat of 1926." *Journal of Asian Studies* 27, no. 3 (1968): 585–602.

———. "A Review of the Wuhan Debacle: The Kuomintang–Communist Split of 1927." *Journal of Asian Studies* 29, no. 1 (1969): 125–143.

Xu Guoqi. *China and the Great War: Pursuit of a New National Identity and Internationalization*. Cambridge: Cambridge University Press, 2005.

———. *Strangers on the Western Front: Chinese Workers in the Great War*. Cambridge, MA: Harvard University Press, 2011.

Yoshihashi, Tekehito. *Conspiracy at Mukden: The Rise of the Japanese Military*. New Haven, CT: Yale University Press, 1963.

Young, C. Walter. *The International Relations of Manchuria*. Chicago: University of Chicago Press, 1929.

Young, Ernest P. *The Presidency of Yuan Shih-kai: Liberalism and Democracy in Early Republican China*. Ann Arbor: University of Michigan Press, 1977.

Young, Louise. *Japan's Total Empire, Manchuria, and the Culture of Wartime Imperialism*. Berkeley: University of California Press, 1998.

Yueng King Wah (Yang Jing-hua). "Chang Hsueh-liang and the CER Event" [in Chinese]. In Guo, *Chinese Eastern Railway*, 122–131.

Zhang Hongjun. "Japan and the CER" [in Chinese]. In Guo, *Chinese Eastern Railway*, 335–343.

Zhang Xue Ji. *The Warlord Chang Tso-lin and His Lieutenants* [in Chinese]. Hangzhou: Zhejiang United Publishing Group, 2011. Digital edition.

Index